OXFORD STUDIES IN DEMOCRATIZATION

Series Editor: Laurence Whitehead

••••••••••••••••••

THE LEGACY OF HUMAN-RIGHTS VIOLATIONS IN THE SOUTHERN CONE

OXFORD STUDIES IN DEMOCRATIZATION

Series editor: Laurence Whitehead

••••••••••••••••••

Oxford Studies in Democratization is a series for scholars and students of comparative politics and related disciplines. Volumes will concentrate on the comparative study of the democratization processes that accompanied the decline and termination of the cold war. The geographical focus of the series will primarily be Latin America, the Caribbean, Southern and Eastern Europe, and relevant experiences in Africa and Asia.

OTHER BOOKS IN THE SERIES

The New Politics of Inequality in Latin America:
Rethinking Participation and Representation.
Douglas A. Chalmers, Carlos M. Vilas,
Katherine Roberts Hite,
Scott B. Martin, Kerianne Piester,
and Monique Segarra

Human Rights and Democratization in Latin America:
Uruguay and Chile
Alexandra Barahona de Brito

Citizenship Rights and Social Movements:
A Comparative and Statistical Analysis
Joe Foweraker and Todd Landman

Regimes, Politics, and Markets:
Democratization and Economic Change in Southern and
Eastern Europe
José María Maravall

Democracy Between Consolidation and
Crisis in Southern Europe
Leonardo Morlino

The Bases of Party Competition in Eastern Europe:
Social and Ideological Cleavages in Post Communist States
Geoffrey Evans and Stephen Whitefield

The Democratic Developmental State:
Politics and Institutional Design
Marc Robinson and Gordon White

The International Dimensions of Democratization:
Europe and the Americas
Laurence Whitehead

The Legacy of Human-Rights Violations in the Southern Cone

Argentina, Chile, and Uruguay

....

LUIS RONIGER

and

MARIO SZNAJDER

UNIVERSITY PRESS

*This book has been printed digitally and produced in a standard specification
in order to ensure its continuing availability*

OXFORD
UNIVERSITY PRESS

Great Clarendon Street, Oxford OX2 6DP

Oxford University Press is a department of the University of Oxford.
It furthers the University's objective of excellence in research, scholarship,
and education by publishing worldwide in

Oxford   New York

Auckland Bangkok Buenos Aires Cape Town Chennai
Dar es Salaam Delhi Hong Kong Istanbul Karachi Kolkata
Kuala Lumpur Madrid Melbourne Mexico City Mumbai Nairobi
São Paulo Shanghai Taipei Tokyo Toronto

Oxford is a registered trade mark of Oxford University Press
in the UK and in certain other countries

Published in the United States
by Oxford University Press Inc., New York

ISBN 0-19-829615-0

To the memory of our grandparents and parents, who crossed
the Atlantic Ocean and came to the Southern Cone,
in search of fulfilment and a life in freedom

....
Preface
....

The home arrest of General (r.) Augusto Pinochet in London in
October 1998, and the legal tug-of-war over his possible extradition to
Spain, where he faces charges of crimes against humanity, triggered
again what many consider the 'ghosts of the past'. Once more, the public sphere focused on the images of past polarization and violence,
of the disappeared, of the tortured, and of those who spent time in
concentration camps and prisons under the General's military rule
between 1973 and 1990. As supporters and foes of the aged senator-
for-life clashed in Chile and elsewhere, the images of national reconciliation and of a consolidated and stable Chilean democracy
appeared tainted.

As the legal tug-of-war continued in the United Kingdom and the
debate mounted on the feasibility, wisdom, and fairness of bringing
former rulers to trial for their responsibility in human-rights violations, writer Isabel Allende, the niece of Salvador, evaluated in the
New York Times Magazine that justice had been done, in the form of
the opprobrium that fell upon the man who 'had the gall to pose as
his nation's savior.' In a nation traumatized by past terror and apprehensions about the future, Isabel Allende saw in the detention of
Pinochet the beginning of the end of the reign of fear in her country.

In Uruguay the popular Carnaval troupes, the *murgas*, captured in
their 1999 lyrics the idea that this case was emblematic of their expectation of justice at home. Some talked of the inherent connection between
the military's work and torture, while others addressed Pinochet's
Uruguayan peers, who 'from now on, will have to live on the run.' They
too, the *murgas* chanted, had much to hide and could expect to be captured one day, like the Chilean retired general. With avenues of institutional justice closed, popular culture kept collective grievances and
expectations alive.

In Argentina, the news about Pinochet found a wide echo. In parallel, legal changes made possible the arrest of General Videla and
Admiral Massera, accused of being responsible for the kidnapping of
new born babies of disappeared persons, when they ruled Argentina
in the late 1970s. The claims for justice, upheld during many years

almost only by human-rights organizations and activists, were again at the center of the Argentinean public sphere.

In late March 1999, the Lords of Law ruled that Pinochet was extraditable to Spain, for crimes committed since 1988, when the International Convention Against Torture and other Cruel, Inhuman or Degrading Treatment or Punishment (1984) was incorporated into UK legislation as part of the Criminal Act of Justice. The treaty had been signed also by both the governments of Spain and Chile. The ruling of the Lords of Law reduced the charges against Pinochet to one for torture and some others for conspiracy to torture. It is on these grounds that the Lords recommended that the British Home Secretary should reconsider the case and decide whether to allow the extradition procedures against Pinochet, or let him free. Some saw in this decision further proof of the protracted and perhaps irresolvable character of many of the issues raised by the legacy of human-rights violations.

As analyzed below, this is only one of many cases that have re-surged, and future cases that can be expected to resonate in the midst of national and transnational public spheres in the Southern Cone and elsewhere. These cases encapsulate the tragedy of the legacy of human-rights violations in Argentina, Chile, and Uruguay in the last three decades. In the framework of the Cold War and propelled by extreme ideological doctrines of national security, military dictatorships 'fought' what they perceived as a global enemy by controlling and persecuting those citizens and foreigners suspected of leftist activities or leanings. Repression acquired a regional character through the cooperation between the repressive apparatus of the different countries. It acquired further international projection as 'the enemy' was persecuted into neighboring countries, the US and Europe, breaking considerations of national sovereignty. Re-democratization brought various attempts to close the issue of the legacy of human-rights violations, presented as 'the' past crisis, whose lessons had to be learnt and whose wounds had to be healed, while avoiding the destabilizing impact of a direct confrontation with the perpetrators of those crimes. The non-closure of this legacy had different manifestations in the form of recurrent crises, unfinished legal confrontations, legislation and counter-legislation, heated discussions about historical memory, socialization of the new generations, and problems in the reconstitution of collective and national identities, themes that constitute the main axes of this book.

It is the character of repression as a traumatic individual and collective experience, and the difficulties that these societies faced in coming to grips with its implications beyond the formal adherence to international human-rights legal principles that bring us back to the recent developments in the Pinochet case. In this case, the international law on human rights has been upheld as superior to the principles of state immunity and restriction of crimes treatment within the boundaries of national sovereignty, thus invalidating self-amnesties, pardons and institutional arrangements of impunity that preclude the exercise of justice. In a world in which globalization seems to be affecting not only markets, the mass media and management, the new projection of international norms of accountability promises to re-centralize the demand of justice by the victims of repression, and to keep the legacy of human-rights violations at the center of the public spheres of the Southern Cone for years to come.

....

Acknowledgements

....

We owe a debt of gratitude to many individuals and institutions, who contributed in various ways to the completion of this work. We are indebted to the Minerva Center for Human Rights of the Hebrew University and its Director, David Kretzmer, for the financial support of this project from its inception, as well as to the Truman Research Institute for the Advancement of Peace that has provided a grant for the completion of the project. We are grateful to Stanley Cohen of the London School of Economics, Victor Azarya, Shmuel Eisenstadt, Florinda Goldberg, and Fionnuala Ni Aolain of the Hebrew University, Tulio Halperin Donghi of the University of California at Berkeley, David Lehmann of the University of Cambridge, Carlos Waisman of UCSD, Alexandra Barahona de Brito of the Institute for Strategic and International Studies in Lisbon, Michael Feige of Ben Gurion University, Edy Kaufman of the Truman Research Institute, María Ruiz of the University of Maryland, and Emilio F. Mignone of the Centro de Estudios Sociales y Legales in Buenos Aires for reading and commenting parts of the manuscript. The research assistance of Mario Schejtman and Daniel Schwartz was essential for this work; they began collaborating with us from the project's genesis and contributed ideas and initiatives, in addition to technical assignments. In later stages, Avi Blinder and Haim Portnoy assisted in compiling the index and completing the bibliography. Many friends and colleagues have accommodatingly collaborated with us. We would like to mention the kindness and patience of all those who agreed to share with us their personal, intellectual, and academic knowledge on the legacy of human-rights violations in the Southern Cone, in interviews conducted in the three countries and elsewhere. In addition to the latter, whose contribution is recognized in different parts of the book, special thanks are due, in Uruguay to Rossana Altman, Gerardo Caetano, Israel Creimer, Carlos Disevo, Elina Fabius, María Luisa González, Enrique Holcman, Ernesto Kesler, Teresa Porzekanski, Julio Schwartz, and the directors and staff of Serpaj in Montevideo; in Chile, to Pinchas Avivi, Manuel Antonio Garretón, Hugo Frühling, Teresa Gaisinsky Link, Rodrigo Guendelman, Abraham Magendzo, Juan Pablo Moreno, Leah Paz, Daniel Pinchasi and José Zalaquett; in Argentina, Itzhak Aviram,

Atilio Borón, Mariano Grondona, Jorge Cohen, Daniel Hugo Costilla, Sergio Kiernan and Manuel Mora y Araujo. Of great importance was the support received from the associations of Friends of the Hebrew University and especially of Roberto Paz and León Schimmel, presidents of the associations in Chile and Uruguay. In Israel, thanks are due to David Cohen, Daniel Gazit, Luis Jaimovich and his associates in Memoria, Alona Kamm, former Argentine ambassador José María Otegui, Leonardo Senkman, Hana Shúa, Alberto Spektorowski, and former Chilean Ambassador Jorge Tapia Valdés. We owe a debt of gratitude to our spouses Shuli and Laura, and to Susana S. de Belfus, Mónica S. de Spangenthal and Diego Vinacur, for their continuous support and help. We are also grateful to Dominic Byatt, senior editor at Oxford University Press who invested time and energy to bring this project to completion. David Bartram did a superb job of editing the manuscript. Parts of this work were presented in several forums and later appeared as articles in *Human Rights Quarterly*, 19 (1997); *Social Identities*, 3 (1997); *Journal of Historical Sociology*, 10 (1997); and *History and Memory*, 10 (1998), the permission of which to reproduce parts of them here is gratefully acknowledged.[1] We are indebted as well to the all those who commented on this work in seminars at the Minerva Center for Human Rights in January 1995, March 1995, and March 1997; in the Latin American Studies Association annual conference in Washington in October 1995; in the workshop on Collective Identities and the Shaping of the Public Sphere, held by the Van Leer Jerusalem Institute and the Truman Research Institute in January 1996; at the School of History of the University of Tel Aviv, in May 1996; at the Euroconference on Collective Identities and Symbolic Representations, in Paris in July 1996; at the departmental seminar of Sociology and Anthropology of the Hebrew University, in October 1996; and at the 49th Congress of Americanists in Quito in July 1997.

[1] Thanks are due to the following: Johns Hopkins University Press for using materials from 'The Legacy of HRV and the Collective Identity of Uruguay' (*Human Rights Quarterly*, 19/1 (1997), 55–77); Carfax, www.carfax.co.uk, for using 'HRV and the Reshaping of Collective Identities in Argentina, Chile and Uruguay' (*Social Identities*, 3/2 (1997), 221–46); Blackwell Publishers, for 'Paths of Citizenship and the Legacy of HRV: The Cases of Redemocratized Uruguay and Argentina (*Journal of Historical Sociology*, 10/3 (1997), 270–309); and Indiana University Press, for 'The Politics of Memory and Oblivion in Redemocratized Argentina and Uruguay' (*History and Memory*, 10/1 (1998), 133–69).

....

Contents

....

·················

Abbreviations

·················

AFDD	Asociación de Familiares de Detenidos-Desaparecidos/ Association of Family Members of Disappeared-Detainees
AFEP	Agrupación de Familiares de Ejecutados Políticos/ Association of Family Members of the Executed on Political Grounds
AFPD	Agrupación de Familiares de Prisioneros Desaparecidos/ Association of Families of Disappeared Prisoners
AMSAFE	Asociación del Magisterio de Santa Fé/Santa Fe Teachers Association
APDH	Asamblea Permanente de Derechos Humanos/ Permanent Assembly for Human Rights
CALEN	Centro de Altos Estudios Nacionales de las Fuerzas Armadas/Centre of Higher Studies of the Armed Forces
CCDH	Comisión Chilena de Derechos Humanos/Chilean Commission of Human Rights
CEJIL	Center for Justice and International Law
CELS	Centro de Estudios Legales y Sociales/Centre of Legal and Social Studies
CEMIDA	Centro de Militares Democráticos/Centre of Democratic Military Personnel
CEPAL	Comisión Económica para América Latina/ECLA (see below in the list of Spanish Abbreviations)
CESOC	Centro de Estudios Sociales/Centre of Social Studies
CGT	Confederación General de Trabajadores/General Confederation of Workers
CNI	Central Nacional de Información/Information National Centre
CNP	Comisión Nacional Pro-Referéndum/National Pro-Referendum Commission
CNRR	Corporación Nacional de Reparación y Reconcilación/ National Reparation and Reconciliation Corporation
CODEPU	Comisión de Derechos del Pueblo/People's Rights Commission

CONADEP	Comisión Nacional sobre la Desaparición de Personas/ National Commission on Persons Disappearance
COPESA	Consorcio Periodístico Sociedad Anónima/Journalistic Consortium Limited Liability Company (the parallel term to PLC)
CORREPI	Coordinadora contra la Represión Policial e Institucional/Co-ordinating Committee Against Institutional and Police Repression
CPP	Comité Pro Paz/Pro-Peace Committee
CREJ	Comité Representativo de las Entidades Judías/Jewish Entities Representative Committee
CUT	Central Única de Trabajadores/Central Workers Union
DINA	Dirección Nacional de Inteligencia/National Intelligence Directorate
DSN	Doctrina de Seguridad Nacional/National Security Doctrine
ECLA	Economic Commission for Latin America/Economic Commission for Latin America
ERP	Ejército Revolucionario del Pueblo/Revolutionary People's Army
ESMA	Escuela de Mecánica de la Armada/Mechanics School of the Navy
FAMUS	Familiares y Amigos de Muertos por la Subversión/ Family Members and Friends of the Dead Victims of Subversion
FPMR	Frente Patriótico Manuel Rodríguez/Manuel Rodriguez Patriotic Front
FREPASO	Frente del País Solidario/Solidarity Country Front
HIJOS	Hijos por la Identidad y contra el Olvido y el Silencio/ Daughters and Sons for Identity and against Oblivion and Silence
ICHR	Interamerican Commission for Human Rights/Inter-American Commission for Human Rights
IELSUR	Instituto de Estudios Legales y Sociales del Uruguay/ Uruguay's Legal and Social Studies Institute
LASA	Latin American Studies Association/Latin American Studies Association
MAPU	Movimiento de Acción Popular Unitaria/Unitary Popular Action Movement
MEDH	Movimiento Ecuménico por los Derechos Humanos/ Human Rights Ecumenic Movement
MIR	Movimiento de Izquierda Revolucionaria/Revolutionary Left Movement

MLN	Movimiento de Liberación Nacional/National Liberation Movement
MPP	Movimiento de Participación Popular, Frente Amplio/ Popular Participation Movement (Frente Amplio-Wide Front)
MRO	Movimiento Revolucionario Oriental/Oriental Revolutionary Movement
MTP	Movimiento Todos por la Patria/All for the Fatherland Movement
NGO	Non-Governmental Organization
OAS	Organization of American States
OPR-33	Organización Popular Revolucionaria-33/Popular Revolutionary Organization-33
ORP	Organización Revolucionaria del Pueblo/People's Revolutionary Organization
PCU	Partido Comunista Uruguayo/Communist Party of Uruguay
PPD	Partido por la Democracia/Pro-Democracy Party
PRN	Proceso de Reorganización Nacional/National Reorganization Process
PSOE	Partido Socialista Obrero Español/Spanish Socialist Workers Party
RN	Renovación Nacional/National Renovation
SERPAJ	Servicio de Paz y Justicia/Peace and Justice Service
UCC	Unión de Centro Centro/Center-Center Union
UCR	Unión Cívica Radical/Radical Civic Union
UDI	Unión Democrática Independiente/Independent Democratic Union
UP	Unidad Popular/Popular Unity

········

Introduction

··········

This book is about one of the long-term legacies of authoritarianism in redemocratized Argentina, Chile, and Uruguay: human-rights violations. To talk about human-rights violations in terms of a legacy may sound strange, especially as people tend to think of legacies as something they wish to preserve and cherish. Indeed, the new democracies in the Southern Cone of the Americas have publicly professed to reject and condemn the uses of state power in various forms against citizens under military rule, thus dissociating themselves from their predecessors. And yet the experiences of military rule have become a grim legacy, bringing major issues and dilemmas to the forefront of the public agenda.

During the transition from authoritarianism and following redemocratization, these societies had to define in what ways and through which channels to thoroughly ascertain and confront the knowledge of what happened in the past, and how to agree upon some version of it ('truth'); how to make those involved in human-rights violations accountable for their past deeds; whether to ask forgiveness from the victims and expect expiation from the perpetrators; along what lines to elaborate mechanisms of expiation and compensation; and how to prepare the grounds for reconciliation.

In dealing with these issues, the citizens and the civilian rulers of the redemocratized societies of the Southern Cone found themselves trapped in their course of action and policy options, as in Franz Kafka's parable of the individual caught in time:

He has two antagonists: the first presses him from behind, from the origin. The seconds blocks the road ahead. He gives battle to both. To be sure, the first supports him in his fight with the second, for he wants to push him forward, and in the same way the second supports him in his fight with the first, since he drives him back. But it is only theoretically so. For it is not only the two antagonists who are there, but he himself as well, and who really knows his intentions?[1]

The civilian rulers and the different sectors of society were caught between contrasting and sometimes polar versions of the past, between normative expectations and the constraints of political contingency, and between their will to consolidate democratic rule and the impossibility to do so without grappling with the past legacy of human-rights violations.

The research design of this book is intended to provide a systematic comparative study of how three countries in the Southern Cone of the Americas have confronted this legacy of past human-rights violations and attempted to reshape the domain of human rights in several areas ranging from institutionalizing acceptable patterns of public accountability to mechanisms of expiation and compensation, from educational policy to constitutional reform, and from policies of national reconciliation to debates about history and collective memory.

Such a comparative analysis is made possible by the fact that the countries analysed share a relatively common background and have recently faced common issues concerning human-rights violations, while at the same time they differed in the institutional paths and in the actual interpretation of these issues among different social sectors.

We analyse these different paths and interpretations systematically in terms of, first, the specific institutional mechanisms adopted by the political leaders in each society; second, the balance of forces between the different social and political actors, namely, the government, the military, the Church, the intellectuals, and the political actors who opposed the military rule and took over government after the transition to democracy, and various non-governmental organizations. We analyse the attitudes of these social actors towards the problems attendant on the processes of political change, especially problems of accommodation between the old and the new forces during and after the transition; and the political problems generated by the experience of repression under the military. In this context, we analyse the struggles, debates, and crises and institutional formations that took place in these societies following redemocratization in the 1980s and 1990s; the concrete policies adopted by the elites in dealing with these problems and the impact of these policies on the processes of reconciliation between the different sectors of these societies. We lay special emphasis on the tensions between the new normative expectations which crystallized with the establishment of the democratic regimes and the constraints of political contingencies as they developed during this period. We show how social actors engaged in strategic interactions as they made choices in critical junctures while confronting the past experience in ways that shaped the legacy of human-rights violations for years to come.

In this comparative framework, we identify a series of parameters which were of special importance in shaping the variations in institutional patterns and in patterns of interpretation in these societies. The most important among these parameters are the social, political, and legal traditions of each country; the constellation of social and political forces within it; the timing of the transition and the sequence of choices following it; the way in which each society reacted to the experience of the neighbouring countries; the patterns of public mobilization and debate; the symbolic involvement and collective catharsis of the different sectors of population in the recurring crises.

The book relies on a large corpus of primary sources (including dozens of interviews and unpublished documents) and publications from the three countries collected *in situ* during several visits to the field. In parallel, it aims to make a general comparative contribution rather than a historicist analysis and, consequently, it relates to works in the social sciences, addressing some recent developments and controversies, particularly in three major domains, which we hereafter detail.

The first domain concerns studies devoted to the third wave of democratization. This literature has posed major theoretical challenges to comparative research, as democratization has become a transnational phenomenon since the late 1970s and 1980s. As democracy was adopted in many areas, from Southern Europe to Latin America and from Central and Eastern Europe to parts of Asia, it became increasingly evident that any analysis of the democratizing processes had to take into account the role and impact of external models and international forces upon the reformulation of domestic politics and cultural change. In Latin America in general and particularly in its Southern Cone, this has meant a continuous confrontation with the Western models which are part and parcel of their own origins rather than alien models imposed from the outside, as in Asian and other post-colonial countries. One of the main illustrations of this trend was the fact that military rulers considered it their duty to implement policies aimed at saving the Western, Christian soul of their nations, even by means that society eventually identified as gross violations of human rights. Later on, with redemocratization, and partly as a result of the authoritarian experience, these societies professed to have finally found their democratic souls. Yet, the democratic authorities had to balance normative principles with political contingency, thus preparing in unintended ways the ground for partial institutional solutions and recurrent aftershocks, controversies, and waves of inner reflection.

Secondly, we address some of the issues raised by the literature on globalization, especially those dealing with the changing cultural landscape, the enhanced concern with globality and the worldwide adoption of new languages (e.g. the human-rights discourse and neo-liberalism), and the transformation of public commitments and conceptions of self-interest variously expressed in public life, as analysed by Roland Robertson, Ulf Hannerz, Ulrich Beck, and many others. Here, the book's contribution is to show how the current global spread of human-rights discourses has been articulated through the specific local processes, dilemmas, and crises that shaped the agenda and public culture of the redemocratized Southern Cone societies.

By carrying out this analysis, we move beyond mere institutionalist studies that focus on the spread of Western culture as a causal factor that constitutes actors, defines their objectives, and shapes organizational and behavioural similarities across the globe. While recognizing this process of diffusion, we would like to avoid leaving the political and social constellations of forces out of the analysis. Specifically, we aim to indicate, first, how these global cultural premises are incorporated locally; second, the political dimensions and struggles involved in this process of incorporation; and third, the changes operated thereby in the very character of these idioms and understandings as they are mediated locally and become institutionalized in different contexts. Furthermore, we aim to contextualize how the human-rights discourses were incorporated through the experience of military rule and redemocratization in Argentina, Chile, and Uruguay, without relativizing the universality of human-rights, which should be enjoyed by all individuals as human beings, as bearers of dignity and value which are not derived from any instrumental consideration.[2]

The book also analyses how the regional character of military cooperation in political repression during the 1970s provided grounds for the eruption of public aftershocks in the 1990s, triggered by developments in neighbouring countries and followed by pending international legal suits.

Last but not least, we relate to the burgeoning literature on collective memory and identity, which has stressed the distinctiveness of collective memory from historical flow and epistemology. Whereas there is a tendency to construct the past in linear fashion as distinct from the present, studies on collective memory have placed images of the past within the present, identifying them as meaningful factors in current visions and decisions. These dynamic interactions between past and present also characterize legacies of human-rights violations. As these images are ensconced in the public culture, they retain a force of their own and contribute to shaping the public agenda. We trace the struggle and politics over memory and oblivion; the meaning-making processes by which people have approached current concerns within their framework of cultural images, normative commitments, and concepts of legitimacy that were encoded differently by their country's past experiences; and the ways in which the latter were elaborated in the Southern Cone.

Beginning with the inevitability of confronting the legacy of human-rights violations under military rule once the public spheres of these societies were opened by redemocratization, this book analyses how key actors reworked the tensions between principles and political contingency into public discourse and policies, into initiatives and counter-actions. The adopted policies only partially treated the legacy of authoritarianism, setting the stage for serious repercussions, imposing constraints on governments and opening the door to a varied politics of oblivion and memory, in the framework of national reconciliation. The debate in the public sphere created, in turn, the possibility for questioning and reformulating some of the basic tenets of collective identity and public life in Argentina, Chile, and Uruguay.

The book addresses these issues by following a multi-levelled approach, which combines the political-institutional approach, the sociological and comparative approach, and the approach through the eyes of political and cultural actors. Such multi-level character is dictated by the nature of the issues under consideration, which have carried on a multiple impact in these redemocratized societies.

The first chapter, 'Repression and the Discourse of Human-Rights Violations in the Southern Cone', presents an overview of the democratic breakdowns of the three countries in the 1970s and its sociopolitical background, as well as the military rulers' use of repression, which was progressively interpreted in terms of the discourse of human-rights violations. In connection with the latter, the chapter analyses several vantage points to interpret the specific forms of incorporation of this discourse and its relevance for the region. The second chapter follows the countries into their periods of redemocratization, and traces their respective treatment of past human-rights violations in the tug-of-war between normative principles and political contingencies.

Chapter 3 deals with the destabilizing threat of the legacy of human-rights violations to the newly re-established democracies, their national reconciliation and free public spheres, while many citizens demanded justice and an acknowledgement of the past, in connection with the principles upon which the new democracies should be built. The fourth chapter considers the dynamics of restructuring the realm of human-rights in the Southern Cone during the new democratic period, including material reparations and demands, constitutional and legal frameworks, ongoing human-rights violations, and educational reforms as part policies for dealing with the legacy of human-rights violations. Chapter 5 reviews that legacy comparatively through several illuminating lenses: regional trends and historical timing; collective catharsis; legal-constitutional frameworks; and civil mobilization.

Chapters 6 and 7 discuss how the confrontation with the legacy of human-rights violations implied problematizing the prevailing images and premises of these societies, and contributed to redefining identity and collective symbols of representation. More specifically, Chapter 6 approaches these issues from the perspective of the political uses of memory and oblivion by the military, politicians, intellectuals, and human-rights activists in each of the three countries, concluding with a discussion of the politics of memory and oblivion over the confinement and expansion of collective memory under democracy. The seventh and final chapter explores how the cultural elites articulated in their work core symbols and models of cultural and social order by reflecting the experience of human-rights violations and, in such manner, reshaping the identity of their societies through such a confrontation. Analysis focuses in particular on how they approached history to explain or reconstruct identity and public life; and how they related to earlier and new forms of patterning of membership, values, and their connections to the re-enactment of inclusion and exclusion during the redemocratized period.

Repression and the Discourse of Human-Rights Violations in the Southern Cone

Repression of political opponents and of co-nationals has characterized much of the history of the countries of the Southern Cone. Nonetheless, the magnitude of repression during the last wave of military
rule in Argentina, Chile, and Uruguay, and its interpretation in terms
of the recently incorporated discourse of concern for human rights have
singled out this recent phase in these societies' institutional and cultural development. As they were interpreted through the internationally projected prism of human rights, accountability, and justice, the
recent experiences of repression emerged as having a distinctive impact
on these societies' self-understanding, reconstruction of public spheres,
and politics of reconciliation, oblivion, and memory.

During the last wave of military rule in the Southern Cone, the repressive policies were legitimated on the basis of organicist nationalist
ideas. According to these ideas, protecting the collective well-being, in
a context of internal struggle, justified the infringement of individual
rights. In reaction, the international discourse of human rights—developed in the aftermath of the crimes against humanity committed in
the Second World War—provided a new vision in which individual rights
were given primacy as the basis for (re)shaping civilized and democratic public life, as sanctioned by international legislation and treaties.
The antinomy and confrontation between these two visions of constructing public life and of defining the role of individuals vis-à-vis society
and the state generated debate and struggle over the legacy of human-
rights violations in the process of redemocratization.

To substantiate the significance of the legacy of human-rights violations inherited by the new democracies, this chapter presents an overview of the democratic breakdowns in the 1970s and the subsequent
patterns of repression under authoritarian rule in Argentina, Chile,
and Uruguay. Authoritarian repression created in these societies
a grim legacy, which could be interpreted through a wide range of

interpretations, including the increasingly respected international discourse of human rights, the incorporation of which added imbalances as these societies returned to democracy, given the prevalence of contrasted visions and interests.

The Sociopolitical Experience of the Southern Cone

Argentina, Chile, and Uruguay evolved as highly articulated and politicized nations, which shared a basic history of Spanish colonization, of Catholicism, of political independence in the early nineteenth century, of mass European immigration (more prominent in Argentina and Uruguay than in Chile) since the late nineteenth century, and a basic modelling of society according to Western ideas of development.

These societies share a dual cultural dynamic. On the one hand, there is a substratum of respect for hierarchy, authority, and order, of Roman Catholic origins, with corporatist leanings. On the other hand, from an early stage, elites have looked to the centres of world development, absorbing from the latter secular Western ideas and ideologies, adapting them as part of their models of nation-building, as befitted their views and local realities. This has been reflected in the way local elites have interpreted foreign models and ideas. For instance, the European tradition of Enlightenment was introduced into the society of late eighteenth century Rio de la Plata without discussing the relationship between religion and society, since religion was perceived as the framework of values holding society together.[1] In the mid-nineteenth century, when European liberalism was introduced in the region, it was oriented towards the de-establishment of the Church, but, at the same time, it was also used against the native populations and their models of social organization and collective land tenure. The European-oriented elites, both Liberals or Conservatives, interpreted their societies in terms of a struggle between civilization and barbarism, which legitimated their policies of annihilating rural social forces, the privatization of communal lands, and their marketization and appropriation by large landholders.

With the adoption of formal models of constitutional liberal democracy, the elites interpreted the models in ways which stressed their authority and allowed the implementation of formal equality before the law in a manner that did not affect the hierarchical structure of society. For instance, while they responded to popular pressures by widening the scope of suffrage laws, elites organized the electoral processes in ways tainted by fraud, patronage, clientelistic manipulation, and vote buying, in order to keep control over the polity, its institutions and resources.[2] Later on, Anarchist, Fascist, and Socialist orientations of European inspiration were re-elaborated and incorporated into local politics. These ideologies, developed and voiced by intellectuals and politicians, had the capacity to mobilize wide sectors of the middle and lower classes.

One of the most radical attempts to change the pattern of mass incorporation into public life was populism. Latin American populism was related to the local patterns of modernization and industrialization, which differed fundamentally from the European or North American paths. In Latin America, these processes were accelerated by populist leaders who occupied the seats of state power. Populist movements and leaders constituted very important agents in the restructuring of public order, very often under the auspices of authoritarian regimes and styles of government. State policies of development changed the sociodemographic structure of the countries and created a multi-class alliance, within which large-scale lower-class political mobilization was instrumental to deflecting interclass strife and could be organized to help reinforce the 'nation' and the state. The strong populist inclusionary drive brought the middle and lower classes into the process of nation-building and participation. It also served as a basis for the interclass alliance that promised to replace the old organic social model of Catholic origins, thus allowing societies to function with lower levels of conflict during their specific path of modernization.[3]

Argentina, Chile, and Uruguay lived through intensive processes of social change and modernization. After the Second World War, the three countries experienced increasing socio-economic and political pressures. While in Chile and Uruguay the normative framework of formal democracy managed to contain these pressures until the 1970s, in Argentina it was biased towards the populist framework of symbolic and effective incorporation created by Peronism and was shattered by the dislocation of social and political order. These trends produced an intermittent pattern of civilian and military rule in Argentina, along with another coup in 1976. All three societies were marked by a basic dissonance between formal sociopolitical and cultural frameworks within shared Western traditions, on the one hand, and the 'real' workings of social life, which contained strong elements of violence, authoritarianism, clientelism and repression, on the other. The latter constantly modified and sometimes threatened to shatter the existing institutional format of these societies.

To understand the public culture of these societies, we thus have to look at the background of intensive social change and modernization and at the tensions inherent in the varied intellectual and cultural trends, which became frameworks for interpreting reality and forming policy in societies characterized by socio-demographic diversity and high levels of inequality.

The political realm was organized in a Republican presidentialist way, with electoral systems that allowed greater electoral participation by widening the scope of suffrage and by generating popular mobilization among substantial sectors of the middle and lower classes. The models incorporated by the political classes formally ensured the recognition of basic rights and liberties, according to the European and North American pattern, and yet for many decades politics was accompanied in practice by fraud, clientelism, and the manipulation of the electorate by the political elites, either in the form of a 'particracy' (a political system centred on parties, as in Uruguay and Chile) or in the form of contention between an elitist pattern and a populist mobilization pattern (as in Argentina). The pivotal force in the political system has been traditionally the executive, which has often overridden the formal powers of the legislature and has exercised strong influence on the judicial system, attenuating the autonomy of the latter in many occasions.

Beyond this shared background, each society developed distinctive institutional paths. In Argentina, the conservative and elitist trend of late nineteenth- and early twentieth-century politics rapidly changed, beginning in the 1910s. The country experienced political and social instability and conflict, which led to the emergence of Radicalism and, since the 1940s, of Peronism as the major axis of politics. Despite its authoritarian patterns of leadership, Peronism combined strong inclusionary features, recognizing the interests of the popular classes and other sectors, such as women, in drafting its social policies. The political instability that followed Perón's ousting in 1955 and the country's economic regression triggered recurrent waves of authoritarian rule and successive attempts to restore democracy. Uruguay attained a form of democracy, based on consensual resolution of political conflict, that lessened the tendencies toward polarization and blurred ideological differences between the major political parties. This form consisted of a system of political rule shared by both majority and minority political forces and institutional forms of reaching consensus among elites. This system, created by José Batlle y Ordóñez in the early twentieth century, and sustained by resources appropriated by the state, upheld civilian rule and instilled the values of citizenship, republicanism, and consensus in the population. This model entered a period of crisis after the socio-economic model became less viable in the 1960s. In Chile, a tradition of political stability based on the autocratic presidentialist model established by Portales was liberalized and, after the 1891 revolution and civil war, replaced by a model of oligarchical parliamentarism. Throughout these changes, a highly legalist and constitutionalist view of the public sphere was nonetheless maintained. Developments in the socio-economic and demographic composition of the country were accompanied by inclusionary policies in the 1920s that destabilized the political order and led to a series of military interventions that lasted until 1932. The return to democratic rule initiated a long period of institutional stability and mobilization, which ended in September 1973 with renewed military intervention. The democratic decades were characterized by presidential rule balanced by a highly 'particratic' parliament and by tensions rooted in political demands and the constant attempts to limit or exclude Communists and Marxists. Modernization and mobilization went hand in hand, creating a very politicized and polarized constellation of forces, which in the early 1970s failed to sustain any legitimate mechanisms of consensual resolution of conflicts.

In the three countries, institutional building was supported by the development of an agro-export economic model, which was coupled with financial markets in the Argentinian and Uruguayan cases (more open in Uruguay than in Argentina) and, in the case of Chile, with a mineral-export model in the late nineteenth century. The agro-export and mineral-export models provided the resources for the growth of state bureaucracies and the financing of social welfare systems, which in the case of Argentina had strong populist characteristics. It also provided resources for policies of import substitution industries (ISI) which facilitated initiation of processes of industrialization in all three cases. These changes in economic structure form the backdrop for the increasing socio-economic mobilization and political polarization in the 1960s and early 1970s.

In Argentina, for most of the twentieth century, the central political elites failed to develop a model with wide-ranging support among opposed political forces, while various political communities with opposing interpretations of political behaviour and different visions of the collectivity (e.g. populist traditionalist vs. liberal modernizing visions) struggled for dominance and cultural hegemony at the very core of the Argentinian polity. Conflict and polarization occurred in all three countries. But, while Argentina lacked any shared, consensual vision about the nature of the political system and the collective identity of society, the situation was different in Uruguay and Chile. In Uruguay, the two core political forces—Batllism and its conservative counterpart, Herrerism—contested with one another, but neither proposed a model of antidemocratic takeover or restrictive nationalism as basis for attaining of hegemony.[4] The basic model developed in the early twentieth century in Uruguay was inclusive, predicated upon the protection of universalist and secular values. This model depended upon the maintenance of political stability, the regularity of democratic procedures, growing financial and economic markets, and the progressive development of a large urban class. In Chile, a tri-polar political system (right, centre, and left) evolved, in which deep ideological disagreements were balanced by a basic commitment of all political forces to maintaining the democratic framework. Still, ideological and socio-economic differences created, after the 1970 election of Salvador Allende, high levels of mobilization and increasing polarization between the government and the opposition, leading to the breakdown of the model.[5]

As these nations entered a period of radicalized unrest and political disorder in the 1960s, the respective armed forces stepped in, displacing democracy. Civil societies failed to develop the capacity to overcome state and political crises. The states failed to maintain governance in the face of mounting, polarized demands raised by different social sectors, especially as protest took on confrontational and violent forms. In Argentina, the military takeover was one in a long series of military interregna that began in 1930; the civilians themselves pressured the military to launch their coup in March 1976. In Uruguay, with the partial exception of the Terra dictatorship in the 1930s, the phenomenon of military appropriation of power was novel. In the early 1970s, the Uruguayan armed forces entered the government and took power over a protracted period, after being invited by the civilian president to 'protect the institutions'. Many decades of more or less uninterrupted civilian rule, which had buttressed the self-image of Uruguay as 'the Switzerland of the Americas', came to an end as the military gained increasing power beginning in 1972–3, took power and controlled the polity and society until March 1985. Similarly, with the exception of the dictatorship of Carlos Ibáñez in 1927–31 and the great instability of 1931–2, Chile enjoyed relatively sustained democratic rule until Pinochet's coup in 1973. The civilian path of Chile came to an end following social deterioration and political unrest in the early 1970s, which led to military rule from September 1973 to March 1990.

Within a shared process of breakdown of democracy and transition to military rule in the three countries in the 1970s, each country entered the authoritarian period in a different way. Many factors affected the ways of breakdown of democratic rule, foremost the character of political struggle and polarization; the high levels of mass mobilization; the increasing political violence and the perceived menace of leftist onslaught; the prevailing doctrines of national security diffused during the Cold War; and the relative capacity of the political classes to confront the ongoing crises. All these factors affected the specific timing and road to authoritarianism, as they were played out against the background of distinct political paths and patterns of civil–military relationships.[6]

In Uruguay, by the end of the 1960s, economic decline coupled with inflation and labour unrest fuelled political activism and urban guerrilla activities, primarily of the Movimiento de Liberación Nacional-Tupamaros, founded in 1962. The response of the government of President Pacheco Areco was to impose martial law in 1968, to which the Tupamaros responded by increasing their actions. In a political system characterized until then by the search for consensus and power-sharing, Pacheco Areco introduced non-party technocrats to the cabinet, used the military to repress strikes, limited media coverage of terrorism, and in September 1971 suspended the right of habeas corpus on the basis of a declaration of internal war. The old system of power-sharing between the two major political parties (the Colorados and the Blancos) was shattered as the country became destabilized. In this climate of increasing violence and repression, Colorado presidential candidate Juan María Bordaberry was elected in 1971 and took power in March 1972.[7] The armed forces were put in charge of the campaign against the urban guerrilla and shortly obliterated the Tupamaros' effective military capacity.

After concluding the military operations against the guerrillas, the army leadership became more interested in its politico-ideological roots—or in what they saw as such—in order to avoid any chance of reappearance of left-wing insurgence. Their behavior and demands were unacceptable for a civilian independent legislature, and the first important rejection of the army's demands produced the coup. The president had chosen the army's side.[8]

The international context of the Cold War played an indirect though important role in buttressing the will of the armed forces to intervene in politics:

American policy towards Uruguay stimulated the military takeover. By attaching growing importance to the military in antisubversive campaigns, by legitimatizing and advising them in their initial steps into politics, and by courting them after each political success, the United States undoubtedly performed an important role as an indirect source of strength.[9]

In June 1973 the President closed the Parliament and dissolved the CNT, the union confederation of Uruguay. The Communist Party and other left-wing organizations were banned; repressive measures and media censorship continued; army officers were placed at the head of the major state-owned enterprises. Bordaberry continued as symbolic head of state until June 1976, albeit under increasing military control. He was replaced by another civilian, Dr Aparicio Méndez, who ruled under the military after being nominated by the Council of State for a period of five years. Political persecution continued. From 1976 to 1980 an attempt was made to establish a system of limited democracy within the parameters of the national security doctrine. Institutional Acts, amending the constitution and formalizing military power, were introduced. 'The defining characteristics of Uruguay's regime as it stabilized after 1976 were its collegiality (there being no dictator to rival Pinochet in Chile) and the methodical (but rarely radical) influence of technocrats in policy-making.'[10]

A new constitution was drafted and brought to a popular referendum in November 1980, but was rejected by 57.8 per cent of voters. In September 1981, retired General Gregorio Alvarez assumed the presidency and a slow transition to full civilian rule began.

Chile lived through a period of democratic, constitutional rule between 1932 and 1973. Socio-economic polarization and political mobilization conferred a radical tenor to Chilean politics in this period, with recurrent attempts to exclude the radical left.[11] Chilean politics functioned within a multi-party system, ranging from the Conservatives and the Liberals on the right, Christian Democrats and Radicals at the centre, to the Socialists and Communists on the left. Unlike the Uruguayan two-party system, the Chilean parties were ideological and not multi-sectoral political organizations. After the Second World War, and notwithstanding the large number of presidential candidates and of parties winning seats in Parliament, a three-pronged political scenario emerged. In the 1960s and 1970s, the Christian Democratic Party, led by Eduardo Frei Montalva, replaced the Radical Party as the major force at the centre of the political map, with clearly defined left-wing and right-wing coalitions on its sides.

In the 1970 presidential elections, Salvador Allende, leader of the left-wing Unidad Popular (UP) coalition won by a small margin over Jorge Alessandri, leader of the right-wing coalition.[12] Allende's UP coalition was composed by his Socialist Party, the Communists, a section of the Radical Party, the Christian left (MAPU), and an array of smaller leftist organizations. His election in September 1970 was contested violently by the extreme right, which assassinated General René Schneider, commander-in-chief of the Chilean armed forces, in an attempt to destabilize the polity and provoke a military coup in October 1970. After signing with the parliamentary centre and right-wing forces a commitment of respect for the Constitution, Allende received the necessary congressional vote to assume power. In the three years of his term, President Allende attempted to carry out social and economic reforms of Marxist inspiration within the existing legal and constitutional frameworks. Reforms included agrarian reform and nationalization of the banking system, of major industries, and of the mining sector. Allende confronted increasing political and social opposition. The announcement of a government plan to reform the public educational system caused strong reactions from the Catholic Church and the opposition. Economic policies of a collectivist nature generated strong opposition, capital flight, strikes, and a deterioration in economic performance. An international, US-led boycott of Chilean mineral exports aggravated the situation.[13] The right-wing and Christian Democratic opposition conducted a unified policy of blocking UP parliamentary initiatives. Attempts to reach political compromises failed. Polarization and mass mobilization both of the right and the left widened, acquiring violent overtones.

[The UP government] expanded the limits of liberal democratic legality to breaking point, bringing it into conflict with the judiciary, the Constitutional Tribunal and the increasingly ideologized opposition of the right and [the] centrist PDC ... The government was caught in the cross-fire between an increasingly aggressive reaction from a traditional elite ... and a radical [revolutionary] minority ... The Armed Forces became involved in the conflict. They were called on by the government to put down strikes, to repress illegal armed activity ... President Allende requested that they mediate the conflict between the government and the opposition in Congress. The right actively encouraged them to depose the UP government.[14]

In the winter of 1973, economic deterioration and political strife created a major crisis, while political options narrowed. The Chilean armed forces, traditionally respectful of constitutional rule and highly disciplined and hierarchical, did not remain immune. During General Carlos Prats' tenure as commander-in-chief, the armed forces constitutionally backed Allende's government, as shown during their repression of the staged military coup of 29 June 1973. Still, there was a feeling of growing unease within the ranks. Many officers perceived the dangers of open social confrontation leading to a civil war, seen as imminent unless the military intervened.

The anti-communist officers and the group which Augusto Varas called, the institutionalist officers, agreed that a coup d'etat was necessary. The latter feared that supporting the Allende government would prompt an internal division of the armed forces, threatening institutional cohesion. . . . [The former] feared infiltration by the left, and perceived that chances for changing the situation without a military takeover had disappeared.[15]

US attitudes towards Allende's government were negative and contacts between American officials and agencies and the Chilean opposition created an atmosphere of support for a change of government;

they instilled confidence in those involved in coup-plotting. General Augusto Pinochet replaced General Prats as commander-in-chief in late August and became the leader of the coup on its eve. On 11 September 1973 the armed forces overthrew the civilian government of Allende, who refused to resign and leave the country for exile, and instead committed suicide at the presidential palace of La Moneda. A sixteen-and-a-half-year period of military rule ensued, which carried out systematic repression against the left as part of a wider foundational drive. In parallel to its systematic use of repression, the military junta led by General Pinochet managed to institutionalize its rule and a future limited democracy through constitutional acts, the 1978 amnesty law, and a new constitution approved by 67 per cent of the voters in a non-controlled referendum in September 1980.[16]

In Argentina, the political system existed from 1955 to 1973 under the shadow of the ban imposed by the military on the majoritarian popular political force, Peronism. Following the overthrow of Juan Domingo Perón in 1955, Argentina lived through a period of political instability and intermittent military uprisings and interventions. By the end of the 1960s, under military rule, guerrilla activities of the Trotskyist Ejército Revolucionario del Pueblo (ERP) and the leftist-Peronist Montoneros began. After years of inconclusive military rule, defined by Guillermo O'Donnell as bureaucratic-authoritarian,[17] the military president, General Alejandro Lanusse, allowed the formal return of Peronism into Argentinian politics and called for elections in March 1973. Perón designated a relatively unknown politician, Héctor Cámpora, who won with 49 per cent of the votes and paved the way for Perón's return from exile. In July, Cámpora resigned the presidency and, in new elections, in September 1973, the ticket of Perón and his third wife María Estela ('Isabelita') Martínez de Perón won with 62 per cent of the vote. The return of Perón raised expectations beyond the prospects of democratization. Public opinion assumed that the unions, which in the past had been able to block economic reforms, would cooperate with the government and be tamed for the sake of stability. Perón was also expected to control the guerrillas, while counting on the support of the business and industrial community and on the loyal opposition of the main opposition party—the Unión Cívica Radical—as accorded in the Radical-Peronist 1972 agreement that led to the electoral reopening. Faced with social tensions and unrest, some of these expectations proved void.[18]

Once in power, the new government of Perón adopted austerity policies which, combined with sky-rocketing inflation, provoked widespread strikes and brought workers and activists to demonstrations and clashes with the police. After Perón's death in July 1974, the tenuous social and political understandings woven around the leader and his image of strength disintegrated. Unions opposed governmental policies and internal repression within Peronism grew. The strategy of preventing sliding violence and subsequent military public intervention, followed by the UCR, proved increasingly ineffectual. The Montoneros and other left-wing guerrillas resumed violence in order to advance revolution. José López Rega, Minister of Social Welfare, personal secretary to Perón, and strongperson during Perón's wife's presidency, used a right-wing terrorist group, the Triple A, to annihilate the left. The situation became chaotic and violent. The government ordered the armed forces to carry out anti-subversive operations, for the first time against the guerrillas in the Tucumán province in February 1975 and on an all-national plane from October of that year.[19] After the military defeat of the guerrillas already in 1975–6, and facing a power vacuum after the loss of governance by 'Isabelita' Martínez and her government, the army took power in March 1976, beginning the Proceso de Reorganización Nacional (PRN). National Reorganization Process was the name used by the military to define their period of rule, in which a new model of social organization was envisaged. This model was based on political demobilization and enforced consensus, carried out through ferocious repression of subversives and internal enemies. Early parallel projects such as those of Admiral Emilio E. Massera, who wanted to create a popular–military alliance and movement and those of Finance Minister José Martínez de Hoz, of incorporating civilian politicians in administrative positions and moving back to open elections after three or four years of military rule, did not prosper. The military junta, led by General Jorge R. Videla, made substantial changes to the constitution, dissolved Parliament, intervened in public agencies, suspended political and trade union activity, and carried out policies of persecution, torture, and assassination of the sectors defined as 'enemies of the Nation', while it carried out liberal economic policies of stabilization, adjustment, and opening of markets.[20]

The timing of the Argentinian takeover determined a different international set-up of reaction to the military policies of repression in Argentina, distinct from that which surrounded the coups of Uruguay and Chile in 1973. The repressive policies in Uruguay and Chile, along with their projection to the international arena by local NGOs, political exiles, and the international media, had created an awareness which played against the military rulers of Argentina since the beginning of the PRN.

The impact of the Argentinian human rights movement's contact with international actors was magnified by the existence of an 'international human right regime' that was greater than the sum of its constituent states, international organizations and NGOs. The international human right regime created an international network and the principle of 'moral interdependence' that helped propagate the human rights movement's concerns across national boundaries. This new pattern of international cooperation on human rights developed critical strength during the era of the Argentine Proceso (1976–1983): the Carter administration displayed a new commitment to human rights by the regional hegemon, multi-lateral human rights forums grew stronger, and—most important—non-governmental transnational organizations played an increasing role.[21]

In 1981 the ruling junta under the presidency of General Roberto Viola initiated a dialogue with politicians towards an eventual transfer of power. Increasing economic instability and social unrest led his successor, General Leopoldo Galtieri, to embark on a failed war over the Malvinas–Falkland Islands with the UK in April 1982. Following the humiliating defeat and the disclosure of inefficiency and corruption, the military were forced to accelerate transfer of power to the civilians, leading to the return to democracy in December 1983.

The military governments of the Southern Cone systematically violated human rights within the framework of political repression. The National Security Doctrine (Doctrina de Seguridad Nacional, DSN), shared by the military establishments of the three nations, posited a link between the concepts of nation and state, and the role of the army towards both.[22] Because of their functional role, their formation, and their professional training the military saw themselves as guardians of the nation's values and traditions, especially in times of crisis.

The basic parameters for defining policies were security needs (external and internal) and defence of national interests, and the military considered themselves the most qualified and perhaps the only capable institutional actor for achieving these goals. In times of crisis they considered themselves entitled to assume the power to execute national objectives. According to their views, military rule would channel the nation's real spirit through the state's machinery. According to the DSN, the basic values of the nation are anchored organically within Western civilization (including Christian values), the defence of private property and initiative, and opposition to Communist and Marxist ideas.

In this process of identification and reduction, the concept of national unity plays a key role. National unity is viewed not as the historical product of social consensus, but as a fact that is 'natural' and meta-social, one derived from an 'essence,' a 'national soul,' or a tradition. But the tradition will not be the one imagined by the citizens, however. It will consist of freezing certain historical facts or universalizing particular features that are defined outside the freely expressed collective will. Consequently, when the collective will strays from the 'essence' of the nation or from 'tradition', it falls to the armed forces, the depository of that tradition, to restore order and take into its hands directly the destiny of the nation and reestablish national unity.[23]

The organic conception of the nation implied eliminating the enemy, since no 'organs' or 'cells' should be allowed to deviate from the basic parameters of the national values and traditions. If necessary, the armed forces would extirpate the threat, following the ideological visions they incorporated from the French theorists of counter-insurgence developed in the Algerian war and reinforced by the strong anti-Communist visions taught in the School of the Americas and other US training centres of anti-guerrilla warfare attended by Latin American officers. The local idioms of organicism gave further credence to the DSN view of the primacy of the national well-being over individual rights and needs. According to this logic, individual rights, including the most basic human rights, can be subordinated to national aims whenever necessary.[24] Particularly in Argentina, the DSN was linked with an integralist vision prevalent among substantial parts of Catholic hierarchy:

For the most part, our bishops have not disentangled themselves from integralism and they often reduced Catholicism to the level of a national ideology. This underlying set of ideas conditioned the reaction of the bishops to the military dictatorship. How were they going to stand up to a regime that in their eyes appeared to be one essential element of 'the Catholic State', protected the Church and was ready to eliminate heretics and enemies of the faith? It was a new alliance of throne and altar. The armed forces—whatever the personal conviction and moral behavior of officers—regarded Catholicism as an element that bound the nation together and an instrument of social control. The armed forces stood in agreement with national Catholicism.[25]

In contrast, the Chilean Church on the eve of the military coup was characterized by stronger internal divisions between its conservative and progressive wings that supported the different political parties, from the National Party on the right to the Christian Democracy at the centre-left.[26]

The state of protracted civil disorder and polarization of the late 1960s and early 1970s was perceived by the military establishments of the Southern Cone as a threat to the respective 'national beings' and as such required intervention into and reorganization of public life. In order to accomplish this, the security forces took power and, once in government, used abductions, long-term imprisonment, torture, summary executions, disappearances, and assassinations. The violation of individual rights was easily framed, recognizing the primacy of national collective interests over the individual. Large sectors of the military command perceived democracy itself as corrupt, inefficient, and leading to greater suffering and eventually to a wider curtailment and even the annihilation of civil and political rights by the Communists and their allies, if the latter were allowed to take hold of the reins of the state.

As the crisis deepened, the formal mechanisms for consensual resolution of conflict broke down. Patterns of authoritarian control and systematic repression were adopted by the military rulers. Unlike in Western Europe and North America, democratic state reformism proved unviable in the context of the Southern Cone during this period.

Patterns of Repression: Singularities and Legacies

Besides the parallel extensive use of repression and strategies of public control under the military governments, some secondary but significant differences can be traced in the various situations. The generalized and decentralized pattern of repression was typical of Argentina. This pattern was related to the previous history of violence and, in particular, to the activities of the nationalist paramilitary groups that acted against the left in coordination with the military already prior to March 1976. During military rule, the para-legal and decentralized character of violence persisted, albeit with some changes. The decentralization and lack of coordination, which in military terms could be related to the direct responsibility of area commanders following general orders concerning the 'destruction of subversion' and 'the liquidation of the enemy', produced an uneven pattern of repression.[27]

In hunting their enemies, the armed forces divided the country into five military areas under the command of the different corps, replicating the organizational design of an international war. Within each command there was a further subdivision into operational brigades and batallions located near almost 200 urban areas. Concurrently, and in coordination with the federal and provincial police forces, more than 300 clandestine centres of detention were established. The chain of command in charge of the repression was parallel to the formal chain of command of the armed forces. The operations against the enemy were conducted by 'task forces' (*grupos de tareas*) composed of different members of the armed and security forces. A pattern of rotation was established by the high commands, which resulted in the delegation of responsibilities and in the diffusion and displacement of guilt. This created a relatively long-lasting 'pact of silence' among the security forces and heightened the levels of fear and lack of personal security of the civilian population. As in a war, the security forces were requested to pursue 'total victory' against the 'leftist networks' and their supporting circles in a rapid and efficient manner.

The criss-crossing character of the division of responsibilities implied obeying orders that emanated ultimately from the juntas, and yet were enacted by task forces responsible to batallion commanders and subordinates in charge of the detention camps. The vague character of the formal directives, coupled with the operational subdivision of the forces and the placing of direct responsibilities on the local commanding officers, generated a pattern of uncoordinated autonomy in the implementation of the military strategy. This produced in turn a very intense and relatively undiscriminating use of violent repression, which affected both activists and random individuals. In some areas, repression was tightly focused on targeted sectors and individuals. In others, such as the province of Buenos Aires, repression was strategically oriented to an ever-spreading periphery that included the subversives' ideological allies and unwitting sympathizers. As General Ibérico Saint-Jean, governor of Buenos Aires during the first junta regime, boasted: 'First we kill the subversives; then we kill their collaborators; then . . . their sympathizers; then those who remain indifferent; and finally we kill the timid.'[28] Such totalizing views sustained an unpredictable pattern of repression, according to which some sectors were clearly targeted, but which threatened also individuals only tangentially connected with the left and some that were beyond the slightest suspiscion of subversion. People were made to disappear as they worked on behalf of other missing detainees; others were abducted in lieu of their relatives, and some by mistake; still others for profit-seeking interests or merely due to personal enmity. The number of missing and presumedly assassinated individuals is nearly 9,000 according to conservative assessments and between 20,000 and 30,000 according to more radical estimates.[29]

The profile of the Argentinian victims indicates that the sectors most severely affected were the blue-collar working class and wide sectors of the middle class, especially students, professionals, and white-collar employees. Professionals suspected of belonging to a radical discipline, such as psychiatry, psychology, sociology, or political science, were especially targeted. Nearly a third of the victims were women, with a representation of housewives, greatly exceeding the percentages of such victims in Chile and Uruguay (On the background characteristics of the victims in the Southern Cone countries see Tables 1.1–1.4). The pattern of repression involved the disregard for due legal process, the massive use of torture, flagrant personal abuses in the secluded detention centres, murders without trial and the phenomenon of the disappeared (*desaparecidos*), whose fate the military authorities claimed

TABLE 1.1. *Victims of Military Regimes' Repression*
(a) Occupational Distribution of Victims

Occupation (Percentages)	Argentina[a]	Chile[b]	Uruguay[c]
Working class	30.2	30.1	20.0
Peasants	n.a.	2.85	2.0
Drivers	n.a.	1.45	2.0
Industrial workers	n.a.	25.05	11.0
Other workers	n.a.	0.75	5.0
Students	21.0	14.22	7.0
From which University students	n.a.	7.24	3.6
White-collar employees	17.9	13.38	26.0
Clerks	n.a.	13.38	25.0
Auxiliaries	n.a.	n.a.	1.0
Professionals	18.3	11.06	21.0
Teachers, professors	5.7	3.99	n.a.
Legal profession	n.a.	0.57	n.a.
Engineers	n.a.	1.62	n.a.
Journalists	1.6	0.44	n.a.
Social sciences	n.a.	0.57	n.a.
Health professionals	n.a.	1.14	n.a.
Administrative positions	n.a.	1.97	1.0
'Technical professionals'	10.7	n.a.	20.0
Clerics	0.3	0.13	n.a.
Architects	n.a	0.61	n.a.
Self-employed and miscellaneous	10.1	25.45	24.0
Business people	n.a.	4.48	5.0
Self-employed	5.0	6.40	n.a.
Artists	1.3	0.31	n.a.
Housewives	3.8	0.75	'0.x'[d]
Unemployed	n.a.	2.72	4.0
Full-time militants	n.a.	n.a.	12.0
Others	n.a	10.04	2.0
Retired	n.a	0.75	1.0
Members of armed forces	2.5[e]	5.79	2.0

[a] Data for Argentina from *Nunca más: informe de la Comisión Nacional sobre la Desaparición de Personas* (Buenos Aires: EUDEBA, 20 edn. 1995), 296.
[b] *Informe de la Comisión Nacional de Verdad y Reconciliación* (Santiago: Talleres de La Nación, 1991), 887.
[c] Data for Uruguay, from *Uruguay: nunca más: Informe sobre la violación a los derechos humanos (1972–1985)* (Montevideo: Servicio Paz y Justicia, 1989), 25. Data refers to a sample composed by 'long-time detainees', n=313, for more details about the survey see ibid. 15–32.
[d] Less than 1%.
[e] Refers to 'Recruits and Low-Ranking Military Personnel'.

TABLE 1.1. (*cont'd*)
(*b*) Occupational Structure of the Southern Cone Societies (Included for
Comparative Reasons)

Occupation (Percentages)	Argentina EAP 1970	Chile EAP 1984	Uruguay EAP 1984
Working class	34.3	35.9	33.1
Peasants/farmers	14.4	14.7	3.3
Students			
Percentage of students being university students (1983)	0.9	0.4	0.7
White-collar employees	24.8	25.7	29.1
Professionals	7.5	6.5	10.2
Self-employed and miscellaneous			
Unemployed (metropolitan, 1980)	2.3	12.0	7.3
Members of armed forces (1980)	0.5	0.79	1.04

Sources: *Statistical Abstract of Latin America*, 22 (1981) and 26 (1985). UCLA Latin
American Center Publications. EAP: Economically Active Population.

TABLE 1.2. *Demographic Characteristics of Victims*
(*a*) Gender

	Argentina[a]	Chile[b]	Uruguay[c]
Men	n.n. (70%)	2,153 (94.5%)	272 (78.6%)
Women	n.n. (30%)	126 (5.5%)	74 (21.4%)

(*b*) Age

	Argentina[d]	Chile[e]	Uruguay[f]
Below 16	1.65	2.1	—
16–25	43.23	36.2	32.0
26–35	38.16	35.0	44.0
36–45	10.13	13.9	18.0
Over 46	6.83	9.4	6.0
Unknown	—	3.4	—

[a] *Nunca más*, 294 Argentinian data refers to disappeared.
[b] *Informe de la Comisión Nacional de Verdad y Reconciliación*, 884. Chilean data
refers to victims of political violence and repression.
[c] Uruguayan data refers to dead and disappeared.
[d] *Nunca más*, 294. Data appears originally in five-year categories.
[e] *Informe de la Comisión Nacional de Verdad y Reconciliación*, 885. Data appears
originally in five-year categories.
[f] *Uruguay: nunca más*, 23. Data refers to 'long time detainees' sample. Age
categories are 18–24; 25–34; 35–44; and 45 and older.

TABLE 1.3. *Sociopolitical Background of Victims*

(*a*) Concentration

Area	Argentina	Chile[a]	Uruguay[b]
Metropolitan	57	56.95	72 (Montevideo)
Urban	22	42.03	22
Exterior	n.a.	1.01	2
Rural	n.a.	—[c]	4

(*b*) Nationality

Argentina	Chile[d]	Uruguay
A 'majority' of Argentinian nationality, however 18.6% of disappeared Uruguayan 'vanished' were abducted abroad, especially in Argentina	97.7% of Chilean nationality	98.3% of Uruguayan nationality

(*c*) Political activity

Argentian	Chile[e]	Uruguay[f]
n.a.	'a majority' (46% without mention)	80% yes (62% of them were active militants)

[a] *Informe de la Comisión Nacional de Verdad y Reconciliación*, 886.
[b] *Uruguay: nunca más*, 120. Data refers to the survey.
[c] Subsumed together with urban victims.
[d] *Informe de la Comisión Nacional de Verdad y Reconciliación*, 884.
[e] Ibid. 885.
[f] *Uruguay: nunca más*, 31, Table 21.

TABLE 1.4. *Place of Detention of the Victims*

	Argentina[a]	Chile	Uruguay[b]
In the streets	24.6	n.a.	23
At home	62	n.a.	61
Workplace	7	n.a.	9
Studyplace	6	n.a.	1
Military or police locals	0.4	n.a.	n.a.
Political centre	n.a.	n.a.	4
Religious centre	n.a.	n.a.	1
Other	n.a.	n.a.	1

[a] *Nunca más*, 17.
[b] *Uruguay: nunca más*, 121. Data refers to the survey.

not to know. As in the other Southern Cone cases, and perhaps more so, the security forces used sadistic methods of torture, mutilation, and murder.

Argentina underwent a massive wave of terror and brutal repression, in which the repressive apparatus succeeded in paralysing the legal and social frameworks which could have diminished the impact of the blatant policy of human-rights violations. One example is the reluctance of lawyers to present habeas corpus appeals in cases of abduction of citizens, especially after the disappearance of some of those lawyers who dared to present them. Another characteristic was the silence of most Church dignitaries, despite their influence upon governmental circles, and upon General Videla. In *Witness to the Truth*, Emilio Mignone shows that, beyond the inner diversity of the Argentinian Church, most of the bishops actively supported military dictatorship after 1976:

The Argentine bishops made a purely political option. They aligned themselves with temporal power, rejecting the witness of the gospel, which demands that crimes be denounced, those responsible be accused and the victims, actively helped, even at the risk of persecution. The bishops knew the truth and they hid it in order to aid the military government. Faced with a choice between God and Caesar, they chose Caesar.[30]

Uruguay, too, had experienced a previous wave of violence between the left-wing urban guerrillas of the MLN (Tupamaros) and the security forces. The Tupamaros had been severely attacked and defeated during the last phase of President Bordaberry's civilian government, before the military assumption of power. Following the latter, the country witnessed massive arrests conducted mostly in the open; long-term reclusion of convicted prisoners; torture, albeit more controlled and limited; and assassinations of political opponents, though in smaller numbers than in Argentina, and mostly with clearly targeted victims. At least 157 nationals 'disappeared' and 95 political prisoners were killed, died from illness, or committed suicide in detention centres between 1972 and 1985. On average, for every 10,000 Uruguayans, 31 were detained for political reasons (many were abducted in Argentina), and most of them were subjected to torture. There are sources that place this rate at even higher levels. Many believe that Uruguay has had in this period the highest record of political prisoners per capita in Latin America. In the same period 15 children were kidnapped with their parents by military personnel, and the destiny of many of them is still uncertain.[31] In addition, tens of thousands of people left the country, driven out by the combined effects of economic decline and repression.[32]

Here, we didn't have the terrible quantity of killings, as in Chile. We didn't experience a sinister operation as in Argentina. But we also lived through difficult times. There was indiscriminate torture. We had among the highest number of prisoners in Latin America. There were some disappearances. There were Uruguayan-Argentinian and Uruguayan-Brazilian joint operations. There was an extremely totalitarian handling of repression, eased by the small size of the country. In a sense, the spaces left open in Uruguayan society were minimal, especially in the hardest years of repression.[33]

The majority of the victims of repression were political militants; many of them were professionals and white-collar employees. Most of the victims were males, while a fifth of them were women. In Uruguay, the urban nature of repression was pronounced, according to the demographic concentration and the urban pattern of political mobilization. In contrast with Argentina, the lower ranks of the armed forces and the police were subjected in Uruguay to more precise orders concerning the methods and focus of repression. This was related to the fact that the Uruguayan armed forces maintained their pattern of corporative deliberation during their rule, thus elaborating their policies of control in a more regulated and yet flexible pattern fit to current developments.[34]

More like the Brazilian way, they operated as a social police force that, correcting, disciplining, and cutting the ill branches, are pruning the tree and afterwards 'let's see' . . . They wanted a system in which the tree would not get infected anew, but basically they liked the tree they had, they thought it was a good tree.[35]

Motivated by their faith in society and hoping to control it rather than merely eliminate the 'subversive enemy', the military rulers of Uruguay instituted a system that on the one hand did not reach the scale of atrocities typical of Argentina, but that, in many senses, was more coercive and penetrated society and culture in a semi-totalitarian way.[36]

The Chilean case can be considered closer to Uruguay in terms of the number of arrests, while similar to Argentina in the scope of repression and the pattern of torture, killing, and disappearances: 2,920 cases of killing as a result of human-rights violations and political violence were examined by the Rettig Commission; another 508 cases were presented but were considered beyond the mandate of the commission; and, in another 449 cases, only the name of the person was known and the commission did not make further inquiries. The successor to the Rettig Commission, the National Corporation for Compensation and Reconciliation (CNRR) published in August 1996 a final report, which confirmed 899 cases in addition to those documented by the Rettig

Commission, bringing the total number of victims of killing and disappearance to 3,197.[37] In the case of Chile, the murdered were mainly people belonging to clearly targeted sectors: political leaders and militants, individuals active in the labour movement, both urban and rural, students and intellectuals. These were mostly the sectors targeted in Uruguay, although in Uruguay many of these managed to survive in prison. The number of people tortured is calculated by human-rights organizations to be in the tens of thousands.

The structure of the Chilean armed forces was highly vertical and non-deliberative, which implied that in each corps and branch a complete subordination to the higher commands was the rule. Compared with Argentina, the Chilean repressive apparatus was accordingly more hierarchically coordinated. In the first months after the September 1973 takeover, acts of repression were carried out in separate channels by the respective intelligence services of the different branches of the armed forces and Carabineros. Moreover, there were initial differences in the approaches of the various branches, with the air force commander favouring a legalist approach (intended to carry out repressive actions within the lines of the 1925 constitutional provision of 'states of emergency' and military law) as opposed to the Army commander, who was more persuaded by the need to carry out a total war against the forces of subversion. Nonetheless, in early 1974 hierarchical coordination was attained by creating the National Directorate of Intelligence (Dirección Nacional de Inteligencia, DINA), the security organ in charge of coordinating and implementing repression. General Augusto Pinochet delegated operational autonomy to the DINA with its commanding officer, Colonel Manuel Contreras, which was directly subordinated to the President of the Junta.[38]

In addition to conducting repressive operations inside Chile, the DINA also operated abroad. It acted, similarly to the Argentinian and Uruguayan intelligence agencies, in the neighbouring countries, and, unlike their neighbours, in the USA and Europe as well. Its most notorious actions abroad were the assassination of General Carlos Prats and his wife in Buenos Aires; the attempted murder of Bernardo Leighton, former Vice-President of Chile, in Rome; and the killing of the former minister of Foreign Affairs, Orlando Letelier, and his American aid, Ronnie Moffit, in Washington. In August 1977, under international pressures and as a result of criticism within governmental and military circles, the DINA was dismantled and replaced by the National Intelligence Centre (Central Nacional de Informaciones—CNI). Both the DINA and the CNI operated by recruiting their personnel from the ranks of the armed forces, thus creating a generalized and officially sanctioned involvement of all armed sectors in repression.

Whereas the DINA had a very high level of operational autonomy, the new body was statutorily defined and operated accordingly. After 1977, repression continued in Chile but was even more clearly targeted (e.g. against the Movimiento de Izquierda Revolucionario—MIR—the Frente Patriótico Manuel Rodríguez—the military branch of the Chilean Communist Party—and later on against the Lautaro group) and enacted in the framework of the military state hierarchy. Among the specific characteristics of the Chilean repression was the fact that a large number of individuals were imprisoned in concentration camps and torture centres, and that many Chileans went into exile in Europe, other Latin American countries, and North America.[39]

The comparative variance in the specific patterning of repression indicates that, although we analyse three nationalist military dictatorships that operated within the shared ideological framework of doctrines of National Security, there was in each case a different constellation of factors that affected the ways in which the pattern of domination was implemented through repression. On the basis of previous and current research, it is possible to trace some of the most salient conditioning factors and their varying constellations in these societies.

It is necessary to keep in mind that the development of collective trauma cannot be automatically inferred from the variable extent and modes of repression. Indeed, there are many differences in the number of victims, their percentage within the general population, their sectorial distribution, their composition in terms of age, gender, and education, the geographic concentration or spread of repressive violence, variations in the specific methodologies of torture and assassination used, and the scale of assassinations.[40] But all these do not explain the ways in which the collective trauma of these societies developed and was treated. Such inference would be faulty, for the impact of repression is mediated by the different format of civic culture and the variable scope of violence and tolerance for violence that prevailed in each society, shaping collective expectations.

The public demonstration effect of repression

A common denominator exists in the three countries in the use of repression as a means for creating a situation of generalized fear, which was instrumental in demobilizing the population. A large corpus of literature, drawing mainly on social psychology and humanistic studies, suggests that, as fear induced distrust, it led to depoliticization and the unwillingness to acknowledge repression. It generated a parallel privatization of concerns and a restriction on the political issues that reached the public sphere. The concentration of feelings, thoughts, and commitments within minimal sets of relationships, mainly but not only within familial links, was another feature of the prevalence of fear in society.[41]

A no less important feature is the relationship between these forms of psychosocial privatization and social disintegration, on the one hand, and on the other, the policies of economic privatization carried out by the military regimes. These policies too were built upon the restriction of public concerns, as individuals concentrate their efforts and concerns on survival and personal advancement. This connection between the societal visions and the economic neoliberal policies of the military governments is the crux of the processes that weakened social solidarity and collectivistic public discourse and marginalized earlier visions of voluntaristic revolutionary change.[42]

The long-term effects of these processes on the personal plane have been eloquently described both by anthropologists and other social scientists as well as in literature and the arts. Often, they are described in terms of a 'culture of fear'. Even when, following democratization, there was a psychological process of elaborating the scars of repression, various forms of 'low-intensity fear' were likely to persist.[43] For instance, Marcelo Suárez-Orozco reports that in mid-1988

a psychiatrist working on the psychological sequelae of terror among the relatives of the *desaparecidos* calmly and convincingly tells me to be careful what I tell him when I call him over the telephone. He noted that his telephone had been bugged . . . for at least two years. A few days later, a Mother of Plaza de Mayo tells me as I am chatting with her in their official house across the street from the Plaza Congreso that they no longer receive much of their overseas mail because they are under surveillance by security forces who want to subvert their international human rights campaigns. In early 1989 *The New York Times* reports that the president of the Mothers of Plaza de Mayo, Hebe Bonafini, was almost killed as a car chased her down a sidewalk in her native city of La Plata in Buenos Aires . . .[44]

Whether substantiated or not, such developments fit into interpretations of reality and reinforce discursive plots which were shaped through the persistent scars imprinted during the period of military rule. Low-intensity fears are perceived in these societies under democracy.

For various generations of Uruguayans, the sequels continue marking our culture and our style of life. From the greatest topics to the most minuscule and mundane. Like the anguish that possesses us as we touch our pockets going out and realize we did not take the documents. Or the desolation we feel at night fearing the sound of a siren, a knock at the door or an unexpected telephone call.[45]

Probably the most sensitive fictional reflection of the emotional state in which former victims find themselves after the ordeal is to be found in writings about encounters and re-encounters of women by women or feminist writers such as Marta Traba's or Alicia Kozameh's works. Kozameh, herself a political prisioner, who at a certain point was released into 'freedom under surveillance' for two additional years before leaving for exile, portrays in her stories the difficulties of former prisoners to reclaim their lives, the nightmarish possibility of further harassment and even renewed incarceration, and the empowerment to be potentially found in the sisterhood that emerged among female prison inmates. In 'El encuentro: Pájaros', the persisting threats take the form of motorcycled men running over three women who decided to meet again, this time outside prison.

Let us cross the street now that nobody is coming. The three almost run, the cars seem far away but they come closer with that peculiar style in which the city expresses its rancor, they display their smoke, their exhaust systems, the capacity of their almighty brakes, that never cease to take into account their intrinsic and reserved right to fail. And they run, Sara and Cristina forward, Elsa behind them, and from behind she sees them, she can distinguish them, recognize them, the motorcycles as they come closer, the same ones, the same types, that speed up. Be careful, shouts Elsa, and the motorcycles pass between them as a flash of light, erasing Elsa's scream, beating and scratching the bottoms of Cristina and Sara, who only realize their presence after they have passed; they hear as they seem to move away You be careful, idiots, you expose yourselves too much, you better stay home and cook, it's better, don't tell afterwards you were not warned. Why do you stare with those faces, you don't understand? They brake and they slow down as Sara and Cristina manage to reach the pedestrian alley, with less than half the books they carried. And they turn their bodies of spasmed muscles, turn their heads . . . And they don't answer, where do they go with so many books the three, are they pushing themselves again into the university, they seem not to learn, be careful what you do, idiots, in what little secrets are you involved, be careful, the wheels advancing and they taking steps backward, confused, in that first stage of fear, of the fears. Don't think we don't know who has children, who has parents, and who suffers more for one or the other. And the one in the red motorcycle speaks for the others Let's go, these idiots won't forget it . . .[46]

Remnants of terror, repression, and horror are also embedded in the transformed language, thus imprinting all communicative flow. As Marguerite Feitlowitz has written:

Dictatorship is alive in these aberrations of the language, in the scars that it left in the language . . . Language, public and intimate at the same time, is a borderline between our vulnerable inner identity and the external world. When, as with the skin, language is mutilated, wounded, or burnt, the borderline disappears. Then we are defenceless, without protection. What we knew we do not know anymore. Names that emerged from a shared experience as true sound false now . . .[47]

As a result, the public culture of these societies is imprinted with fear for years to come. This is especially visible in those cases where there is a high likelihood of renewal of crises and social insecurity.[48]

The opening of the public sphere under democracy created an opportunity for the public to learn about the mechanisms of misinformation, repression, and fear formation. Institutionalized mechanisms should pre-empt future violations and guarantee the protection of human rights in the long term, but knowledge of past atrocities may also be a deterrent, as the fear carries over into the democratic period. Research has indicated also that, in order to survive, many of the individuals who suffered violations of human rights and struggle against them could not avoid adopting a dichotomous view that paradoxically mirrored in inverted terms that of the repressors.[49]

The analyses above focus on the way repression was used as a means to attain a 'public demonstration effect'; a parallel analytical line emphasizes instead the expressive use of violence by the repressors. Typical of this approach is Frank Graziano's elaboration of René Girard's thesis on the 'divine' character of violence. Graziano elaborates the thematic structure of Dirty War violence as the emotional and erotic expression of those individuals who had militarized control over Argentinian society. According to this interpretive line,

the phallocentrism of 'dirty war' torture and mythology, the 'castratability' and transferability of the *picana*[50] (as phallus, word, power), the dynamics of Junta desire, the insistent presence of Christian doctrine with its hierarchical relation within a Father–Son deity together suggest an Oedipal structure of 'dirty war' violence . . . [In this interpretation, Graziano follows] the extension of the complex to politico-familiar structures, [in particular] René Girard's development of mimetic rivalry . . . in place of the Oedipal father, Girard posited any model-rival; in place of the mother, any object valued by the rival; and in place of the unconscious, mythic mentality.[51]

According to Graziano, when society seemed on the verge of collapse, the military 'saviours' of the nation drew a mythic map and began carving into the victims' tortured bodies depending on their location on that map; the victims, of course, were silenced from the start under the repressors' paradigms and violent erotic impetus.

To look at repression from the perspective of the repressors' emotional drives for omnipotence and power may lead us to recognize its presence in the three situations as part of the prevailing strategies of domination, with differences related to the psychological make-up of the repressors.[52]

Notwithstanding the importance of this psychosocial dimension, it does not enable us to provide a systematic account of how distinctive patterns of repression crystallized in the three settings, for it was the cultural and sociological framework that determined in each case how and to what extent these drives crystallized into more or less institutionalized paths of repression.

The frameworks of repression

An explanation of the variable patterns of repression is to be found in terms of the presence or absence of various conditioning factors, which were shaped with differences in the institutional development of these societies. When analysing the institutional set-up of the different patterns of repression, four clusters of such factors seem to be of special importance: first, the image of threat posed by the radicalized left at the onset of military rule; second, the patterns of legitimacy that developed in these societies, especially regarding military interventions in public life; third, the scope of legitimate dissent and the existence or absence of a tradition of demonizing political opponents; and fourth, the organizational dimensions of the repressive apparatus.

The first cluster relates to the projection of threat posed by the radicalized left and revolutionary sectors in each society at the onset of military rule. The activities of the guerrillas (urban and rural) and the mobilization of popular sectors committed to various left-wing and populist radical ideas provided the background for initiating a repressive project of 'national salvation' by the security forces. This projection of threat has to be analysed on two levels: first, how the political leadership and the security forces perceived the threat themselves; and second, how the political leadership and the security forces projected images of threat to the society. These images were represented in terms of threats to personal security, life and private property, and of a generalized threat to the 'Nation', its values and the society at large. In Uruguay, the defeat of the Tupamaros prior to the military takeover diminished the imagined threat to that society. As these events occurred under presidentialist-parliamentary democracy, institutions such as the Parliament could exercise some supervision over the military's treatment of political prisoners. As they took power, the Uruguayan military commands could be confident that they had already mortally wounded the guerrillas and their attitude was accordingly less messianic than in the neighbouring countries. This background conditioned the subsequent legal framing of most repression in Uruguay.

The objective relation of forces between the military and the revolutionary groups was mediated by the images of threat perceived and projected publicly. In Argentina, before the 1976 coup, a perception of threat and chaos was generated by kidnappings, assassinations, bombings, and other terrorist attacks by both extreme rightist paramilitary and leftist guerrilla groups. The armed left hoped that repression would prompt the massive support of the population for their revolutionary cause.[53] Despite military victories over the guerrilla organizations and the mobilized sectors during the last phase of the civilian government, the armed forces continued to function under the operational definition of threat once they took power. Such a threat, relating to underground organizations such as the Montoneros, Fuerzas Armadas Revolucionarias (FAR), Fuerzas Armadas Revolucionarias del Pueblo (FARP), and the ERP, was perceived as acute, even though the armed forces had defeated these organizations in Tucumán and other places during the last years of Martínez de Perón's rule.[54] Even as the real threat of the guerrilla forces disappeared, the image of threat persisted.

As it turned out, the two terrors needed one another to feed their own perverse aims: the armed left needed the repressive right in its fantastic plan for a popular uprising. The armed forces, following the coup of 1976 that ushered in the dirty war terror, perpetuated and carefully fed the myth of a subversive threat, *even after the armed left had been virtually annihilated in the field.* Even years after the threat of the armed left had been crushed, innocent civilians continued to be haunted in the name of 'national security.'[55]

Following the 1976 coup, the military curtailed the possibilities for monitoring their repressive actions, and their messianic vision was translated into a *carte blanche* to eliminate any vestige of subversion, leading to flagrant violations of individual human rights. In Chile, the confrontation between the armed forces and the organizations that supported the government of Allende began with the coup. The government of the Unidad Popular (UP) had wide support in different sectors of civil society: in the large trade union movement, student unions, professional associations, neighbourhood associations (especially in the *poblaciones* around the big cities), intellectuals, sectors of the Church, and even within the armed forces. The military believed that the industrial belts of the major cities were organized in paramilitary units by the UP activists to serve the Revolution and to resist any move by the armed forces against the Socialist government. Following the coup, the capacity of the leftist sectors and organizations to resist the military takeover proved ineffective. Nevertheless, the armed forces and Carabineros perceived and confronted the left as an extremely widespread, organized, and dangerous enemy. Thus, when assuming power, they occupied the offices of the political parties and organizations, imprisoned their leaders and killed many of the activists, and overtook the latter's strongholds such as the industrial areas and the universities.[56]

Second among the factors that conditioned the different patterning of repression is the extent of legitimacy granted to participation in and control of the public sphere by the military, crystallizing in the presence or absence of traditions of armed forces' intervention in public life. On a general plane, a common background may be perceived: in all three cases, the military maintained a distinction between the concepts of the 'nation' and of 'state'. Whereas the state was conceived as a temporal and changing entity, the nation was posited as the eternal collective subject of history. According to their views, the basic commitment of the armed forces was given to the nation, defending its values and interests, while constitutionalism, or the defence of the state institutions, was respected as long as these institutions did not threaten the nation.[57] A situation of polarization, conflict, anarchy, civil war, or any serious menace to the nation, as interpreted by the military, might prompt military intervention, even in those countries where the armed forces had traditionally been reluctant to assume power.

Nonetheless, some countries showed a pattern of recurrent interventions in public life, while in others that pattern was nearly absent. In the case of Argentina, the military had very early adopted a tutelary attitude toward politics, the state, and the public sphere. The Argentinian armed forces had taken power in 1930, 1943, 1955, 1962, and 1966, and once more as they initiated the PRN in 1976. Their public vocation was sustained by their disdain for civilian politicians and their self-image as the saviours of the nation. As stated by Alain Rouquié, 'The armed forces do not intervene as a last resort or in exceptional conditions, but as a military [political] party and in order to impose the political line rejected by public opinion or by another military sector.'[58] Once in power, the Argentinian armed forces acted with almost complete disregard for legal constraints in carrying out the 'dirty war' against subversives and their supporting circles.

In Uruguay and Chile, in contrast, the armed forces had stayed outside the political centre and developed a vision of 'civilism' and of their constitutional role as central to their professional position. In Uruguay, the post-1971 growing involvement of the armed forces in politics under presidents Jorge Pacheco Areco and Juan María Bordaberry and the coup of 1976 were perceived as being the exception.[59] Once in power, they used long imprisonment and torture in their war with the radicalized political opposition and killed a number of prominent politicians, although they refrained from a systematic policy of mass illegal imprisonment and killings as in Argentina. After having been in power for years, the Uruguayan military rulers decided to reform the civilian constitution by submitting a proposal to a general referendum by the citizenry; once defeated in the polls in November 1980, they accepted the defeat of their constitutional reform.[60] In Chile, the armed forces were traditionally respectful of the constitutional framework and of electoral results. In relation to their introduction in the state apparatus, since the 1930s the civilian authorities had attempted to limit the military to their professional duties, assigning them no political or developmental functions. The military received meagre budgets and had limited influence on Chilean elites. The increasing polarization of the late 1960s and early 1970s created a situation in which the military was progressively absorbed into politics. Already in 1969 the attempted rebellion by General Roberto Viaux (the so-called *Tacnazo*) was triggered by feelings of corporate inferiority among the Chilean officers corps vis-à-vis the armies of Argentina and Peru, countries with which Chile had pending and potentially explosive border disputes. The assassination of the commander-in-chief of the army, General René Schneider, and the constitutionalist attitude of his successor, General Carlos Prats, increasingly pushed the military into politics and into the government.[61] In September 1973, weeks after Prats presented his resignation and was replaced by Pinochet, the military finally took power in order to 'save the nation'. A systematic policy of illegal imprisonment and killings was carried out under military rule, especially in the early years, under the coordinated command of the intelligence body, DINA. In Chile, the military authorities used the basic legal patterns that had existed for decades, attempting to frame authoritarian rule on the basis of legality and constitutionality, but with a strong dose of authoritarianism.

Closely related to the preceding factor in monitoring military intervention and repression was the variable extent of autonomy of the civilian political systems. In Argentina, the primacy of the Peronist camp (formally ostracized from the military coup of 1955 until the democratic elections of 1973) was a major factor in the interweaving of the army in politics. As orderly public life deteriorated after the return of Peronism in 1973, the armed forces were widely seen as the proper agents of stabilization of the political system. The low level of autonomy of the Argentinian political class, compounded with calls from some civilian sectors for the military to intervene in the state, again brought about the demise of democratic rule in 1976. Afterwards, such low levels of autonomy were a major hindrance for the civilian political forces' ability to retain legal protection of individual rights and for their prospects of regaining power during military rule before the Malvinas–Falkland debacle. In Uruguay, the civilian politicians then in power called on the military to play a central role in combating subversion and progressively surrendered the civilian government's autonomy vis-à-vis the military. In Chile as well, large sectors of the civilian opposition to the UP government pressured the military to put an end to social and political disorder; they intended for such intervention to be short-lived, but of course this expectation was disappointed. Following the 1973 coup, those civilian sectors who collaborated with Pinochet retained a high level of influence in economic and constitutional matters. Although these sectors could not prevent the military from engaging in extensive repression, they seem to have been instrumental in bringing Pinochet to reconsider the pattern of repression around 1977, convincing him to demand more regulation of the activities of the internal intelligence apparatus.[62]

A third factor that differentiates the patterns of repression is the extent to which political dissent was legitimate, i.e. whether political opponents were demonized. As Jeffrey Alexander has indicated, politics involves important meaning-making processes:

Political fights are, in part, about how to distribute actors across the structure of discourse, for there is no determined relation between any event or group and either side of the cultural scheme. Actors struggle to taint one another with the brush of repression and to wrap themselves in the rhetoric of liberty. In periods of tension and crisis, political struggle becomes a matter of how far and to whom the discourses of liberty and repression apply. The effective cause of victory and defeat, imprisonment and freedom, sometimes even of life and death, is often discursive domination, which depends on just how popular narratives about good and evil are extended.[63]

Variations in these respects are evident in the spectrum of political banning of oppositionary forces, whether the latter covered the activities of the extreme left alone or included also other political forces such as Peronism. Both in Chile and in Uruguay multi-party politics had attained legitimacy, thus enabling the institutionalization of conflict management and regulating the contest for power and allocation of resources. Thus in Chile and in Uruguay major power holders were more likely than in Argentina to concede defeat and hand over power peacefully, and opposition groups were more likely to refrain from resorting to threats or violence in expressing their political demands. In Argentina, the demonization of the political opposition probably facilitated more lethal patterns of repression, once authoritarian rule began.

It is important to reflect on this variability in connection with the varied interpretation of the National Security doctrine the military establishments shared in the three countries. As discussed above, this doctrine suggested a comprehensive war against the forces of subversion and for the defence of the nation and its 'organic' values, conceived in Catholic, nationalist, and anti-Marxist terms. Nonetheless, the doctrine was interpreted in slightly different ways in the various countries. In Argentina, it was a guideline for eliminating the enemies of the nation; the terms used were organicist and projected a medicalized discourse that demanded the 'extirpation of ill tissues' from the national body:

During the dictatorship, a 'medical' story circulated: the country was ill; a virus had corrupted it; a drastic intervention was needed. The military state defined itself as the only surgeon able to operate without delays and without demagoguery. To survive, society had to endure major surgery. Some parts had to be operated on without anaesthetic. That was the kernel of the plot: a sick country and a group of physicians ready to save its life. In fact, the story covered up a criminal reality of mutilated bodies and bloody operations. But at the same time the story referred to that reality explicitly. The structure of the terror story [at that time] conveyed and secluded everything.[64]

Military nationalism evolved as a central rallying cry for defending the nation, as evident in the December 1978 near state of war with Chile and in the 1982 war with Great Britain. Despite the brutality of the repression and the lack of active internal opposition, no systematic institutional model was developed, as apparent in the military's failure to replace the 1853 Constitution. In Uruguay, the armed forces opted to act harshly but to implement policies aimed at returning to normalcy in terms of authoritarian and limited democracy submitted to popular approval, according to Uruguayan political traditions. Failing to gain such approval in the 1980 referendum, the Uruguayan armed forces accepted the popular verdict. In Chile this doctrine was interpreted in terms of a merciless war against subversion, but also led to the reformulation of the institutional frameworks in the 1980 Constitution, in terms that prevented populist or radical mobilization linked to Marxist or other foreign ideologies. The evolving model portrayed a neoliberal vision of economic life, the idea of the 'subsidiarity of the state', and the notion of civil society organized through associations representing the different social sectors, all imbued with the national pride so dear to the military.

Fourth among the institutional factors differentiating the patterning of repression in the cases under consideration is the structure of the security forces command through which repression was carried out. With a population of only three million, heavily concentrated in Montevideo, Uruguay was unlikely to experience widespread covert violence or overt denial of such violence; such policies were more possible in Chile and Argentina, with their larger populations and vast geographic size.

This factor in itself cannot, however, explain why the Chilean army resorted to overt repression while the Argentinian forces pursued a different strategy of repression and denial. Here the command structure conditioned how strategies adopted by the supreme commands were carried out at lower operational levels, that is, actual repression and violation of human rights. The armed and security forces of Chile stood out by virtue of their adherence, within their own doctrinal terms, to a more coordinated and rigid structure of command and implementation of repression. At the opposite pole stood the Argentinian armed forces, which were characterized by a highly uncoordinated pattern of repression. In between stood the Uruguayan armed forces, with a coordinated pattern of repression.

In decentralized structures such as that of the Argentinian armed forces, the specific subculture of the repressors and their latent values and orientations were far more important than the orders they received from above; in Chile, on the other hand, the centralized and legalistic structure of command ensured that orders were applied literally. This dimension has important implications for the question at the centre of the public agenda following redemocratization: who should be punished? Those who gave the orders? Those who carried them out? Only those who distinguished themselves in carrying out the repression?

The patterns of repression that evolved in these countries have in a certain way affected the treatment of human-rights violations following redemocratization. For example, they affected the possibilities for punishment, excusation, compensation, and reconciliation during democratic rule, as we will indicate in later chapters. They also affected the reformulation of the institutional and symbolic models and discourses these societies used to confront the recent past.

Throughout the transition to democracy, the experiences of repression thus became an 'inheritance' for the redemocratized countries; this legacy both sustained a discourse of human-rights violations and was interpreted through that discourse.

The Discourse of Human-Rights Violations in the Context of the Southern Cone

The extent of repression, and the international publicity achieved through the work of local NGOs and international bodies, brought the discourse of human-rights violations to the centre of the public spheres of the Southern Cone polities, already during military rule. In this period, when censorship and political controls were fully in place, the governments reacted to this discourse mostly by denouncing it as part of a policy of defamation inspired by their leftist political enemies at home and abroad. The military governments rejected the discourse of defending human rights on two grounds. First, according to their views, situations of crisis allowed for the exceptional derogation of civil rights as envisaged by the human rights treaties (e.g. article 27 of the Inter-American Convention on Human Rights). From their perspective, coercive violence had been used, if at all, to the same extent as during previous civilian governments, in order to guarantee social order. In a principled line, they justified using violence in order to save their societies from a greater evil, namely, the annihilation of all civil and political rights as part of a Marxist totalitarian takeover.[65] Second, international pressures concerning the human-rights issue were perceived by the military rulers and presented to the public as a blatant violation of sovereignty. The supporters of the military government rejected the absolute criteria advanced through the discourse of human rights and favoured a vision that suggested the need to contextualize actions to understand their significance. Accordingly, they claimed that what the opposition to the military presented as human-rights violations should have been relativized and interpreted as measures taken to prevent the disintegration of these societies, in the context of anarchy.

While certain minorities progressively adopted human rights as their banner for opposing military rule, wide sectors of the demobilized societies of the Southern Cone accepted the official versions and others reacted with apathy. Part of that 'acceptance' was related to the lack of a 'rights consciousness', thus allowing violations to be contextualized, thereby making the official positions easier to push on public consciousness. It was during the transitions to democracy and following redemocratization that the discourse of human rights became the central idiom for dealing with the legacy of authoritarianism and for reshaping the identity of these societies, in terms of individual rights.

The approach of human rights was first projected to worldwide prominence in the early post-war period, when it was enshrined in the 1948 Universal Declaration of Human Rights. The ensuing 1966 international covenants on Economic, Social, and Cultural Rights and on Civil and Political Rights were followed by a long series of general and regional conventions, topical conventions intended to guard against particular human rights abuses, conventions on group protection, and conventions that prohibited discrimination based on race or sex, or based on education, employment, and occupation. But, as a discourse of wide appeal, it became meaningful only as regional and international changes occurred in the 1970s. Since then, transnational institutions have emerged and movements have been organized that promoted the language of human rights and the monitoring of human-rights violations on a universal scale.[66] Although the universal standards set by the international community have not been fully implemented, they reflect a wide consensual recognition of certain minimal rights of individuals and groups, which

member states of the UN have agreed to recognize, promote and protect, and for which, therefore, states are properly held accountable. Today, the legitimacy of political regimes—hence their capacity to rule non-coercively—is judged less by the old standards of divine right, revolutionary heritage, national destiny, or charismatic authority, and more by new standards informed and refined by the language of international human rights.[67]

The growing international status of the human-rights discourse has been unevenly connected with a varied degree of political conditionality and effective implementation of human rights and entitlements in local settings. Such implementation hinged upon the specific historical experience of different societies and, particularly, to how past human-rights violations have been confronted in each setting following political changes, regime transitions, and democratization. In this sense, the impact of a universal concern with human rights and entitlements is compounded by differing visions of citizenship and patterns of legitimacy encoded historically in each society as well as by its current political and social context.

In Argentina, for example, the idiom of human rights—as inalienable rights inherent in individuals by their human 'nature'—was and (at the same time) was not an innovation in its political culture. The countries of the Southern Cone had indeed developed highly sophisticated legal systems and written constitutions with explicit rights protection that very early recognized legal provisions such as the habeas corpus. In the twentieth century these societies entered international forums and signed international treaties that made formal commitments to human rights. Nonetheless, until recently the discourse of human rights was alien to the local political culture and conceptions. Indeed, before the PRN, neither the military nor the forces of the extreme left recognized the primacy of human rights as the foundation of public life. For elites and popular strata alike, the language of human rights was devoid of substantial significance.[68] Concurrently, the striving for equality was inherent in the imagery and language of the Argentinian state and of major social sectors at least from the early Peronist period. However, this language of equality was embedded in anti-liberal principles and in communitarian ideas, especially within an organic imagery of the nation and its people and within a hierarchical conception of political authority that sustained a heavy concentration of power and decision-making in the hands of the leader. The organic vision of the nation had roots in the country's political culture and appealed to sectors beyond Peronism, at both the left and the right ends of the political spectrum. According to this organic vision of state and society, the political community and its centre stand above private interests. In principle, therefore, any reliance on the factional expression of private interests can be precluded, inasmuch as the ruler interprets the popular will, works towards the common good, and carries out the public mission in order and harmony, thus precluding anarchy and struggle.[69]

Within this framework, major political actors tended to fight for power not only for partisan purposes, but also to remake their societies according to these conceptions; in Edward Shils's terms, they wanted to create a societal centre that promotes the common good and safeguards social and political order.[70] Such were the motives cited by the military men who launched the *coups d'état* of the 1960s and 1970s in Argentina, Uruguay, and Chile as well as in Brazil. This vision of public life supported the military governments' policy of repression, which implied high individual costs for the supposedly higher benefit of preserving society as a whole. This is particularly exemplified by the role of the Argentine courts in rights enforcement during the military regime. There existed a formal language of protection to promote a 'rights'-based approach, but the balancing acts engaged by the judiciary gave greater weight to commonality, security, and *raison d'état*, assisting military rule.

Under the military governments and then during the fight for democracy, human-rights ideas exploded into the public sphere. The rising status of these ideas was not the result of changes in legal concepts effected by the state, as in Canada. In the latter, the idea of individual rights was institutionalized through a Charter of Rights and Freedoms as part of Prime Minister Pierre Trudeau's attempt to reinforce the unity of the country and the primacy of the federal structure and its direct appeal for individuals, over the interests of the provinces, such as Quebec.[71] Nor did the rising status of human rights in the Southern Cone express the enshrinement of a language of individualism, as in the United States. In the latter, the format of American constitutionalism, using amendments and legislation, enabled the progressive implementation of an individual human-rights discourse in the public sphere in general and the legal domain in particular.[72]

In the Southern Cone, the discourse of human rights exploded as the language that, anchored in internal experiences and international principles, served to express the need to (re)construct the institutions and the collective identity of society, as monist military rule was replaced by pluralist democracy. Such (re)construction or change was to be elaborated around two factors: first, the tacit or explicit condemnation of authoritarian rule; and second, the commitment to basic principles of ethical behaviour in the field of human rights, which were presented as antithetical to the principles followed by the military governments. This trend projected a new dimension of public life, which went beyond the formal and traditional understanding of substantive democracy in the Southern Cone, towards a vision of it as the framework in which the individual can expect full protection of human rights.

The human-rights issue is a relatively new theme. Neither in Chile nor in Latin America does the recognition of human rights have a long history. In these societies the question is not how to recover something lost. It is how to create something that did not exist before. On top of that, the theme entered with political banners and, therefore, there are many occasions in which we are forced to look for synonymous terms and avoid direct reference to the human-rights wording.[73]

Father Luis Pérez Aguirre, leader of SERPAJ, a victim of imprisonment and torture himself, reckons that the human-rights discourse entered these societies under tragic circumstances: 'Unfortunately, it was only with the dictatorship that people here [in Uruguay] began to talk about torture, about arbitrary imprisonment and other abuses.'[74] The incorporation of the human rights discourse is significantly connected with the fact that the violations were 'gross, massive and systematic', that is, that they constituted a collective experience of violation of human rights.

This path of incorporation poses a series of problems concerning the theoretical analysis of the diffusion and globalization of discourses beyond the Western poles of development. Concerning the Southern Cone, the major problems seem to have been: first, the problem of recognizing and bridging the traditional gaps or disjunctures that existed between the formal endorserment of such principles and their actual implementation in daily life; second, the problem of connecting the discourse of human rights to the core agenda of redemocratization, while avoiding its identification with partisan political positions that could relativize it; third, the problem of retaining the universalist grounding of a discourse of respect for human rights, while making it relevant to local political and social circumstances, thus avoiding the claims of cultural relativists who accused human-rights activists of bringing foreign discourses into local realities; fourth, the problem of reconciling a discourse of individual rights with social concerns that historically were geared to organicist rhetoric and ideas in these societies.

In the literature at least three major approaches have been offered to reflect on this process of diffusion and incorporation of the idiom of human rights, which need to be addressed with the context of the Southern Cone in mind.

The first approach, by John Rawls, tries to address the problem of elaborating a world consensus between different societies and states, with varied conceptions of justice, partly liberal and partly non-liberal, partly egalitarian and partly hierarchical. Basing his approach on procedural justice as the regulative principle holding together individuals with competing values, as he moves to the international arena, Rawls raises the issue of what could be the minimum common denominator for the generalized (i.e. global) recognition of human rights. This common denominator could be acceptable both to non-liberal societies in terms of their own conceptions and to liberal societies, as the minimal requirements for the acceptance of non-liberal countries as legitimate members of the 'civilized well-orderedness' of a Law of Peoples. According to Rawls, even non-liberal societies enable all human beings to be dutiful members of their societies and dutiful members of their statuses. Accordingly, he considers as minimum requirements keeping their members alive and protecting them against degrading practices that would destroy the ability of the individuals to maintain full membership in their communities.[75]

Rawls's views have been criticized on different grounds.[76] Of particular interest for our arguments are the criticisms by Thomas Franck and María Pura Sánchez, for whom Rawls's approach represents an ideal theory that, in practice, justifies the state's preference for order over justice and condones different levels of rights across and within societies. According to Franck, this approach basically reflects a logic of legitimacy which prescribes non-intervention in the face of injustice. This logic could only be changed if the world system would be transformed from one based on states to one based on the primacy of global citizenship and transnational governance. Only under such circumstances, representatives of people would be able to respond to the needs of prisoners of conscience, relatives of detainees-disappeared, disentitled minorities and torture victims of their own governments.[77] Similarly, Sánchez indicates that Rawls's approach seems problematic, as it can tolerate harsh conceptions of domestic well-orderedness, idealizing the toleration of human-rights abuses as part of the intra-state status quo, of the cultural set-up of 'undeveloped' societies, and of distinct traditions. This theory is also unable to explain how the minimal contents of world 'well-orderedness' would be enforced as part of a global (amoral) modus vivendi in settings where the rule is dictated by alliances of authoritarian or oligarchical governments and elites.[78]

Rawls's analytical model is especially problematic in the context of the Southern Cone, in which a long tradition of disjuncture has crystallized between the formally accepted and publicly proclaimed legal rules and the substantive enactment of norms, policies, and attitudes, analysed above. This gap between principles of political philosophy and policies has universal validity, as Michael Sandel has observed: 'Political philosophy seems often to reside at a distance from the world. Principles are one thing, politics another, and even our best efforts to "live up" to our ideals typically founder on the gap between theory and practice.'[79] In the Southern Cone, this trend is compounded by the persistent hold of organicist ideas that contest the principles of Liberalism as core values in these societies, which have viewed themselves as representative of Western civilization. In the context of these societies, the Rawlsian approach's wide margins for condoning regulative action could have been endorsed by those involved in repression as a philosophical basis for justifying some of their deeds for the sake of organic well-orderedness. During military rule, the power holders considered that the decadent Liberal values (which included preserving individual human rights) were useless in confronting the anarchic and revolutionary pressures they faced. They represented, so they claimed, a truer carrier of the values of Western Christian civilization which served as the basis of their legitimacy. Under democracy, a shift occurred from political and ideological enemies to the threats posed to the system by impoverished and marginalized sectors of society. In societies with sharp social polarization, wide sectors are often willing to condone once again harsh treatment toward suspects and criminals; these sectors hold that such practices are necessary to protect society and maintain order. Under such conditions, regulative and repressive deeds can be interpreted not in terms of an infringement on human dignity but in terms of safeguarding the fabric of society. It should be noted that the human-rights standard (normative) position accepts such stand with strict limitations. It is unclear how the Rawlsian approach can help limit the authoritarian trends that prevailed during military rule and which have survived—albeit with some significant shifts—during redemocratization.

A second approach has been suggested by Richard Rorty. According to Rorty, the ideals of procedural justice, human equality, and human rights are a 'parochial, recent, eccentric cultural development' of the West and have been variously adopted in other contexts as a matter of expediency. Rorty recommends Rawlsian procedural justice (justice 'as fairness') as the criteria to regulate the interactions among different peoples, cultures, and discourses. Within each society, Rorty suggests respecting local norms and vocabularies as long as the different cultures, even when they are ethnocentric and exclusivist, cooperate in respecting the global rules (what he calls keeping 'the world bazaar' open). That is, he suggests public pragmatism in the global arena. Different cultures should be respected even when phrased in outdated terms as long as these terms are implemented inside each society or 'club'. The latter is portrayed as composed of elements living in harmony and sharing the same views. Such cultures are 'fanatical' when they are in conflict with human dignity and equality 'outside the club'; in this case, the appeal to local culture is not enough to protect it from outside condemnation.[80]

We will aim at nothing stronger than a commitment to Rawlsian procedural justice—a moral commitment when made by members of some clubs (e.g., ours) but a matter of expediency when made by members of others. The ultimate political synthesis of love and justice may thus turn out to be an intricately-textured collage of private narcissism and public pragmatism.[81]

María Pura Sánchez considers this suggestion as 'just a recipe for human rights violations', pointing out that such an approach disregards considering the inner struggles and cultural debates that are inimical to any complex society:

Who speaks for the home ethnos? Do we consider the ethnos' conception of justice moral because it imposes 'duties on all' and protects the members against slavery, coercion, and forced occupation (Rawls)? Do we require more than that? Do members have choice about whether to continue their membership? These (human rights) questions are incompatible with ours (and theirs) neither knowing nor caring what the people in the club over on the other side of the bazaar are like.[82]

In the polarized societies of the Southern Cone, Rorty's approach could overlook domination, coercion, and violence. During military rule, politics were played out not in terms of consensus and negotiation but in terms of a zero-sum game aimed at the annihilation of other human beings. Against such a static approach of the ideal world order, the discourse of human rights and of rejection of human-rights violations served in this context to challenge the domestic conception of justice as hegemonically diffused by the military governments.

A third analytical approach to the diffusion and incorporation of the discourse of human rights has been suggested by Abdullahi An-Na'im and Alison Dundes Renteln. Dundes Renteln allegedly aims to reconcile human rights and cultural relativism, by looking for basic common principles that most cultures share and anchoring human rights in cross-cultural universals.[83] In a related line, An-Na'im points out that

the lack or insufficiency of cultural legitimacy of human rights standards is one of the main underlying causes of violations of those standards. . . . The general thesis of my approach is that, since people are more likely to observe normative propositions if they believe them to be sanctioned by their own cultural traditions, observance of human rights standards can be improved through the enhancement of the cultural legitimacy of those standards.[84]

According to An-Na'im, universal cultural legitimacy is necessary and also possible to develop through enlightened interpretations of cultural norms and cross-cultural dialogue. Indeed, respect for human dignity can be found along with contrasting principles also in the cultural background of societies beyond the core of the Liberal West. The standards set in the International Declaration of Human Rights can be pushed to expansive meanings and implemented in different societies by letting cultures reinterpret them in terms of the principles that exist in their own cultural frameworks and which point to such converging directions. This approach indicates that, out of divergent cultural idioms and visions, a shared commitment to human dignity can evolve if local forces take the initiative in leading the process of cultural change.[85] Accordingly, this approach provides a perspective on the prospects of global incorporation of human-rights principles, which takes into account the local cultural make-up. Nonetheless, this approach does not provide guidelines for understanding how, for instance in the Southern Cone, the formal recognition of human rights can be translated into policies and implemented substantially, acquiring, through practice, a new presence in society. These societies have long proclaimed their adherence to Western principles of human dignity and rights. The local elites conceived Western idioms and ideas as part of their own cultural heritage, and as such, they incorporated the visions and terminology of civil and political rights, at least on a formal level. Thus, human rights were formally and academically discussed in the period that preceded the last wave of military rule, albeit mostly in legal terms.[86] What singles out the last period of transition to democracy are the debates that took place—perhaps for the first time—on implementing such principles around issues of truth, accountability, and justice. Whereas An-Na'im focuses on cross-cultural dialogue to enhance the hold of the discourse of human rights, it seems to us necessary to emphasize the interplay of the institutional and cultural factors, and particularly the role played by international human-rights organizations and activists in their dialectical interaction with the local forces interested in enforcing or rejecting the discourse of human-rights.

The study of the institutional frameworks seems fundamental in understanding the levels of receptivity to the international discourse of human rights at the local level. Paul J. Di Maggio and Walter W. Powell have provided a framework for analysing the interaction between the local and the international arena, in terms of institutional isomorphism.[87] The authors identify three major mechanisms of institutional change, which focus on the forces that bring societies to adopt global discourses and practices. These mechanisms are (*a*) coercive isomorphism that stems from political influence and the problem of legitimacy; (*b*) mimetic isomorphism resulting from standard responses to uncertainty and which brings organizations to model themselves after those similar units abroad that are perceived as more legitimate or successful; and (*c*) normative isomorphism, associated with professionalization and involving the growth and elaboration of professional networks that span organizations and polities, and across which new models diffuse rapidly.

Taking these mechanisms into account, the enhancement of the hold of human rights as a legitimate internal discourse seems to have been advanced in the Southern Cone as a result of combined coercive and normative isomorphism. Already in the late 1970s, the discourse of defence of human rights became a central factor in international politics, through the converging actions of Amnesty International, US governmental agencies under the Carter administration, the Inter-American Commission on Human Rights, the UN, some of the EU governments, and associations of political exiles. These frameworks were instrumental in putting pressure on the Southern Cone dictatorships to stop gross violations of human rights. In this connection, it is worth stressing the interplay between international political conditionality and domestic results, based significantly on the fractured structure of the UN and other international agencies.

In the UN, the Commission for Human Rights was particularly active, led since May 1977 by the Dutch diplomat Theo Van Boven, who had himself been active in the follow-up of the Chilean situation since 1975. On 20 December 1978, the General Assembly issued a resolution of concern with the fate of the detained-disappeared. The effective impact of these efforts was minor, indicating the secondary role played by mimetic isomorphism in this context.

By contrast, the decisions of the Carter administration had far greater impact, especially until 1978. Carter based his presidential campaign on the call to return to moral standards in policy drafting, that is, on the antithesis of the corrupt Machiavellianism he attributed to the preceding Republican administrations. Patricia Derian, who was appointed assistant on human rights to the Secretary of State, came to play an influential role in framing international assistance and commerce between the USA and Argentina in the context of the monitoring of the human-rights scene.

A series of reports by commissions of inquiry sent in the 1970s to gather information *in situ* were a crucial influence in the realm of policy.

In the case of Argentina, commissions were sent by Amnesty International (November 1977), the UN Commission for Human Rights, the USA (three visits by Patricia Derian took place in 1977), and the Interamerican Commission of Human Rights (in 1979), among others. In Chile, the most important visits were those by Amnesty International after the 1973 coup and a 1978 report by the UN Commission for Human Rights. In Uruguay, two reports were made by the International Red Cross and by the sub-Secretary General of the UN, Javier Pérez de Cuellar, in 1979. Save for the last mission, the commissions returned from the Southern Cone outraged by the gross violations of human rights witnessed and reported to them on the spot, radicalizing the attitude of the international community towards the military regimes. This fuelled, in turn, the activism of the local organizations of human rights, such as the Madres de Plaza de Mayo and the Argentinian Committee of Human Rights (CADHU) that brought their pleas to the US Congress, the UN in Geneva, and other European capitals.

Having 97,000 members in 74 countries by 1976, Amnesty International was especially instrumental in disclosing the veil of misinformation and secrecy that surrounded these regimes' persecution of citizens on political grounds. Amnesty International's denunciation of disappearances, disclaimed by the military governments, attained global respectability following the award of the 1977 Nobel Peace Prize to the organization as well as the subsequent selection of the Argentinian human rights activist Adolfo Pérez Esquivel as the 1980 laureate.

As for the disappearances, the international community had two different versions, one from the Junta, the other from Amnesty. Nine months after the Amnesty report on Argentina was released, the verdict was rendered: Amnesty won the 1977 Nobel Peace Prize. International human rights groups were indeed beginning to flex their muscles. It was just a matter of time before they took the case of the relatives to the world stage, at the United Nations.[88]

Although President Reagan seemed to endorse more pragmatic considerations related to the final stages of the Cold War, the US institutional structures—such as the State Department—remained unchanged during his tenure and US policies favoured redemocratization paths in Eastern Europe, the USSR, and Latin America. The networks of local NGOs in Latin America were connected with international NGOs and organizations at the OAS and the UN, with parliamentary committes for human rights, and with associations of exiles that generated awareness of the extent and gravity of human-rights violations in the Southern Cone. Through these connections, the local NGOs were able to prompt a wide concern with the issue abroad and at home, and at the same time acquire resources and improve organizational skills, in what may be interpreted as a process of mimetic isomorphism in the Southern Cone. All these learning processes transformed the NGOs that worked in the field of human rights into central actors in promoting human-rights policies during and after the transition. They had to confront, however, alternative visions and contrasted views that denied legitimacy to a discourse anchored in the external frameworks of reference. In their work, the connections they established with international organizations and networks has been fundamental in attaining a proper institutional and social recognition for human rights as a theme that could not be put aside.

Conclusion: A Legacy of Human-Rights Violations

Each of the three countries examined in this work have had to confront, with the transition to democracy, a parallel grim legacy of massive human-rights violations: of abuse of force, arbitrary imprisonment, abductions, torture, and executions without trial. Emerging from recent fratricide, large-scale official and unofficial brutality, public complicity, and betrayal of trust, these societies had to reassess their basic beliefs and reconstruct their social fabric.

Rapid institutional change brought these societies to function as democracies in a relatively short period. Censorship was abolished, representativeness was established through elections. The military went back to the barracks, civilian governments took over. Policies could be changed and complaints voiced once again. However, the massive human-rights violations constituted a long-term open wound in the bosom of these societies. Even in the utopian case of reaching full truth, acknowledgement, and justice, these societies would have to confront the irreversibility of torture, fratricide, and forced disappearances.

The redemocratized societies of the Southern Cone had to confront this legacy in the framework of different constellations of forces, contrasted visions and interests, and given gaps between the formal and the real workings of politics and public culture. Under these circumstances, the discourse of human rights promised to provide a normative and moral framework to address the legacy of state-related repression and shape it in terms of human-rights violations.

In Argentina, Uruguay, and Chile, the main problem in incorporating the discourse of human rights did not exist in the formal adoption of principles but in their implementation, which hinged upon the agency of social and political actors in shaping the public agenda and upon the relationship between the state in its various functional branches and those social and political actors, elites, and organizations interacting in the public spheres reopened by redemocratization.

The ways of adoption of the discourse of human rights and human-rights violations, closely connected with a political project and its ethical message, also implied the fragility of this discourse in the Southern Cone. Whereas parts of these societies fundamentally accepted a commitment to human rights, for others the discourse of human rights was politically tainted with adversarial intent and as such was unacceptable. For many observers, it had to be balanced with more general needs and constraints at the centre of the public agenda.

The uneven perception of social and political actors to what ought to be done was revealed when, following redemocratization, the civilian governments had to confront the legacy of repression in terms defined by the discourse of human rights, accountability, and justice. Under these circumstances, civil societies and the civilian governments proved too weak to resist the demands of political contingency.

Shaping the Public Sphere and the Legacy of Human-Rights Violations

Redemocratization projected the legacy of human-rights violations onto the centre of the public spheres of Argentina, Chile, and Uruguay. Historically, public spheres developed as the arena in which private sectors come together for the purpose of interacting discursively and of engaging with the state 'in a debate over the general rules governing relations in the basically privatized but publicly relevant sphere of commodity exchange and social labor'.[1] In Nancy Fraser's words, it 'is the space in which citizens deliberate about their common affairs, and hence an institutionalized arena of discursive interaction. This arena is conceptually distinct from the state; it is a site for the production and circulation of discourses [and, we may add, actions] that can in principle be critical of the state.'[2] The concept has cross-cultural and cross-societal importance, since it highlights social dynamics both in Western and non-Western societies and wields heuristic force for analysing varied situations of autonomization and de-autonomization of society and sectors thereof vis-à-vis the state.[3] It is in the public sphere where contestation and participation, the two major processes that ensure the workings of democracy, may take place.[4]

During military rule, the public spheres of these societies were severely constricted and controlled to varying extents. The governing juntas closed the political arena, excluding the opposition's politicians and persecuting the radical left and its sympathizers, and tried to reorganize society, in each case according to its own ideological model and all within the Doctrine of National Security. These societies, which in the 1960s and 1970s had experienced processes of popular massive mobilization and increased (disordered and almost 'anarchical') participation, were forcefully demobilized under military rule. Political parties had been banned or their activities frozen by decree; educational systems were regimented and disciplined after major military interventions in the universities and school programmes were reshaped according to the new ideological parameters; heavy censorship was imposed upon the media and cultural expression was 'purified' of any leftist orientations; trade unions were attacked, with many of their activitists jailed and assassinated; professional and entrepreneurial associations were co-opted, 'cleansed' of hostile elements; and self-censorship crystallized as the result of a highly repressive situation.

Under different circumstances, local resistance and protest, backed by international action, would have affected the governments. Social and political protest was not the primary cause of the demise of the military in Argentina, Chile, or Uruguay. But such action, in tandem with deteriorating economic performance, declining regime legitimacy, international pressures, and political manœuvring, led the military administrations to open the political arena. These openings developed into more or less controlled transitions to democracy, which were characterized by an opening of public spheres that had been closed or limited during military rule.

Shaping a Democratic Public Sphere in Societies with a Legacy of Human-Rights Violations

Following the demise of the military governments in Argentina (1983), Uruguay (1985), and Chile (1990), the possibility arose to restructure the public sphere in democratic terms. Doing so involved recognizing both the centrality of legal principles, of basic human and civil rights, and of the possibility of autonomous action by citizens, even when this action is opposed to the state. But, in tandem with the prospects of reshaping the basic parameters of public life, all the issues suppressed during military rule, including human-rights violations, came to the fore. The full extent of massive human-rights violations was made public. The disclosure did not carry with it an acknowledgement of past deeds by the societal sectors involved in repression. It triggered a debate and confrontation around the legacy of human-rights violations and around issues of justice, accountability, and attainment of public knowledge and acknowledgement.

These issues, related to the construction of democracy, acquired special importance in the transitional period. They were significant particularly for the victims who survived repression and for the relatives and friends of those assassinated and made to disappear. Their recognition could contribute to healing the trauma suffered by societies emerging from fratricide and human-rights atrocities, providing a substantial basis for any claim to reconciliation. Accountability leading to public knowledge and justice may have served as a strong deterrent for future human-rights violations. These principles could provide a viable channel for rehabilitating those who violated human-rights. In addition to the above consequentialist arguments in favour of enshrining accountability in societies with legacies of human-rights violations, there was also an expectation for a general and righteous moral condemnation of the crimes committed.[5]

The confrontation with these issues opened a wide range of policy alternatives, and created serious problems for the new democracies, as the public agenda was dominated by matters of principle that demanded political solutions, in which elements of contingency weighed heavily.

Against this background, the political leaderships of these countries attempted to deal with the human-rights violations legacy through channels of resolution that best fitted each case, hoping to overcome the experience and memory of crisis. In Argentina, the transition to democracy occurred following the defeat in the Malvinas–Falkland war. The poor military performance in the war and the discovery of corruption shattered the legitimacy of the governing armed forces, already weakened by their mismanagement of the economy.[6] As Argentina entered the democratic period, the Alfonsín government (1983–9) adopted a radical policy for treating the country's legacy of human-rights violations. This policy was carried out through parallel channels. First, a 'truth commission' was charged with clarifying the extent and depth of human-rights violations, including the fate of the thousands of victims who 'disappeared' (the *desaparecidos*). Second, the new government put on trial members of the governing juntas and other high-ranking officers, who were responsible for conducting the 'Dirty War' against the radicalized and mobilized sectors of society. Third, a special governmental body was created for dealing with human-rights affairs, and mechanisms were established to deal with material compensation for the victims of repression.

The radical character of some of these channels, especially the trials, was diminished following a series of partial military upheavals. As a result of military pressure, a series of laws was adopted (the Full Stop Law and the Law of Due Obedience), beginning a dilution of the government's policy of exemplary trial and punishment, a process that ended with the total pardons and comprehensive amnesty granted at the beginning of the 1990s by the subsequent government of Carlos Menem.

In Uruguay, the transition to democracy resulted from an agreement between the military and the main political parties; after democratization, the government passed legislation designed to close the human-rights violations issue completely. Different sectors of civil society exercised their constitutional right to request a national referendum on that legislation. A two-and-a-half-year-long process of collecting signatures and campaigning for the ratification or the annulment of the law produced much mobilization on both sides. It also generated a prolonged discussion on the dilemmas of normative principles versus the constraints created by political contingency. In the referendum, conducted in April 1989, the forces interested in annulling the law were defeated by a very narrow margin. The results of the referendum were widely interpreted as signalling the end of the debate and the definitive closure of the issue.

In Chile, a transition controlled by the military limited the possibilities of treating the legacy of human-rights violations comprehensively. The institutional authoritarian enclaves that the military retained (through the 1978 Amnesty Law, the 1980 Constitution, and the organic laws of the 1980s) maintained restrictions on the issue in the redemocratized public sphere. Governmental policies comprised a series of parallel mechanisms: an official commission of inquiry to reveal the general and individual circumstances that produced the loss of thousands of lives; symbolic actions to vindicate the victims and provide material reparations to their families; and trials in those cases not covered by the military amnesty. The latter generated tensions that moved the issue back to the arena of political decision-making, in which limited democracy did not allow for legislative changes and decisions.

Shaping a democratic public sphere implies opening the agenda to issues that may be contested by actors holding irreconcilable positions. Such democratic public sphere enables participation as a major mechanism of working through social, political, economic, and cultural problems. In democracy, institutional principles and procedures provide the framework for such participation and open contestation. In turn, it is through the latter that those procedures and institutions may be changed in an orderly fashion. In practice, during the transitions and the new wave of redemocratization, the civilian political classes have sought to reposition themselves at the centre of institutional life and hold power. Once in power, these forces have tried to guide, if not control, the public sphere and channel the public agenda away from issues that could be conflictive or destabilize the new democracies. Within the variable institutional limits inherited from military administrations and the constrains posed by conflicting pressures and existing power relations, the civilian governments launched policies aimed at consolidating the new democracies in the Southern Cone. Under these circumstances and against the background of the local political culture, the capacity of different social actors to affect the public agenda, for instance regarding the legacy of authoritarianism, was limited.[7]

The legacy of authoritarianism operated in different ways in the public spheres of Argentina, Chile, and Uruguay. On the one hand, the close relationship between repression and human-rights violations and the format of military-authoritarian rule made human-rights one of the goals of redemocratization. The revelations of the extent of past abuses generated extensive mobilization of civil society and placed the issue at the centre of the political debate. The debate revolved around a series of topics basic to the consolidation of democracy: first, in what ways and through which channels to confront the knowledge of what happened in the past, and how to establish an official truth or at least a shared version of the past; second, how to make offenders accountable for their past deeds; third, whether to ask the victims for forgiveness and require acknowledgement and expiation from the perpetrators; fourth, along what lines to elaborate mechanisms of reparation and compensation; and fifth, how to set the grounds for reconciliation.

On the other hand, through the processes of inquiry, trial, legislation, and/or debate, individuals, associations, and actors experienced the prospects and limits of their capacity vis-à-vis the state and the political elite over the issue. And, concomitantly, the opening of the issue generated broad awareness of the horrors inflicted on fellow citizens, instilling or recreating fears concerning political participation and activism.

In spite of the specificities of each case, the three settings have shared this dynamic of widening the scope of the public sphere and, at the same time, discovering the limits of possible change. In some cases, the expectations of the early democratic period were disappointed. In others, achievements went beyond initial expectations. Whatever the concrete results of state policies and initiatives of civil society, all actors had to confront the issue as central to shaping a democratic public sphere after military rule. Beyond the concrete paths followed in each case, by confronting the issue of past human-rights violations, a principled concern with respect for human-rights decisively entered the public spheres of Argentina, Chile, and Uruguay.

Argentina: The Progressive–Regressive Cycle

Argentina's transition to democracy preceded those of neighbouring Uruguay, Brazil, and Chile. Following the failure of its economic policies and its defeat in the 1982 Malvinas–Falkland war (which had generated a nationalist 'dream of grandeur' and high expectations), the self-image of the armed forces as the major defenders of the nation, both in its material and moral dimensions, was totally undermined and the military regime disintegrated. The armed forces lost both power and professional and ideological legitimacy. The dream of a strong and united Argentina able to revindicate its sovereignty against Great Britain lay shattered in front of a society already deeply shocked by economic crisis and by the disclosure of massive corruption and military inefficiency. The organicist vision of the Doctrine of National Security, put into practice in the Process of National Reorganization (PRN) since 1976, was bankrupt. The military, divided among themselves, could not agree on an orderly transition that would preserve some elements of their ideological and institutional model upon the return to democracy. Military rule disintegrated as a result of the military's own mistakes and not because of pressures originating in civil society, even though some mobilization had occurred. Public debate began on one additional sign of Argentine failing 'dreams of grandeur'.[8]

The circumstances of military defeat and the previous mismanagement of the economy provided the framework for the political agenda during the transition, from June 1982 to December 1983. These factors created wide possibilities for reshaping Argentina's public sphere completely, while forcing Argentine polity and society to confront without delay the legacies of the PRN: the socio-economic crisis, and the massive human-rights violations committed under military rule.[9]

The public acknowledgement of the systematic, gross human-rights violations during the 1970s thus became a major theme in the agenda of the transition. The legacy of human-rights violations disclosed during the transition was of such unprecedented magnitude in the history of Argentina that it necessitated and enabled decisive policies when democratic rule was re-established. Historically, Argentina had known many waves of violence, political upheavals, and military dictatorships, as well as socio-economic crises. However, the violations committed during the PRN exceeded by far past Argentine experiences. The magnitude of human-rights violations could be used by the incoming democratically elected authorities as a political tool to reshape the traditional format of civil–military relationships, in which the military had recurrently played a major role in politics and controlled the public sphere.

Argentina's return to democratic rule, after one of the most turbulent decades in its history (ending with the military PRN), was perceived as a 'foundational' moment in the modern history of that country. This perception of being at the beginning of a qualitatively different era was reinforced by the new government's attempt to confront the country's past experience and implement radically new democratic patterns of behaviour. In President Alfonsín's view, the foundational thrust of the period would conclude more than a century and a half of misunderstandings and lead towards national integration.

Argentina is experiencing a new foundational era. . . . We want to found . . . a society that should be at the same time pluralist and tolerant, characterized by solidarity and cohesion; that is, a society in which we become richer through diversity and in which we help one another to reach our own objectives . . . through collective deliberation; ample, open and logical debate; in which decision-making is regulated by the rule of the majority and judicial procedures. In this way, the various groups agree to submit their differences to the mediation of a shared normative order that establishes mechanisms to solve eventual conflicts peacefully . . . and consolidate social cohesion.[10]

These foundational expectations had to be translated into effective policies for dealing with the legacy of human-rights violations in a way that would establish the primacy of the rule of law and reshape the character of the nation. With relatively powerful leverage in decision-making at the beginning of democratic rule, the Argentine political class had a wide range of options about the course of action to be followed regarding human-rights violations. At the same time, the lack of compromises resulting from a non-bargained transition with the armed forces implied that the civilian administration could attempt to confront head-on the military system of repression.[11] In doing so, it did not have external referents from the region and had only the more remote precedents of the Nuremberg and Tokyo trials. In parallel, the military could also be expected to try to influence the decisions of the new administration in all available ways, to reshape their position in society, and to recover their legitimacy and prestige.

The promulgation of a law of self-amnesty by the military government on 25 September 1983, shortly before handing over power (Law No. 22924), was an implicit recognition that members of the armed forces had committed acts that were punishable and could, in principle, be judged if these acts were not covered by that law.[12] The military wanted to prevent debate concerning the different aspects of repression, but they were unable to find political sectors willing to make a commitment in that direction. The two main presidential candidates had adopted different approaches towards the issue. The Peronist candidate, Italo Argentino Luder, preferred a pragmatic attitude that would respect the central arguments of the armed forces. His opponent, Radical Party candidate Raúl Ricardo Alfonsín, took a principled approach, expressing his opposition to any compromise that would leave human-rights violations unpunished.[13] Alfonsín's clear stand helped him receive 52 per cent of the votes in the general elections of October 1983. For some, this was surprisingly strong support for a candidate of the

UCR, even more so as he confronted the force that had been dominant until then, Peronism. Alfonsín assumed the presidency on 10 December 1983, on the day of the Universal Declaration of Human Rights. The immediate prosecution of the perpetrators of such actions could be perceived and be presented as one of the major commitments of the first redemocratized government. Expectations were high. In December 1983, Argentina's society was overtaken by euphoric feelings produced by the return to democracy. This time, the basic vision of the country's grandeur was focused on rebuilding democracy.

The results of the confrontation with the roots and branches of authoritarianism in Argentine society were uncertain following redemocratization in 1983. This confrontation implied integrating the views of social and political forces that had totally opposed visions of the past. Moreover, it implied setting up the principles of the new democracy by balancing normative principles (the rule of law and the primacy of equality before the law) and the constraints posed by political contingency, in what David Pion-Berlin calls a 'strategic calculation' in terms of costs-and-benefits writ large.[14]

Post-dictatorial justice

From his first day in office, Alfonsín began to implement an unprecedented policy aimed at prosecuting those who had committed crimes against their co-nationals in the framework of the PRN, and aimed at transforming the armed forces, as he had promised during the electoral campaign.[15] Under the cross-pressures of the relatives of the repression victims and the NGOs committed to human-rights on the one hand, and of the armed forces on the other, the government initiated a series of actions both substantial and symbolic in character.[16]

While dealing with the military, Alfonsín opted to minimize the full institutional implications of the policy of punishing human-rights violators, as he tried to reassure them that it was not directed against the institution of the armed forces as a whole.[17] The President even adopted one of the main theses of the armed forces: namely, that human-rights violations were a consequence of the state of internal war fought against the leftist guerrillas during the 1970s. And yet, on 13 December, three days after assuming the presidency, Alfonsín issued two decrees ordering the arrest and prosecution of the members of the three military 'juntas' as well as that of former guerrilla leaders. This was a very bold initiative. For the first time in the history of Argentina and of Latin America as a whole, a civilian government ordered the armed forces to bring to trial the heads of the former military juntas. The government also ordered the arrest and trial of seven leaders of the guerrilla movement Montoneros.[18] Later on, it ordered the arrest of general Ramón Camps, former chief of police of the Province of Buenos Aires, under whose command a considerable number of victims were abducted.[19]

On 15 December 1983, only five days after taking office, Alfonsín decreed the formation of a national commission of inquiry (CONADEP), comprising some of the country's most prominent human-rights activists, journalists, and well-known personalities, and led by the renowned writer Ernesto Sábato. The CONADEP was charged with clarifying the fate of the victims of military repression.[20] The inquiries and especially the commission's final report became central for placing the human-rights issue on the public agenda and for the attempted reshaping of Argentina's public sphere in democratic terms.

Alfonsín's policy of dealing with human-rights violations also involved reforming in early 1984 the military Code of Justice. According to the reform, the Supreme Council of the Armed Forces would remain the first court to prosecute military personnel, and civilian courts would intervene if no progress was made within six months. This measure represented an attempt to restrict the autonomy of the military. Still, it was opposed by all the human-rights organizations. The initiatives of the government were interpreted as making compromises with the armed forces, since military justice retained control over the first stage of prosecution. Alfonsín's basic approach to establish responsibility distinguished between the heads of the armed forces, the officers and soldiers bound by their duty to obey the directives issued by the higher commands, and those among the latter who had committed 'excesses' while fulfilling duties.[21]

The decision to demand responsibility from the highest officers of the military governments was unprecedented. It implied that no impunity would be granted to those responsible for issuing orders that caused human-rights violations. Nonetheless, from the perspective of the victims, the relatives, comrades, and concerned NGOs, the decision to prosecute only the top military elite and those who committed gross abuses of human-rights was a sign of compromise. It implied accepting the principle of due obedience by the lower ranks of the armed forces. The situation was, however, ambivalent. It could be interpreted as a commitment to pursue full justice and demand the submission of the military to the principles enshrined in democracy. This both reflected and provided grounds for the rising expectations in civil society. But the decision could also be interpreted as a very partial attempt to institute principles of equal accountability and respect for legality. This was evident in the deliberate avoidance of any explicit attack against the military and security institutions as a whole, and particularly against the middle and lower ranks implicated in viola-tions.[22] Alfonsín's message to the armed forces seemed to be that, if they cooperated and purged themselves of the highest officers respons-ible for the systematic abuse of human-rights, the government would not prosecute every soldier, officer, and policeman implicated in human-rights violations.[23] The highest ranks of the armed forces refused to cooperate with the civilian authorities. They assumed institutional responsibility and claimed that their actions had been justified by the country's state of anarchy on the eve of their coup and that the attack against them was an institutional attack motivated by the same polit-ical interests that the armed forces had defeated in the internal war. Before the initiation of the trials, General Jorge R. Videla defended the honour of the armed forces and criticized the new attempts of those 'subversives' to discredit the invaluable contribution of the armed forces to the security and stability of the country.[24]

On the basis of the DSN, the armed forces were convinced that Argentina had gone through a special kind of war, in which the enemy was disguised inside the society and aimed to destroy the moral values and spirit of the nation. In an extreme situation like that, all means are legitimate and the armed forces had no choice but to fight the threat. Having won the war, to which they had been pushed by politicians and other sectors of society, they felt that the current critique was unjust, if not hypocritical. As admiral Emilio E. Massera stated dur-ing the public trial:

I did not come to defend myself. No one must defend himself for having won a just war. And the war against terrorism was a just war. Nonetheless, I am being prosecuted due to our victory in that just war. [Imagine] if we had lost that war, we wouldn't be here—neither you nor we—, since the Supreme judges would have been replaced long ago by the turbulent popular tribunals, and a menacing and irrecognizable Argentina would have replaced the old Fatherland.[25]

A similar critique was made by the first commander-in-chief of the army under democracy, General Jorge Arguindegui, who after his retirement declared: 'This is a Nuremberg but inverted; in Nuremberg they judged the vanquished, not the victors.'[26]

The hypothesis of internal war, used by the military in defence of their deeds, has since then been rebuked by the review of undisputable documentation: 'The war theory is absolutely indefensible . . . There is a report made by General Rivero of the Interamerican Commission of Defence, stating that the military power of the guerrillas ended in December 1975, with the attempted takeover of the Buen Viejo region [in Tucumán].'[27] Estimates of the guerrillas' real strength point to a total of 2,000 activists of the Montoneros and the ERP, 400 of which were really armed in the heyday of their activities.[28]

The opening of a democratic public sphere and the centrality of the legacy of human-rights violations acquired by the public agenda brought the military to address the issue openly by defending their actions. In the process of redemocratization, the military lost control of the public sphere and had to argue their case according to democratic rules of multiple representation. They had become another actor and were not able to use state power as a shield, as they had done during most of the twentieth century. The liberalization of the press and the activities of human-rights groups generated a new climate of political freedom in which politicians of most parties addressed human-rights issues to amass political capital.[29]

Alongside the issue of military responsibility, the format of civil–military relationships in democracy was affected. A plan to reform the military was enacted by Alfonsín's government. The main goals of these reforms were the subordination of the armed forces to the civilian authorities; the professionalization of the army; and the replacement of the Doctrine of National Security that had guided the minds and actions of the military during the previous decade. These reforms involved reducing military budgets; transferring industrial and technological assets from the military to the Ministry of Defence (e.g. the transfer of the navy's nuclear programmes); reasserting the civilian president's high command over the armed forces; civilian control over promotions and retirements of officers; and state supervision of the military's international links.[30]

The trials of the military officers involved in human-rights violations, together with the attempted reform of the armed forces, alienated the military and increased their distrust of the civilian authorities. The military perceived the actions taken against the former commanders (three of whom were former presidents) as a direct attack against the institution and as a means of tainting the good name and status of the security forces through the indictment of its members. The trials were perceived as the spearhead of a policy of delegitimation used to weaken the institutional capacity of the armed forces to withstand the reforms.[31]

The two institutional paths opened by the President, the CONADEP on the one hand and the legal track on the other, remained a focus of controversy during 1984. Given that those leading and/or personally supporting each path were totally opposed to the views and interests of the other path, they had the effect of a 'distorted mirror'.

The CONADEP was investigating, interviewing, and opening files about human-rights violations, victims, and victimizers during the 'Dirty

War'. The commission was helped in its initial phases by the information collected before by several NGOs—particularly the Centro de Estudios Legales y Sociales (CELS) and the Asamblea Permanente de Derechos Humanos (APDH)—on thousands of victims and hundreds of perpetrators.[32] Meanwhile, the Supreme Military Court was endorsing the practices of the security services not only as necessary measures, but also as legal and moral ones. Two opposing images were emerging from the confrontation of the same reality from opposite points of view.

On 4 July 1984 the CONADEP broadcast a two-hour TV testimonial programme, with the participation of survivors of repression and close relatives of the disappeared. The contents were so shocking that the government considered the possibility of preventing the broadcast. The final decision was Alfonsín's, after he watched it privately. Despite the fact that Sábato's and Minister of Interior Antonio Tróccoli's declarations in the programme reminded the public that revolutionary violence had triggered repression, Alfonsín faced military insubordination following the broadcast. As a result, he decided to replace the commander-in-chief of the army, General Jorge Arguindegui.[33]

In September 1984, both the CONADEP and the Supreme Military Court presented the results of their work. The CONADEP report, forwarded to the President on 20 September, contained 50,000 pages of files and documentation, with a confidential addendum detailing the names of 1,351 members of the armed and security forces mentioned by the victims and their relatives and friends as authors of gross human-rights violations.[34] During its work, CONADEP tried in vain to obtain the testimonies of officers singled out by the victims. Lacking the cooperation of the security forces, the report could not provide a case-by-case indication of the fate of all disappeared and of the deeds of the agents involved in each case. Nonetheless, the commission collected information on a substantial number of military and security forces, forwarding the names of forty of them to the Ministry of Justice for possible prosecution. The report also included a detailed enumeration of the repressive tactics, methods, places of detention and torture, and lengthy quotations of dozens of victims' testimonies. It tried to portray both the institutional apparatus of state-related repression and the voice and suffering of the victims.

As soon as a summary of the report was made public as a book published by Editorial Universitaria de Buenos Aires, under the name of *Nunca más* (Never Again), it exploded like a bomb in the midst of the public sphere. The citizenry was shocked when it learned of the atrocious extent of human-rights violations committed by the security forces following the March 1976 coup. The book revealed to the wide public the horrifying facts and the dimensions of the repression. A supplement sold with the book contained the names of the 8,961 missing detainees and of 365 clandestine detention centres, in which tortures and assassinations had taken place. The disclosure of the detention centres was crucial for clarifying the scope of the enormous repressive apparatus during the PRN. The report had the credibility of an impartial source, independent of the traditional political forces and representing all sectors of civilian society. The impact was of such magnitude that the book became the major publishing best-seller of all time in Argentina, selling since 1984 over 250,000 copies.[35]

The long-term impact of the report may be open to alternative interpretations. On the one hand, it was a forceful document necessary to establishing an authoritative account of human-rights violations under military rule and a first step to reshaping public opinion and bringing those responsible to justice, making them accountable for their deeds. From an alternative perspective, while giving voice to those who suffered the atrocities of repression, the report's format lacks a comprehensive historical and political contextualization of the master plan behind repression. In parallel, the aggregate impact of the testimonies projected an image of terror that contributed to the aggrandizement of fear in public culture. Coupled with impunity and democratic instability, such an image could be counter-productive to the explicit aims of the drafters. While the report contains recommendations for precluding future human-rights violations, these recommendations were conditioned by the implementation of full legal accountability under democracy. Yet, the lack of stability, corruption, and political contingency were about to create situations in which the lessons of the CONADEP report could be interpreted as a warning not to mingle in public affairs, while those 'know how', secure order.

On the institutional level, the government accepted the recommendations made in *Nunca más* and created a Subsecretary of Human Rights as a permanent agency of the presidency to continue with the investigations, to bring its results to the judiciary for prosecution, and 'to promote the knowledge, acceptance and diffusion of human-rights'.[36]

However, the report had little effect on reshaping the entrenched positions of both the most radical groups of human-rights activists and the military. The Mothers and Grandmothers of Plaza de Mayo refused to see the commission's work and its report as final. They continued to demand the creation of a parliamentary bi-cameral commission with wider powers of inquiry as well as the application of the law's full weight on those responsible for torture, disappearances, and assassinations.[37] The armed forces witnessed the publication of *Nunca más* and declined to accept its line of interpretation and conclusions, after having refused to cooperate with the commission. Their concern and perception of being hunted worsened with the publication of the report. Shortly after the publication of *Nunca más*, the Supreme Council of the armed forces sent a document to the Federal Court of Justice, stating that it could not continue the military prosecution against the former heads of the juntas because the orders imparted to the subordinates were legitimate beyond any possibility of objection ('inobjetablemente legítimas').[38]

The wave of outrage and moral repulsion that this document generated in every sphere of society contrasted with the fact that the military judicial path had reached a dead end. Using the authority that the new military Code of Justice granted, the Federal Appeals Court decided to take over the trials of the former junta members. The reformed military code specified that even after the Federal Appeals Court took over the case, it still had to apply the Military Code in its deliberations.[39] Nonetheless, Eduardo Rabossi estimates that the military lost then a precious opportunity to investigate autonomously the most serious cases of human-rights violations. By carrying out limited actions, the Supreme Council could have pre-empted civilian intervention on substantive issues, beyond mere formalities of procedure.[40]

The military refused to testify in front of civilian judges and tried to provoke (without success) the dismissal of federal prosecutor Julio César Strassera.[41] The cohesion of the ex-commanders was undermined, especially in the case of the members of the first military junta. When requested to give their first responses to the charges, each commander followed a different strategy. In the press, the most common interpretation alluded to the personal differences and approaches that had divided the commanders in the past. On a more principled level, the strategies of defence reflected the involvement of each branch of the armed forces in the carrying out of human-rights violations. The largest measure of responsibility fell upon the army, represented by General Jorge R. Videla. The least involved was the air force, represented by Brigadier Orlando R. Agosti, while the navy—and its commander, Admiral Emilio E. Massera—was in the middle. The prosecution had accused the commanders of the military juntas of being responsible for the disappearance of 711 individuals ('desaparecidos') abducted by the armed and security forces. Videla refused to recognize the authority of the Federal Court. Massera accepted it but made minimal declarations, whereas Agosti presented a full statement in which he stressed that each branch had acted separately.[42]

The trial, although of enormous juridical importance (it was the first time that these procedures were applied in Argentina), transcended the judicial domain and became a focus of public interest and political concern for months. The media coverage of the trial attracted great

attention and intellectuals saw in the trial 'an insurmountable landmark in the difficult elaboration of a collective moral consciousness to
accompany the process of cultural and social transformation needed
for a new cycle in national life'.[43] The wide public interest was partly
due to the context of the public expectations and the new legalistic
effervescence that swept the country after the inauguration of the civilian government. People trusted that the truth could be clarified, and
that those responsible for horrendous crimes would be punished. This
was the new basis for the society's hope that democracy would deliver
its promises of justice. Both the prosecution and the military participated in a media-led public debate about the nature and significance
of the trials. Prosecutor Strassera stated that the trial was not meant
to become a 'new Nuremberg'. In Argentina, he remarked, the institutions were not on trial and the trials were not politically motivated. Rumours about the possibility of issuing, after the trials of the
ex-commanders, amnesty to the other participants of the 'Dirty War'
began to reach the newspapers. The term used was 'due obedience'—
obediencia debida—which signified the lack of responsibility of the
medium- and low-rank officers and soldiers who had complied with
the orders of their commanders. Even one of the main human-rights
organizations, the Permanent Assembly for Human Rights (APDH),
issued a press declaration in which it reaffirmed the importance of the
trials as a means to reinvigorate the institutions, including the honour of the armed forces.[44]

After receiving all the evidence that the prosecution and the defendants presented, the Federal Appeals Court decided to enter the final
phase of trial, the oral and public phase, in April 1985. With the
new phase of the trial, the terms of the public debate regarding the
developments that took place during the late 1970s were transformed
by the new loci in which that debate resided. Also, the main actors
that had attempted to influence the course of governmental actions
stepped aside, leaving the main focus of attention to new participants,
mainly the judges, the lawyers, the usually discredited judicial system,
and the witnesses. Whereas most legal proceedings are conducted on
paper and witnesses are examined in a protracted rather than sequen-
tial manner, the uninterrupted oral phase of the trial was thought by
Alfonsín's legal advisers to be of pedagogical and public significance.
It was meant to be of 'dramaturgical' importance in confronting past
events, in settling responsibilities and in re-educating the population
in public morality.

The potentially imposing effects of such a trial on collective catharsis and consciousness were mediated as the court decided not to
permit live broadcast of the trial, whether on radio or television (it

only permitted television cameras to capture the images without the sounds). This decision shifted the intepretive locus to the media, which gave high priority to covering of the events and from the beginning explained the legal terminology unfamiliar to the general public. A major role was played in this respect, in addition to the regular media, by a special weekly, *El diario del juicio* (The Journal of the Trial), that began appearing a few weeks after the initiation of the open phase in the trial. This publication reported on the proceedings, presented the testimonies of the witnesses at court verbatim, reproduced documents, and published public interviews with key actors in the drama. *El diario del juicio* appeared for 36 weeks between May 1985 and January 1986, selling out its 250,000 weekly copies and becoming an item sought by collectors in later years.[45]

From the beginning of the trial, both the defence lawyers and the prosecutor tried to define the terms of the legal discussion, by constructing discourses and counter-discourses of the PRN. The defence based its strategy on the view that the actions of the accused were part of their response to a serious threat to the country's integrity. Keeping this argument continually at the fore, they tried to discredit the testimonies of most witnesses by disqualifying them as former terrorists or subversives. At first, the prosecutor objected to this kind of questioning, but the judges sometimes accepted it, to establish whether the victims of the gross human-rights violations had engaged in any activity that could have been perceived by the armed forces as subversive.[46] On the other side, the prosecutor's strategy centred on establishing the responsibility of each commander for the human-rights violations presented to the court.[47]

Of special importance to the respective goals of each side was the identity of the witnesses called during the trial. The defence concentrated its initial effort on substantiating the chaotic situation of the country at the time the actions took place. To this end, the defence summoned public figures (such as politicians, syndicalists, and journalists) who had played central roles in the country ten years earlier. The prosecution's witnesses, on the other side, were mainly ex-detainees, family members of the *desaparecidos*, journalists, politicians, and even armed forces personnel. The latter were requested to explain their participation in the anti-subversive war and the nature of the orders they had received from the commanders. Their responses were sometimes evasive, appealing to the impossibility of recalling details such as names, places, or procedures.

For the first time, and not directly at the trial but more in the debate that surrounded it, military men with democratic convictions began to step forward publicly. Some had been separated from the armed forces at the beginning of the military dictatorship for opposing the methods of the regime. Others had defied the military hierarchy during the PRN. Many of them later joined the 'Centre of Democratic Military Personnel' (Centro de Militares Democráticos—CEMIDA). The reaction of the armed forces towards these expressions was always harsh, and they never accepted them as legitimate.[48]

The verdicts of the trials were made public in December 1985. In their decisions, the judges provided both the victims and the military with some grounds for disappointment and relief. They accepted the prosecution's thesis that human-rights violations were part of a systematic design articulated by the armed forces and carried out under supreme secrecy and with public denial, albeit in a decentralized pattern in which the officers in charge of the operations were free to determine the fate of the victim, that is, whether he or she would be liberated, passed to the Executive (and thus publicly acknowledged as prisoner), judged by a court, or assassinated. The judges concluded that the responsibility for this plan and its execution resided, mainly, with the members of the first ruling junta. This vision suited the defence line of the members of the second and third juntas, and the judges used this argument in finding four out of the nine defendants not guilty. In the verdicts, the judges also distinguished the role played by each branch of the armed forces. The army and the navy were found by the Court to be much more implicated in gross human-rights violations than the air force. The terms of the sentences corresponded to this disparity.[49]

This grading of punishment was severely criticized by most human-rights activists. Their disappointment was expressed in recriminations towards the executive. On the day the verdicts were published, the Mothers of Plaza de Mayo organized a public demonstration to denounce the injustice of what they perceived as lenient verdicts, irreverent to the martyrdom of their beloved. Human-rights activists more pragmatic than the Mothers were also upset by the result of the trial.[50] Their reactions were influenced by the high expectation they had had that the trials could provide an authoritative and conclusive historical judgement. Mark Osiel considers that the courts are incapable of fulfilling the aspiration to combine matters of legal and historical judgement and settle them at once by the apparatus of the state. By its own logic, the legal system enforces civility rules, a logic of individualization of acts and responsibility, and an adversarial structure in proceedings that can seldom fulfil the totalizing expectations of either side.[51]

The judges recommended prosecuting every officer and soldier suspected of bearing responsibililily for human-rights violations. The Court decision confirmed the fears of the armed forces that the trials against the members of the juntas were only the beginning of an escalation in the civilian persecution against the armed forces.[52] Though designed to heal the wounds of the recent past, by judging only the commanders who had embodied the spirit of the PRN, the government's strategy failed to assess the role played by the judiciary. Being at the centre of public attention and expectations, the courts exercised a high degree of autonomy.

Each side in the trials disliked the verdicts and accused the judges of being too sympathetic to the other side, but the party that suffered most from this unexpected independence of the judiciary was the government itself. After the verdicts, Alfonsín remained isolated from the rest of the actors. Human-rights organizations felt betrayed by the government's policy and stopped cooperating with it. The non-governmental organizations diverted most of their resources and efforts to achieving the indictment of the greatest number of military personnel possible and generating more pressures on the military. The strategy of restricting the punishment to a central symbolic trial was threatened by the joint impact of the judicial recommendations and the militant attitudes of the NGOs and part of the media. At the same time, the government's credibility with the army reached its lowest level yet. Until a political solution was reached, the military would refuse to accept the full supremacy of the civilian authorities.[53]

Increasing demands and policies of closure

The trial of the commanders vitiated the initiative of the executive. In the public sphere, the NGOs and the military assumed the central protagonist roles in dealing with the legacy of human-rights violations in and out of the courts. The polarization that divided Argentine society in the past was re-enacted within the public debate, threatening the stability of the new democracy. The process of inquiry and indictment generated waves of unrest in the armed forces. Signs of resistance were visible from the beginning of the trials. Already in April 1985, rumours abounded of possible military coups, followed by a campaign of destabilizing violence waged by groups on the extreme right. These groups planted bombs and instigated social disorder with the goal of undermining Alfonsín's human-rights policies.[54]

The deterioration of the economy and the failed attempts to carry out a deep and long-awaited structural reform of the armed forces created mounting pressures and a loss of momentum in the treatment of human-rights violations, while the costs of carrying out these policies rose from month to month. Until the verdicts against the members of the juntas Alfonsín's government had succeeded in creating an image of the progressive implementation of policies leading to the resolution of human-rights violations, but a reversal of policies was initiated following the dramatic peak of the publication of the CONADEP report and the trial of the military commanders.

Concurrently, a series of trials was opened against lower-ranking officers identified by the victims and relatives as responsible for gross human-rights violations. According to the Argentine penal procedures, it is not a prerequisite for opening a process that full information should be forwarded on the identity of those who committed a crime or felony. The judicial system must begin an inquiry and a trial would be opened if evidence that substantiates the denunciation is present. Those with a special interest in the case (e.g. the victim or some relatives) can take part in the trial, albeit supporting the initiative of the public prosecutor. They can appeal before higher courts if they disagree with the decisions of the lower court. They can demand material reparations, either at the criminal court or separately, by filing a complaint at a civil court. Already in mid–1984 around 2,000 denunciations had been forwarded to the courts, including over 400 presented by the CELS.[55]

As the courts advanced through these files, Alfonsín's capacity for political action was increasingly restricted vis-à-vis the armed forces. The President tried to limit the unrest of the armed forces by reducing the number of military personnel accused. He thus issued in April 1986, special ordinances for the military prosecution, the Instrucciones al Fiscal General del Consejo Supremo de las Fuerzas Armadas. In these ordinances, the government had expressed the view that only officers that exceeded the orders received from their commanding officer were to be held responsible for their actions in court.

The ordinances generated public outrage. The Federal Court of the Capital District of Buenos Aires threatened to resign unanimously if the Instructions were not cancelled immediately, demonstrating the increasing political isolation of Alfonsín. Among the military too, the instructions were viewed with suspicion, as hinting that the inquiries and decisions of the Supreme Council of the Armed Forces would be appealed in civilian courts, as had already occurred in the cases of General Camps and several policemen, of Astiz, and of personnel of the army First Corps. Unrest mounted accordingly in the middle ranks of the officers' corp.[56]

The President tried to appease the armed forces and avoid an institutional crisis by enacting in December 1986 a law of expiry, popularly known as the 'Full Stop Law' ('Ley de Punto Final'). Most of the parliamentarians opposed to the proposed law absented themselves from the vote. In the lower chamber, 40 per cent of the members were absent, ranging from those identified with the Renovador wing of Peronism to dissident Radical representatives. The coalition supporting the Full Stop bill was composed of Radicals loyal to the President, Peronist conservatives, and small provincial parties. The law established a deadline of thirty days for presenting new charges concerning human-rights violations, and a time limit of sixty days for initiating trials.[57] The law clearly signalled that the regressive trend was fully under way. The government expected that by 22 February 1987, when the deadline would pass, only thirty to forty members of the armed forces —mostly retired officers—would stand trial.[58]

The enactment of this law generated three parallel processes. First, a wave of popular protest ensued. Demonstrations were organized all over the country. In Buenos Aires a demonstration that united various organizations—political, syndical, economic, and those dedicated specifically to the human-rights issue—drew at least 32,000 participants (according to police sources) and probably between 55,000 and 80,000 participants (according to the newspapers and the CELS). A similar protest took place in the southern province of Río Negro, and Alfonsín blamed both right and left extremists for undermining efforts to achieve social peace.[59] Other expressions of protest against the law took place in the Senate when a group from the Madres de Plaza de Mayo organization verbally accosted senators, calling them traitors and accomplices to the armed forces.

Second, the enactment of the law led to hundreds of legal suits being laid before the courts within the time limits set. This avalanche reinforced society's perception that the judicial system endorsed the independent approach of the Federal Court, despite efforts made at the highest levels of the government to stop the process.[60]

Third, the law paradoxically hardened the positions of wide sectors of the military that opposed the government's policy on human-rights. Following redemocratization, these sectors identified that policy with revanchism and signs of political immaturity on the part of Argentines. Among others, this view was voiced by Fr Daniel Zaffaroni in a sermon during a mass of FAMUS, the Association of Relatives and Friends of Victims of the Subversion, in June 1984:

One of the errors into which we cannot lapse is that of the revanchism that generates a movement of infinitely increasing violence, nor ought we to fall into the error of attributing to democracy the virtues of a panacea. Even admitting that it is the best political system known up until now. It is very far from being the cure for all evils. We ought not to forget that here and in other countries subversion was born under democratic governments. The social injustices that provided the pretext for subversion also occur with democratic governments. Democracy is the government of the people, as a result of which if the people are not mature enough to govern, democracy makes the people the author of their own disgrace. Would that not be their own ruin? Democracy, as does liberty, supposes adultness and responsibility.[61]

In early 1987 these sectors considered that the government was giving in to pressures and that the law had merely hastened the legal prosecution of members of the security forces. In March 1987 the commander of the navy, Vice-Admiral Ramón Arosa, declared before Alfonsín's Minister of Defence, Horacio Jaunarena, that the inquiries into human rights had exceeded 'all permissible limits'. FAMUS demonstrated in favour of those accused of human-rights violations, hailing the condemned General Jorge R. Videla, head of the first military junta in 1976, under whose rule most of the violations were committed. The Military Circle, a club of military officers, awarded honorary membership to any officer condemned on grounds of 'human-rights violations'. A bomb was planted in the house of one of the Federal Appeals Court's judges, where cases of human-rights violations were heard at that time. The commander-in-chief of the army, General Ríos Ereñú, declared publicly that the war waged against the left-wing subversion was totally just and legitimate.[62]

The refusal of a military officer—Major Ernesto Barreiro — to appear before the court in Córdoba triggered the military uprising of Semana Santa (Easter) 1987, led by Lt.-Col. Aldo Rico in Campo de Mayo, Buenos Aires. The rebels demanded a 'political solution' in the form of an amnesty and the discharge from the army of twenty-three generals (including the commander-in-chief of the army, Ríos Ereñú), perceived by the middle-rank officers as collaborators with Alfonsín in his policies both concerning the military responsibilities in the 'Dirty War' and towards the military as an institution.[63] The middle ranks of the armed forces believed that, within the framework of the democratic government, they were being forced to pay a price for having performed their military duty. In the framework of their ideological indoctrination—within the Doctrine of National Security—they considered themselves victors in a just war against international communism. In democratic Argentina, they were told that what they considered a heroic and dutiful performance was nothing but a series of horrendous crimes against their co-nationals and against humanity. The middle ranks considered that although the top military elite was judged and condemned and they themselves would not be promoted and might be even judged on human-rights abuses; their commanding officers were too lenient toward the civilian authorities, in exchange for being promoted by the latter.

As Alfonsín failed to gather the immediate active support of the armed forces for repressing the rebelling garrison, he opted to talk with the rebels in his capacity as President of the Republic. He discarded the subsequent commitment of the air force commander and of other high-ranking officers to repress the rebels. He was also reluctant to rely on public support and the formal support of all the political class to face the rebels or to punish them after they gave up the use of force. During the 1980s, public opinion polls showed systematic public support of democracy and persisting demands for post-dictatorial justice, in the range of 70 to 80 per cent of representative samples.[64] Alfonsín's lack of accountability in the decision to talk (and negotiate) with the rebels and condone their actions, and the highly authoritarian style he adopted in dealing with the crisis, backfired. Alfonsín affirmed that the crisis was over without concessions having been made on his side, a position that the media adopted. Whenever somebody suggested that the Semana Santa rebellion ended as a result of a transaction between the President and Lt.-Col. Rico, Alfonsín indignantly rejected the claim. Nonetheless, as time passed, the demands of the rebels were fulfilled. Four generals and, later on, another fifteen were made to retire; the subpoenas of military officers under trial were suspended; all the rebels—with the exception of Rico himself—were freed and reassigned to new commands; former Major Barreiro was freed; civil trials initiated and pending before the Supreme Court were halted and rumours about possible presidential pardons spread. Civil–military relationships were tense, with the high commands of the armed forces pursuing a policy of revindication and promising not to relinquish the positions gained in Semana Santa. The supporters of the military on the extreme right threatened and attacked branches of left-wing political parties. Unknown individuals placed a bomb at the Secretariat of Human Rights of the Confederación General del Trabajo, Argentina's main trade union confederation. Shots were fired at the tomb of Ricardo Balbín, the UCR leader who preceded Alfonsín at the head of the Radical Party. The hands of the corpse of former president Juan Domingo Perón were amputated and made 'to disappear' from his mausoleum at the Chacarita Cemetery.

As a result of what were perceived as governmental concessions to the rebels and as result of the climate of violence and confrontation, Alfonsín lost prestige and credibility with the general public.

This society, especially the middle class and the sectors close to Alfonsín, lived the events of Semana Santa as a televised Greek drama, in a very tragic way . . . The obscure negotiations, the lack of transparency and the legislation that ensued were very harsh for the Radical Party and most sectors of society, even though Due Obedience was contemplated in the policies of the ruling party.[65]

Alfonsín was viewed with suspicion by the army, for other reasons. These events and the personal promotions and demotions in the ranks of the armed forces did not appease the unrest of the officers, which stemmed from inner rivalries and a sense of vulnerability on the part of the military institutions, whose officers were accused of crimes concerning their role in the previous decade. Politicians all over the country began approaching the local army commanders and repositioning themselves in the light of the Semana Santa aftermath and the mounting power of the military.

By June 1987 Alfonsín's government submitted a Law of Due Obedience to the Parliament, which was intended to absolve from responsibility for human-rights violations all those who, with the rank of Lieutenant-Colonel and lower, had committed such acts. Balbino Zubiri, president of the Defence Commission of the Chamber of Deputies, justified the need to support the bill in the following terms:

Any country in which the armed forces and the whole people regard each other as foes is seriously ill. It is necessary to sanction this law because today we are in a country in which, as the President of the Republic himself stated a few days ago, the phantom of civil war is constantly above our heads.[66]

Zubiri explained that the law was not intended as an amnesty:

Whereas amnesty prevents punishing the deed and the social claim operative in its connection, this bill transfers culpability from the actual executor of the decision to those who conceived and dictated those decisions; but the social and moral questioning of the action remains . . .[67]

The bill was approved as Law No. 23521 on 4 June 1987, by parliamentarians under the strong feeling of being under military pressure. One of the leaders of the Peronist Renovador sector, Antonio Cafiero, recognized that 'we are not deliberating freely . . . there are new lists of citizens [to be repressed] circulating . . . we know that there is an invisible army pressuring . . . to compel us to legislate against conscience'.[68] Torture, assassination, arbitrary detention, and false testimony in court were covered by the law. The bill did not 'cleanse' those suspected of rape, kidnapping children, and stealing or destroying material property. Under the new law, only about 40 of the nearly 370 officers hitherto due to be prosecuted for alleged human-rights violations were now to be tried.

The Law of Due Obedience generated a new wave of debate. Those who supported the government's initiative used the following arguments: any policy should take into account political and social implications; those who committed gross violations of human-rights were not exceptionally sadist monsters acting within a culture of respect for liberal principles, but instead were part of a general tradition and social climate that encouraged the use of violence; if these actions reflected the organizational culture of the military institutions as a whole, then the set-up of that subculture required reform; accordingly, the task of democracy should be to teach the rule of law and to build trust in the autonomous role of the judiciary rather than to launch a policy of vengeance against the old authoritarian style of doing things; after the indictment of the high commanders, the democratic lesson that nobody is beyond the law had been internalized; to continue reprisals would impair the rebuilding of collective solidarity. The President, too, used the latter arguments as he emphasized in particular that the country was on the verge of destabilization and even civil war; that blaming the military alone was a very partial reading of the role of the civilian sectors in the PRN; that the government's policy was intended to create a new role for the army rather than to destroy it; that the society was eager to heal the wounds and polarization of the past; that although many of those who had committed human-rights violations would go unpunished, those responsible for creating the systematic pattern of violation had been subjected to the rule of the law.

Those who rejected the policy of pardons used opposing arguments. They claimed that the Law of Due Obedience was the result of improvisation rather than a deliberate attempt to redefine the relationships between society and the armed forces; that there was no justification on earth to release people involved in blatant violations of the most basic individual rights; that the law enshrined the principle of inequality before the law; that it gave primacy to property over life, as it condoned crimes against humanity but excepted robbery committed during such acts; that the law wasted the political goodwill of civil society shown in the widespread mobilization during the events of Semana Santa; and that the concessions resulted from the weakness of the political system as it faced the restrengthened sectors of the armed forces.[69] As emphasized by Member of the Chamber of Deputies Diego R. Guelar:

For some 'this is the beginning of the move backwards', 'the beginning of civil war', 'the removal of the mask of the petit bourgeois regime', 'the cheating of popular will'. For others, it is 'the beginning of reconciliation among Argentines', 'the prospect of incorporation of the armed forces without past rancors', or 'an act of justice with those that vanquished subversion . . .' [Above and beyond these polarized views] what is significant is not that the military was forgiven—which might be a decision that brings dignity to those who enact it—but the fact that forgiveness was dictated by the military establishment, despite the [political] will not to sanction it.[70]

Some courts initially refused to apply the law, declaring it unconstitutional. However, the Supreme Court decided, in the appeal of the Camps case, that it withstood the criteria of constitutionality (23 June 1987). Later on, it reconfirmed this interpretation when it exonerated Generals Benjamín Menéndez, Antonio Domingo Bussi, and Luis Martella, who had been accused of committing gross human-rights violations in Tucumán.[71]

That development led to the UCR's defeat at the legislative and provincial governors' elections of September 1987. Contributing to that defeat were also the strict austerity measures adopted by Alfonsín's administration in July 1987, meant to cope with the deep economic crisis affecting the country. Towards the end of the Alfonsín government, the inept policies failed to stabilize the economic situation in Argentina. Hyperinflation, after being controlled through the Austral Plan in 1985, returned and climbed to unprecedent heights. Under these circumstances, the government was losing control of the country in general and the army in particular. Very little was left of the intended policies, and civil–military relations continued to be dictated largely by the acts and demands of groups of army officers totally opposed to the official policies. Political contingency was prevailing more and more over principles.

Democratization had opened the public sphere to a wide debate on the main problems of Argentina, placing the legacy of human-rights violations at the centre of the public agenda. No agreement existed on these problems, neither between the military and the civilians, nor among civilians themselves. The original policy of Alfonsín's government played on both sides of the fence. Rhetorically and symbolically its policies seemed to be as progressive as those demanded by the NGOs, and, indeed, the CONADEP report and the very fact that the members of the military juntas were brought to court imprinted the democratic agenda with a progressive vision of accountability and the rule of law. Eventually, the government's intention to treat only crimes committed by those who stood at the head of the juntas backfired. NGOs and relatives of the victims mobilized in protest, while the judges' recommendations in the trial of the junta members opened the courts to massive numbers of cases. The Punto Final law only created a snowball effect by establishing a deadline for presenting cases. The reaction of the military brought the progressive moves to a halt and initiated the regressive stage in the cycle of treating past human-rights violations. Having failed to take into account the full strength and impact of public debate in a democratic public sphere, the first civilian government lost the initiative on human-rights issues. The policies became reactive due to the deteriorating situation, and then became regressive in order to avert the possibility a new breakdown of democracy.

The military uprising of Semana Santa and the subsequent legislation of the Law of Due Obedience in 1987 were only the first stage in the regressive cycle of dealing with the issue. Public opinion was increasingly concerned with the socio-economic crisis, eroding the bases of civilian support for Alfonsín's government and deepening the disaffection of the NGOs most concerned with the trend taken by the human-rights policies. In December 1988 a small number of troops led by Colonel Mohammed Alí Seineldín rebelled once more against the government, demanding amnesty for those condemned on human-rights violations, larger budgets, better wages, and personnel changes in the army's top echelons. While the rebellion was repressed by other sectors of the army, the government satisfied some of their demands.[72]

The election of Carlos Saúl Menem and his rapid inauguration in July 1989 further tested the ongoing format of civil–military relationships and policies. In August 1989 the Minister of Defence, Italo Luder, suspended the ongoing trials against dozens of officers. In September, rumours spread of Menem's plans to grant full pardons to those officers who had been condemned. The rumours triggered very large demonstrations of citizens hoping to pre-empt such an initiative, and to prevent further erosion in the treatment of human-rights violations.

These activities, which included petitions, publications, and demonstrations, proved ineffective. Pardons for most condemned officers were granted in October 1989.[73] Further mobilization by NGOs concerned with human rights[74] did not prevent the extension of pardons to the top figures of the Dirty War and the Process of National Reorganization—General Videla, Admiral Emilio E. Massera, General Roberto E. Viola, Admiral Armando Lambruschini, Brigadier Orlando R. Agosti, General Ramón Camps, General Ovidio P. Ricchieri, General Carlos Suárez Mason, together with Montonero leader Mario Firmenich and former Finance Minister José A. Martínez de Hoz.[75] Immediately following his pardon, ex-General Videla sent an open letter to the Chief of Staff, General Martín Bonnet, stating that the armed forces deserved an apology. Sectors of the civilian population continued to demonstrate against the pardons, although there was a clear reduction in the size of protest. Despite the opposition of substantial parts of civil society and of the NGOs and the criticism of part of the media, Menem was able to move ahead with national reconciliation and strengthen the executive, since by 1989 the Argentine public agenda had shifted completely to the ongoing economic crisis, with its hyperinflation and huge external debt.[76]

At the same time, Menem managed to subordinate the armed forces. The President acted firmly—with the support of the high commands —against acts of rebellion such as those led again on 3 December 1990 by Colonel Seineldín, thus clearly indicating that no insubordination would be tolerated. On a more structural dimension and within the general programme of economic stabilization, the President continued the trend initiated by Alfonsín of reducing and restructuring the armed forces. The armed forces were required to 'contribute their share'. They had to conduct budgetary cuts, personnel downsizing, and privatization of military industries and other corporate assets. On 31 October 1991, the commander-in-chief of the armed forces, General Martín Bonnet, who opposed these trends, asked to be discharged from service and was replaced by General Martín Balza, who had repressed the Seineldín uprising one year earlier. These developments were further confirmation of the levels of subordination of the military to the civilian authorities achieved by Menem's policies.[77] Mandatory military service was reduced and finally abolished in 1994, following the Carrasco case. Omar Carrasco was a young conscript mistreated brutally and beaten to death by his superiors. His body, initially hidden, was finally produced, and a loud uproar against the armed forces ensued.[78] The connection between this individual case of a human-rights violation and the twofold confrontation between civilians and the armed forces eventually led to the abolition of mandatory military service and its replacement by voluntary enrolment, after over ninety years of compulsory service.

Unlike the failed military reform under Alfonsín, President Menem succeeded in reformulating civil–military relationships. This was accomplished using presidential pardons in exchange for military subordination to the elected President. Menem sacrificed the principle of primacy of the law in treating human-rights violations, to the principle of civilian government's primacy over the armed forces. The executive thus emphasized its status as the central and unchallenged decision-maker, well above the sectorial interests of the military and of the other branches of the Argentine state, namely, the judiciary and the Parliament.

The subordination of the military should be seen as directly related to a series of reforms undertaken by Menem's administration. With economic stabilization and reduction of hyperinflation as primary objectives, the executive proceeded to apply strong neo-liberal policies, ideologically distanced from the electoral platform of Menem in 1989. The strong parliamentary opposition was handled by governing by decree, in what was euphemistically called 'decreto-cracy'. Between 1989 and 1993 President Menem issued 308 decree-laws, which were put

into effect without parliamentary discussion and approval.[79] Menem
also overcame possible legal opposition by increasing the number of
judges in the Supreme Court from five to nine, with judges loyal to the
government. This move neutralized one of the foci that in the past contributed to the loss of governance during Alfonsín's period.[80] Another
path of reform was taken by Menem through an agreement with former
President Alfonsín. Through this agreement, known as the Olivos Pact,
presidential periods were shortened from six to four years, consecutive presidential re-elections were made possible, and a reform of the
national constitution was agreed upon and enacted in 1994.[81]

Under Menem's policies, laws were enacted for the compensation
of victims of repression under the military dictatorship. Civilian demands for compensation were presented to the courts, which produced
verdicts favourable to the victims at least in one case (see Chapter 4).
These policies were part of the formula Carlos Menem used of national
reconciliation, conceived as a mechanism to ensure social peace. Institutionally, President Menem completed the regressive turn initiated
in Semana Santa, hoping that the legacy of past human-rights violations would be removed forever from the public sphere of democratic
Argentina. Although in the short term these policies prevailed, the seed
for future crises was planted in Argentina's institutional path.

Uruguay: The Vitality of Civil Society and Resolutive Referendum

In Uruguay, the transition to democracy resulted from an agreement between the military and the main political parties. Prior to this,
on 30 November 1980, the military rulers attempted to get popular
approval for their project of constitutional reform. The reform envisioned a model of domination and articulation that demobilized civil
society, restricted autonomous debate, and limited political participation to those elite circles supporting the military and their views.
The rejection of this reform in the 1980 ballots was respected by the
military rulers. In spite of their defeat in the referendum, the military retained both a large measure of control over the political process and internal cohesiveness. This allowed them to move towards
democracy in a transition negotiated with most of the political class,
partially dictating their own terms. Even though civil society was nar-
rowly restricted in its expressions, it supported the politicians' efforts
towards redemocratization. NGOs dealing with human-rights, and
especially the Servicio de Paz y Justicia (SERPAJ), found a willing
audience among the political class. During the long period of political

proscription, the human-rights banner had been carried almost solely by the NGOs and their leaders. As pointed out by David Lehmann, these organizations proliferated in this period as part of a series of new social movements rooted in civil society and autonomous from state controls.[82] In the early stages of political opening, these leaders were in touch with all civilian political sectors, enabling contacts between them, both on account of the former's record of opposition to the military and on the universality of the human-rights issue. During the negotiations between the military and the politicians in 1983, Father Luis Pérez Aguirre worked for the coordination between a myriad of associations of human rights.

We, the team of human rights, tried to coordinate, during a time when the number of groups multiplied. The movement was not yet centred in the political parties, which were not organized [since most leading politicians were proscripted], and were still uncertain about the political space that would be open for their action. Everything was concentrated under the banner of human rights, since all political sectors had their human-rights commissions as did the churches, trade unions, and everybody else too.[83]

Pérez Aguirre denounced the hypocritical attitude of the military, which continued to torture prisoners at the very same moment that it negotiated with the politicians. The potentially explosive character of such denunciations is illustrated by their impact on the military, which stopped the negotiations as a reprisal. A fifteen-day hunger strike by Pérez Aguirre and two other SERPAJ activists, supported by the politicians, brought about the reconvening of negotiations. Another critical event was the death of physician Vladimir Roslik, as a result of detention and torture, on 15 April 1984. This case was covered in detail by the media, which, along with the main political forces and the international community, demanded explanations from the military administration. The military responded by harassing the media. It arrested the editorial secretary of the weekly *Jaque,* which denounced Roslik's murder and published the names of other assassinated victims; it also temporarily closed television Channel 10 for reporting on the case. As a result of the Roslik affair, the Colorado Party adopted the banner of human rights, and a wide public consensus emerged against the violation of human rights. The Colorados' role was also strengthened relative to other forces in the opposition to the military, and the Communist Party, recognized as a victim of the repression, was included as a legitimate participant in the political arena.[84]

The Naval Club pact, signed in August 1984, was intended to enable elections and the transition to civilian rule. The main negotiators, General Hugo Medina and Colorado Party leader Julio María

Sanguinetti, had to balance contradictory pressures. The hardliners in the army demanded explicit impunity. Such a move would have pushed the leftist forces of the Frente Amplio out of the negotiations. A rejection of impunity by the politicians would have ended the whole transition to democracy. Public statements by General Medina at the time made it clear that only military personnel who had committed 'disqualifying actions' (e.g. theft and rape) could be brought to trial. The army would not allow any legal or extra-legal move against those who had followed orders. Thus, one of the main costs of the political opening was the implicit understanding that the perpetrators of human-rights violations would go unpunished.[85]

The democratic government instituted in 1985 had to deal with the legacy of human-rights violations. At the same time, it had to face the tasks of consolidating democracy against a background of military forces that retained a powerful position in the system. This situation was typical of transitions to democracy conducted by the military high commands from a position of relative strength. Still, formal democratization implied opening the public sphere to actors excluded during the military rule.

Like the other Southern Cone countries, Uruguayan society and the political system faced serious problems incorporating the experience of human-rights violations into the agenda of the transition. The political framework of the democratic transition and the limitations imposed by the potential threats to the redemocratized regimes conditioned the possibility of treating the legacy of human-rights violations from a legal, political, and institutional perspective. That is, the new democracy could neither ignore the issue nor deal with it efficiently and in a comprehensive way without endangering the newly structured democratic system. Accordingly, the expectations of wide sectors of the population for a solution of 'justice' were compounded by the pragmatic context of political expediency.

Following redemocratization and shortly after the inauguration of elected President Julio María Sanguinetti, the Parliament approved in March 1985 a law sanctioning the release of political prisoners jailed since 1 January 1962, with the exception of intentional homicides. Courts of appeal were requested to review the cases of the prisoners within 120 days, to decide whether the prison terms were justified. In cases in which imprisonment was justified, the terms of sentences were reduced by two-thirds (article 9 of Law 15737). Article 5 excludes from this amnesty all those 'crimes committed by military or police personnel ... who were perpetrators, co-perpetrators or accomplices of cruel or degrading unhuman deeds or of detention of individuals, afterwards "disappeared."' This article was extended to crimes committed on the basis of political motivations by people who had acted on behalf of the state and/or protected by the state.[86] In terms of military–civilian relationships, this law would create the need for an equivalent law of amnesty to cover the actions of the military and the police.

Concurrently, in April 1985, a National Commission of Repatriation was created to facilitate the return of exiles. The commission assisted 16,000 returning exiles in obtaining work, in funding medical insurance and housing, and in financing labour-related ventures. The Amnesty Law provided the reinstitution of public employees fired by the military rulers on the basis of political considerations (article 25). A law which regulated this issue was enacted in November 1985.[87]

In April 1985, the Chamber of Deputies established two inquiry committees to investigate the kidnapping and assassination of two Uruguayan MPs in Buenos Aires, Colorado Senator Zelmar Michelini and Speaker of the Chamber of Deputies Héctor Gutiérrez Ruiz; and to investigate the kidnapping and disappearance of over 150 persons, kidnapped mostly in Argentina and Chile. Although President Sanguinetti would have preferred that the judiciary carry on with the investigation of human-rights violations, by August 1985 the Chamber of Deputies awarded special powers to its committees to investigate the events that had occurred between 1973 and 1985.[88]

By October 1985 an agreement was reached between President Sanguinetti and the commander of the armed forces, Lt.-Gen. Hugo Medina, according to which the military courts had to try and punish those who had committed the worst violations of human rights, to serve as exemplary cases. Nonetheless, this agreement did not lead to any effective steps. The connections with General Medina as the leader of the military were nurtured by the civilian executive, with the purpose of overcoming the mistrust of the armed forces and their staunch opposition to any attack on the basis of the human-rights issue.[89]

In early 1986 the parliamentary committee on human-rights violations presented to the judicial system a list of forty-six cases of military and police personnel involved in extreme human-rights violations. President Sanguinetti presented in August 1986 a bill designed to grant immunity from trial to the members of the security and armed forces that were involved in human-rights violations. Such a law would have been equivalent to the pardons granted in March 1985 to the Tupamaros. The popular reaction to that bill was strong. A mass gathering of over 10,000 demanded its rejection, an action the Parliament took in September 1986.[90] This pattern of resolving the legacy of human-rights violations differed strikingly from the Argentine precedent. The Uruguayan Parliament took the initiative in elaborating ways of closing the issue by legislation. Whereas in Argentina one of the first steps of the democratically elected administration was to annul the law of self-amnesty legislated by the military, in Uruguay the political class was looking for a device to grant amnesty to the military, reinforcing Ferreira Aldunate's thesis of the understandings reached at the Naval Club. Another contrast concerned the search for establishing the 'truth' about the experience of repression under military rule. While in Argentina an official commission of inquiry (the CONADEP) worked out a report that was endorsed by the government, in Uruguay parliamentary committees took upon themselves the investigation of human-rights abuses between 1973 and 1985. Within the terms of Uruguayan civility it was the politicians who almost completely took over the issue.[91]

In October 1986, nineteen generals warned that lack of legislation involved 'serious risks' for the democratic system. The political forces were divided on the issue: whereas the National (Blanco) opposition party favoured a partial amnesty, the Colorados demanded a wider amnesty, and the left-wing coalition of the Frente Amplio rejected any compromise of that kind. The armed forces indicated that no member of the armed and security forces would obey the judicial subpoenas being handed down.

Finally, the Parliament approved the *Ley de Caducidad* or 'Law of Expiry' which covered delinquent acts due to political motives or acts committed by members of the armed and police forces before 1 March 1985.[92] Article 1 of the law states,

It is recognized that, as a result of the sequence of events originated in the agreement between the political parties and the armed forces in August 1984 and aiming to accomplish the transition to the full enforcement of the constitutional order, the exercise of the punishing right of the state will not be used with respect to the crimes committed before 1 March 1985, equally by military and police personnel, for political reasons or while fulfilling their duties and as a result of actions ordered by the commands acting during the *de facto* period.[93]

The legal proposal presented by the government enjoyed the support of the coalition and of wide sectors of the National (Blanco) party opposition. The law granted pardons for human-rights violations, save in extreme cases that included also illicit profit on the part of the violators.[94] At the same time, the government maintained the right to investigate the disappearance of 164 citizens during the repression, as well as the fate of the children of the *desaparecidos*. The Senate acquired control over the promotion of military officers; the Ministry of Defence was put in charge of the placement of the intelligence services; and the parliament was granted supervision over the military academy.

The political process had been shaped to that moment in the traditional way of doing politics in Uruguay during democratic periods. The politicians were used to reaching agreements on central issues by deliberating within the political class. Traditionally, Uruguayan social movements had been weak and did not exert significant influence on their country's 'particracy'.[95] Around the legacy of human-rights violations a new scenario emerged, in which the initiative was taken by civil society, involving mass participation. The Law of Expiry could be interpreted as an attempt to re-enact this pattern of political action and preclude contestation and debate in the public sphere around an issue with explosive implications for the consolidation of democracy.

The referendum and its implications

Under the Uruguayan constitution of 1967, a referendum on a legal decision such as the Law of Expiry could be held if 25 per cent of the electorate requested it. Those who opposed granting impunity to the perpetrators of human-rights violations mobilized to collect the required number of signatures petitioning for a referendum on the issue of the amnesty. Massive mobilizations took place parallel to gathering the necessary signatures. The protest was initiated by the MLN-Tupamaros, and was soon led by the Committee of Mothers and Relatives of Disappeared Persons (represented by María Esther Gatti de Islas), together with the widows of Héctor Gutiérrez Ruiz and Zelmar Michelini, Matilde Rodríguez and Elisa Dellepiane. NGOs, SERPAJ in particular, were instrumental in the coordination. Beginning in January 1987, the campaign was carried out under the umbrella of a National Committee for the Referendum (Comisión Nacional Pro-Referendum—CNP), led by the three women mentioned above.[96] With the sequence of human-rights violations fresh in the minds of many Uruguayans, civil society associations found it possible to challenge the administration and the ruling parliamentary coalition, by moving the issue to the centre of the public sphere.

After an initial period of enthusiastic signing that led to the collection of 305,000 signatures in three months, a piecemeal strategy was carried out, consisting of door-to-door visits and popular gatherings both in urban and rural areas. On 17 December 1987, the Pro-Referendum Committee presented a total of 634,792 signatures to the Electoral Court. This number was well over the 555,701 signatures required to sanction the referendum. A dramatic months-long interlude followed, marked by the protracted verification of the signatures. The promoters of the referendum accused the Electoral Court of trying to discard tens of thousands of signatures. The media broadcast dramatic events such as the punishment of those members of the armed forces and the police who had signed the petition. On 28 November 1988, the verification came to an end with the validation of 529,110 signatures and 4,591 fingerprints. Another 36,834 signatures were suspended until those citizens appeared before the Electoral Court for further verification. Slowly these citizens were located and appeared before the court, and by 19 December 1988, the additional required 23,000 signatures had been obtained.

During the gathering of signatures, the forces pushing the referendum tried to project an image of self-organizing networks and pluralist forces of civil society, dissociated from the traditional parties, although supported by individual politicians. Signing the petition for the referendum, they stated, did not imply how the citizen would vote in the referendum itself, but was rather designed to enable the people to decide. The slogan of the campaign reflected this emphasis on popular sovereignty: 'I sign for the people to decide'.[97] The CNP was portrayed as 'integrated by Uruguayan citizens inspired by the basic principles of our nationality: liberty, democracy, justice and peaceful coexistence'. The Law of Expiry was portrayed as an affront to the democratic feelings of the Uruguayan people, for whom justice and equality before the law are fundamental. It was also seen as directly contradicting universally recognized legal principles. Furthermore, the law was portrayed as antithetical to the 'purest traditions of the nation', traditions rooted in the actions of Gervasio José de Artigas and other founding fathers of the country. The CNP emphasized that the reaction to the law was a 'spontaneous, popular uproar'. Similarly, it emphasized that the mobilization was motivated by a 'free civic consciousness' of the Uruguayans, and that it was part of a fundamentally important process of overcoming fear and learning again to trust the people's own capacity for decision-making after the military interregnum.[98]

This message was phrased in terms of ethics, truth, and justice; hope, happiness, life; reaffirmation of the basic values of society; and social regeneration from below. These themes were emphasized during the long process of popular mobilization. The events included musical and food events in local congregations, meetings bringing back the memory of popular forms of organization, and door-to-door visits.[99] Tension developed in later stages of the campaign, when the need to organize through central coordination became clear. This trend was much resented by rank-and-file activists.[100]

Several major issues became central in the debate that followed, both before and after the collection of signatures. These issues were addressed by both the supporters of the Yellow banner who favoured ratifying the law and by the supporters of the Green banner who wanted to defeat it. And yet, supporters and opponents addressed these core issues from diametrically opposed perspectives.[101]

The first issue was the need to uphold democracy. The theme of democracy was shared by both the supporters and the critics of the Law of Expiry. According to the former, the contribution of responsible citizens to democratic consolidation should be to keep the thorny issue of past human-rights violations off the political agenda. The green banner supporters declared that only a direct acknowledgement and treatment of the issue would allow democracy to develop fully.

Second, both sides recognized the need to avoid a return to dictatorship. The 'yellow' supporters awarded priority to political realism: any attempt to bring members of the armed forces to trial over past human-rights violations would prompt military intervention. The 'green' supporters declared that only upholding the primacy of law over considerations of political contingency would preclude the recurrence of a de facto military government.

The third theme was the need to support justice and equality before the law. For the supporters of the Law of Expiry, this implied granting the members of the armed forces the same treatment that was given to the members of the Tupamaros in March 1985. For the opponents of this law, no equality could be claimed on the above grounds. The implicated members of the armed and security forces had acted beyond what was necessary in terms of threats to the system. Moreover, the political activists detained, jailed, and liberated following the 1985 amnesty had already suffered from imprisonment, loss of liberties and tortures, while the members of the security forces had not even been brought to trial. Granting impunity for the sake of pragmatic considerations would defile the principle of equality before the law.

Fourth, both sectors shared the will to move towards the future. The priority of the 'yellow' was to erase the traces of past dissent and violence in order to preclude a new stage of uncertainty and instability.[102] For the 'green', a comprehensive clarification of the past was a sine qua non for leaving the past behind.

Fifth, the need to reinforce and define the professional role of the armed forces was also perceived by both sides. The yellow supporters claimed that reopening the issue would harm the institutional position of the armed forces. The green supporters stated that there was a need to cleanse the image of the armed forces by individualizing and punishing those who committed human-rights violations. Any attempt to ignore those actions would stain the image of the entire institution.

The weakening of a peaceful consolidation of democracy and the erosion of institutional trust were major themes in the arguments brought by the supporters of the Law of Expiry. President Sanguinetti declared that defeating the law would affect the process of pacification since 'the armed forces would feel excluded from the spirit of reconciliation of the democratic transition'.[103] Sanguinetti attacked time and again those who challenged the validity of the Expiry Law and displayed a vast array of arguments for supporting its ratification. During the collection of signatures, he declared:

I call from here the whole country to alert. That signature stands for resentment and revenge. That signature is simply to return the country to the phantoms of confrontation. The call made today [for supporting the referendum] by deceit in the name of a supposed justice only carries the spirit of revenge. No more signatures for rancour! No more signatures for the past! . . . Many of those who defend human rights do not believe in them, because under democracy they are members of subversive and violent organizations . . . The political organizations and trade unions of Marxism in Uruguay evoke human rights simply to validate subversion and, at the same time, to weaken the forces that serve the state for its own defence.[104]

Before the vote at the referendum in 1989, the Uruguayan President considered the referendum 'like the plebiscite of 1980, a crossroads. Either we continue to advance forward, or we change direction [and go backwards].' He also stated that the referendum was not 'an issue debated between the government and the opposition, between the military and the extremists', but a problem 'of the whole Uruguayan society that will have to decide whether it wishes to consolidate and strengthen the democratic peace in which it is living today or, on the contrary, to go back to the past'.[105]

Interestingly enough, the military themselves resented the arguments that portrayed them as the threatening factor behind the need to enforce the Law of Expiry. In the official organ of the Military Circle, *El soldado*, they stated time and again that their basic position was to contribute to social peace. They also rejected the argument about the need to apply a criterion of equality between the amnestied Tupamaros and the members of the armed forces. According to the military perception, the comparison was faulty and demeaning.[106]

The issue was presented by the supporters of the yellow vote as having broader implications than the imbalance in civil–military relations. Members of the government and the Colorado Party emphasized the negative impact a green victory would have on the judiciary. The phrasing of the question presented in the referendum was ambiguous: 'to leave the Law of Expiry without effect'. This ambiguity, the 'yellow' supporters emphasized, could have far-reaching implications. According to a legal interpretation, as indicated by Vice-President Enrique

Tarigo on 4 April 1989, a green victory would imply annulling the law and reopening the cases initiated at the time of its enactment in 1986. According to another interpretation, such result would imply derogating the law, thus enabling the opening of new cases but not producing a *pre-ante* situation.[107] Eventually, according to this second interpretation, the ambiguity of the referendum would lead to litigation in which the judiciary would inevitably produce contradictory judgements that both sides would perceive as political. It was claimed that this situation would polarize Uruguayan society, leading to the erosion of trust in the judiciary, one of its central institutions.

The supporters of the green position rejected the thesis of institutional destabilization. They shifted the discussion to the emotional and ethical dimensions of the reconstruction of Uruguayan social texture. On these terms, the political class could hardly answer the claims of the leading figures of the CNP. Naturally enough, many of the politicians refused to confront Matilde Rodríguez and other leaders of the CNP in public debate. The argument used was that since Matilde Rodríguez was not a 'presidential'—a possible presidential candidate —that is a professional politician, she did not have the same kind of commitment toward a code of political responsibility.[108] The authority of Max Weber, distinguishing the ethics of responsibility of the politician as opposed to the ethics of conviction, was cited by President Sanguinetti to justify his refusal to debate the issues with the widow of Gutiérrez Ruiz. The politicians' own image was one of mediators between two irreconcilable visions of society, one held by the victims of the repression and the other by the armed forces, both confident of their absolute rightfulness.[109]

Despite the emphasis on the mobilization of civil society, the discussion in the weeks preceding the referendum (1 to 16 April 1989) were led mainly by politicians and a few of the leaders of the CNP. The role played by the organized sectors of civil society was relatively minor. The Church called for a search of conscience. The Jewish community organized panels to discuss the issue. The unions preferred to take a secondary role in the green campaign, probably to discredit the Colorados' claim that the mobilization against the law was organized by the Communists and the Tupamaros.

The ruling party, the Colorados, played on a dual message. It portrayed the call for a referendum as genuine proof of the vitality of Uruguayan democracy, and yet it warned that those pushing and financing the green position included Communists and former guerrillas. Similarly, it reassured the population that the government would find a political solution in the eventuality of a green victory, and yet it warned that this result could be harmful to Uruguayan democracy. The

TABLE 2.1. *Perception of the Issue as Moral or Political (Montevideo Rep. Sample)*

Perception of the Issue	All	Yellow vote	Green vote	Undecided
Moral Issue	68	52	80	56
Political Issue	17	35	7	21
Does not know/No opinion	15	13	13	23

Source: *Búsqueda*, 6 Apr. 1989

Colorados tried to turn the confrontation into a party issue, a political matter, in which the major opponent would be another political actor, the left-wing coalition of the Frente Amplio, rather than the National Committee for the Referendum, which was ignored as a partner in the debate.

The main opposition force, the National (Blanco) Party, did not speak in a unified voice. In general, it left to the Colorados and especially to Tarigo, the Vice-President, the unpopular task of defending the Law of Expiry. Aware that such a defence carried with it the price of falling popularity, the Blancos seemed to be conscious of the institutional dangers implicit in the green option and were unwilling to pay the price involved in promoting the ratification of the law.[110]

The Frente Amplio kept a low profile, aware of the need not to politicize the issue. It was, however, critical of those who tried to instil fear in the population in order to lead to a yellow victory. Groups related to the left-wing forces, such as student associations and unions, were very active on the side of the green option. In Montevideo, ten days before the referendum, only a small minority of the population viewed the issue as merely political (see Table 2.1).[111]

On 16 April 1989, a compulsory referendum took place. The participation rate was 84.78 per cent. The voters ratified the law by a majority of 56.65 per cent against 43.34 per cent. Despite the identification of the issue as a moral one, the majority of the population decided to follow the pragmatic instead of the ethical option. In Montevideo, the capital and main urban centre of the country, 56.60 per cent of the voters rejected the law. The supporters of the green vote were a majority in Montevideo, and a minority in the rural and minor urban areas. Occupationally, they had a majority among the unemployed, white-collar workers, and professionals, and received fewer votes from housewives, retired people, and unskilled manual workers. The green vote was supported by urban workers, especially by those with ten and more years of schooling.[112]

The Colorados' position won. They managed to emerge as the stabilizing force able to close the rift between the military and those sectors of civil society that demanded justice and opposed impunity. But, on the political front, the terms of the campaign eroded the support for the Colorados. The Blancos would reach the November 1989 elections with a cleaner image and win the elections.

Immediately after the polls closed, President Sanguinetti expressed satisfaction with the demonstration of civility by the Uruguayans. He declared that 'to decide in the polls instead of shouting; this is the true meaning of being Uruguayan. Serenity, peacefulness of spirit . . . The Republic stood to the heights of its best traditions.' Sanguinetti added that taking the road of legitimate resolutions of conflicts had been typical of the country: 'We must listen to the voice of the People, . . . as the majority voted for Peace beyond the profound disparities of opinions.'[113]

Significantly, the leading political figures behind the 'yellow' option had declared time and again that their victory would not be followed by public rejoicing. In the referendum, there would be neither victors nor defeated.[114] Rhetorical figures were used to reaffirm the unity of the Uruguayans and to declare the issue definitively closed.

A series of meetings was convened by retired high military officials following the referendum. Some, including the Minister of Defence, retired Lt.-Gen. Hugo Medina, expressed their satisfaction with the massive civilian support of the Law of Expiry. However, high-ranking officers such as retired General Hugo Posse, head of the military forces during the 1973 coup, attacked on 20 April, in an address to the Military Circle, the view that the results of the referendum represented a picture of 'no victors or defeated'. According to Posse, the struggle against sedition conducted between 1973 and 1985 was morally correct, as it preserved order, fostered authority, and saved the Fatherland. No call to public courtesy should obscure the fact that those who use the terminology of human rights and justice are [still] trying to 'disarm the Nation both in a material and a spiritual sense', he added.[115]

The forces supporting the annulment of the law needed an explanation for the defeat. Most commonly mentioned were the fears of the population and their own failure to overcome the propaganda of government forces, which used the media on a much larger scale than the opposition, creating a sense of danger to democracy in the event of a green victory. In an interview on 18 April, Matilde Rodríguez said that those who cast a yellow vote did so because of their evaluation of the present situation rather than because of their approval of the military's and police force's actions. The opponents of the law accepted the results, but they promised not to forget the martyrs and stated they would continue the struggle for morality. They added that the forces of the yellow option won the day without convincing society. They added that the ultimate judgement belongs to history.[116]

The major success of the green campaign had been the wide mobilization of civil society that had turned the issue into a major focus of public debate for months. The human-rights issue, instead of remaining secluded in the private or sectarian realms, had dominated the public sphere. The CNP reached every stratum and gained much respect. The mobilization of the green option forced professional politicians to meet this challenge by turning to all sectors of the population, reinvigorating democracy through debate and participation in a direct way. According to this view, the main benefit of the campaign was the mass mobilization. For the first time in Uruguayan modern history, popular mobilization was conducted without the hierarchical leadership of professional politicians. Sure enough, this change was only an interregnum in the control exercised by professional politicians over the public sphere. The electoral price paid by the Colorados in the November 1989 elections seems to indicate that politicians cannot merely build on arguments of political contingency but must recognize the validity of moral principles in public life as expressed by popular demands. For at least once, for a period of 784 days leading to the April 1989 referendum, the sentiments expressed by wide sectors of civil society had concrete implications for the future of the democratic public sphere and the direction of the political system.

Many share the view that the referendum sealed the problem from a political and legal point of view. The fact that civil society mobilized widely and had the chance to challenge the decision by the political class to close the issue at the centre of the public sphere has given further legitimacy to the formal way of resolving conflicts. The wide acceptance of the referendum's results did not preclude future crises. No indictments of repressors took place due to the Expiry Law, which closed the judicial track in hundreds of pending cases. Impunity was imprinted within the articulated ways of resolution. Although there were institutional mechanisms elaborated for material reparations, no official revindication and preservation of the memory of the victims ensued.

The Uruguayan report, *Uruguay: nunca más,* was elaborated by a team of eight SERPAJ activists. Lacking the support of the state and, therefore, facing a lack of representation and legitimacy, they opted to attain public credibility by relying on the testimonies collected over several years by the NGOs and on a poll of 313 prisoners processed by military justice, residents of both Montevideo and the rural areas.

What we tried to do was to commission a [polling] firm, Equipos Consultores Asociados, to carry out a poll with a representative sample . . . in order to ask people a series of questions related to our hypotheses. The result was a enormous amount of statistical information . . . The book is not only about opinions; there are facts that are irrefutable according to the applied scientific methodology. . . . We are certain that everything in it is true.

We tried not to talk with adjectives, not to use inflammatory statements, and in the cases where the reader could make up his own mind, we remained silent.[117]

The unofficial character of the commission's work, the reduced size of the team, and the scant material resources available for the inquiry and writing of the report prolonged the work for three years. The report was finally published in September 1989, after the referendum, and in an edition of 1,000 copies. Two more editions of 1,000 copies each were published later. The report published by SERPAJ thus had a limited distribution.

Against this background, the unclarified fate of the missing individuals and their disappearance as the result of cooperation between the armed forces of Uruguay and the neighbouring countries provided ground for future revelations that triggered crises and rekindled the public debate over the legacy of human-rights violations.

Chile: Principled Policies and Authoritarian Enclaves

Chile was the last country in the Southern Cone to democratize, after Argentina, Uruguay, and Brazil. The economic situation had improved significantly since the economic crisis of 1982. The military led the transition to democracy from a position of strength, reinforced by an economic boom that produced unprecedented rates of growth in the Chilean economy. Pinochet and his supporters took significant steps to institutionalize a model of limited democracy, sustained by neo-liberal economic policies. Authoritarian enclaves established through the 1980 Constitution were meant to ensure that the new democracy would preserve a model based on neoliberal philosophies in which rights of property and the principles of the free market would be the undisputed parameters of development. In social life, the model favoured the erection of voluntary associations charged with orderly public action and subject to the general guidelines of the state, which, while politically controlling the public sphere, was intended to become a 'subsidiary' of society, that is, some sort of minimal state. Efficiency and strength were to become the pillars of the state, in which the military— enjoying a large measure of autonomy and power—is a virtual fourth branch of government.[118] The model of limited democracy in Chile was constitutional and rigid and awarded (through such enclaves as the appointed senators, the Council of National Security, the Constitutional Court, and a special binominal electoral system) the right-wing forces the capacity to veto any legislative changes that would dismantle the framework inherited from the years of Pinochet rule.[119]

In the Chilean case, although Pinochet lost the 1988 plebiscite and democratic elections held in December 1989,[120] the military retained a large measure of power and autonomy, making them to some extent arbiters of the new democracy. Whereas in Uruguay, the military's attempt to institutionalize limited democracy failed and the transition to democracy was the result of an agreement, and in Argentina, the transition to democracy followed the disintegration of military rule, in Chile the military government succeeded in imposing its own model and led the transition.

During Pinochet's rule between 1973 and the late 1980s, the public sphere was severely constrained, although with intermittent openings. Despite the high levels of repression, contestation and even violent resistance persisted. When, in the campaign for the ratification of the 1980 Constitution, the military government allowed restricted political participation and debate, the opposition received immediate support from large segments of the citizenry. In the 1980s, as a result of the deep economic crisis of 1982, protest against the government gained momentum. In spite of repression, different associations concerned with civil and human rights functioned throughout the period of dictatorship, proving again the strength of Chilean civil society. The Asociación de Familiares de Detenidos-Desaparecidos (AFDD); the Agrupación de Familiares de Ejecutados Políticos (AFEP) and the Agrupación de Familiares de Prisioneros Desaparecidos (AFPD) operated since October 1973. These associations worked in close coordination with the Committee for Peace (Comité Pro Paz—CPP), which evolved by 1976 into the Vicaría de la Solidaridad, which became the spearhead of moral opposition to authoritarianism, as analysed by Pamela Lowden.[121] In 1977, SERPAJ was established in Chile and the following year the Comisión Chilena de Derechos Humanos (CCDH) was founded, under the leadership of two prominent Christian Democrats, Máximo Pacheco and Jaime Castillo, serving as a network for internal and international political action on human rights. Other voluntary organizations were created later on, functioning as opposition bodies to the dictatorship, on the basis of the defence of human rights. Academic research on human-rights issues was undertaken by scholars of different affiliations in the Academia de Humanismo Cristiano.[122] Progressively, 'Chile developed one of the longest lived, strongest and largest human rights movements in Latin America, with deep links to the major opposition parties.'[123]

In the transition to democracy, seventeen parties entered a broad coalition to confront Pinochet politically within the constitutional constraints imposed by the military and win the electoral contest, under the leadership of a single presidential candidate, Patricio Aylwin. This coalition, the Concertación de Partidos por la Democracia, included such varied parties as the Christian Democrats, the Christian Left, MAPU, the Party for Democracy, the Radical Party, the Social Democracy, and two sections of the Socialist Party.

Human rights became a central issue for the opposition political forces that led the process of redemocratization. In the platform of the Concertación, the human-rights issue figured prominently. The experiences of the dictatorship years, especially the persecution of political activists from the left, along with the links between the human-rights organizations and political parties, contributed from the 1980s to the progressive diffusion of the human-rights discourse as a cornerstone of any future democratization. When the political opposition to Pinochet recovered from the initial blow of repression, the issue of human-rights violations and the centrality of the respect for human rights became a factor unifying political forces deeply divided over other issues. Chilean politicians were deeply divided by ideological visions concerning the development models they favoured for the country. The learning process resulting from the destruction of Chile's democracy by the military led politicians to be sensitive about the perils of political polarization. Socio-economic disparities and political divisions were overlapping cleavages that polarized the Chilean public sphere in the late 1960s. In the late 1970s, the revolutionary platform of the Unidad Popular and the policies of Allende's government collided with the staunch defence of property rights and traditions by the liberal and conservative wings of Chilean politics. The Christian Democrats had tried earlier to balance these diametrically opposed positions, in their model of 'Revolución en Libertad' (Revolution in Liberty), aimed at creating a bridge between pressures for social change and the defence of traditional values, pledging economic development with and through evolutionary social reform.[124]

These different visions of social and economic development sustained by various political forces persisted during military rule, but most of the Chilean political class had become well aware of the destructive power of polarization over socio-economic issues and demands. Only by referring to broad values, as represented in the discourse of human rights, could former political enemies such as the Christian Democrats, the Socialists, and the Communists find common ground for concerted action and overcome ideological disagreements. Eventually, local events and international pressures over the abuse of human rights in Chile produced recognition also by part of the civilian political forces supporting Pinochet of the need to take this issue into consideration.

Nonetheless, for a very large segment of Chilean citizenry the issue was not paramount relative to socio-economic considerations. The performance of the Chilean economy was for many more important than the authoritarian dimension of the military government. Thus, in the October 1988 plebiscite on the continuity of Pinochet's rule under limited democratic terms, Pinochet received more than 43 per cent of the popular vote, in spite of the grim record of human-rights abuses during his rule. Pinochet's campaign relied on the success of Chile's economic development model, a model that was endorsed by the political forces of the Concertación with minor changes related to increasing taxation to finance social programmes.[125]

The different forces of opposition to Pinochet shared a common aim: the recreation of Chilean democracy and the end of authoritarian rule. Most of these forces, allied in the Concertación, expressed their commitment to carry out, if elected, a policy of truth and justice regarding past human-rights violations.[126] The main obstacle to tackling the issue of human-rights violations in the most comprehensive manner, as the Concertación professed and intended, was the power and autonomy retained by the military during the transition and early democratic period, bolstered by the organic law of the Armed Forces. The actual power of the military lent credit to General Pinochet's reiterated statements that 'the rule of law [i.e. democracy] would be over if anybody touches one of my men [the members of the armed forces]'. The institutional bases of such a power equation were the rules of the game established by the military and enshrined in the 1980 Constitution and the 1978 Amnesty Law (Decree Law 2191), together with the provision that Pinochet would remain commander-in-chief until March 1998.[127]

Another factor in shaping the policies related to the human-rights violations legacy was that, by 1990, the whole spectrum of the Chilean political leadership—both in the opposition and in governing circles—had witnessed the experience of neighbouring Argentina and Uruguay in dealing with similar situations since 1983 and 1985 respectively. The Argentine way seemed to exemplify the shortcomings of a bold frontal treatment of human-rights violators followed by regressive policies and pardons. The Uruguayan way indicated to Chilean political elites the vitality and dangers of popular mobilization, which was observed with apprehension in the Chilean context. The lessons to be drawn from these parallel experiences were varied, but they seemed to show the Chilean political elites the need for moving cautiously within the framework of the local relation of forces and the local constitutionalist, legal traditions.[128]

The inauguration of the first civilian administration after sixteen and a half years of military rule was followed by a massive gathering in the National Stadium in Santiago. The stadium had served as a concentration and torture camp following the coup of September 1973. In March 1990, Patricio Aylwin decided to begin his mandate in that locale, with the symbolic presence of some of the victims, the families of the executed and missing, their friends, and the mass presence of supporters of the Concertación. The act evinced the characteristics of a purifying ritual in which the former opposition paid public tribute to the victims. In the act, President Aylwin—in a clear continuation of the line adopted in the political campaign for the plebiscite of 1988 and for the elections of 1989—reiterated his government's commitment to address the human-rights issue. He stated:

'[T]he moral conscience of the nation requires that the truth about the disappearance of persons, horrendous crimes and other grave human-rights violations that took place under the dictatorship should be clarified. We have said, and today I repeat it, that we should address this complex issue conciliating the virtue of justice with the virtue of prudence and, when the necessary personal responsibilities are established, the hour of pardon will come.'[129]

It was clear, then, that the limits on Chilean democracy by the military and their supporters precluded any frontal and comprehensive judicial treatment of those 'horrendous crimes' that Aylwin mentioned in his presidential address. The civilian government had to develop a delicate balance between the professed principles of centrality of human rights, on the one hand, and on the other, the total rejection by the military (led by Pinochet) of opening issues covered by the Amnesty Law. This position of the former power holders, coupled with the blocking parliamentary power held by the right-wing parties and the appointed senators,[130] dictated the need for moderation and delicate political steering in that most explosive pending issue, the legacy of human-rights violations.

Limited democracy in Chile created a situation in which a ruling coalition of parties that had internalized the human-rights issue as a main component of its democratic vision, and was conscious of the dangers of social-political polarization, had to deal with the legacy of past human-rights violations from a position of constraint. They lacked, for instance, the necessary parliamentary majority for changing the legislation that granted impunity to most of those that had committed the abuses. In addition, the road to justice was blocked by the 1980

Constitution, the organic laws and a judiciary that had cooperated with the military. Furthermore, in order to clarify the truth about the victims' fate, the cooperation of the armed forces was vital but also difficult to attain. The armed forces of Chile had traditionally been extremely disciplined and hierarchical. The army, which constituted the pillar of Pinochet's power, had been formed in the strictest Prussian tradition, which stressed internal cohesion, non-deliberation, and complete loyalty to the force's high commands. In Chile, a widespread perception existed that the armed forces were guarantors of the constitution, at least from the early 1930s to the early 1970s. During the military rule beginning in 1973, the armed forces were indoctrinated along the lines of the Chilean version of the Doctrine of National Security. The 1980 Constitution incorporated many of the ideological parameters of this vision into the framework of limited democracy, institutionalizing the armed forces as the formal guarantors of national security and institutional order.[131]

The lack of definition of the concepts of national security and institutional order strengthened military power and autonomy vis-à-vis the state. With the transition to democracy, the armed forces found themselves facing a civilian administration that demanded their cooperation in clarifying the open questions about the fate of the missing and their remains. They were driven legally to comply with the norms they themselves had set up, while they were fully in disagreement with the policies of the new government over human rights. Accordingly, they responded formally to the requests of information but evaded supplying substantive information. Disagreements between the different branches of the armed forces did not break the unified front they presented to the civilian authorities when dealing with issues of human rights.

Facing this situation and trying to act to confront past human-rights violations, the civilian administration tried to create public recognition of 'the truth', in its general and individual dimensions, and to attain those forms of justice deemed possible in the concrete setting of Chile's return to civilian rule. For all parties involved, human-rights issues were part of a wider equation, closely related to the main issues of the democratic transition and consolidation. Undoubtedly, the problem of truth and justice about the legacy of human-rights violations directly confronted the main 'authoritarian enclaves' created by the military.[132]

The treatment of the legacy of human-rights violations touched upon the reformulation of the public sphere and the collective identity of society as Chile moved from military-authoritarian to democratic rule.[133] The new authorities opened the public sphere, addressing the central problems and legacies of Chilean experience, including the legacy of human-rights violations and the authoritarian enclaves. Once the public sphere was opened, NGOs representing victims' relatives conducted a wide array of activities to centralize the issue and demand truthful knowledge and justice.[134] The government consciously maintained a dialogue with these associations and took their plight into consideration as it drafted policies. Members of these NGOs were hired into the public service and their status changed from opponents to those who could articulate their former demands into policies.[135] At the same time, the authorities consciously had to avoid re-enacting the pattern of polarization that had destroyed Chilean democracy and fostered authoritarianism in the early 1970s. Due to limited possibilities for action, the democratic administration relied on several symbolic and pragmatic steps to proceed in shaping a democratic public sphere, while refraining from radical moves and retaining the legitimacy needed to consolidate democracy and hopefully to open the road for future reforms that would lift the limits imposed by the military.

The bulk of the Aylwin government's inquiry was assigned to the National Commission of Truth and Reconciliation, established in April 1990 under the presidency of Raúl Rettig. The commission was charged with investigating cases that resulted in death as a consequence of state and political violence.[136]

The Rettig Commission included experts in human rights and legal affairs who represented a wide span of opinions, including personalities who were close to the former military government such as Ricardo Martín Díaz (one of the senators nominated by Pinochet and former president of the Human Rights Commission of the military government) and Gonzalo Vial Correa (Minister of Education under Pinochet in the late 1970s). The commission also included José Luis Cea Egaña, a well-known expert in constitutional affairs with conservative views; Jaime Castillo Velasco, who had founded and led the Chilean Human Rights Commission under the dictatorship; lawyer Laura Novoa Vásquez, a personal friend of Aylwin; Mónica Jiménez de la Jara, a Christian Democrat activist; and José Zalaquett Daher, a former president of Amnesty International and an expert and activist in human-rights issues. The president of the commission, Raúl Rettig, was a former senator, president of the Radical Party, and a highly respected judicial expert in the domain of human rights. The high status of the commission was manifest in the nature of its formation: the expertise of its members; its non-partisan character; the presence of personalities identified both with the forces that opposed military rule and with those that supported it; and its non-parliamentary character, resulting from the presidential nomination and its high level of autonomy in performing the goals set in the Supreme Decree 355 by which it was designated.

The goal of the Rettig Commission, as stated in article 1 of that decree was

> to contribute to the global clarification of the truth about the most grave violations of human rights committed in the last years, be it in the country or abroad, if the latter are related to the Chilean State or with national political life, with the purpose of contributing to the reconciliation of all the Chileans and without impairing the justice proceedings related to them.[137]

The definition of 'grave violations of human rights' included deaths resulting from 'disappearances', tortures, and executions where the state was responsible because the acts were committed by its agents; the definition also included deaths resulting from kidnappings and other acts where the persons responsible were motivated by political considerations. This definition was part of the careful balance self-imposed upon the policies of the Concertación government.

The commission was ordered 'not to assume jurisdictional functions of the Courts of Justice or to interfere with pending legal proceedings . . .'. It would not be able to establish individual responsibility for deeds it came to know about, nor would it be able to single out the persons who actually committed human-rights violations. When criminal deeds came to its knowledge, the role of the Rettig Commission would be to bring the facts to the respective courts of justice.[138]

The commission did not have the right to subpoena witnesses. At the same time, the status of the commission established its clear organizational autonomy. The commission would be able to dictate its own working rules within a mandate of six months, extendable for another three (by articles 7 and 5), and its proceedings would not be held in public. It had the right to keep secret the identity of those who provided information or cooperated with it. State departments were called to cooperate with the commission, provide needed documents, and arrange visits to places, as necessary (article 8). The armed and security forces resorted to formalisms to avoid forwarding substantive information, claiming in some cases rights of jurisdiction and in others that the relevant information did not exist anymore. Since witnesses could not be called to testify before the commission, formal replies were the only response on the part of those who knew most about the fate of the victims and especially of the missing.

The Rettig Commission was charged, simultaneously, with establishing a comprehensive truth and an individual truth for each victim of human-rights violations between 11 September 1973 and 11 March 1990, by:

establishing the most complete possible picture of the grave deeds referred
to, their antecedents and circumstances . . . collect antecedents that would allow
to individualize the victims and establish their fate and whereabouts . . . to
recommend measures it believes just for reparation and revindication . . .
recommend legal and administrative measures to impede or prevent deeds
similar to those mentioned . . .[139]

The nomination of the National Commission of Truth and Reconciliation represented a major policy step with which the first democratic
government of Chile in seventeen years tackled the legacy of human-
rights violations. Nonetheless, the remit to cases resulting in death
left a huge number of violations beyond the purview of the commission. This restricted the work of the commission to a list of 3,400 cases.
This list resulted from the information forwarded by different NGOs
and the inscription of the victims' families.[140] Of these, the commission
reached conclusions about 2,279 individual cases, of which 2,115 died
as a result of human-rights violation by state agents and 164 as result
of political violence. The decision not to deal with the issue of the direct
responsibility and authorship of the killings a priori protected those
that had committed them.

To establish some sort of 'comprehensive truth', the report of the
commission included a 20-page first chapter on the political framework
that traced the events leading to the 11 September 1973 *coup d'état*
back to the 1950s, thus attenuating, in some measure, the responsibility of Chile's military rulers between 1973 and 1990 for initiating
a legacy of human-rights violations. This trend was reinforced by the
commission's inclusion of deaths resulting from left-wing political violence on an equal footing with human-rights violations committed by
state agents.

The Rettig Commission had been charged with uncovering the truth,
as a sine qua non for national reconciliation, a fundamental building block of the democratic public sphere as conceived by the civilian
leadership. The truth included an analysis of political violence of all
sorts. The commission would hand over information on new and pending cases to the judiciary, asking it to proceed and prosecute within
the limits of existing law. The Rettig Commission had great symbolic
value. Nonetheless, the courts were left in charge of producing legal
substance (prosecution, verdicts, and sentences), when possible, while
those responsible for issuing the orders and those who committed gross
human-rights violations during military rule could not be brought to
trial in most cases.

The Rettig Commission had a large measure of legitimacy due to
its presidential origins, its balanced personal composition, its high level
of professionality, and its inquiry into human-rights violations due both

to state violence and to political violence. In addition, its mandate of contributing to national reconciliation implied that it was very difficult for any sector in Chile to oppose its goal. Nonetheless, during the months of the commission's work, extremist opposition groups and circles close to the military claimed that the real purpose of the commission was to reopen healed wounds and get even with the military. This stance was severely weakened when mass graves containing the remains of repression victims were discovered in Colina, Pisagua, Copiapó, and Calama during 1990. The democratic opening provided—with the lifting of censorship and controls—new possibilities for searching for the missing independently and in parallel to the work of the Rettig Commission, weakening public and political opposition to it. 'The public horror and outrage provoked by this finding(s) proved that a truth-telling commission was truly necessary and not just an example of state sponsored vengeance against the outgoing regime', claimed Alexandra Barahona de Brito, adding that by the beginning of 1991, the Chilean Parliament had unanimously declared its support for the Rettig Commission.[141]

The plight for knowledge and justice

President Aylwin received the 1,350-page report of the Rettig Commission on 8 February 1991 and made it public on 4 March 1991. The announcement was broadcasted by radio and TV through a voluntary joint transmission of TV channels and radio stations from La Moneda's presidential palace in Santiago. The message, transmitted through all networks, had all the weight and legitimacy associated with presidential rank in Chile.

The President addressed the nation, presenting the Rettig report as aiming to bring about 'reconciliation based on truth and justice', in its widest scope and detail. Aylwin stressed the recognition of the state's responsibility in the events leading to the killings of thousands of Chileans, who were entitled to the restitution of their good name and honour and whose relatives should receive moral and material reparations. 'The process of reparation encompasses the courage to confront the truth and the realization of justice. It requires generosity in order to avow mistakes and attitudes of pardon to achieve the reconciliation (*reencuentro*) of Chileans.'[142] Reflecting on the basic criteria of a democratic public sphere, autonomous participation and public trust, President Aylwin stated that 'truth is the foundation of social life', while the lack of truth leads to hatred and violence. Lies are incompatible with social peace. As the extent of human-rights violations was concealed for a long period of time, Aylwin remarked, hatred and tensions mounted. Aylwin perceived the truth about human-rights violations in Chile as the precondition for defusing polarization and attaining social peace in a democratic way.

The state agents caused so much suffering and the responsible bodies of the state could not or did not know how to preclude or sanction it, while the society failed to react properly. The state and society as a whole are responsible by action or by omission.[143]

In a voice broken by emotion and almost in tears, Patricio Aylwin addressed the nation:

This is why I dare, in my position as President of the Republic, to assume the representation of the whole nation and, in its name, to beg forgiveness from the relatives of the victims. This is why I also ask solemnly of the armed and security forces, who have participated in the excesses committed, that they make gestures to acknowledge the pain they caused [and] to contribute to lessening that pain.[144]

Aylwin's policies of dealing with the legacy of human-rights violations in Chile are embodied in this message. As President, facing the living victims, the relatives and comrades of the dead and the whole country, he accepted the responsibility of the state for deeds of his predecessors, whose policies he strongly opposed and criticized before.

Driving towards national reconciliation within the democratic framework he wanted to consolidate, he respected the limits imposed by the military concerning impunity. Without renouncing the basic principles his administration supported, the President asked the former rulers of the country and their rank-and-file to acknowledge voluntarily the wrongs they had done to the victims. While still preserving impunity, by this act of acknowledgement, he wanted to heal the personal and social wounds and recreate a sense of community.

The public apology to the victims was one of the recommendations of the commission, which the President endorsed publicly as a necessary moral step. The government was resigned to the fact that the military had placed limits on the legal system, preventing prosecution in most cases; but the government still emphasized national reconciliation, partly through publication of a comprehensive report detailing the history of political killings, as a way to instil total respect for human rights as a central axis of Chile's democratic consolidation. The revelations about the scope and horror of their deeds and the public rejection of their actions by the democratically elected authorities, and by large segments of public opinion, would set the norm for future common life. The compromise between the moral principles and political contingency had produced a symbolic solution meant to recognize the total validity of moral principles and at the same time preserve the political viability of Chile's limited democracy.

In sum, the link established between truth and reconciliation included two major tenets of constitution of the public sphere: first, the political goal of the government of building democracy through national reconciliation by uncovering the truth, with all the above-mentioned limitations; and, second, the attainment of justice, which had to be extremely partial, because most cases involving human-rights violations were excluded from the commission's mandate and because the legal and institutional framework inherited from the military imposed limits on policy options.

Since nearly 700 cases remained inconclusive, and in order to instil in the population full respect for human rights, Aylwin decided to create—following another recommendation of the Rettig Commission —an autonomous public corporation, the Corporación de Derecho Público. This organization was charged with further inquiry into the fate of the victims of the unsolved cases, the creation of a central archive, and the provision of legal advice to the relatives of the victims. These steps were to be combined with material reparation to the families, including pensions, education grants, housing, forgiveness of debts, and the possibility of exemption from obligatory military service for the victims' children, to be carried out through the Corporación de Reparación y Reconciliación.[145] Aylwin also endorsed creating the office of ombudsman (the Defensor del Pueblo) to prevent future violations of human rights and state abuses of power.

Another commission recommendation accepted publicly by Aylwin was the need to educate the armed forces and security agencies of the country concerning the value of human rights and the commitment to their respect. Terrorism had been recognized by the Rettig Commission as a form of human-rights violations, which had produced 132 deaths of members of the armed and security forces, facilitating some acceptance on the latter's part for a discourse that until recently they had resented as identified with the Communist opposition.

The publication of the Rettig Report, and in no lesser measure, the way it was announced to the nation, was a peak in the government's strategy for dealing with the legacy of human-rights violations inherited from the period of military rule. Three elements were intertwined and carefully played by the main actor, the President of Chile: symbols, pragmatic mechanisms of reparation, and politico-legal actions.

The symbolic elements were present in Aylwin's policies since his inauguration in the National Stadium in Santiago in March 1990. Other symbolic acts followed, such as the public mass ceremony of burying Salvador Allende's remains in the Santiago General Cemetery and the inauguration of a mausoleum for the victims of repression, in a very central location in that cemetery, by the country's Vice-President. The way in which Aylwin presented the Rettig Report in his public speech of 4 March 1991 culminated this process of symbolic elaboration of the grim legacy of human-rights violations. While offering a principled defence of human rights as a mainstay of present and future democracy Aylwin placed the full weight of his office behind the commission's findings, establishing them as the truth about the cases investigated and clarified.

Following the commission's recommendations, the government of Chile created a series of pragmatic steps of reparation. Another dimension of action was to implement a series of politico-legal steps and initiatives that followed closely the recommendations of the Rettig Commission. These included a demand on the Supreme Court to move forward with pending cases. Aylwin had accused the judiciary of not having acted appropriately under the circumstances of military rule, since the justices, by omission, did not curtail human-rights violations. He thus pointed to the need for reforming the judiciary, not only because modernization made it necessary but also to ensure future protection of human rights by this branch of the state. Well aware that there were narrow limits to judicial action against perpetrators and that victims and their supporters felt strong needs for justice, Aylwin widened the concept of justice to include truth, moral restitution, and reparations, extrapolating justice from the realm of legal interpretation. He proposed to reinterpret the Amnesty Law of 1978 by allowing the courts to investigate the cases of disappeared persons to reach the truth about their fate without threatening to punish those responsible. Aylwin pointed out that national reconciliation and social peace would be achieved through executive actions and policies but that the other powers of the state, the armed institutions, spiritual authorities, social organizations, and the whole national community should see it as their role, too, to contribute to social peace.[146] By asking the courts to clarify the fate of all the victims in the unsolved cases, he clearly signalled that institutional limits should not impede proceedings whenever possible. His respect for the constitutional rules set by the military, which made it impossible for legislation to change the terms of impunity, was the political-pragmatic element designed to defend existing stability and future democracy by signalling that the political game was being played in the constitutional terms the armed forces had designed, even if the results were unsavoury for them.[147]

For instance, releasing political prisoners following the return to democracy constituted a complex legal problem. According to the 1980 Constitution, individuals sentenced on charges of terrorism were not eligible for 'amnesty or pardon, or provisional freedom for those tried for such crimes . . . For all legal purposes, such crimes will always be regarded as common offences and not as political ones.'[148] In March 1990 there were 417 convicted political prisoners and nearly 1,300 detainees awaiting trials on political grounds. During the Aylwin administration, political prisoners were slowly released from jail, mostly on the basis of presidential pardons, but also through the Cumplido Laws and within the framework of an agreement between the political forces of the Concertación and the Renovación Nacional (RN) Party. On 15 March 1994, six of the remaining nine political prisoners had their prison sentences commuted to exile.[149]

The acceptance of the practical recommendations of the Rettig Commission about continuing the investigation into the unsolved cases, the establishment of the ombudsman's office to defend human rights and of the Corporation of Reparation and Reconciliation, the material reparations, and Aylwin's appeal to the courts to proceed in the spirit of the above-mentioned steps translated the ethical dimension into pragmatic lines. These lines were designed to transform the defence of human rights into one of the pillars of consolidated democracy in Chile, in spite of the constraints posed by limited democracy.

The President's public acceptance of the report placed the military and their supporters in an uncomfortable position. Until then, Pinochet and many of his supporters claimed ignorance of the facts or accused those raising them of malintent. For instance, when asked in 1989 if executions without a trial had taken place, Pinochet answered:

Never. How can you imagine that I would accept letting my people be shot for the fun of it [*Cómo se le ocurre que iba a aceptar que me fusilaran gente por amor al arte?*] I am a military man, not a member of a SS troop. How could I accept being told 'we shot a prisoner'? On what grounds? The guy had surrendered . . . Many things were invented, like the story of the Mapocho river red with blood.[150]

The publication of the Rettig Report in March 1991 created much unrest among the military. General Augusto Pinochet harshly attacked the report, saying that it was 'an unpardonable refusal to recognize the real causes that motivated the action to rescue the nation on September 11, 1973. . . . The Chilean army certainly sees no reason to ask pardon for having fulfilled its patriotic duty.'[151] Nonetheless, those who opposed the report had to admit that the data collected proved the massive extent of life lost under military rule. The public announcement of the report by the President signalled the formal acknowledgement of the facts. From then onwards it was nearly impossible to deny the extent and gravity of these killings committed under military rule.

The publication of a comprehensive truth by an official non-partisan commission about these events, which had been hidden by censorship under military rule, was needed to start 'a social catharsis in order to overcome a schizophrenia in which some sectors of society claimed it did happen and others that it did not happen'.[152]

The argument of those opposed to the thesis of human-rights violations was narrowed subsequently to the problem of interpreting and possibly justifying the loss of life in terms of a war situation. Unión Democrática Independiente (UDI) Senator Jaime Guzmán, one of the most sophisticated advocates of military rule and the political architect of the model of limited democracy in Chile, argued that the situation of civil war provoked by Allende's mismanagement of Chile, a fact recognized widely in 1973, formed the basis of the actions adopted by Chile's armed forces:

The attempts of the Popular Unity to infiltrate and divide the armed forces were the final straw. Then, the overwhelming majority of the people looked to the institutions trained for war, expecting them to take over a country [living] in a state of internal war, with the aim to put an end to it and save Chile. The violations of human rights that took place then can and should be justified by none. But the main people responsible—more than the people in uniform who committed them—were the top leadership of the Popular Unity that led us to this pre-civil war, a situation in which historical experience demonstrates that such painful events inevitably take place.[153]

The armed forces reacted by rejecting the conclusions—if not the facts—of the Rettig Report and by raising again their thesis of having acted the way they did because the situation was one of internal war.

The global truth was generally accepted by the whole Chilean society, since people do not talk [anymore] about presumed missing people, not even the right-wing press. The disappearances are clear. The only one rejecting that truth is the army, but it does not deny the concrete facts but instead sends an implicit message: 'do not ask us for accounts, we saved the country'.[154]

Aylwin's appeal for acknowledgement of truth and responsibility, and for cooperation with the courts in clarifying the fate of the missing people, was accordingly unanswered. Pinochet and the hardliners claimed that the Rettig Commission was unconstitutional and that its conclusions were partial and biased. They called for a meeting of the National Security Council on 27 March 1991. Although the military did not constitute a totally united front, the air force and Carabineros commanders being more moderate than those of the navy, the army, and Pinochet himself, no one presented apologies, or made 'gestures of acknowledgement of the pain they caused', as they were called upon to do. The military hardliners rejected also the measures recommended to prevent future human-rights abuses as well as reparations to the victims. They interpreted these measures as an attack against the honour and integrity of the armed forces. The commission was accused of partiality and anti-military sentiments. The historical interpretation of the report was considered by the military to be narrow, biased against them, and vengeful. The juridical validity of the report was totally rejected, while the military adhered to the thesis that the amnesty law precluded investigating the open cases.[155] As the Chilean political parties reacted to the military declarations, the debate was further centralized in public opinion.[156]

Terrorism came back to the centre of Chilean politics with the assassination of senator Jaime Guzmán, on 1 April 1991. This dramatic event added to a long chain of violent acts by extreme leftist extraparliamentary organizations that took place in the first year of democratic rule. FPMR—Frente Patriótico Manuel Rodríguez—and two branches of the Lautaro movement, had carried out acts of 'popular justice', attacking military personnel, judges, and supporters of Pinochet and robbing banks to finance their activities.[157] The assassination of Guzmán moved the political focus from the main contents of the Rettig Report towards the issue of leftist terrorism, and threatened to revive polarization. The contemporary resurgence of violence supported the military's claim of having been fully justified in the past, when they acted to defend the stability of institutions and social order against the same revolutionary, destructive, and terrorist left.[158]

The public discussions and political shifts generated by the Rettig Report's publication and by the subsequent assassination of Jaime Guzmán did not affect the fact that Aylwin had sent to the Supreme Court a request to speed proceedings in the pending cases and in unsolved cases being investigated.

The judiciary had to decide whether the Amnesty Law implied an automatic pardon that prevented opening proceedings, as the military argued, or rather, whether it implied the need to clarify the details of each case, including the authorship of the acts, before granting the pardons, as argued by Aylwin and the president of the Supreme Court. The latter claimed that, from a strictly legal perspective, amnesty could not be granted before there was wide proof that a crime had been committed, although this did not necessitate establishing personal responsibility for it.[159]

In 1991, the courts were calling military personnel as witnesses to testify in different cases. Interrogations became frequent. Since the proceedings were known to the public, journalists frequently harrassed military witnesses, looking for interviews with them. Military personnel were subjected to the usual procedures in the courts, including long waiting periods, and they felt they were being treated in dishonourable ways. This situation augmented the tensions in the ranks of the military.

On the occasion of Aylwin's trip to Europe, on 28 May 1993, the army mounted a military exercise, the *boinazo* (or 'beret coup') in downtown Santiago, deploying special troops, the Black Berets, in full combat gear. This was a clear message to the civilian authorities that continuing the judicial inquiries into human-rights violations was unacceptable to the military. The Minister of the Interior and acting Vice-President of Chile, Enrique Krauss, had to negotiate with the army to defuse the crisis. Upon Aylwin's return to Chile, Pinochet presented him with a long petition addressing the tense relations between the military and the civilian authorities. The demands strongly opposed the policies of Defence Minister Patricio Rojas and were especially focused on the need to put an end to the 'insults' (*vejaciones*) inflicted upon military personnel when called to the courts to testify.[160] The military themselves had set the 'rules of the game' of limited democracy, but the military personnel felt that they were being treated in dishonourable ways, as they were subject to the same judicial procedures as the civilian population, while they saw themselves above any public reproach and imputation. Aylwin's response was twofold. He replied to Pinochet that the key to resolving the tensions was the military's strict cooperation in solving cases of human-rights violations pending in the courts. Institutionally, Aylwin and those who backed his human-rights policies, as well as the victims, the NGOs dealing with these issues, and the left, rejected any possibility of a Full Stop (Statute of Limitations) law of the kind adopted in Argentina or Uruguay under similar conditions. The government elaborated a negotiated option: cooperation in clarifying the unsolved cases in exchange for an acceleration of the proceedings. A special law was prepared and sent to Chile's Parliament. The main idea of this law, popularly known as the 'Ley Aylwin', was to designate a number of judges—*ministros en visita*—to take care of all the pending prosecutions, and to ensure expertise and the speeding of procedure by freeing the designated judges from other obligations. Furthermore, these judges would be able to designate assistant judges—*ministros suplentes*—to help them in rapidly processing the pending cases. Special procedural rules would be enacted. Giving testimony would be permitted out of the courts, through the good offices of priests, lawyers, or other people whom the witnesses trusted, in complete secrecy. Aylwin thought that these measures could induce military personnel, possessing knowledge on the fate of missing victims, to reveal the places where the bodies could be found. The aim was again to reveal the whole truth while respecting the limitations imposed by the Amnesty Law and by military autonomy and power.

The political debate generated by the draft of the law was dominated by mixed feelings and contrasted positions. The left wanted less secrecy in the proceedings, claiming that secrecy was contrary to the aim of reaching truth and public recognition. It also wanted to avoid the nomination of military judges as *ministros en visita*. Part of the right supported the idea of speeding up the judicial path and, consequently, voted in favour of the project. Since the debate around enacting the law was breaking the Concertación's consensus and political unity, and because the army opposed any reforms to the bill (e.g. by the Socialists), Aylwin withdrew the bill from Congress.[161] As no political solution to the problem was viable, the courts had to continue dealing with the pending cases, according to the pre-existing pattern. More cases were sent to military justice and were covered by the Amnesty Law, but some of the most explosive, such as the *Letelier* and the *Degollados* cases, still proceeded though the civilian courts on their way to Supreme Court for final verdicts. All this created the grounds for further confrontations between the military and the civilian government.

The pattern of resolving the human-rights violations legacy in Chile consisted of respecting the impositions of limited democracy and the balance of power between the military and the civilian authorities. Within these limits, Aylwin's administration followed a policy of obtaining 'all the truth and as much justice as possible'. By revealing the truth that had been secluded until then, and by transferring, whenever possible, individual cases for the judiciary to prosecute, the public sphere remained open to pending institutional crises. Although trials were focused on individual responsibility, without demanding general accountability from the branches of the armed forces, their prosecution generated the closing of ranks around the accused according to the patterns of loyalty, internal cohesion, and discipline discussed above. The possibility also existed of individual trials raising the question of commanders' responsibility in a way that would eventually implicate the higher ranks. The seeds of future crises were thus imprinted in the pattern of addressing the legacy of human-rights violations in Chile, just as in the other Southern Cone countries.

···············
3
···············

National Reconciliation and the Disruptive Potential of the Legacy of Human-Rights Violations

In the reshaped public sphere of the redemocratized societies, the theme of the recent abuses of human rights became central for approaching the models of social engineering elaborated by the military. As soon as censorship was removed, revelations about the authoritarian rulers' misdeeds came to dominate the public sphere. Many became conscious of having emerged from a period of deep crisis in the texture of their society and in respect for human rights. In Chile this trend was compounded by the fact that the civilian democratic goverment sustained the military's basic socio-economic model.

At the same time, the experience of repression turned into a legacy with a disruptive potential for the democratic frameworks. The breakdown of democracy in the 1970s was preceded and justified by the deepening socio-economic and related political-ideological cleavages. In the 1980s and 1990s the legacy of human-rights violations threatened to add to current problems and to become a source of renewed polarization and systemic destabilization under democracy. In this context, policies of national reconciliation were elaborated and a series of public aftershocks surfaced around the significance and implications of the past repressive wave in the three societies of the Southern Cone.

As in many radical sociopolitical transformations, the public sphere of the new democracies was dominated by debate over the principles upon which to build a consolidated democracy. This debate had practical consequences for the realignment of political and social forces.

National Reconciliation and the Seeds of Crisis

Faced by considerations of political contingency, the leaders of these countries attempted to balance principles with an ethics of 'public responsibility'. Their vision of politics was not radically different from the visions of the past, as they expected to dominate the political arena. Their strategy was to move beyond the experience and memory of the past and to consolidate democracy. Sectors of civil society, especially the NGOs that had been active defending human rights under conditions of duress, as well as the military continued to play an active role in the public sphere. Each side sustained a polar vision of the repression years and expected the democratic government to accept its views and elaborate political solutions accordingly. Various pragmatic approaches were adopted by the political leaders for resolving the tensions between normative priorities and political contingency. Yet these paths could not prevent confrontation generated by the past legacy, and in fact they became part of the problem in future crises.

In all three settings, national reconciliation was explicitly or implicitly perceived as a requisite for orderly democratic life. The terrible lessons of past polarization had taught that democratic life requires consensual methods of conflict resolution. The recent experience of massive human-rights violations was a critical issue at the centre of the public agenda in the reconstituted democracies. The political leadership could not ignore the issue. Nonetheless, any attempt to punish those involved in such acts could trigger the destabilization of the polity.

The issue of the legacy of human-rights violations remained a source of conflict and polarization, similar to the situations and confrontations that preceded the previous wave of military takeovers. From the point of view of the political leaderships, it was imperative to tackle the issue as soon as these countries returned to democracy. The political class was in the difficult position of trying to balance the demands for impunity put forward by the military—who perceived themselves as 'saviours of the Nation'—with the demands for justice voiced by the victims, their relatives, friends, and public supporters. The demand for justice by the latter could not be ignored by political systems committed to a rule of law and equality before the law. The policies adopted were designed to clarify the fate of the victims and grant them public recognition, while moving unevenly and under serious legal and practical constraints to punish in very limited ways (if at all) some of those responsible, without impairing the web of delicate civil–military relationships.

The political leaderships used national reconciliation as a constructive political formula to overcome the above contradictions. Many of the leaders emphasized that the delicate situation necessitated the kind of compromises they were pursuing. The arguments pointed to the impossibility of applying a politics of pure principles. In many cases, strongly ethical and ideological positions were criticized as triggers of the kind of catastrophic anarchy these societies had already experienced in the late 1960s and early 1970s. According to this logic, national reconciliation became a goal and a political instrument to overcome polarization and achieve social peace.

These trends were evident in all three countries. In 1988, Uruguay's Colorado Party leader and Vice-President, Enrique Tarigo, claimed that '[t]he country cannot keep looking back because of events that, however regretful and horrendous, happened ten or twelve years ago. It is imperative to live in today's world and provide solutions to current problems and needs.'[1] Following the April 1989 referendum, President Julio María Sanguinetti emphasized, perhaps prematurely, that 'Uruguay has resolved all the problems of the past. The debate about the dictatorship period is over. The country is facing its future.'[2]

President Aylwin stressed time and again that 'Chile has an aptitude for understanding and not for confrontation. We cannot progress by digging deeper into divisions. It is time for pardon and reconciliation.'[3] The Rettig Report clearly indicated that '[t]he Commission understood from the start that the truth that should be established has a clear purpose: to contribute to reconciliation among all Chileans'.[4] José Zalaquett, one of the central figures who designed the human-rights policies of the civilian administration, stressed the principle of political viability: 'In Chile, the guiding line should be—in Max Weber's distinction—an ethics of responsibility rather than an ethics of conviction. All things being equal, forgiveness and reconciliation are preferable to punishment.'[5] The Chilean Church strongly supported the need for reconcilation between all Chileans. Leading dignitaries of the Church have consistently stressed their non-partisan character and yet their support of the democratic government's drive toward national reconciliation. For the Bishops' Conference of Chile such a reconciliation was crucial, since it implied 'closing wounds in a climate of truth, justice, and pardon. It does not mean leaving wounds without healing, but neither does it mean wanting revenge.'[6] The Chilean opposition leader Andrés Allamand declared that the Church's call for reconciliation 'encourages us to leave behind the divisions. Now the most important thing is reconciliation.'[7]

In Argentina, the policy of pardons was strongly defended by President Carlos Saúl Menem, who considered it 'a mechanism to ensure social peace. I won't desist from a move that has had a positive result. With that decision, an end was put to subversion in Argentina and to the tendency towards takeover of many sectors of the armed forces.'[8]

In the three cases national reconciliation was projected as a rhetorical device, which almost everybody could accept at low cost. Even the members of the security forces could profess acceptance of the idea of national reconciliation. The Uruguayan army's commander-in-chief, Carlos L. Berois, was among the first to indicate explicitly the rationale of the armed forces in supporting the policy of reconciliation:

Recently, on the occasion of honouring the memory of those fallen in its defence [of the country], we had stated our will not to reopen those wounds or animosities which many Uruguayans ['orientales'], military and civilians, keep alive, justifiably or not. Today we reaffirm that position, expressing publicly our fervent desire to collaborate in the reconciliation (*reencuentro*) of all Uruguayans in the effort to build a better fatherland, based on the principles and ideals that we cherish, which constitute the essence of our nationality and which are cultivated in all domains of the army.[9]

In societies afflicted by years of instability, polarization, and violence, the general idea of reconciliation was perceived by the civilians and the military alike as crucial for attaining stability, consensus, and peace. However, the disparate interpretations of both sides had widely varying implications and political costs, which the political leaderships tried to control in the public sphere.

Tensions arose when the legal and extra-legal treatment of human-rights violations had to be incorporated into the general framework of reconciliation. In Uruguay, almost immediately after the referendum of April 1989 ratified the Law of Expiry, some political sectors noted that 'we have to give an answer to the pain of the families of the *desaparecidos*. This answer . . . is basic for achieving an equilibrium and reconciliation.'[10] In Argentina, the problem was exacerbated by the existence of thousands of *desaparecidos*, which posed insurmountable difficulties to national reconciliation.

Exiles come back or stay abroad, but are alive. Some succeeded better than others to survive dictatorship. Dead are buried and we pay them homage, according to our customs. But the disappeared are neither dead nor alive. They constitute a tragedy, something that has wounded Argentine society and that makes reconciliation difficult.[11]

Menem's support of pardons for the sake of national reconciliation was harshly criticized by those sectors demanding full justice:

Reconciliation? What an absurd pretension! This will take several generations. How can a mother reconcile with the person who killed her son? What is important is to share the idea of living in peace, respecting the democratic rules and institutions.[12]

In all three countries the uses and the timing of the attempt to create national reconciliation were elaborated according to the balance of forces between the armed forces, the government, and the NGOs and sectors representing the victims since the onset of democracy.

The sectors most affected by the repression and their supporters had varied success in keeping the issue of human-rights violations at the centre of the public agenda. In Chile, President Aylwin worked in close cooperation with the major NGOs, while respecting the limits imposed by the constitutional set-up inherited from the military period. In Argentina, these social sectors had wide public resonance until April 1987 and then lost strength as the government succumbed to military pressures and initiated the regressive stage in its policies. In Uruguay, the sectors most affected by the repression and their supporters succeeded in mobilizing large segments of the population against granting impunity but failed in their constitutional attempt to annul the Law of Expiry in the April 1989 referendum.

The armed and security forces, for their part, managed to different degrees to affect the official policies and resist the legal and extra-legal attempts to make them accountable for the human-rights violations committed during military rule. In Argentina, while justifying their actions with the thesis of having fought and won the war against subversion, the armed forces began defending their interests from a position of weakness. They progressively managed to gather strength and resist, inducing a reversal of policy that led ultimately to closing the legal path and to pardons. In Uruguay and in Chile, the armed forces also clung to their traditional theses of having waged a legitimate war against insurrection, from a position of relative power and autonomy. The Naval Pact agreement, which enabled the transition to democracy in Uruguay, entailed not prosecuting those who had committed human-rights violations. The Uruguayan political leadership promoted legislation aimed at avoiding state trials against the military for human-rights abuses. In Chile, the armed forces enjoyed the impunity provided by the 1978 Amnesty Law as well as an autonomous status granted by the 1980 Constitution and the subsequent organic laws.

In between stood the political leaderships of the redemocratized countries, which resorted to the formula of national reconciliation or its equivalents (e.g. social peace) to create a difficult pragmatic equilibrium between diametrically opposed positions of the military and the concerned sectors of civil society.

As institutional partial solutions were implemented, national reconciliation fulfilled a dual role. It was used to legitimate impunity granted to past violators of human rights, and it was a source of legitimacy for political leaders trying to minimize the public impact of the legacy of human-rights violations. The partiality of the institutional solutions provided the grounds that bred future destabilizing repercussions.

Repercussions in the Public Sphere

The efforts of the political leaderships in Argentina, Chile, and Uruguay did not preclude a series of consecutive repercussions which centred on the legacy of human-rights violations in the public sphere. The repercussions were of different weights, and, although in none of the cases did they shatter democracy, they reopened the debate and brought the issue of the authoritarian legacy once more to the centre of the public agenda. The political leaderships could not easily brush aside these triggers by using rhetorical figures or by adopting measures of little substantive content. In each case, the developments pointed to the inconclusiveness of the previous institutional mechanisms for dealing with the human-rights violations legacy. They reflected as well how the issue of human-rights violations was compounded following democratization with the question of whether it was possible to change the format of relationships between the armed forces, on the one hand, and the state and civil society sectors, on the other.

In Argentina, the first trigger, in 1994, indicated the apathy of the public. The senatorial approval needed for the promotion of navy officers Rolón and Pernias brought about an inquiry concerning their participation in the infringement of human rights during the previous regime. They confirmed their participation as part of their duties during the military dictatorship. However, these revelations did not generate wide interest. The climate around human-rights violations had changed radically since the first democratic government. The generation that came to age after the period of trials and public coverage of human-rights violations in the mid-1980s lacked basic knowledge of the past, and was mostly unconcerned about the legacy of the military period.[13]

However, by March 1995 the climate had changed, when retired Captain Adolfo Francisco Scilingo, an ex-navy officer, made a series of public appearances and confessed to having participated in the operations leading to the 'disappearance' of political prisoners in the years 1976–7. According to Scilingo, the victims were sedated, flown in navy planes to mid-ocean and thrown alive into the sea with heavy burdens so that their bodies would not be recovered and brought ashore. The declarations he made to human-rights activist and writer Horacio Verbitsky resulted in a book, *El vuelo* (The Flight), which immediately sold thousands of copies.[14]

Scilingo, tormented by his participation in these acts, had previously written letters to the high commands, trying in vain since 1983 to convince them to publicly recognize the acts committed at centres of detention such as the infamous Navy School of Mechanics (ESMA) in which he served. Scilingo claimed that he and many other members of the Navy acted according to explicit orders issued by the high commands of the force, and that the latter had to acknowledge they ordered the use of such a methodology of war against subversives. Scilingo was convinced that 'unless we tell the truth regarding the disappeared, no peace will be possible'. As he told a Uruguayan reporter later on, from his cell in prison where he was serving a sentence for fraud:

Was it a war? Was it not? . . . We are to blame for the mystery, since there remain the [9,000] disappeared, of whom 4,000 [disappeared] from the ESMA. . . . The Navy is responsible. What is to be hidden? Those who criticize me say that the dirty war was a service to the nation [*una patriada*], to save the country from the hands of communism. So, if they are so proud, why do they hide the issue of the disappeared? What is the problem? This is not consistent: I am proud of having participated in the war against subversion and on the other hand I keep hiding the truth. Then it is right: we feel ashamed, they are ashamed, of telling what we have done.[15]

The revelations, made also in TV interviews with Mariano Grondona in the country's highest-rated talk-show, and reproduced in numerous press reports and articles, precipitated an agitated debate, acts of remembrance and public demonstrations over the legacy of human-rights violations, the fate of the *desaparecidos*, the nature of civil–military relations, and the significance of democracy.[16] The renewed centrality that human-rights abuses had acquired in the public sphere was related to the game of civil–military relationships and interests and the scandalous nature of Scilingo's revelations. The new generation, mostly unconcerned about the legacy of the military period, heard for the first time about that experience and was shocked as the previous generation had been shocked a decade earlier. Although the case did not change the development of the ongoing presidential electoral campaign, which was conducted mainly around the concern for macroeconomic stability, it threatened to recreate the confrontation and polarization over the legacy of human-rights violations in the public sphere.[17]

These revelations could have recreated the tensions that accompanied earlier revelations, but these were deflected by the declarations of General Martín Balza, commander-in-chief of the Argentine army. Following Scilingo's public appearances in the media and the publication of the book, President Menem and the commanding officers of the navy tried to denounce Scilingo as a petty criminal and untrustworthy individual. Unidentified death threats reached Scilingo and his family in the following months. General Balza adopted a completely different attitude. He recognized that major crimes and human-rights violations had indeed been committed during the military government. He also declared that the Argentine armed forces should act in the future within the strict limits of constitutional legality and morality.[18]

The Army, instructed and trained for classical war, did not face crazy terrorism within the law . . . The mistake of the Army was to privilege the individualization of the adversary, his location above dignity through obtaining information by illegitimate means, even to the extent of suppressing life, confusing the road that leads to every just objective. I repeat: the end never justifies the means.

Nobody is forced to fulfil an immoral order or an order that is removed from the law and the military regulations. . . . Whoever makes the Constitution vulnerable, or uses injust, immoral means to achieve a 'just' aim is delinquent. I assume our part of responsibility for the errors committed in the fight [fought] among Argentines.[19]

This position was in stark contrast with the traditional attitude of the military elite in Argentina, which justified any action done in the service of the nation and the institution as morally correct and as patriotic. Balza's position was not unanimously endorsed. Admiral Massera, a member of the first military junta in 1976, declared that no crimes had been committed and no one was illegally killed. Massera was not alone in endorsing the position that the armed forces had won a legitimate war against subversion. General Mario C. Díaz, second in command after General Balza, was the main officer on active duty to take a stand against Balza's statements. Other retired officers made similar declarations.[20]

The debate was reopened, involving wide circles, from the political class, the military and concerned NGOs, to intellectuals, the Church, and the public in general. Balza's declarations won significant civilian support, although some human-rights activists demanded an even more critical stand. Nobel Prize winner Adolfo Pérez Esquivel sent an open letter, in which he declared that 'Balza's declarations are important but they are not enough; we disagree with the statement that all of us share the blame for the tortures, rapes and disappearances. We do not support the collective allocation of the blame. The victims were not responsible and neither were we.'[21] Human-rights activists also disagreed with Balza's claim that the armed security forces' files of the period were no longer available or that the commander-in-chief could not order their reconstruction, in case they were destroyed before democratic rule.

The Madres de Plaza de Mayo also considered Balza's speech insufficient. Hebe de Bonafini, president of the NGO, characterized Balza's declarations as 'hypocritical'. They declared that if he really was against human-rights violations, he would have removed from the armed forces all those with proven records of involvement in the Dirty War. If he was really sincere in his commitment, she added: 'Balza would not look the other way and he would imprison the murderers of those soldiers who were assassinated in the military camps [under democratic rule].'[22]

The chain reaction initiated by Scilingo produced a debate over the role of Argentina's Catholic Church during the military rule. The bishop of Viedma, Miguel Hesayne, and the bishop of Quilmes, Jorge Novak, well known—together with the late Bishop Jaime de Nevares—for their exceptional defence of the persecuted, condemned the apparent involvement of church ministers who had supported the armed forces and provided spiritual comfort to repressors, as Scilingo claimed.[23] Following a series of external and internal pressures and many declarations on the need for a 'mea culpa' by priests and bishops, the Argentine Church issued after days of debate a declaration that expressed remorse 'for mistakes, infidelities, incoherences, and delayed response'.[24] The bishops' statement was diffuse and was not followed by any disciplinary measures within the Church. The most active human-rights NGOs reacted to these declarations with disapproval, rejection, or scorn.[25]

The 1995 revelations served as a prelude to the acts commemorating the twentieth anniversary of the military coup, which produced a wave of condemnation of the security forces' past policies. Concurrently, violent attacks were carried out against some of the former members of the security forces, known for their involvement in the repression. Captain Alfredo Astiz, whose extradition has been requested by the French authorities because of his involvement in the assassination of French nuns in Argentina, was attacked on the streets of Bariloche and Buenos Aires by people who recognized and identified him as a former torturer. For the following three years, Astiz was the focus of a series of international and local incidents until his final demotion from the navy.[26]

Jorge Bergés, a police doctor known for torturing imprisoned women and abducting their newborn babies for adoption by military families in the 1970s, was another focus of continuing confrontation with past atrocities and inhumanity. In May 1996, Jorge Bergés was seriously wounded while walking near his home in Quilmes, in the Province of Buenos Aires. Allegedly, the attackers were members of the ORP—Organización Revolucionaria del Pueblo—who inflicted fifteen wounds upon him.[27]

A few weeks before the commemoration of the twentieth anniversary of the military takeover in Argentina, Enrique Arancibia, an ex-member of the Chilean intelligence agency, DINA, was detained in

Buenos Aires as the perpetrator of the 1974 bombing which killed the exiled ex-commander of the Chilean armed forces, retired General Carlos Prats, and his wife; the detention was part of a judicial inquiry pending in Argentina and generated pressures against amnesty in Chile.[28] These declarations, stressing again the scope of the DINA's international operations, added to the political turmoil generated in mid-1995 by the final verdict on the *Letelier* case. This case was the most notorious and protracted case dealt with in military and civilian courts in Chile since the 1970s.

The assassination of Orlando Letelier had been excluded by Pinochet's government from the 1978 Amnesty Law. Letelier, a former Minister of Foreign Affairs during the presidency of Salvador Allende, and his secretary, a North American national, Ronnie Moffitt, were killed in Washington, DC, on 21 September 1976, by a bomb planted in Letelier's car. During the late 1970s and 1980s the *Letelier* case was a source of constant tension between the military government of Chile and the USA, especially after the courts in the latter found ample proof that the crime had been committed by anticommunist Cubans collaborating with Chilean DINA intelligence agents. The Chilean military courts declared the *Letelier* case closed, and in 1989 they rejected a petition by lawyers Fabiola Letelier and Jaime Castillo to reopen the case. The courts declined at that period—when Chile was still under military rule—to convict General Manuel Contreras, the founder and commander of the DINA, and his second in command, Brigadier Pedro Espinoza, on charges of homicide and of providing false passports to the authors of the assassination. In Chile the case seemed to have come to a stand-off.

In the wake of the publication of the Rettig Report, on 12 March 1991, Aylwin's government petitioned the Supreme Court to reopen the case on the grounds that the falsification of passports is a crime to be investigated by civilian and not by military courts. In July 1991, the Supreme Court finally designated judge Adolfo Bañados to conduct the trial. By September 1991, Contreras and Espinoza had been charged, in the civilian courts, with homicide and falsification of documents.[29]

The final verdict of the *Letelier* case, in May 1995, sentenced the founder and commander of the DINA, General Contreras, to seven years and his second in command, Brigadier Espinoza, to six years of imprisonment.[30] In spite of the fact that the *Letelier* case was explicitly not covered by the 1978 Amnesty law, the idea of sending a general and a brigadier to jail seemed repulsive to wide circles in the Chilean armed forces and generated much uneasiness in the ranks of the army's officers corps. Contreras's refusal to comply with the Supreme Court's final verdict generated a crisis involving the armed forces, because he found safe haven in an army battalion and later on in the navy hospital in Talcahuano.[31] Public and political pressure on the government increased, especially after Espinoza's decision to go to jail, after a short period of resisting the sentence. The Letelier family, human-rights activists, and politicians of different backgrounds demanded full compliance with the verdict. Meanwhile, large groups of army officers manifested their solidarity with Espinoza by visiting him en masse in the Punta Peuco prison. After five months of resisting, Contreras accepted the verdict, as elite army troops were to be placed in charge of his surveillance. He was secluded in Punta Peuco with Espinoza, the two sole inmates of a very special wing of a small prison, which was constructed especially for this kind of prisoner and whose standards of comfort are outstanding in the Chilean penitentiary system.[32]

Also in 1995 new unmarked burial sites were found in Colina, Copiapó, and Peldehue, creating high tension and expectations among the relatives of *desaparecidos*.[33] Declarations in August 1995 by Supreme Court judge Roberto Dávila about the imminent declarations of a former security agent, who supposedly would become 'the Chilean Scilingo', remained unfulfilled.[34] In mid-1997 new revelations about cases of paedophilia in the German agricultural community of Colonia Dignidad (Villa Baviera) triggered media attention to the location of a torture centre at the place operated jointly with DINA in the 1970s and to the Nazi styles of members of that community.[35]

In Uruguay, Scilingo's confession reopened the wounds of the human-rights violations, especially since most of Uruguay's *desaparecidos* were abducted in Argentina after 1976, with cooperation of the Buenos Aires military authorities.[36] Here, as in Argentina, one of the main issues was the fate of children of the victims. In 1995, a child related to the notorious trade unionist José D'Elia was located.[37] The proceedings for his return to his biological family reopened—in tandem with Scilingo's declarations—the unsolved dilemmas of the legacy of human-rights violations. In March the commemoration in Argentina of the twentieth anniversary of the military *coup d'état* was widely reported in Uruguay, with more than a passing reference to the local lack of political will to do something similar.[38]

In late April, members of the Naval Fusiliers batallion declared anonymously that they had participated in acts of human-rights violations.[39] Nonetheless, the Uruguayan military has preserved a high measure of internal cohesion around the defence of the thesis of having saved the country from communism and anarchy. This cohesion was damaged in early May 1996 by the declarations of retired Navy Captain Jorge Néstor Tróccoli. Tróccoli, who was a student of anthropology at the time, recognized that although he had not participated in the worst acts of torture and assassination, he had fought a war in which the armed forces 'treated their enemies inhumanely', alluding to the torture, disappearance, and murder of many of them.[40] In September 1996, Tróccoli published a book, *La ira de Leviatán* [Leviathan's Fury], in which he presents his vision of the country between 1963 and 1996. Based partially on interviews with former military servicemen and civilians, the book portrays a spiral of violence that dragged the armed forces into confrontation and war. In the book's concluding section, Tróccoli called upon the former guerillas and the armed forces to sign a peace treaty, something they have not formally done yet. Such a formal peace, based on mutual recognition and respect between former enemies, would lead to dialogue and national reconciliation.[41]

The position and statements of Tróccoli, who was expelled from the Faculty of Anthropology in Montevideo by a decision of the student assembly, generated wide interest and represented the first public fissure in the ranks of Uruguay's military about the legacy of human-rights violations. Rafael Michelini praised the former member of the armed forces for acknowledging his responsibility. For the first time there was some recognition of what had happened by somebody who had been directly involved in the repression. This was, according to Michelini, a partial but important step in establishing the truth.[42] By contrast, the war hypothesis offered by Tróccoli was harshly criticized by retired Navy Captain Oscar Lebel. 'It was not a war. It was hunting time . . . The citizens who suffered did not call it a war. They were innocent victims. It is as if the Jews defined the Holocaust as war . . .'[43] Among those who praised the willingness of Tróccoli to come forward and reflect on the role of the armed forces in repression, some expressed reticence about his call for national reconciliation, considering it premature:

The country has many pending issues concerning the dictatorship. To search for truth on the 'disappeared', how they died and where their remains are. To locate the missing children. To have the institutional acknowledgement of the armed forces on their deeds during the dictatorship and their commitment not to repeat such behaviour in the future. And, of course, the critical revision of all those among us—organizations, leaders, and activists—that have had any direct or indirect role in the process that turned out to be so different from what we expected. What does stand in the current agenda is the reconciliation with the torturers. To absolve them ethically is out of question. Not even the missing truth can be achieved by legitimating torture.[44]

A debate ensued within the opposition as well. Some, like Michelini, seemed to be advancing the same thesis as Tróccoli: the thesis of confrontation between two violent evils; the military and the radical left. Others, like former MLN-member Eleuterio Fernández Huidobro, considered that a thorough review of conscience requires a comprehensive perspective, without forgetting the role played by the civilian majoritarian forces—and foremost by the Colorado party—in condoning the use of repression and violence against co-nationals.[45]

The march for the Truth, Memory, and Never Again (popularly known as the March of Silence), which took place on 20 May 1996, honouring the memory of Colorado Senator Zelmar Michelini, Speaker of the Chamber of Deputies Héctor Gutiérrez Ruiz, Rosario Barredo, and William Whitelaw, assassinated in 1976, was a further indication of Uruguay's unending confrontation with that legacy of authoritarianism.

In the three societies, policies of national reconciliation did not achieve the closure of the issue nor were they able to avoid reverberations and repercussions that strained the processes of democratic consolidation and recentred the legacy of human-rights violations in the public agenda.

Human-Rights Violations: A Regional Problem

The legacy of human-rights violations errupted once more in the centre of the public agenda in Argentina, Uruguay, and Chile more or less simultaneously, in 1995–6. The developments were different in each case, as were the strategies for handling the legacy of authoritarianism within the redemocratized framework.

In past years, the legacy of human-rights violations was publicly debated on several occasions, in each of the countries, especially in Argentina in 1984–5 and Uruguay between December 1986 and the April 1989 referendum. Since mid-1995, the public agenda of the three countries focused again on the legacy of human-rights violations. A feeling of unfinished business was becoming apparent. Indications of the regional character of the problem abounded through the revelations of the *Letelier* case, and through other revelations on the DINA's activities outside Chile; the detention and trial of Arancibia for his implication in the assassination of General Prats and his wife in Buenos Aires; revelations in 1996 about the assassination in Buenos Aires of Michelini and Gutiérrez Ruíz; the disappearance—and probable assassination—of more than 100 members of the Uruguayan opposition to the military as well as nearly eighty Chilean nationals in Argentina in the 1970s; and the disappearance and assassination of Argentine members of the opposition to the Argentine military, in Uruguay.

These and related events put flesh and bones on the existence of the 'Plan Cóndor'. This framework, built on the ideological basis of the national security doctrine (different versions of which were adopted by the Southern Cone's and Brazilian military dictatorships) secured the security forces' cooperation in persecuting and killing left-wing activists.[46] According to a 1976 classified report by FBI agent Robert Scherer,

Operation Cóndor is the code name for the gathering, exchange, and storage of intelligence data about the left, the communists and Marxists, who have recently been set up among the participating forces in South America, in order to eliminate the Marxist terrorists and their activities in the area. Furthermore, Operation Cóndor promotes joint operations against terrorist targets in the affiliated countries . . . Chile is the center of Operation Cóndor which also includes Argentina, Bolivia, Paraguay and Uruguay. Brazil has also, supposedly, agreed to turn over information to Operation Cóndor. A third and more secret phase of Operation Cóndor includes the formation of special teams of the member countries to travel anywhere in the world, into non-affiliated countries, carrying out sanctions which include the assassination of terrorists and collaborators of terrorist groups belonging to Operation Cóndor's member countries.[47]

In August 1995, Nilmario Miranda, chair of the Human Rights Commission of the Brazilian Parliament's Chamber of Deputies, suggested the creation of a 'Mercosur of the *desaparecidos*'. The idea was that since repression had had a regional character under the military dictatorships, the time had come to establish regional mechanisms for exchanging information to clarify the fate of citizens who were abducted and made to disappear in one of the neighbouring countries. The network would be composed of parliamentary human-rights commissions of the member countries of the Southern Cone Common Market—Mercosur (Argentina, Brazil, Uruguay, and Paraguay) and eventually Chile and Bolivia.[48] Accordingly, the Paraguayan government has handed over part of its secret archives to the government of Argentina. These archives, popularly known as 'the archives of terror' contain documents which prove that within the framework of the Condor Operation nearly 170 Uruguayans and an equivalent number of Chileans, Paraguayans, and Brazilians disappeared or were assassinated in Argentina during the PRN.[49]

The authoritarian states had annihilated their enemies without regard for national borders or areas of jurisdiction, and thus whenever the issue of disappearances, torture, or assassination became critical in one country in the region after democratization, strong echoes resounded in the others. Against the background of partial knowledge of the truth and restricted acknowledgement of the process's implications, the revelations of former members of the security forces rekindled wide claims for justice, spearheaded by the NGOs and the families of the victims. The complexity of civil–military relations explains the extreme sensitivity to this issue on the side of the military. This background, shared by the three cases, explains why, once the crises are initiated in one country, they reverberate in the neighbouring settings. For example, Arancibia's declarations and trial in Buenos Aires had clear repercussions in Chilean politics, adding to the pressures accumulated during the crisis over the *Letelier* case verdict.[50] Similarly, the refusal of Contreras to serve the jail sentence handed down by the Chilean courts in the *Letelier* case raised the whole issue of DINA's operations outside Chile. In Argentina, Scilingo's declarations, preceded by the Rolón and Pernias testimonies in Parliament, raised the issue of the *desaparecidos* not only in Argentina but also in Uruguay.[51]

Another dimension of the regional character of the problem was the common refusal by the three armed and security forces to allow civilians the knowledge the latter had requested on the fate of the disappeared. The armed and security forces have rejected the possibility of opening their records or of providing the testimonies of those who were involved in acts against civilians, that is, of those who know the fate of the *desaparecidos*. The high commands of the armed forces have systematically declined having any information about the missing individuals.[52]

The pattern of cooperation of the three armed and security forces was reinforced by their similar ideological visions. In the view of the military of the three countries, they had fought a war to 'save the [respective] nation'. Despite the national specificity of each case, carrying out the goals set by the National Security Doctrine required fighting against an international phenomenon: the revolutionary left-wing threat. Eradicating the political and military opposition required regional cooperation, using methods that the military establishment had internalized during the height of the Cold War. Once they had cooperated in actions that came to be portrayed by the redemocratized societies as flagrant violations of human rights, again, the members of the three security establishments found themselves partners in an unwritten pact of silence with regional implications.

Once fractures appeared in the implicit wall of military silence, an international demonstration effect took place, even if in partial and distorted ways. The declarations of Scilingo in Argentina, followed by General Balza's review of concience set a precedent for the neighbouring countries that had to be addressed even by those opposed to a new evaluation of the past.

In the democratic period, the armed and security forces of the various countries continued to work under the common perception that there were subversive enemies, which according to the military still continued to represent a regional threat. Argentina resented Enrique Gorriarán Merlo's passage through Uruguayan territory as he travelled to Brazil, after he led the assault on the military base of La Tablada. Argentine journals reported about the connections between the Uruguayan Tupamaros and the Movimiento Todos por la Patria that had attacked La Tablada. When the attack was made known in the neighbouring countries, the armed forces of Uruguay expected a domino effect in their home country. As a result, the Uruguayan armed forces performed an exercise of rescuing a military camp from an initial attack and capture by subversive forces. The Uruguayan political forces that had opposed the Law of Expiry saw in this exercise an attempt to intimidate and menace the people shortly before the referendum.[53]

The institutional constellations and previous mechanisms of dealing with the legacy of human-rights violations created different situations in each country. The path of resolving past crises condition the ways in which the triggers of new crises operate.

In Chile, the path of the institutional treatment was symbolic and legal. The verdicts reached in the mid-1990s in the *Degollados* and *Letelier* cases (not covered by the 1978 Amnesty Law), and the difficulties in implementing the sentences, initiated crises. In Uruguay, the path of the institutional treatment was political, centring on initiatives led by the political class and the oppositional mobilization of civil society, until the 1989 referendum. The echoes of Argentine events and the initiative of local politicians and public figures (Rafael Michelini, Matilde Rodríguez, and others) have recently reopened the issue, placing it at the centre of the public agenda. In Argentina, the path of resolution was a legal-political building of indictments, amnesties, and pardons, which in the late 1980s left an intense sense of frustration among the concerned actors in the field of human-rights violations and an unfulfilled claim for national reconciliation. The widely different character of the paths followed in Argentina (of legal, political, symbolic, and cultural character) and the high—presidential —source of the pardons complicated the situation. This is perhaps the reason why the impasse is being broken from within the ranks of the military, by retired navy captain Scilingo and the subsequent declarations of General Balza. These declarations, which broke the wall of silence, found an echo among retired military and security personnel of neighbouring Uruguay (Tróccoli) and Chile (Arancibia), whose declarations became replicate crisis triggers or added to existing critical situations.

The regional dimension and the partiality of the early ways of confronting the legacy of authoritarianism are brought together when a new crisis develops. The regional ties among the countries mean that crisis is never entirely local but spreads to the other countries. The partiality of the early knowledge and the treatment of human-rights violations conditions the mounting threats that any revelations—as minor as they might be—create. Revelations by members of the security forces signal the fragility of the wall of silence the military established as a norm concerning the violence employed in repression. They signal as well the relative accessibility of the knowledge requested by NGOs, victims, relatives, and friends.

In the above cases, a crisis is triggered when a former or current member of the armed forces breaks ranks with the military and security institutions regarding the legacy of human-rights violations. In the cases of Scilingo, Tróccoli, and Arancibia there was recognition of gross human-rights violations, with direct or indirect participation of the officer who goes public with information previously denied; there was endorsement of the military thesis that the armed and security forces had no alternative at the time but to face a brutal enemy in the latter's own terms of violence; and there was an uneven and partial remorse that led to opening the issue.

Tróccoli's statement is paradigmatic of this ambivalence:

I assume responsibility for having combatted the guerrilla band with all the forces and resources at my disposition. I assume responsibility for having done things which I am not proud of now, nor was I proud of then. I assume responsibility for having participated in a war, as I understood it at that moment. After all, the situation of war is most of the time a juridical status and humanity sees itself wrapped up in death and injuries even when a war is not declared. I assume responsibility most of all for having been submerged in violence. Only now, from this [my current] perspective, can I understand the norms and values that prevailed in that situation, set and determined by the [state of] war . . . If one could dignify the evil involved, we could say it was a dirty war, but not less heroic than others, both on one side and the other. For the most part, only to your judgement will I lend the true value. Even when somebody is full of hatred, I will be able to understand it.

In the case of Contreras and Espinoza in Chile, both officers stuck to the basic thesis of the military. The 1978 Amnesty Law, itself an exception to normal democratic practice, included an exception to its own spirit. It sanctioned the possibility of bringing to trial those responsible for assassinating Letelier in the USA. When the political and judicial systems tried to implement that provision, both officers, and particularly retired General Contreras, triggered a crisis. They resisted the jail sentences, claiming that no exceptions should be made if the principle of having won a war against subversion was recognized by Chileans.

The crisis is triggered by individuals variously motivated. The motivations include: disagreements with the line of commands; a problem of conscience, which usually begins as the individual who had participated in the actions matures and reviews his activities under military rule; rejection of judicial verdicts; the search for fame and money; and the will of individuals to redefine the problem of human rights in the spirit of mutual approachment and reconciliation.

Nonetheless, as the individual goes public, his declarations rapidly take the centre stage of the public agenda on the national level. They are quickly reproduced by the media of the neighbouring countries, in which they find an echo, due to the regional character of the issue and the parallel partiality of past institutional solutions. General economic, social, and political considerations may add to the extended ramifications of the crisis, but these considerations are minor in the initiation itself. The diverse economic and political performances of the new democracies in Argentina, Chile, and Uruguay is ample proof of this point.

Major sectors of civil society, throughout the whole spectrum of the socio-economic scale, are only slightly concerned with reopening the human-rights abuses issue. This is related to the contemporary socio-economic set-up, which is characterized by rising poverty, social marginalization, widening income gaps, and mounting levels of crime. All these have combined to create the perception of personal insecurity among both the well-off and the lower strata, who demand greater social control by the police, even at the price of ignoring contemporary human-rights violations.[54] Many sectors of society, along the whole socio-economic scale, are interested in economic and social stability as well. Against this background, any threat to institutional stability is seen in a negative light.

These attitudes are also widespread in the political classes that have reacted to the issue when placed at the centre of public attention, but have tried to minimize its impact and downplay its potential for crisis. In Uruguay, following the 1989 referendum, human-rights demands have almost disappeared from the political platforms of the major parties and their internal sectors (*lemas*). Only Michelini's Nuevo Espacio party and small circles within the left are interested in obtaining knowledge about the fate of the disappeared or in advancing socio-economic entitlements as part of a wide conception of the relationship between human rights and democracy.[55] In Argentina, following the 1994 constitutional reform resulting from a political pact between Menem and Alfonsín, both the Partido Justicialista and the Unión Cívica Radical treat the issues related to rights and freedoms as part of their views on justice, internal security, sectorial issues, and foremost their concern for institutional policies. The third major political force, the FREPASO (Frente del País Solidario), has taken a more contestarian position, proposing to enshrine human rights as a central part of Argentine institutionality, throughout a series of reforms and structural changes. Many of these proposed reforms originated in the FREPASO's proposal for the drafting of a constitution for the city of Buenos Aires, which enjoys federal autonomy. In this draft, special emphasis was placed on the guarantees suggested to ensure human rights, which included innovative procedural guarantees.[56]

In Chile, the beginning of the transition in the 1990s and the presence of authoritarian enclaves in the formal democratic framework have preserved a closer link between politics and human rights. Being aware of the lack of closure of the pending constitutional reforms and of the legacy of human-rights violations, all political forces have related to both issues and their connection. In the 1993 platform of the ruling Concertación coalition, there is a whole section devoted to human rights, which are seen as the moral basis of political thought and action and democracy, while they are also to be pursued as concrete measures, such as promoting the return of exiled Chileans or making local legislation compatible with international legislation and treaties.[57] The parties at both the right and the left express a basic commitment to human rights, with differences in their view of the need to restrict rights in case of crises. Both RN and the UDI consider that the 1973 military intervention was justified by the perils of anarchy and civil war; large sectors of RN are prone to reach an agreement on the closure of the legacy of human-rights violations that would allow constitutional reform, thus opening the limits on Chilean democracy. In the centre-left, Christian Democrats and other Concertación forces are willing to approach RN toward constitutional reforms, and Socialists and Communists cling to intransigent positions regarding human rights.[58] In spite of the above differences, in all three countries most political parties have incorporated formally, though in various ways, the language of human rights and downgraded the potential for crisis of the legacy of past human-rights violations.

The repercussions around the past erupted against the will and interests of the majority sectors in each society. The impetus of the aftershocks stresses how difficult it is to incorporate the legacy of past human-rights violations into collective memory and identity. Though most of these societies would prefer to forget the past and march toward the future, whenever the crisis is triggered it is extremely difficult to close it in the terms of the past paths of resolution.

At the political level, repeated rumours circulate about the cooperation between leading political figures of the Southern Cone countries

to close pending cases related to the legacy of human-rights violations. One such case has been attributed to the links between presidents Menem and Sanguinetti, focusing on a quid pro quo agreement,
according to which Sanguinetti agreed in June 1989 to provide shelter
for Montonero leaders in Uruguay until amnesties were enacted in
Argentina, and Menem included in the Argentine list of pardoned the
names of José Gavazzo and other members of the Uruguayan security forces implicated in the assassination of Uruguayan politicians
Michelini and Gutiérrez Ruiz on Argentine soil. While Gavazzo and
the others were residents of Uruguay at that time, they had been under
trial *in absentia* in Argentina for crimes committed there. Argentine
demands for extradition had never reached or were not processed by
the Uruguayan authorities without any reasonable explanation.[59]

The formula of national reconciliation, which explicitly or implicitly sustained the attempts of the political classes to bring the issue
to a close, was unevenly implemented. In each case it tacitly recognized the thesis of the armed forces as partially valid and provided
the perpetrators with substantial answers to their plight, in the
form of amnesties and pardons, or the recognition of the status quo
ante. Much of this was done under military pressure. At the same time,
the paths followed provided partial truth (and in the case of Chile,
also partial acknowledgement) concerning the role of the state and
society—but not that of the military and its supporters—in the victims' plight.

National reconciliation was used as a formula, which according to
the political forces in power presaged an era of social peace, in which
the issue of human rights would acquire positive connotations, becoming one of the pillars of democracy. The majority of the population took
a passive position and neither actively supported the victims nor
endorsed the position of the military. But as the governments of redemocratized Argentina, Chile, and Uruguay acted and reacted trying to balance principles of legality, justice, and political contingency,
the result was the perpetuation in the public sphere of old attitudes
by those directly concerned, far into the democratic period.

A situation has arisen in which the issue of human rights tends
to be marginalized in the public sphere, without being comprehensively addressed, until new testimonies and evidence place the legacy
of human-rights violations again at the centre of the public agenda.
This script of crises beyond past crisis is encoded in the patterns of
partial treatment of the authoritarian legacy by the new Southern
Cone democracies. Paradoxically, these aftershocks are bringing these
societies closer, in a tortuous way, to establishing knowledge and
acknowledgement of past human-rights violations.

Pending International Cases

Repression of political opponents in the form of human-rights violations did not recognize frontiers. The same techniques of torture, disappearance, and assassination were employed against co-nationals and aliens suspected of direct involvement or indirect assistance to 'subversion'. Concomitant local networks of counter-insurgency also tracked 'enemies' beyond the national frontiers, in the neighbouring countries as well as in Europe or the USA.

The international dimensions of repression have brought third parties located outside the Southern Cone to play an active role in determining the fate of their own disappeared citizens or the character of acts of terrorism committed in their territory by security forces sent by the Southern Cone countries. The difficulties inherent in the Southern Cone legal systems for suing military personnel implicated in serious human-rights abuses (amnesty and impunity laws and pardons) have reinforced the symbolic and institutional import of the judicial actions initiated in such countries as the USA, Spain, Italy, or France.

Each of the countries of the Southern Cone mobilized repression forces in somewhat distinct ways against co-nationals abroad and against aliens residing in their territory. Uruguay has been the least involved in such extra-national patterns of repression, with their forces working mostly within the national frontiers and refraining from any significant direct role in the disappearances (most cases of missing Uruguayans involved abductions and assassinations on Argentine soil by Argentine security forces). Despite the collaboration of Uruguayan security forces with their Argentine and Chilean peers, no cases of international scope have been made abroad in the democratic period against Uruguayan officers.

In Argentina, the main international impact of repression has been related to the murder of foreign countries' citizens during their stays in Argentina (as political exiles, permanent residents, or tourists). Several legal suits have been filed abroad in the democratic period against those involved in the assassination of such civilians. First, a trial was held in France against navy captain Alfredo Astiz for his involvement in the disappearance and murder of two French nuns, Leonie Duquet and Alice Domon. Astiz was found guilty and sentenced *in absentia* to life in prison. In March 1995 the French authorities filed an international arrest order against Astiz, a move that was countered in Argentina by the support of Astiz by his superiors in the navy, thus creating international tension between both countries. In addition to the nuns, there are at least another thirteen French nationals, missing since the PRN, whose 'disappeareance' has been reported to the

CONADEP.[60] A second trial was initiated in Spain by Judge Baltasar Garzón in September 1996 to determine the whereabouts of 320 missing Spanish citizens during the PRN. As 97 Argentine military officers were implicated in the disappearances of at least 266 individuals and the kidnapping of 54 victims' children, reports appeared in the press that the Spanish Foreign Affairs Ministry was contemplating the possibility of demanding the extradiction of those officers if the courts require it. A precedent for such procedure was set when Argentine courts granted the extradiction to Italy of Nazi war criminal Erich Priebke. In accordance with Argentine constitutional recognition of the primacy of international treaties on Genocide and Human Rights, no time limits could affect bringing to trial or extraditing persons accused of having committed such crimes.[61] Nonetheless, Argentine courts made it clear that they would not accept any such demand, since the Law of Due Obedience and the pardons had closed the issue from the point of view of Argentine justice.[62]

A third judicial process was initiated in Italy in 1983 for the disappearance of Italian nationals in Argentina; the trial has been protracted but still threatens to implicate at least forty Argentine military officers.[63] Commenting on the trials on human-rights violations against Argentine nationals in Spain and Italy, Alicia Pierini, Argentine subsecretary of Human Rights, stated the problem in terms of national sovereignty, which is being infringed by trials abroad.[64] This shows how deeply embedded is the resistance to the implications of globalizing trends in the realm of human rights, in spite of the declared adherence of the political leadership to globalization in general.

Other legal suits have been filed in Sweden, in connection with Astiz's role in Dagmar Hagelin's murder, and in Germany, where relatives of German nationals who were made to disappear in Argentina initiated legal action under the aegis of a 'Coalition against Impunity', formed by local and international NGOs and led by the Evangelical Church.[65] In Honduras, human-rights ombudsman Leo Valladares has accused Argentine military officers of training local military in repressive methods that violate the international human-rights law. In the USA, private lawyers have made effective use of the alien tort claims act to prove civil liability and to win large awards for damages against Argentine military personnel involved in human-rights violations.

Chile is the only country among the three in which a trial initiated abroad (the case *Letelier–Moffit*) has led to the trial and indictments of military officers (Contreras and Espinoza) on Chilean soil. Similarly, Chile seems to be the only case in which military personnel have been implicated as seemingly co-responsible for the assassination of Berríos, a Chilean national, in Uruguay, after the return to democracy. This case seems to be an example of post-dictatorial collaboration between the Chilean and the Uruguayan security forces behind the backs of elected governments. Chemical engineer Eugenio Berríos Segafredo was an agent of Chilean Intelligence requested by Chilean courts to testify on the assassination of Letelier. Berríos disappeared from Chile in late 1992. A year later, a man claiming to be Berríos complained in the police station of the Uruguayan town of El Pinar that he was being held there against his will in a nearby house by Uruguayan and Chilean personnel. After leaving the station, the man was never seen again. Two years later, in March 1995, a forensic doctor identified the remains of a body found on the Uruguayan coast as those of Berríos.[66]

These disparate developments are related to the dual character of current controls over the repressive military apparatus. On the one hand, repression has been highly coordinated and Chilean armed forces have established clear-cut thresholds for the attribution of responsibilities for human-rights violations, mostly dismissing them as part of necessary actions done in a state of internal war. On the other hand, the legal frameworks which the military administration adopted (e.g. the 1978 Amnesty Law) established both time and other parameters for attributing responsibility for repressive actions committed after 1978, as well as exceptional cases such as the assassination of Letelier.

In judicial cases initiated abroad, the attitude of the Chilean armed forces has been to disclaim any institutional responsibility, declaring that those standing trial are attributed with personal responsibility. Three major trials have been initiated which may have institutional spillovers. First, there is the case of the 1974 assassination of the former commander-in-chief of the Chilean army, General Carlos Prats and his wife, in Buenos Aires, where they were living as exiles after Pinochet's assumption of power. In January 1996, a former officer of the Chilean DINA, Enrique Lautaro Arancibia Clavel was arrested in Buenos Aires and accused of involvement in the murder. As a result of his declarations, other individuals such as Colonel José Zara Holger, Brigadier-General Raúl Eduardo Iturriaga Neumann, Captain Armando Fernández Larios, and Agent Michael Townley have been implicated in the case.[67] Arancibia's defence lawyer, Alberto Ottalagano, was state-nominated Rector of the National University of Buenos Aires in the early 1970s and was considered an enthusiastic admirer of Fascism, holding extreme anti-democratic views.[68] In another trial, conducted in Italy, General Manuel Contreras and

Iturriaga Neumann were found guilty of the attempted assassination of former Chilean Vice-President Bernardo Leighton and his wife in Rome in October 1976. Contreras and Iturriaga Neumann were sentenced *in absentia* to twenty and eighteen years in prison, respectively. It is highly unlikely that the sentence will be carried out since there is no agreement of extradiction between Italy and Chile.[69]

Another case with international implications concerns the trial of two DINA officers for the assassination of Carmelo Soria, a Spanish citizen and CEPAL official (who therefore had diplomatic status) in Chile in July 1976.[70] In the same manner as during the military administrations, the Chilean democratic government neither recognizes the jurisdiction of foreign courts on crimes committed on Chilean soil nor the possibility of extraditing alleged perpetrators of such crimes committed against foreign nationals in Chile.[71] The Spanish judge Manuel García-Castellón has recognized a complaint which names General Pinochet with late Admiral Toribio Merino and Generals Gustavo Leigh and the late César Mendoza, all members of the military junta, as well as General Manuel Contreras as defendants. After the Chilean authorities refused to comply with the Spanish request for subpoenas and extradition, Judge García-Castellón invoked the mutual Treaty of Legal Assistance between Spain and the USA to request information from American agencies. Attorney-General Janet Reno has given her approval for the declassification of FBI and CIA documents and for the appearance in the Spanish courts of FBI and CIA personnel possessing information in the case.[72]

In a democratic public sphere, the existence of hundreds of unsolved cases of missing persons sets the stage for potential 'aftershocks'. The media has been effective time and again in giving public resonance to individual pain and personal claims for full knowledge. One such case that incited the Chilean public attention in 1996 was the disappearance of Jacobo Stoulman and his wife Matilde Pessa in Buenos Aires on May 1977. Thanks to the research work of Juan Pablo Moreno and Iván Cabezas, major questions were raised concerning the whereabouts and fate of this couple and the international implications of Chilean nationals abducted in Argentina. Stoulman was a wealthy member of the Jewish community, partner in a Santiago travel agency and in a foreign exchange agency, which apparently also handled funds of the then proscribed Communist Party of Chile. Stoulman himself had no known political affiliation. Once they disappeared in Argentina, the family tried unsuccessfully to inquire about their fate with the Foreign Affairs Ministry, the Vicariate of Solidarity, and NGOs. They also hired the services of several prominent Chilean lawyers who travelled to Buenos Aires, where they were warned not to continue their search on behalf of the Stoulman family (a fact they did not convey to their clients). In an official cable in 1977, General Videla informed the Chilean Foreign Affairs Ministry that the couple had been detained and released shortly after, and continued their trip to Montevideo (in a flight that was proved to be non-existent). The cable itself was lost, never reaching the family. The Chilean Foreign Affairs Ministry did not continue the investigation into Uruguay. Following the abduction, all Stoulman's bank accounts in the USA and Europe were emptied, and nearly one million dollars disappeared. Moreno and Cabezas have suggested, on the basis of a wide array of partial evidence, that the Chilean and Argentine security forces coordinated their actions to abduct the couple and obtain access to their bank accounts. The pragmatic intentions were ideologically veiled by a DINA agent in Argentina, Enrique Arancibia, who suggested that Stoulman was connected with the Montoneros-Graiver case of links between the guerrilla and a well-known Jewish financier, as part of a 'Jewish-Bolshevik conspiracy against Argentina and Western civilization'. Despite the efforts of the family, no specific knowledge was obtained in the following nineteen years, save for a mention in both the Chilean Rettig and Argentine *Nunca más* reports. In 1996, the publication created a mini-scandal involving some of the Chilean diplomats involved at that time, especially the current Chilean ambassador to Denmark, as well as other officials who apparently covered up the case.[73] An unexpected development in pending international cases related to human-rights violations occurred in late 1998, as retired General and Senator (for life) Augusto Pinochet arrived in Great Britain for medical treatment. Following an international warrant of arrest signed by Spanish investigating judge Baltasar Garzón on a criminal process conducted in Spain, Britain's judicial and state authorities were forced to decide on the prevalence of divergent principles of accountability. Namely, the principles of sovereign immunity and international law as they relate to the alleged crimes against humanity perpetrated by the former supreme powerholder of a country, Chile, against citizens of third countries, in this case Spain.

On 25 November 1998, the Lords of Law of the United Kingdom overruled a prior High Court decision that recognized the immunity of Augusto Pinochet as former head of state. By a majority of three to two, the judges in charge of the appeal process decided that the principle of Sovereign Immunity—recognized by the British Immunity Act of 1978—does not stand when the respondent is accused of crimes against humanity.[74]

This decision, which could bring Pinochet to face extradition, was seen by many as a watershed in the delayed efforts to bring the former head of state to trial beyond the boundaries of the Southern Cone, where the frameworks of constitutionality inherited from military rule and the constraints of political contingency have precluded it. The decision by the Law Lords was greeted with delight by human-rights activists in Britain and all over the world, whereas it was strongly resented by the general's supporters, both in Chile and in Britain.

While the position of human-rights advocates was articulated in terms of justice, accountability, and international law, the opponents made use of a wide range of political and humanitarian arguments against the extradition and in favour of the unconditional release of Pinochet. Among the reasons invoked for the latter were British economic, political, and military interests and special relations with Chile, primarily the support given to Britain during the Malvinas–Falkland conflict in 1982; Pinochet's frail health at age 83; and the claim that in eleven ongoing trials against Pinochet in Chile, no evidence had been found of the general's personal involvement in the crimes of which he is being accused. In more political terms, many Chileans feared that Pinochet's arrest and the subsequent legal procedures would affect their country's public stability and democratic consolidation. Indeed, as the news broke in Chile, polarization was re-enacted. Demonstrations in favour and against Pinochet erupted and, mainly verbal, attacks against Spain and Britain took place from mid-October, especially in Santiago. Perhaps fearing further destabilization, Chile's democratic government demanded the unconditional release of the General, basing its claims on the principle of sovereignty, as Senator Pinochet was travelling abroad supposedly on an official mission, and arguing that crimes committed on Chilean soil cannot and should not be tried before foreign courts. At the time of writing, the events around Pinochet's possible extradition from Britain are being dealt with with intensity in the national as well as the international public spheres. In Chile, they have brought all sides to consider new political options about the terms of the transition from authoritarian rule and democratic consolidation. Now, the centrality of the legacy of human-rights violations is being stressed more than ever, as linked to the democratic future of the country.

Beyond its immediate results,[75] the new aftershock around past human-rights violations has deep implications for the redefinition of responsibility and accountability in a globalizing public arena. It stresses that the legacy of human-rights violations as a public problem cannot be contained within national borders for various reasons, foremost due to the international character of repression, as discussed above, and in addition, due to the separation of powers and judicial autonomy inherent in Western liberal democratic arrangements, which make more difficult the application of political contingent criteria. Moreover, the massive publicity of these issues in the global mass media adds another dimension of difficulty in any attempt to cover up, favouring public accountability. Accordingly, politicians from different parties and beliefs tend to comply with court decisions in spite of the discretionary power they possess to rule otherwise. Once the wheels of the legal system start moving, all the process, though still carrying political as well as legal implications, moves according to the cadence of an autonomous judiciary, which opens the way to the penetration of global standards of condemnation and trial of human-rights abuses, even if these occurred decades ago, as in the case of Chile. These cases are illustrative of a long series of cases that may be reopened in later years, pressuring both those who played any role in the events and those who are currently in charge of dealing with the institutional legacy of human-rights violations.

The regional and transnational character of repression has been replaced by the international impact of its treatment under democracy. The open character of the redemocratized public spheres in all three countries have precluded the confinement of the legacy of human-rights violations to internal dimensions and effects. Therefore, the subject has been publicly reopened time and again by developments taking place in other countries, while each state resists foreign judicial action by resorting to arguments about the defence of national sovereignty. The disruptive potential of the numerous pending cases, though not a source of immediate destabilizing impact, can be expected to return to the Southern Cone, not necessarily triggered from within.

Restructuring the Realm of Human Rights in the Southern Cone

Following the repression under military rule, the issue of human rights was promoted to the fore of social life. Regardless of the political and economic performance of the various military governments, human-rights violations tainted the dictatorships and became an important tool for those oppositionary political and social forces that were striving to redemocratize their countries. With the return to democracy, the legacy of human-rights violations was openly addressed by all sorts of social and institutional actors in the uncensored public spheres.

Three dimensions emerged as central for confronting that legacy: first, the problem of the victims and the personal and institutional responsibility for the acts of repression; second, the effort to prevent massive human- and civil-rights violations in each of these societies in the future; and third, the incorporation of the repressive period into the collective memory and identity of these societies.

The third dimension will be addressed below, in the chapter on memory and oblivion (Chapter 6) and the chapter on the transformation of collective identity in Argentina, Chile, and Uruguay (Chapter 7). In the present chapter we continue addressing the first and second dimensions, reviewing the policies and changes introduced by the democratic governments and adopted by social actors. Many of these policies were reactive and did not touch the many traces and pockets of authoritarianism left in these societies, as seen in current abuses of human and civil rights. In the sections that follow we analyse the elaboration and limits of institutional mechanisms and policies for addressing the afore-mentioned dimensions in the legacy of human-rights violations.

Material Reparations and Demands

Following redemocratization, the governments of the Southern Cone faced the problem of reparations and compensations to the victims of repression of the previous administration and to their relatives. In dealing with reparations, the civilian administrations adopted policies according to how much responsibility they accepted for the deeds committed by their military predecessors. In Chile, following the Rettig Report, the Aylwin administration assumed complete material responsibility towards the victims of human-rights violations, as part of the former's vision of truth, justice, and national reconciliation. According to this vision, the civilian state should establish mechanisms for reparation and compensation for the damages inflicted by the previous administration. Argentina went through two stages concerning reparations. In the first stage, Alfonsín's administration initiated a policy of prosecuting the high commands and other officers involved in human-rights violations. The establishment of culpability was seen as a precondition for any claim of compensation or reparation on the part of the victims or their relatives. This path was blocked by the Punto Final Law, due to mounting tensions between the civilian government and the military after the trials of the heads of the Juntas. Subsequent legislation in the form of the Due Obedience Law further blocked the possibility of automatically transferring the cases to civilian courts for compensation. In the second stage, the administration of President Menem completed the regressive cycle by pardoning all those sentenced or under trial since the mid-1980s. Between 1992 and 1994, the administration passed three laws regulating state compensations for the victims of human-rights violations and their relatives.

In Uruguay, the democratic government refrained from assuming direct state responsibility for the violations of human rights under the previous government. It only established, by law, the restitution of material property and of employment, or compensation for the loss of both.

The previous trends were reflected in the specific legislation and policies. In Chile, the state compensated victims' families through the Reparation Law of January 1992, granting monthly allowances of nearly 400 US dollars to over 4,600 relatives of victims. According to the mandate of the National Corporation of Reparation and Reconciliation, education scholarships were granted in the order of tens of millions of US dollars to the children of the victims (known as the Rettig scholarships). Liberated political prisoners were also entitled to and received financial assistance for their labour force reabsorption and studies. In September 1993, the Parliament enacted the *Ley de exonerados*, which provided compensation to 55,000 public employees who had lost their jobs during the period of military rule. The administration established mechanisms for the return of the political exiles and their reabsorption in Chilean society by creating the Oficina Nacional del

Retorno, which granted recognition to studies, academic and professional titles acquired while in exile, and an exemption from import taxes on the exiles' belongings when returning to Chile.[1] As a result of the trial over the assassination of Orlando Letelier and Ronnie Moffit, and following the Chilean–US (Brian–Suárez Mujica) agreement, the Chilean state paid 2,611,800 US dollars to the families of the victims.[2] Some other trials resulted in court decisions ordering the defendants— military and security personnel—found guilty of disappearances and assassinations to pay reparations for sums ranging from 2 and 3 million pesos (c.5,000–7,500 US dollars) in the Temuco case, to a joint sum of 30,500,000 pesos (c.76,000 US dollars) to the relatives of Manuel Guerrero, Santiago Nattino, and José Manuel Parada, the three victims in the *Degollados* case. In this latter case, the state was also ordered by the Supreme Court of Chile to pay 74,700,000 pesos (c.190,000 US dollars).[3]

In the case of Argentina, the legal framework organized between 1992 and 1994 included Law 24043 (1992), which indemnified illegally detained persons; Law 24321 (1994), which recognized the legal status of the *desaparecidos*; and Law 24411 (1994), which granted compensations to the relatives of the missing and dead individuals. According to the first law, the victims of political repression were entitled to receive from the state the sum of 40 dollars per day of imprisonment during the PRN; 30,000 dollars for serious wounds; and 50,000 dollars for the death of a relative. According to Law 24411, the indemnization that relatives of missing persons were to receive was raised to about 220,000 dollars.[4] Already in 1992, six cases were presented to the Interamerican Commission for Human Rights, which demanded the identification of those responsible for human-rights violations against 132 Argentine nationals during the PRN. In October 1992, the ICHR concluded that Argentine legislation at the time was incompatible with the respective articles of the American Convention of Human Rights and with the American Declaration of the Rights and Duties of Man, both of which Argentina had accepted as international treaties binding national legislation. The ICHR also recommended full compensation for the victims.[5] Another international aspect of the problem of the *desaparecidos* was raised as the Brazilian government published its own official list of missing persons in 1996, including three Argentine citizens who had been illegally detained and disappeared in Brazil in the 1970s. The government of President Fernando Henrique Cardoso approved the payment of 105,000 to 160,000 US dollars as reparations. The relatives of another three Argentines who disappeared in similar circumstances appealed to President Menem and received his full support of their case before the Brazilian government.[6]

Recently, several demands for reparation have been brought before Argentine civilian courts. In the case of Hugo Tarnopolsky, whose wife, two children, and daughter-in-law were abducted by military forces, the civil court ruled against two ex-junta members and the Argentine state. The Court granted him $2 million in compensation, one million from the state and one million to be paid by retired admirals Emilio E. Massera and Armando Lambruschini.[7] Braja Kleinrock Havas, a resident of Israel and victim of torture in 1976 sued the Argentine state in 1995 for personal damages suffered during the PRN, for the sum of five million dollars, which she intends to use to honour the memory of the victims of repression.[8]

In Uruguay, the legal framework established in the 1985 Law of Amnesty (Law No. 15737—articles 12, 13, and 24) sanctioned the restitution of property that had been illegally confiscated or appropriated because of the state of emergency under military rule, or material compensation in its default. Some restitution of property and compensations took place in the late 1980s.[9] In 1987, the representatives in Parliament of the Partido por el Gobierno del Pueblo proposed, without success, a bill to confer minimal pensions and social assistance to the relatives of those who had disappeared in the country under military rule.[10] The Amnesty Law also required the state to rehire state employees fired during the dictatorship; in the event this was unfeasible, the state was required to provide them or their relatives with a pension. The law enabled the reintegration of more than 10,000 public employees and provided pensions for more than 6,000 former employees or their relatives, in case the former had died.[11] By and large, the Uruguayan government adopted a piecemeal strategy of individual negotiation rather than comprehensive and regularized legislation. In 1989, Celso Scaltriti, an ex-member of the Communist Party who remained disabled after torture, sued the Ministry of Defence and was granted 480,000 US dollars by a civil court.[12] A few other civil suits were handled in the early 1990s. In one of them, the judicial case of Eduardo Arigón Castells, Judge Dr Pedro Keuroglian recognized in Uruguayan jurisprudence the legal status of 'forced disappearance'.[13] On 28 June 1991, the Ministry of Defence agreed to pay two million US dollars to the families of fifteen victims of human-rights violations, as a result of a compromise. The lawyer of one of the families declared that this was a step forward because the state had recognized its responsibility for the death of political prisoners, in accordance with the country's international commitments of the country. In its annual report, SERPAJ considered the agreement as a transaction in which material reparations functioned as a springboard to close criminal proceedings.[14]

Constitutional and Legal Frameworks

The countries of the Southern Cone have a long constitutional and legal tradition that goes back to the early nineteenth century, at the onset of independence, with further roots in the colonial period. This tradition emphasizes the primacy of law; but the law was very often violated in practice, both during periods of anarchy, civil war, *coups d'état*, and dictatorships, and due to the executives' use of emergency decrees and special powers. Usually, in such 'states of emergency', the legal and judicial systems of these countries have recognized the authority of the *de facto* rulers, in order to maintain the continuity of a state of law following the change of government.[15]

Once these states of emergency end, sometimes via the return to electoral democracy, the new legal and constitutional frameworks have to deal with the question of whether the previous governments had acted legally. One central element in this legal dilemma is whether to grant amnesties to former rulers and political enemies. Before the last wave of military rule, the usual pattern in the three countries was to close the 'states of emergency' by granting amnesties and/or pardons, thus hopefully reaching a state of normality and order.

The history of amnesties and pardons goes back to the period of early independence and nation-building in the nineteenth century. In Argentina, major amnesties and pardons were granted after the uprising of 1874; following the rebellions by the Unión Cívica and the Radicals in the early 1890s; in 1932, when President Justo pardoned the political prisoners from Uriburu's presidency; in 1958, when President Frondizi granted an amnesty to Peronist leaders in prison or exile; and in 1973, when President Cámpora decreed a general amnesty following the access in power of Peronism. In Uruguay, amnesties and pardons were granted in 1835 at the end of the wars of independence and again in 1854 and 1860; in 1872 an amnesty put an end to the rebellion of Timoteo Aparicio; in 1875 those involved in the Revolution of the *Tricolor* were pardoned; in 1897 pardons were granted to those involved in the rebellion of Aparicio Saravia, followed by a formal agreement between the victors and the defeated in 1904; pardons followed the uprising of Cerillos in 1926;[16] in 1935 the Terra Dictatorship was closed by a law of pardon. In Chile, the rebels of 1827, 1841, and 1857 were pardoned; President José Joaquín Pérez granted pardons in 1865 and 1867, covering in the latter case all political crimes since 1851; and President Jorge Montt decreed a new general amnesty after the 1891 civil war.

In 1978 the Chilean governing junta presided over by General Pinochet issued the Amnesty decree to cover acts committed during the 1973–8 period; the idea was to preclude any future judicial actions against personnel of the armed and security forces, with some exceptions (as analysed above).[17] This decree, still in force, is a central component of the framework used to deal with the legacy of human-rights violations in redemocratized Chile.[18] As the law did not cover the military men implicated in the *Letelier* case as well as human-rights violations committed after 1978, trials and indictments followed, leading to the imprisonment of officers such as Contreras and Espinoza. Nonetheless, the indicted military personnel retained their ranks and were imprisoned in special comfortable conditions, under military surveillance and regulated by military codes of conduct, which respected their rank and prerogatives, something unavailable for common prisoners. All this raises serious doubts regarding equality before the law and equal punishment. In Argentina, shortly before handing over power, on 25 September 1983, the military government decreed a law of self-amnesty (Law No. 22924), which was annulled by President Alfonsín in December 1983. After the trials of the commanders and following the rising military tensions and uprisings in the late 1980s, the Law of Punto Final and Due Obedience were approved, and in 1990 a general pardon was issued that covered all those sentenced or on trial because of human-rights violations and political violence. In early April 1998 the two chambers of the Argentine Parliament abrogated both laws; the decision did not carry any practical effects since local legislation cannot be applied retroactively and since the crimes committed were covered under the pardons.[19] In Uruguay the 1985 Law of Amnesty (Law No. 15737) and the December 1986 Law of Expiry (Law No. 15848, ratified by the popular referendum in April 1989) sanctioned the closing of political confrontation by pardon and amnesty.[20] In the three societies of the Southern Cone the issue of human-rights violations came eventually to be treated by recourse to the traditional pattern of closing violent civic confrontations through amnesties and pardons, historically encoded in the political cultures of Argentina, Chile, and Uruguay.

Another element of legal importance in political revamping concerns the judicial branch, which during military rule and previous states of emergency had legitimated what would normally be considered extralegal acts. During the last wave of military rule, the courts showed their cooperation with the *de facto* rulers by failing to enforce most habeas corpus and *recurso de amparo* petitions, customary legal mechanisms for protecting human rights.

Following redemocratization, the duly elected governments have faced the dilemma of continuity or reform. The choice of continuity freezes the previous judicial apparatus, which had cooperated with the *de facto* rulers and maintains its verdicts, thus avoiding serious institutional repercussions. The choice of reform implies questioning previous legal frameworks (both those of the *de facto* rulers and those that did not prevent the breakdown of democracy), but may lead to serious institutional repercussions and to the rise of strong opposition from the established political classes and the judiciary. When governments change, there is also a problem with nominating new judges to the Supreme Court; these judges are identified with the new government, which can upset the balance between the different branches of the state if the court gives priority to the whims of the executive. The normal, slow pace of legal procedures becomes a factor of political importance in the transitions to democracy. In this context, the publication of human-rights violations committed under military rule and the political commitments of the democratic politicians who replace the military in power create expectations of the population for a rapid judicial treatment. Often, these expectations are disappointed by the judicial system's way of working, which is under constraints resulting from budgetary limitations, overload, and lack of personnel. There is a growing consensus in the three countries about the need to reform and modernize the judicial system, albeit in very general terms and beyond the common agreement about the importance of speeding up procedures and verdicts.[21]

These trends and dilemmas, present in Argentina as well as in Chile and Uruguay, developed in different ways in direct correlation with the paths of transition, particularly in connection with the visions and relative power of the different social and institutional actors. As discussed in previous chapters, in Argentina the government abolished the law of amnesty enacted by the military to cover their deeds. In Chile, the amnesty law by the military became part of the legal framework inherited by democracy and could not be abolished. In Uruguay, the pacted transition left to the civilian government the task of legislating an amnesty—the December 1986 Law of Expiry—which was contested by civil society but finally ratified by popular referendum. Uruguayan democracy confronted the above problems and dilemmas within the framework of the 1967 Constitution. In Argentina, the upheavals of the last decades and the post-authoritarian period created in 1994 the conditions for reforming the constitutional framework established in 1853. This reform was made possible by a political pact between President Menem and former President Alfonsín, the respective leaders of the Justicialist (Peronist) and Radical parties. The reformed Constitution of Argentina (1994) establishes that the constitution will prevail over any legislation made during *de facto* rule, and that those who violate the constitution will be punished with permanent exclusion from public office, with no chance for pardons or reduced sentences.[22] Article 36 also recognizes the right of the citizenry to resist by force any act aimed at overriding the constitution.[23] In article 75, the constitution grants constitutional rank to the international treaties on human rights, signed by Argentina, such as the Convention for the Prevention and Sanction of the Crime of Genocide, the Convention against Torture and Other Degrading, Inhumane and Cruel Treatments, the American Convention on Human Rights, and the International Pact on Civil and Political Rights.[24]

The local constitutional status of the international treaties on human rights was tested following Scilingo's declarations (see Chapter 3), as the CELS presented two exemplary judicial demands asking the Federal Penal Chamber of Buenos Aires to request the navy and the army to provide lists of detainees-disappeared. The idea was to force an official and/or institutional declaration of responsibility for the acts alluded to in Scilingo's confession, as well as to prompt the judicial recognition of the Right to Truth (held by the relatives of the victims and by society at large) and the relatives' Right to Mourn, which is denied them by the lack of verifiable details about the fate of the disappeared and the location of their remains. According to the thesis advanced by the plaintiffs, the impossibility of punishing the perpetrators of disappearances (sanctioned by the laws enacted by the civilian governments) does not infringe on the right to have a full and truthful account about their fate, as recognized by the principles and obligations of International Law explicitly accepted by the Argentine state and fully endorsed through the constitutional reform of 1994. The cases, opened in court in April 1995, were supported by the international organizations of Human Rights Watch/Americas (formerly Americas Watch) and the Center for Justice and International Law (CEJIL), which asked and were allowed to function as *amici curiae* and forward a report on international legislation concerning human rights and on the obligation of states to provide information about the fate of the *desaparecidos*. The court recognized the 'standing status' of the case and the rights involved, which CELS considered an achievement on its own. The court advanced requests of information to the navy and the army. However, as soon as the latter claimed lack of jurisdiction and lack of information, the Federal Penal Chamber decided in July 1995 to close the case. Martín Abregú, lawyer and executive director of the CELS, considered the decision as implying that the judicial system

recognized the rights at the basis of the claim and indicated its willingness to inquiry. Nonetheless, once those who are supposed to follow the court's instructions ignored them, the judiciary opted to bow or look the other way instead of imposing its hierarchical will and fulfil its role. [In Argentina] the judiciary does not take a firm stand to guarantee individual rights . . . when there are other [i.e. institutional] interests at stake.[25]

In Chile, the crises generated by the legacy of human-rights violations served the democratic government as a springboard for constitutional reform, in a protracted process that has not yet reached its conclusion. The *Letelier* case and its aftermath actualized the possibilities for constitutional reform. Frei's administration, which had declared in 1994 its intention to reform the Constitution, tied the expectations of the right-wing forces to speed up the judicial process to their accept-ance of constitutional reform and proposed changes in the armed forces' organic laws.

The mainstream forces of the Concertación wanted to use the situ-ation to attempt a dismantling of most of the authoritarian enclaves inherited from the previous military period.[26] Frei's proposal for con-stitutional reform included eliminating appointed senators, changing the nomination system of membership and tenure in the constitutional court, changing the membership of the National Security Council, and awarding the President the deciding vote to 'settle a tie'.[27] The pro-posal of legal change involved transferring all pending trials solely to civilian courts. By November 1995 a deal was reached between Presid-ent Frei and the leadership of Renovación Nacional (RN), the main opposition party, to advance a reform bill by a RN senator. According to the bill, special judges were to deal with these trials; priority was to be given to clarifying the fate of the *desaparecidos*, and incent-ives would be given to those who provided information. Whereas in Frei's proposal cases would remain open as long as no conclusion was reached about the missing victims, the RN proposal granted judges the authority to close cases whenever they believed no further informa-tion was obtainable. Without reforming the Amnesty Law of 1978, the new bill included mechanisms for safeguarding the integrity and hon-our of the members of the armed forces called to testify in court. If accepted, the RN bill would be applied to the mounting number of pend-ing cases (currently about 600) affecting nearly 1,000 individuals.[28] This legal initiative, supported by President Frei, the Christian Demo-cratic Party, the Radical Social Democratic Party, and the PPD, created a schism in the ruling coalition, since it was expressly opposed by the Socialist Party, which considered the proposal to be too lenient toward the repressors. In the right-wing opposition coalition (Pacto Unión por Chile), Pinochet's main supporters from the Unión Democrática Independiente (UDI) opposed the bill on the grounds that it would destroy the institutional framework created under Pinochet, in addition to being useless for the human-rights issues as it did not include deadlines for closing the pending cases. Even within the RN, no agreement was reached on the proposal.[29]

During 1997, most politicians have been avoiding the issue of the institutional closure, even as they tighten their muscles for the parliamentary elections scheduled for December 1997. Observers of the Chilean political scene explain this restraint in terms of the possible replication of seats (due to the Chilean binominal electoral system) and of the continued appointment of the non-elected senators, most of them sympathetic to the right. The retirement of General Pinochet from the supreme command of the armed forces (that took place on 11 March 1998) could open the way for talks between left-wing and right-wing forces, to change the current institutional impasse. The former would be interested in changing the legal status of many political activists who are still in prison or have been forced into exile. The latter could agree to reach a compromise on the human-rights front in order to attain a final closure on the issue, thus precluding any further allegations and suits against members of the security forces and their supporters.[30]

Human-Rights Violations under Democracy

The grim record of human-rights violations under military rule became central in the public agenda of the societies of the Southern Cone following the transition to democracy. The disclosures by the official and unofficial inquiries, journalistic and testimonial reports, and results of the judicial processes raised the consciousness of the population concerning the magnitude of past human-rights violations in these societies. This disclosure generated a widespread rejection of political repression among a substantial part of the population, on ethical grounds. Nonetheless, it also instilled fear by revealing that atrocities are likely to be committed in these societies if clashes over principles are not muted in the public sphere. The interpretations that this disclosure prompted were, however, varied in character, with some sectors defending the necessity of harsh repressive policies for the sake of social order and national integrity. Following redemocratization, when society experienced political destabilization and economic disruption—as under hyperinflation in Argentina—these attitudes became widespread, with substantial sectors of the population giving high priority to stability and order.

The tensions between keeping social order (of a certain kind) and respecting the rights of citizens, which under the military were strictly defined as a function of stability and order, were projected into the democratic period. In this period, these parameters were rethought within the tenets of political contingency and economic constraints, on the one hand, and ethical principles, on the other.

An ambivalent perception concerning human rights developed in the redemocratized societies of the Southern Cone. On the one hand, the focus on human-rights violations by the military generated a widely shared principled rejection of political polarization and violence as the major mechanism of resolving political conflicts. The cycle of political violence-anarchy-coercion-violence and further coercion was largely rejected, with only marginal sectors still willing to use violence to carry out personal revenge. The rejection of past repression was expressed in the newly incorporated discourse of human rights, which provided the public sphere with a conceptual frame with which to address the legacy of human-rights violations and any other forms of abuses under democracy. This trend is strengthening one of the basic tenets of democracy: consensual mechanisms of conflict resolution. Political and intellectual elites profess their commitment to human rights. Legal and constitutional reforms were initiated or attempted in all three countries that aimed to preclude in different ways and degrees any possible recurrence of human-rights violations like those the societies knew in the recent past. The media plays a major role introducing these issues—albeit with short and only intermitent incursions—into the public sphere.

On the other hand, human-rights violations have continued to be reported in these countries, albeit in somewhat new directions and with much public tolerance. The reports identify at least four major dimensions of human-rights abuses under democracy in the Southern Cone societies. These concern, first, abuses by police forces in anti-criminal operations and while interrogating and holding detainees; second, abuses performed in prisons and other reclusion centres; third, actions committed by members of the security forces for lucrative purposes; and fourth, persisting human-rights abuses committed on a political basis or against journalists.[31]

There are differences concerning the prevalence of these various forms of abuses in the three countries. Human-rights violations under democracy have been reported concerning Argentina more often than Chile and Uruguay, even though constitutional reform in the former has buttressed formal guarantees and strengthened personal and collective freedoms. Leading Argentine political figures consider that the reported events of police violence are not part of an endemic phenomenon but constitute specific instances, that should be—and are—treated by the law on a particular basis.[32] We consider that the relatively larger infringement of human rights and greater sense of impunity in

Argentine democracy supports the hypothesis that the greater the real or perceived threat of destabilization in these societies the greater the willingness of the population to support the use of force to keep order and stability, thus encouraging (or at least, not curtailing) instances of police brutality.

Another indication is provided by cases of harassment of journalists, which have proliferated in recent years in Argentina, in connection with the growing (and for some observers, exaggerated) influence of the media in the country's public sphere and criticisms made concerning presidential policies.[33]

In all three countries, there have been reports of police violence and torture in operations and during detention of criminals. In Chile, for example, under democracy dozens of cases of torture by Carabineros were recorded, most of them taking place in 1990–2 at the Third Police Headquarters in Santiago, without leading to trial of those responsible. Between 1992 and 1995 forty-six cases of human-rights violations were reported by Nigel S. Rodley, special UN reporter on human rights. Most of these cases involved brutal treatment of common delinquents and suspects, often leading to torture. According to Rodley, these violations are possible due to the laxity of judges and lack of legislative guarantees concerning the complete subordination of the security forces to the civilian authorities.[34] In Argentina, between 1985 and 1989, more than 400 cases of civilian deaths in police operations were reported for the city of Buenos Aires and the surrounding areas of the province of Buenos Aires alone. Several cases of kidnappings—'disappearances'— by police personnel and army personnel were also noted. Beatings by the police, in order to extract confessions and as part of police control, seem to have been common in the 1980s and 1990s. Between 1984 and 1986, 698 cases of maltreatment were denounced; 879 such denunciations were made in 1989 and 870 in 1990. Between 1989 and 1991, only one person was brought to trial on these grounds. Reports attest to the application of burnings with cigarettes, with less frequent references to the use of *picanas* (cattle-prods), i.e. of torture by electricity.

Dubious cases of suicide have taken place in police quarters and penitentiaries. In Uruguay, three such cases were reported in 1989. Protest and further investigation led to the hypothesis that these deaths resulted from police beatings, producing a scandal and the resignation of the Minister of Interior. Also reported widely has been the indiscriminate detention and harassment of youngsters, without ensuing presentation of charges. Demonstrations and a strike in the educational sector took place in 1990 against Uruguayan police violence and their *razzias* (raids) in popular neighbourhoods. The highest rate of deaths resulted from police operations in which suspects were fired upon and killed on the spot. Some Uruguayan police officers have been tried for their involvement in such events. In Uruguay, the Human Rights Commission of the Parliament has often summoned Ministers of Interior on these grounds, denouncing police abuse.[35] In Argentina, by the early 1990s a substantial number of police officers (estimated at 800) had been discharged as the result of their involvement in human-rights abuses committed while on duty in the province of Buenos Aires alone. In 1991, relatives of citizens affected by police abuses in Argentina created a Commission of Relatives of Victims of Institutional Violence. In addition, lawyers dealing with cases related to police violence have established a coordinating association, Coordinadora contra la Represión Policial e Institucional (CORREPI). Pockets of police violence have continued to appear in certain areas, for example in the province of Buenos Aires. Student protest and demonstrations exploded in different parts of the country around the ratification in early 1996 of a new federal law of higher education in Argentina. In La Plata, a traditional hotbed of student activism, the police of the Province of Buenos Aires reacted with force, detaining over 200 students and repressing a demonstration which pleaded for their release; the police used gas, rubber bullets, and beating sticks, wounding several demonstrators, including Hebe de Bonafini and a TV cameraman. As the students ran to the woods, they were met—according to witnesses —by undercover police personnel in civilian clothes and driving the same unidentified cars used during the PRN. Following harsh criticism, earlier declarations by the governor in praise of the police were followed by the officials' recognition of excessive use of force, by the denial that there was a systematic 'methodology of violence', and by the assertion that individual policemen were responsible, not the institution, and those who had committed excesses were to be discharged. Despite the denial, many instances of police violence have taken place in the province of Buenos Aires; in 1995, for instance, 123 out of the 195 deaths due to police actions country-wide took place there. CELS attibuted the alarming figures to the 'lack of preparation [two-thirds have finished only basic school] and lack of training of the police [courses are 3 months long] and to pressures due to its bureaucratic structure and regulations.'[36]

In all three countries, the conditions of imprisonment for common prisoners have been denounced as inhumane. Acts of brutality and abuses are commonly reported in the overcrowded prisons, where alimentary and sanitary conditions are deficient and overcrowding is the norm. Long periods of detention without trial and lack of proper legal assistance are common. Rebellions in prisons are endemic and their repression harsh. Conditions are especially problematic in the centres of juvenile detention, where cases of suicide and attempted suicide were commonly reported, especially in Uruguay. Members of Parliament and the SERPAJ jointly demanded the humanization of the penitentiary system. In 1991, as a result of continuous reports of mistreatment of prisoners in police dependencies, the Fiscalía Letrada Nacional de la Policía, that is, the Internal Comptroller of the Police of Uruguay, was created. Some officers responsible for mistreatment and torture were demoted as part of the Fiscalía's inquiries, even though many indications were found of police cover-up. In 1992, reports and photographs appeared in the press conveying the suffering of prisoners, tied to their beds as part of routine punishment in the Libertad prison of Montevideo.[37] Beatings of prisoners and abuses were widely reported for Argentine prisons, especially in 1985.

Whereas under military rule, security personnel kidnapped and assassinated individuals for political reasons, under democracy the same techniques have been adopted by some security personnel for extortion and personal gain. In Argentina, in 1985, a number of business people kidnapped by both current and retired officers attracted public attention, concomitant to the planting of explosive devices, threats, and intimidations, which motivated the establishment of a sixty-day state of siege by the democratic administration.[38]

The role of armies in internal repression has disappeared since democratization. However, there have been a few notorious cases in which gross human-rights violations have been reported. In Argentina, a great deal of public attention was attracted by the treatment of those who attacked the Third Infantry Regiment barracks at La Tablada, Buenos Aires. Following the attack and the counter-attack by the army, allegations were made of torture, 'disappearances' and extra-judicial executions of the members of the Movimiento Todos por la Patria (MTP—All for the Fatherland Movement) by the security forces in January 1989.[39] Similarly, there is evidence of use of force within the ranks of the Argentine army, in which informal and non-contractual relationships prevail as a central regulative mechanism throughout the hierarchies of command, and especially in forms of abusive treatment of the lower ranks. The assassination of Private Omar Carrasco in 1994 and other similar cases were made public, creating momentum for cancelling the system of mandatory military service in Argentina.[40] In Chile, a similar case of assassination of a private during compulsory military service produced different institutional results. In March 1997, the remains of Private Pedro Soto Tapia of the Yungay battalion were found in a mine pit. As the inquiry languished, President Frei demanded a rapid and efficient judicial treatment in May 1997. The army reacted in a monolithic manner, rejecting the claim that human-rights violations had taken place in its ranks and supporting instead the thesis of a common crime.[41] Despite the grim dimensions of such events, a major change from previous decades should be emphasized, as these violations of human rights do not go unnoticed nowadays, and they are made public within the framework of the human-rights discourse that the Argentine and Chilean public spheres have incorporated.[42]

Under democracy, there are still signs of persisting use of violence and infringement of human rights rooted in the polarized visions that prevailed in the period preceding military rule and during military rule itself. During the tense periods in civil–military relations in 1989–90, firearm attacks and explosives were used by Argentine right-wing organizations against members of the judiciary, journalists, and politicians. In the 1990s, the headquarters of Mothers of Plaza de Mayo were ransacked several times, and their leader, Hebe de Bonafini, received menacing phone calls. Cinematographic director Francisco Solanas was shot by unidentified persons following the publication of an article in *Página/12*, in which he harshly criticized the government. Politicians, judges, journalists, and correspondents of the foreign media were threatened and some of them were attacked. In Chile, there have been various cases of attack and killing of security personnel and political figures (e.g. the assassination of Jaime Guzmán in April 1991 and the attempt against the life of retired General Gustavo Leigh, ex-member of the first military junta in 1990) by left-wing organizations seeking vindication, revenge, and 'popular justice' for the victims of military repression. More than thirty terrorist attacks on Mormon churches were conducted by the Movimiento Juvenil Lautaro, which considered the Mormonsa spearhead of North American influence in Chile. The son of the director of *El Mercurio* was kidnapped in 1991 by the FPMR. Political violence of this sort has been noted less often in Uruguay. During 1992, clandestine armed organizations closely related to the military appeared in Uruguay, such as Guardia de Artigas and Comando Juan A. Lavalleja. These organizations were allegedly responsible for placing some small explosive devices.

The above violations of human rights have been publicly reported both nationally, by the media, the NGOs concerned, and parliamentary commissions, and internationally, by such agencies as the US Department of State, Amnesty International, the Interamerican Commission for Human Rights of the OAS, and United Nations agencies. The awareness that the reports of these forums and agencies have created in the public sphere creates the possibility of reaching negotiated and normative solutions to the emerging problems in the area of human rights. Nonetheless, societies possessing wide knowledge about human-rights violations committed in their midst can but do not necessarily enact political and normative measures to curtail such violations.[43]

For vast sectors of public opinion, a strong hand against criminals is considered as necessary. Uruguayans, for example, have been increasingly supportive of the need to impose the death penalty for certain crimes and of harsher penalties for other crimes. In 1987, 36 per cent of Montevideo's population supported the death penalty; in 1992, the percentage rose to 42 and, in 1995, to 45 per cent. In 1995, 83 per cent of the country sample favoured harsher punishments for criminals.[44]

Not long ago a Law of Public Security was enacted, which augments the terms of punishment for a wide array of crimes. The law does not lower the minimum age for standing trial, but allows the incarceration of minors . . . The law was easily approved by Parliament without raising public attention, because of the growing demands for personal security voiced by broad sectors of the population, as if personal security could be secured through harsher terms of retaliation.[45]

This demand stands in contradiction with the recent historical experience and the high levels of mobilization against the Law of Expiry.

. . . There is a growth or a change in the types of delinquency that emerge in the city [of Montevideo]. People feel insecure. On the one hand, they abhor policial repression; on the other hand, they need it. This shapes an ambiguity that is very strange, since people trace their attitudes toward repression to their rejection of military dictatorship and, at the same time, they claim that the marginal elements only understand the language of force. We now stand at an ambiguous crossroads.[46]

In Argentina too, there has been a generalized feeling of lack of personal security in metropolitan areas and distrust of the police, which increased in the 1990s. In a June 1990 poll conducted in the capital city and the greater Buenos Aires 76.7 per cent felt 'unprotected'.[47] By mid-1996 the percentage rose to 85.3 per cent.[48] The most widespread reactions expressed towards the police were fear, distrust, and feelings of insecurity, which covered 40.6 per cent and 61.5 per cent of all responses in March and August 1996 polls, respectively.[49] Ninety per cent of respondents in another sample were of the opinion that violence had become more acute from May 1995 to May 1996.[50] In August 1996, nearly 70 per cent pointed out that the major factor contributing to increased delinquency was the rising unemployment. Nonetheless, in terms of possible solutions, people moved from suggesting structural long-term solutions to demanding harsh punitive short-term measures.[51] A criminal case in mid-1996 generated this sort of outcry for harsh punishment, as noted by Gabriel Fernández:

People read the headlines of the evening newspapers and went back home commenting that criminals like Sopapita deserve the death penalty, that the police should enter the shantytown (*villas*) by force since the majority of their inhabitants are thieves and protect the gunmen, that it is hard to understand how we can live this way, and that it is better for the neighbourhood shop owners to pay the police what they ask [to pay them bribes], even if sometimes they overdo it with the kids, but at least they maintain security.[52]

These ambivalent attitudes toward human rights also exist in redemocratized Chile. In spite of the economic boom that began in 1985, there is a perception of rising crime. In a country-wide opinion poll conducted in 1991, 71.8 per cent of the interviewed considered criminality the main problem in redemocratized Chile.[53] In 1996, 84.2 per cent claimed that crime had become more violent in the last year.[54] Maintaining order in the country was an ongoing preoccupation for around 50 per cent of the population in the early 1990s, increasing to around 65 per cent in the late 1990s.[55] Polls have found that an overwhelming majority of the interviewed supported maintaining the death penalty for major crimes. In a poll conducted in April–May 1997 among an urban national sample, 54.5 per cent supported maintaining the death penalty without the possibility of presidential pardon, and an additional 20.6 per cent were in favour of that measure with the possibility of presidential pardon.[56] The demand for harsher punishments is related to the attitudes shown to those in charge of public order and justice. Although there are records of police violence, the close association between the police and the military and the latter's preserved autonomy and strength place the demands for increased personal security and its possible repercussions in the form of human-rights violations, in a somewhat different perspective from that in Uruguay and Argentina. A peculiarity of the Chilean situation is the relatively high level of prestige of the armed forces and the police, reflected in indices of trust in the commanders of the police forces (Carabineros and Investigaciones) higher than those expressed towards the Supreme Court and the criminal courts.[57]

Educational Policies

Argentina, Chile, and Uruguay faced the need to reconstruct their educational systems and programmes, in order to resocialize the younger generations and develop manpower capabilities in directions that would meet the envisaged prospects of redemocratizing their societies and modernizing their market economies. Market-oriented trends are reflected in the new contents and practices of educational reform in the positivist development of skills related to efficiency, quality, and professionalism. At the same time, humanistic contents have been addressed by the educational systems and incorporated in the programmes as part of the political process of redemocratization and rejection of previous military repression. For instance, the theme of human rights has been introduced in the formal curricula. Nonetheless, the inconclusive stage of elaboration of the legacy of human-rights violations brought about a situation in which human rights are formally taught but dissociated from the realities of their implementation or the lack thereof in these societies.

In all three countries human rights have entered curricula in two distinct domains. One includes human rights as part of their formal civic educational programmes. In this manner, students are taught the development and tenets of universal human-rights concepts, as sustained internationally and as formally incorporated by their countries' constitutions and legal systems. In parallel, the legacy of human-rights violations has also been addressed in different ways through the history programmes of these countries.

In the first domain, studies have followed mostly a legal and formal approach, disconnected from local historical experiences and current realities. In the second domain, studies have been elaborated often only in broad strokes in order to fit within the political and institutional constraints of each country. In the students' minds, the disjuncture between the formalistic, legal principles addressed in civic studies and the social and political experiences addressed in historical studies shape a cognitive dissonance, that is challenged only when issues related to infringements of human rights regain public attention from time to time.

Educators who have worked in the Southern Cone countries in the drafting of projects for reforming the curricula have drawn attention not only to the need to recentralize the teaching of human rights, but also about the relevance of looking for dynamic ways of bridging the above disjuncture. Illustrative of this have been the drafts prepared by Argentine teachers for the contents of the General Basic Education framework in 1994. In those drafts, they state in connection with human rights and moral development that

Beyond knowledge, the programme should encourage discussion and shape the required skills for personal and moral development, civil responsibility, and a consciousness about human rights with critical capability.

. . . Although the educational contents may be taught separately in different disciplines, the basic themes should cut in an interdisciplinary way throughout the breadth of the educational work.[58]

The draft conditions the understanding of human-rights issues to a historical contextualization:

Issues related to gender, to children and youth, to unemployment, to cultural and ethnic differences, to hunger and mortality due to lack of health services, all these have their own characteristics, their rates, their own social dynamics and their own histories.

All human rights substance (rights and norms, the constitution and democracy, civil and political rights, economic, social and cultural rights) are directly related to a concrete social background. Rights are there to be implemented, not to remain at the level of formulation of knowledge alone.[59]

Such a comprehensive vision of human rights, which can be found in various projects in Uruguay and Chile too, has met serious difficulties on the road to implementation. Working against their implementation are a myriad of factors, foremost the constraints posed by policies of economic adjustment that reduce available budgets for education; the spirit of economic neoliberalism reducing the appeal of discourses of social solidarity (and of interpretations of human rights moving beyond individual rights, civil and political) and the political contingencies pressing towards the marginalization of human-rights issues.[60] As a result, many worthwhile projects have been rendered inconsequential, being watered down on the road to their official endorsement and implementation.

In Argentina primary- and high-school texts and teachers' manuals stress the value of democracy. At the more general level, democracy forms part of the courses of 'Ethical and Civic Studies' that are taught during the third year of high school (the first year of the so-called *Escuela Polimodal*). In the framework of these courses, democracy is presented as heavily anchored in its ethical value and its capacity for protecting individual human rights. The school has the responsibility to instil the student with 'democratic values' such as 'the pursuit of well being, the search for truth, life, the dignity of human beings, love, peace, harmony, solidarity, friendship, mutual understanding, justice, freedom, tolerance, honesty, intercultural and international understanding'.[61] In one of the official publications of the Ministry of Education for teachers, the major aims of teaching civic and ethical studies are stated clearly:

When the Federal Law of Education establishes that the educational system will enable the integral education of men and women it refers to the need for educating for democratic life, for environmental conservation, health, love, work, the respect and defence of human rights. The reasons to teach ethical and civic studies in the primary educational cycle: In order to shape full persons and citizens who are responsible, critical and solidary, through the development of their moral personality. . . . To promote understanding of the importance of full personal development; the adoption of basic values and the critical, respectful assessment of others' opinions; developing the capacity for arguing, linking ethical principles with actions, values, and social norms; the understanding of the importance of the National Constitution and the legal national and international recognition of human rights for the full attainment of personal and social potentials.[62]

There is a great difference between the above educational aims of citizenship through formal education and the elaboration of the legacy of human-rights violations as a mechanism for instilling such consciousness among the new generations. In the history texts, generally taught to primary-school students aged 11 and 12 and to high-school students aged 15, the transfer of power from Alfonsín to Menem is presented as the most important event in the history of the country in the twentieth century. This event is taught as proof of the consolidation of democracy in Argentina. National history is portrayed as besieged by the continuous intervention of the military in politics resulting from political instability and economic chaos. The cycle of recurrent waves of chaos—democratic breakdowns—and restoration of democracy is depicted as finally interrupted by the great achievement of democratic continuity during the last two administrations. The last three decades, and especially the PRN period, are presented as the antithesis of the current institutionalization of democracy. Repression is portrayed in a rather sketchy and uncritical way, as a natural consequence of the polarization, destabilization, and violence that pervaded society in the 1970s.[63]

In most textbooks the crucial events of the regressive policy trends that concerned the legacy of human-rights violations (the laws of Final Point and Due Obedience and the Semana Santa military uprising) are not mentioned at all. Exceptional in this respect are a few pedagogical works elaborated by private institutions and individuals such as *Historia 3: el mundo contemporáneo* and the comprehensive socio-historical analysis by Torcuato S. Di Tella, *Historia Argentina 1830–1992*.[64]

At the university level, especially in faculties of law, human rights are formally taught. At the University of Buenos Aires, the first chair was Dr Eduardo Rabossi, a member of CONADEP and first subsecretary of human rights under Alfonsín.

An effort in bridging the problems rooted in disciplinary divisions and static emphases on human rights has been accomplished recently, in a book which is intended to serve as an interdisciplinary textbook for high-school teachers and students in social sciences and civic formation. This book, *Haciendo memoria en el país de Nunca más*, touches fundamental issues related to the framework of state and society, youth, violence and tolerance, memory and oblivion, reaching out to the readers through pictures, tables, reproduced documents, questions and tasks for elaboration. This book sets a model of work, the efficiency of which has yet to be tested.[65]

According to the testimonies of young people, in the 1980s students were exposed more intensively to Argentine history of before 1930 than to later events. Children acquired some knowledge of the events that took place under military rule mainly outside school, through films and TV programmes, the *Nunca más* report (which in the 1990s was introduced to the high schools), and public demonstrations and the work of the NGOs.[66]

The impact of formal teaching on the formation of a dynamic and broad interpretation of human rights has been reduced by a threefold process. First, the state has tended to separate civil and political rights from socio-economic rights, not endorsing a cross-disciplinary and contextual approach, as suggested in the programmes of educational reform mentioned above. Second, a dearth of budgets has led to the impoverishment of the educational system, especially in the peripheries, distant from the central cities, resulting in rising levels of student absenteeism. Third, the decentralization of the educational system has granted greater autonomy to teachers, thus creating wider disparity between those willing and those resisting any contextualization of human-rights issues in Argentina. 'Everything is there, written [in the programmes]. In practice, in the courses, it may stay as an abstraction, unrelated to life, unless we teachers concretize human rights by discussing real situations and problems.'[67] Accordingly, the emphasis on teaching human rights within the educational system has hinged upon the specific interests and skills of the teaching staff, especially as the system entered a period of decentralization. Around the twentieth anniversary of the coup a flurry of activities took place. In some cases, such as the Liceo Nueve and the Bet-El Jewish Community School, youngsters prepared their own projects on the legacy of human-rights violations, professing their will not to forget and not to allow the repetition of repression in Argentina:

The pit of terror will never again threaten to devour us. . . . Neither unjust laws nor pardons will ever erase our memory. As long as memory lives, the guilty will still be guilty and those horrendous events will not happen again. . . . We cannot forget the victims, those who fell defending freedom, in order that the sun of democracy and justice will shine again.[68]

The educational authorities have introduced the theme of human rights into the formal curriculum, but the instilling of a broader consciousness about the issue has depended more on its development in the public sphere and on extra-curricular processes than on formal decisions alone.

In Uruguay, the Council of High School Education (Consejo de Educación Secundaria) in 1986 issued new programmes for the courses in Moral and Civic Education, Introduction to Sociology, and Introduction to Law. In Moral and Civic Education, 15-year-old students during their third year of high school are exposed to international documents on human rights (of the ONU, the Interamerican Institute of Human Rights) and to the national provisions in the Uruguayan Constitution, as well as to an analytical classification of types of rights. The emphasis is legal. In Introduction to Law, to be taught during the sixth year of humanistic secondary studies, much attention is given to the topic of human rights, even though the approach begins with a detailed analysis of current legislation, which is decontextualized from past events and present uncertainties and problems.[69] A major shift can be traced in the new syllabus issued by the Council of High School Education for Social and Civic Education in 1993.[70] One of five units in the syllabus is devoted to the study of human rights. In addition to the analysis of the international conventions on human rights and the constitutional guarantees, previously existent, the new syllabus also links the above legislation with the analysis of a democratic order that should ensure human rights. Teachers are encouraged to deal with a local phenomenon affecting citizens' rights (e.g. the housing situation) and to coordinate joint classes with history teachers on the development of human rights in Uruguay. Nevertheless, recent Uruguayan developments are not mentioned in this syllabus, either. In addition, the treatment of human rights occupies the last unit of studies, which increases the chances that students will not reach the topic as a consequence of delays, strikes, and other circumstances.

SERPAJ has played a central role in the pedagogical entrenchment and diffusion of human rights. In 1994 and in 1995, it organized among teachers contests of essays and proposals for teaching human rights. SERPAJ has published a series of teaching manuals and articles for teachers, which provided both a theoretical background and a number of proposed activities that could contribute to learning the subject in both its formal and informal dimensions. The available material includes the first issue of the journal *Educación y derechos humanos, cuadernos para docentes: reflexiones y experiencias*[71] and the book by Francisco Bustamante and María Luisa González, *Derechos humanos en el aula*, which is an encompassing, up-to-date, and easy-to-read guide for secondary-school teachers.[72] Using a friendly graphic design, human rights are dealt with in a practical manner, which enables students to engage in numerous activities and assess autonomously what their rights are and how to use them if, for example, they are raided by the police as they leave a discotheque. Texts of a variety of Latin American writers are used to introduce the students to complex subjects. Human rights also include social, cultural, and ecological rights. Yet, specific references to human-rights violations under the military are absent. Despite its high quality and educational value, author María Luisa González recognizes the book has had a limited impact in the educational system. Of the 1,000 copies published, barely 300 have been sold.[73]

On the other hand, history textbooks tend to leave the normative questions aside. One example is the history textbook by Benjamín Nahum, *Manual de historia del Uruguay 1903–1990* (volume ii). This book thoroughly deals with the dictatorial and democratic periods, dedicating much attention to the transition process, the demands of justice, the Law of Expiry, and the referendum. The account is basically from a political perspective, that is, it analyses how the various political parties reacted to different problems and how solutions were adopted. It is a political history that leaves aside normative questions.[74]

There are many well-documented reference books that focus on modern and contemporary Uruguayan history, which focus on the military dictatorship. An excellent work is the four-volume series *El Uruguay de la dictadura*, written by well-known historians and social scientists.[75] Schools have also prepared extensive lists of reference texts that can be used in teaching the recent history of the country and the human-rights problem as a whole.[76] Nevertheless, the 'freedom-of-education principle' in Uruguay determines that no compelling directives are to be developed concerning the uses of this extensive material. As in Argentina, the teaching of human rights in Uruguay depends on the combined effects of the teachers' will, their capabilities, the students' interests, and other (time and labour) constraints. Consequently, there is disparity in the concrete educational curricula in this field. Human rights are mostly studied by presenting their legal and formal basis at both the international and the national levels, with very few attempts to include the collective and concrete experiences of the last decades in the treatment of the issue. At the same time, SERPAJ has directed major efforts at presenting the topic in a lively and practical way, but has achieved limited results from this endeavour.

As in the other countries, in Chile there is also a basic disjuncture between the teaching of human rights as part of civic education and as part of history. The last few years in civic education has witnessed a slow process of programme and textbook revision. One of the new textbooks on civic education emphasizes the normative and legal approach, referring to the Chilean context through a short but critical discussion of the institutionalization of military rule and the enacting of the 1980 Constitution, which enshrined property rights.[77] In the study of history, there is a great disparity in the contents of textbooks. Earlier texts that were written under Pinochet and, as such, were highly sympathetic to military rule, are being slowly replaced by texts that are variously critical or uncritical to the dictatorship and the problem of human rights.[78] Luis Emilio Rojas's *Nueva historia de Chile*, published in 1991, is a clear attempt to change earlier approaches. Rojas dedicates much attention to showing the illegal nature of the military coup, Pinochet's policies, and their impact on Chilean society and collective memory. Some attention is given to military abuses. According to the author, repression has left Chilean society deeply wounded and in need of reconciliation. The book also deals to some extent with economic recession and damage caused by neoliberal economic polices. The exile, the forces of opposition to the dictatorship and its abuses on human rights, the murder of Letelier and Prats and the DSN are also treated as important issues. As Chile achieves democracy, the rejection of violence toward all political forces is portrayed as a major objective.[79]

The Corporación Nacional de Reparación y Reconciliación was entrusted with the task of structuring the educational and cultural policies affecting human rights. Accordingly, since 1993 this public corporation has carried out a series of activities such as organizing annual contests of essays and seminars for training educational personnel in teaching human rights, collecting and publishing bibliographical lists, dictionaries, and pedagogical guides for teachers, and stimulating research on education and human rights.[80] As a result of the contests, collections of the best essays were published in book format.[81] A series of projects and educational proposals of reforms have also been developed by the Corporation, supported by the government, and by NGOs such as the Chilean SERPAJ.[82] Thus, a duality remains in the educational realm, opposing the advanced character of some of these programmes to the non-consensual character of the study of the military period. This duality is probably connected to the continuing presence and strength of the armed forces as part of the loci of institutional power and to the ongoing inability of the major political and social forces to reach an agreed vision of the past in contemporary Chile.

Another important issue in educating for democratic life, not thoroughly treated in this work, concerns the educational curricula of the security and armed forces. According to the opinions of human-rights experts, shy attempts have been made in Argentina and Uruguay to introduce the theme of human rights in police training. In Chile, the theme is still politically charged and therefore difficult even to discuss in the framework of the security and armed forces.[83] An important project designed to strengthen democratic culture in Latin America is currently being conducted at the Latin American Studies Center of the University of Maryland, under the joint direction of Saúl Sosnowski and Edy Kaufman. The project has begun training military staff officers from Argentina, Peru, and other Latin American countries in the field of human rights.[84]

In all three countries, research and seminars have produced a wide array of proposals on how to advance the subject of human rights in the educational system and in the public culture. This process of proposal creation seems to be stronger and more rapid than the political, economic, social, and organizational capacity of the educational systems to absorb them. There have been serious discussions in these countries about the importance of reformulating education, incorporating the formal study of human rights into the curricula, or enhancing consciousness about human rights. There is still significant dissonance between the scope of the proposals and declaration of principles and their pragmatic implementation in the fields of education and culture.

·················
5
·················

Comparing Paths in the Confrontation with Human-Rights Violations

Comparing Paths and Performances

The institutional paths examined in Chapters 2–4 had distinctive characteristics. Each Southern Cone society looked for ways to address the issues raised by the legacy of human-rights violations. Within its own institutional path and constraints, each society developed detailed policies that dealt with the different aspects of its legacy in ways that made sense in terms of the local forces, perceptions, and trends. Each society looked for precedents and tried to assess the adequacy of the institutional path followed by the other countries, finding inspiration and recognizing dangers in the experience of others.

This chapter attempts a systematic comparative analysis of these paths. It is aimed at understanding how and under what contextual circumstances each society has followed a different path in treating its own legacy of repression in terms of human-rights violations.

We assess four factors as potentially crucial in creating this differentiation, through their relative and variable impact on five key domains and issues to be dealt with in societies with legacies of human-rights violations. The factors are: first, the different social, political, and legal traditions of each country; second, the specific institutional mechanisms adopted by the political leaders in each case; third, the balance of forces between the different social and political actors—the military, the NGOs, the government, and the opposition—and their attitudes towards the process, during and after the transition; and fourth, the relative success or failure of implementing policies for confronting the legacy of human-rights violations inherited from the military period and, particularly, the political steering of the problem. The variable character and combination of these factors have structured the development of distinctive patterns for dealing with this authoritarian legacy in each society. All three countries have had to deal, however, with common issues and problems crucial to the reconstruction of their societies given the legacies of human-rights violations inherited from military rule.

The five key issues that had to be addressed by these societies were: first, the issue of how to achieve thorough knowledge about the past experience and some agreed-upon version of truth; second, where they position themselves in the continuum between accountability and impunity/immunity; third, what can or has to be done in terms of acknowledging wrongs, expiation, official 'excusation' and requests of forgiveness addressed to the victims; fourth, what has been achieved in the domain of reparation and compensation; and fifth, where these societies stand vis-à-vis the prospects of moving beyond the problem of past human-rights violations, through the use of various formulae and mechanisms of reconciliation, memory, and oblivion.

In the following paragraphs we assess the combined impact of the above factors on the detailed issues and domains. In Argentina, the plurality of channels and mechanisms used by the first democratic government, and especially the CONADEP commission report and the trials of the military commanders, prompted widespread and cathartic recognition of the magnitude of the problem after the transition to democracy. Looking retrospectively, writer Ricardo Piglia recalls the psychologically charged atmosphere and the plot that became dominant with democratization:

[With Alfonsín] there is a change of genre towards the psychological novel. Society was encouraged to conduct a review of conscience. The technique of the inner monologue was generalized. A sort of gothic autobiographical style was constructed, with guilt at its core: [There were talks about] the despotic tendency of the Argentines; the fascist dwarf that dwelt inside; the subjective authoritarianism. Political debate was internalized. Everybody had to construct an autobiographical story to see what personal ties he or she had maintained with the authoritarian and terrorizing state. It is hard to find a better built fallacy: To distribute responsibilities in a democratic way . . .[1]

People expected that full justice was attainable and that the CONADEP report could provide comprehensive truth. According to Mark Osiel, the adversarial structure of judicial proceedings could represent to the larger public the drama of ideas and debate around the opposed historiographical interpretations of the experience of repression. But developments defied the foundational expectations of attaining justice: 'If dramatic catharsis and social connection [were] to result, they [had to] emerge from this very process of civil dissensus, rather than from any hope of its immediate resolution by the court.'[2] As time passed, demands for individualized justice mounted in parallel with the increasing pressures exerted by the armed forces on the executive to put an end to those demands and trials. Otto Kirchheimer and Juan E. Corradi referred to the peculiar combination of intense expectations and partial results in terms of transitional justice. According to Corradi, transitional justice is 'a particular and intensive type of political justice: the trial by fiat of a previous regime . . . Such trials are especially intense because they pose before the entire community the ultimate problem: the fact that the exercise of justice is at the same time indispensable and impossible.'[3] It is within these dilemmas that the Argentine public sphere was opened wide to the phenomenon of open-ended catharsis and, later, unfulfilled expectations. Towards the late 1980s a regressive turn of policies was under way. The turning point in dealing with the legacy of human-rights violations and, on a wider scale, with civic–military relationships can be identified in the April 1987 Semana Santa military uprising. During the crisis, the political steering of the problem by President Alfonsín was decisive in eroding the public trust and the massive support of civil society. As a result of this crisis, the civic–military balance of forces changed. The laws promulgated aborted the judicial track and pardons were granted that liberated the convicted military leaders, finally putting to rest the earlier high expectations of civil society about reaching comprehensive truth and justice.

Under the changing circumstances of governance and political steering and the deteriorating macroeconomic conditions, the operative failure of most of the institutional and informal ways of treatment led to discouragement among most social sectors over the treatment of the human-rights violations legacy. In addition, the controversy around this legacy became a source of instability in the already tense civil–military relationships, adding a preoccupying dimension to the chronic socio-economic crisis. The incoming administration of Menem decided to address the whole problem by neutralizing the major source of concern for the consolidation of democracy: civil–military relations, in which one of the key issues was the legacy of human-rights abuses. The Menem government's policy of pardons was intended to create national reconciliation by decree. The 'national reconciliation' led by the authorities was more a result of political decisions and the government's capacity to control the public agenda. It did not effect deep attitudinal change or contribute to achieving consensus over the experience of human-rights abuses.

Towards the early 1990s past human-rights violations were marginalized in a public sphere marked by a series of political compromises, leaving concerned sectors of society with a feeling that neither truth nor justice could be expected and that the struggle to reach them was a Sisyphean task. The combination of the repentant declarations of a retired military officer and the wide coverage provided by central figures of the media generated consternation. The revelations shocked many of the members of the new generation, who had previously ignored the issue, and reminded the older generations of past repression and disappearances. These developments reinvigorated the persistent claim of the Mothers of Plaza de Mayo and other NGOs that the legacy of human-rights violations was of great importance and magnitude for Argentine society and still had to be confronted in serious and radical ways. General Balza's declarations went beyond acknowledgement and reformulated the stand of the armed forces in democracy, centring it on a commitment to respect human rights in whatever situation may evolve. Although Balza's position was contested within the high commands, his public stance in his capacity as commander-in-chief had deep implications for the future of civil–military understandings in Argentina. The combination between Scilingo's declarations and remorse, the debate that once again dominated the centre of the public sphere, and the stand taken by General Balza provided new forms of recognizing truth and acknowledgement by sectors previously in favour of keeping the issue out of the public sphere. The path of Argentine crises brought about a measure of truth implying acknowledgement of brutal acts against humankind and, in Scilingo's case, some form of repentance. Parallel acts of violent revenge against former repressors were part of the scenario of 'unfinished business': lack of official information about the fate of the missing and impunity of repressors that had committed gross human-rights violations.

In the mid-1990s Argentina was still debating in new ways the issues that were relevant in the mid-1980s. Nonetheless, after the closure of the main channels of institutional resolution, which were exhausted in the 1980s, the issue becomes central to the public agenda through individual acts that may enable cathartic reactions in civil society, constituting the core of a new crisis, and leading to institutional reactions.

Uruguay has possessed a public sphere in which the patterns of participation were primarily defined by its rules of civility. Among them, the provision for a popular referendum was especially instrumental in confronting the legal methods used by the political class. Individuals and NGOs challenged the democratic government's policy of legislation for closing the issue. The process leading from the promulgation of the Law of Expiry in December 1986 to the referendum in April 1989 involved high levels of civil contestation, popular mobilization, debate, and a widespread process of social learning about the violations and their social and political implications. During the months leading up to the referendum, the debate dominated the entire public sphere. Civil society contested the power of the particracy of Uruguay, which, according to one of its most prominent members, had negotiated with the military an institutional compromise sealed by the Law of Expiry. As civil society played a prominent role in the institutional moves leading to the referendum, the defeat of those who opposed the Law of Expiry signalled the institutional closure of the issue in ways respected by winners and losers alike. Uruguayans used respected democratic mechanisms to solve one of the most thorny issues left over by military rule. For some, the very process of attaining the referendum, carrying it out peacefully, and the acceptance of its results are signs of the vitality of the civil component of the Uruguayan collectivity. For others, the vitality of civil society singles out this collectivity from others in the Southern Cone, but the results of the referendum reveal the limitations of this component vis-à-vis the logic of the state and its 'raison d'état'. According to the latter interpretation, democracy has only partially delivered on its promises of justice and equality before the law. It provided neither comprehensive information about the fate of the victims nor justice as perceived by the latter. In contrast with Argentina and Chile, the Uruguayan state has not established an official commission of truth to provide a full account of human-rights violations under the military nor assumed corporate responsibility for the suffering of the victims and their relatives.

In post-referendum Uruguay, NGOs moved to follow up the human-rights situation with a prospective vision. Persistent abuses of authority on the part of the police forces and in the prison system triggered recurrent concern with human rights. Together with enhancing civility in the Uruguayan public sphere, the results of the referendum revealed the relative dearth of political space for manoeuvring vis-à-vis the armed forces. The high levels of mobilization and debate over the resolution of the authoritarian legacy during the first three years of the democratic period eroded the centrality of the issue and marginalized it. Past human-rights violators remained exempt from punishment, imprinting a clear message concerning how current issues might be dealt with.[4] The memory of the referendum's results, in which institutional pragmatism trumped principles of accountability and equal standing before justice, has left a mark on Uruguayan political culture.

The potential for crisis in Uruguay has been reduced due to the possibilities for institutional consensual resolution via the legal-judicial track in this country. In a certain sense, different events related to human-rights violations appeared from time to time and attracted wide interest in the public sphere. Nonetheless, they did not evolve into a major crisis with political repercussions, because the institutional path was consensually closed. This is why discussions about the legacy of human-rights violations can be expected to reappear in the domains of memory, historical interpretation, culture, and around particular cases that may be of social concern. On some occasions, events initiated in Argentina were reflected in Uruguay, since most of the Uruguayan victims had been abducted and/or assassinated in Argentina. Ongoing abuses of human rights have provided grounds for continued concern with the human-rights issue. Human-rights violations are still committed, nowadays against criminals, outcasts, and prisoners, for the sake of personal security and social stability. Even those sectors that benefit from the harsh treatment that the police and the authorities use against marginal and criminal individuals must recognize the partial lack of respect of civil rights as central to this democracy. Again, considerations of sociopolitical order seem to overcome normative principles and the respect for humanity.

In Chile, limited democracy imprinted the pattern of confronting the legacy of human-rights violations. The first democratic government's adoption of the human-rights banner secured the support and cooperation of the main NGOs. This awarded further legitimacy to President Aylwin's policies of reaching truth and as much justice as possible.[5] The political class, which after the long military period perceived polarization with apprehension, respected the limitations inherited from Pinochet's rule and took into account the prevailing balance of forces between the armed forces and the civilians. The wide coalition organized by the forces opposed to Pinochet elaborated basic agreements around democratic principles, among which the theme of human rights was central. Even for right-wing politicians, who had supported Pinochet, human-rights violations was an issue from which to dissociate oneself. Commenting on the Rettig Report, Hermógenes Pérez de Arce, said:

The impact was very important. I believe it was devastating for the political right and the former military administration. Thinking in electoral terms, the most cunning right-wing politicians have claimed that human-rights violations is an issue of the military, while modernization—acccomplished under military rule—was theirs. This placed the former government's negative side on the military's shoulders allowing politicians to cash in on the positive side of the balance.[6]

Following the rise to power of the civilian administration, both the military and the civilians followed Chile's tradition of constitutionalism and legalism, thus advancing on the front of human-rights violations where the 1978 Amnesty Law and the 1980 Constitution permitted.

The successful implementation of the legal path implicated some of the high-ranking officers of the previous military administration, thus precipitating crises which the high commands of the armed forces, led by Pinochet, used to reinforce the binding force and status of the constitutional arrangements, in which the institutional position of the armed forces was a basic component.

Regional Trends and Historical Timing

In each of these settings, the key political and social actors took into account the parallel patterns adopted in the neighbouring countries for dealing with the legacy of human-rights violations. In Uruguay, for example, the 1987 military rebellion of Semana Santa in Argentina and especially the concessions made to the military in its aftermath produced a radical shift in how different political forces viewed possible courses of action to be followed in Uruguay. Before April 1987, the Uruguayan left considered the Argentine path as an example to be emulated in their own country, while most of the more conservative forces claimed that Uruguay was a case apart and no inference could be drawn from Argentina or other cases. According to the latter, the path of Uruguayan civility set this country apart within the Latin American setting. General Hugo Medina expressed this view about Uruguayan exceptionalism, arguing that 'the Uruguayan armed forces permitted a bloodless way out, which is an example for all [Latin] American countries. To this we should add the fact that military rule allowed us to save many from death. We do not to have to repent for any drop of blood shed in the country.'[7]

Following the 1987 rebellion in Argentina, on the other bank of the Río de la Plata, the forces trying to close the human-rights issue in Uruguay saw in those events a premonition of what could happen in their own country if attempts were made to bring the military to trial. As perceptively noted by journalist Carlos María Gutiérrez,

From a comparative point of view, it can be argued that, on the issue of military impunity, Alfonsín has finally chosen a Uruguayan solution [*una solución a la uruguaya*]. Until last month, when the Argentine example (in which, at least, members of the Juntas were sent to jail . . .) was mentioned to the pro-government forces, the latter replied by arguing that this was 'another country, other conditions'. The current stand of President Alfonsín erases this image of differentiation, because now it has reached (or is reaching) through a distinct path the same political equation: social peace equals impunity. Now the Colorados and Blancos that voted or supported the Law of Expiry here do not find so many differences between Uruguay and Argentina. They are publicly moved by what they call the democratic courage of the neighbouring ruler.[8]

Similarly, the Uruguayan forces that rejected compromises with the military shifted their earlier view of Argentina in the other direction. According to them, the Uruguayans should not hesitate in adopting decisive policies because of the example of the neighbouring nation, since Argentina had a peculiar tradition of violence and military intervention in politics, which sets it apart in the Southern Cone.

[These are] complex events, not yet clear, which require rigour and avoiding at all costs the risk of abusive analogies. . . . This is not the first time that people tend to simplify realities. We are interested in analysing today those [views] that were launched with the purpose of smuggling—behind this kind of analogy—the impunity, or the purpose of granting impunity, to the war crimes of the Uruguayan dictatorship.[9]

Following the debates and crisis around Scilingo's 1995 revelations in Argentina, the Uruguayan political leadership came back to the thesis of the uniqueness of their country. President Sanguinetti stressed, in a talk with the high command of the armed forces, that 'happily, there is no point of comparison' between the paths of the two nations. In Uruguay, the question of not prosecuting the military was solved by the popular vote that ratified the Law of Expiry on 16 April 1989.[10]

In Argentina, once the results of the Uruguayan referendum were known, the candidate for the vice-presidency of Alfonsín's party, the Unión Cívica Radical, Juan Manuel Casella, had no doubt that a plebiscite in Argentina would bring about 'the support of the People for the decisions of Congress taken in 1983, 1987 and 1988', that is, the trends towards increasing impunity for the military. Communist leader Eduardo Barcecat, of the leftist Izquierda Unida, considered that 'this defeat will be important in all Latin America and especially in Brazil, Argentina and Chile, where it serves as a model for the right-wing regimes and their allies'.[11] Similarly, in Chile, according to Jorge Correa's evaluation,

Aylwin was influenced by the Uruguayan and Argentine experiences. [In Argentina], even in the most favorable circumstances, President Alfonsín had to abandon some of his goals as a result of military resistance. The new Chilean President also took note of the Uruguayan experience, where military officers resisted testifying before courts in cases of human-rights violations. . . . Moreover, the recent Argentine experience showed that the confrontation with the armed forces over this matter could have a hurtful effect on the country's democratic stability as a whole. . . . One of the possibilities considered (to solve the HR issue) had been to form an *ad hoc* investigative parliamentary commission, similar to that of Uruguay; it was finally turned down due to the unsatisfactory results achieved in Uruguay.[12]

Another close collaborator of President Aylwin and member of the Rettig Commission, José Zalaquett, stressed as well that

[T]he Argentine case was telling for Chileans. It proved the importance of a systematic effort to reveal the truth. It also showed the extent to which a government can lose authority when it raises expectations it cannot fulfil. Uruguay also provided an example for Chile . . . In Uruguay the government took too cautious an approach, avoiding not only trials for past state crimes but also any significant official disclosure about past violations. Citizens' opposition to this approach led to a nationwide campaign . . . Taking these lessons into account, the Aylwin government decided to follow a course it could sustain . . .[13]

In the mid-1990s, in the midst of the Contreras crisis, individuals reflected on the paths of Argentina and Uruguay, trying to assess their applicability in the Chilean setting:

We cannot draw positive conclusions for Chile from the many cases in which authoritarian regimes left pardon laws for [dealing with] human-rights violations. We can only avoid mistakes: worsening even further a situation with extremely rapid measures (Argentina) or extremely cautious measures (Uruguay) that generated military and civilian upheavals. . . . The unfortunate Argentine experience is the main example that the Chilean government parades about the way in which these things should not be done. . . . neither can the Uruguayan formula be pointed out as a good example for Chile. In spite of the fact that the measures brought social peace and, since then, in Montevideo the leader of the subversives and the ex-dictator, General Gregorio Alvarez, breathe the same air, the Uruguayan experience is categorized as too cautious by human-rights advocates. It not only abstained from making the names of the guilty public, but also it abstained from investigating . . .[14]

Historical timing determined that the latecomers could benefit from what they perceived as the positive and negative experiences of those countries that initiated redemocratization earlier. In this sense, Argentina had to elaborate the institutional and informal ways of treating the legacy of the previous military government without any previous South American reference and with only the more remote precedents of the Nuremberg and Tokyo trials. As Uruguay entered democracy in 1985 it could already look to the other side of the Río de la Plata in elaborating its own path. The Uruguayans could perceive that even in Argentina, where the new democracy incorporated a defeated and divided military, it was extremely difficult—if not impossible—to obtain the latter's cooperation in uncovering the past. Later on, as the Uruguayan political class began to legislate the closure of the human-rights violations issue, the Argentine regressive trend leading to the Law of Punto Final in December 1986 was a landmark for the former's enactment of their own Law of Expiry.

Following extremely different paths, Argentina and Uruguay arrived almost at the same time at legislation intended to put an end to the issue.

The protest of concerned sectors of civil society led to different institutional results in Argentina and Uruguay. In Uruguay, these sectors articulated a wide mobilization framed within the 1967 constitutional provision that allowed civil society to challenge parliamentary legislation through a referendum. The protest in Argentina was as massive as in Uruguay, but it was channelled through street demonstrations and individualized legal suits which fitted into the time limits established by the Punto Final Law. The pressures generated by civil society in this case tended to recreate polarization through massive judicial demands against the military precipitating military rebellions and eventually forcing a regressive trend in the treatment of past human-rights violations. Uruguayans perceived in the Argentine experience the dangers of disarticulated polarization, which may help explain the consensual acceptance of the April 1989 referendum results by the victors and defeated alike. The final stages of the transition from military rule to democracy in Chile coincided with the most acute point in the regressive trend of the cycle in Argentina and with the closure brought about by the referendum in Uruguay. For all sectors in Chile, the results evolving in the neighbouring societies were interpreted as unacceptable. For the Chilean military and their supporters, the trials and resulting humiliation suffered by their counterparts in Argentina were to be rejected and the kind of popular mobilization witnessed in Uruguay was to be avoided. For the Concertación, the regression of human-rights policies in Argentina indicated the need to follow a cautious path in Chile, and the closure without truth and justice imbedded in the Uruguayan path was antithetical to Chilean principles.

The perspective provided by historical timing played a role in defining the path elaborated in each of these cases, within the local institutional traditions and frameworks. Among the three cases, the late transition in Chile stands out. Whereas the experiences of Argentina and Uruguay evolved through more or less parallel time schedules with distinctive paths and results, the Chileans were able to learn positive and negative lessons from the other two. The lessons from the Argentine and Uruguayan experiences were interpreted within the framework of Chilean experiences, political culture, constitutional and legal traditions, and situational constraints. Interpreting the examples of neighbouring countries both limited the options for treating the legacy of human-rights violations and obligated the Concertación to elaborate new formulae in this domain.

The Perspective of Collective Catharsis

The collective catharsis and debate that dominated the Argentine public sphere following democratization resembled earlier situations, like those developing on the eve of the Malvinas–Falklands War, the subsequent military defeat, and revelations of inefficiency and corruption. As in those situations, the media, the intellectuals, and the political actors regarded these events as crucial and even foundational for redirecting the paths of Argentine history.

The establishment of an official commission of inquiry and the trials of the military commanders were central in this stage of confronting the legacy of human-rights violations. The public agenda of Argentina was totally dominated on a daily basis for a period of two years by revelations in the media and in every dimension of social and cultural life. Along with a continuous preoccupation with the issue, there were some peaks, like the publication of the CONADEP report and the verdicts in the public trials of the military leadership, that monopolized public interest and fuelled high collective expectations. The CONADEP report and the trials implied a symbolic restructuring of Argentina's basic symbols and institutions. The self-proclaimed role of the military as bearers of the essence of the nation and national values was severely questioned, while alternative views of essential values were projected around civility, defence of the law, and respect for human rights. Following the regressive policies in this domain, collective expectations were subsequently replaced by widespread fatigue and disappointment. In the crises of the mid-1990s collective attention was once again captured and emotionally driven by the confessions of former military officers. Tulio Halperin Donghi perceived the highly cathartic overtones of the encounter of Argentine society with the horrors of its recent history:

While it is clear that these horrors have changed the shape of that history forever, it is less clear whether the new Argentine history will have much to say about the horrors themselves ... The notion that the illuminating potential of any historical episode is proportional to its terribleness assumes that history is structured like good melodrama, which does not seem to be the case.[15]

The collective cathartic element was not absent in Uruguay and Chile. Nonetheless, it was channelled differently, mainly as complementary to various institutional mechanisms elaborated for confronting the legacy of human-rights violations in these societies. While in Argentina the passage to democracy generated foundational expectations, in Uruguay redemocratization was rather perceived by the political class and large sectors of the population as a restoration of the older models of Batllist democracy and its values of civility, respect for legality, and political consensual solutions. In Uruguay, according to the existing constitutional framework, there was the possibility of calling a referendum on the basis of popular initiative. The mechanism of referendum had been used by governmental initiative eleven times. In 1986, for the first time in the history of Uruguay, it was civil society that initiated the collection of the required 25 per cent of the citizens' signatures necessary to hold a referendum on the basis of popular initiative. The process of mobilization that followed the initiative of individuals and NGOs involved a massive debate, elaborate meetings, and broad campaigning from door to door and into every corner of the country. An awakened consciousness arose through acts of remembrance, emotional identification with the figures of the abducted children of the disappeared and of the murdered individuals, especially Michellini and Gutiérrez Ruiz, and the involvement of thousands of Uruguayans who had suffered from imprisonment and torture during military rule. Public debate had emotional, intellectual, symbolic, and sensorial elements that interacted in plural forms across the social spectrum. For some, the mobilization re-enacted painful memories, for others it acquired the form of a mass happening, while for others it was evaluated in political and institutional terms. For all Uruguayans, however, it was almost impossible to remain indifferent. In the process of collecting signatures and subsequent mobilization towards the referendum it was difficult to assess whether a poster with the face of an abducted child was a stronger or weaker argument than a general's statement of having saved the country from self-destruction. This stood in sharp contrast to the character of the parliamentary debate on these issues. The emotional and cathartic elements, though similar to those in Argentina and in Chile, were channelled in Uruguay into a definite institutional framework: the collection of signatures, the campaign, and the vote in the referendum. In Argentina, the institutional moves adopted by the democratic administration generated a huge cathartic involvement among civilians, which was predominantly reactive and ineffective in keeping the progressive momentum on its institutional track. While Uruguay expanded from the Expiry Law to the referendum, in Argentina the institutional channels narrowed from the publication of the CONADEP report and the trials of the commanders to the Punto Final Law and the pardons. Broad civilian sectors reacted and protested as the institutional channels narrowed, but they had no civilist pattern like the Uruguayan referendum mechanism by which to challenge institutionally the moves of the government or to resist the pressures of those social actors, like the military, that tried to bring about regressive policies in the treatment of human-rights violations.

In Chile limited democracy posed institutional constraints on the enactment of the basic normative commitment of the political forces of the Concertación, which came to power in 1990. Within the limits of action faced by Aylwin's government, the policies enacted included strong symbolic elements of recognition, acknowledgement, and centralization of the legacy of human-rights violations. In the view of Chile's political class, the need to secure stability required restraining popular mobilization over this issue and lessening the intensity of feelings that in the past had led to polarization and bloodshed. President Aylwin was the main actor, adopting policies to channel these feelings into symbolic peaks taking place in carefully defined sites and dates, such as the inauguration in the National Stadium on 12 March 1990, and the public announcement of the Rettig Report to the nation on 4 March 1991. The purificatory ritual of inversion enacted in the former act was complemented with Aylwin's emotionally charged and authoritative presentation of the report. This act attempted to define a common 'truth' leading to those measures of justice that were possible within limited democracy and to the attainment of national reconciliation. In contradistinction with the Argentine and to a lesser extent the Uruguayan situation, in Chile there were short moments of catharsis rather than long periods of emotional upheaval.

Aylwin had the moral guts and the respect of the population as he established the Rettig Commission and announced the latter's report publicly, on live TV and media broadcast, asking on that occasion for forgiveness and expressing deep remorse about the suffering inflicted on the population. The Presidential address was an act that nobody dared to criticize, not even mildly, and that had great impact . . . Again, when the court announced the verdict in the trial of Contreras, there was a live TV transmission. . . . one could hear the shouting and applauses and the people singing the national anthem. It was a very cathartic situation, very strong, very healthy for Chilean society.[16]

On the basis of principled commitment to human rights (shared by his coalition), the President conducted an intense dialogue with the NGOs and had wide support among the spectrum of political forces that backed his government. He thus nurtured trust in the official institutional treatment of the issue and prevented popular mobilization (excepting occasional acts of 'popular justice' or vengeance by the radical left against military personnel). On the basis of the limiting institutional framework inherited from military rule, the administration conducted a working dialogue with the high commands of the armed forces, and especially a dialogue between Aylwin and Pinochet. This dual dialogue, conducted on different grounds, enabled them to diffuse highly charged situations evolving from the process of dealing with the legacy of authoritarianism, as occurred for example following the assassination of Senator Jaime Guzmán on 1 April 1991. In the Chilean political scenario of redemocratization, contestation came basically from the right, which was not interested in destabilizing the system as long as the constitutional framework dictated by the Pinochet administration was respected. The Chilean forces of the Concertación accepted the rules of the game of limited democracy established by the military, with the built-in Amnesty Law of 1978. Departing from different positions, all political forces and social actors followed the pending legal and institutional avenues opened by the government. The combination between limited democracy and the autonomy and power of the armed forces—coupled with the constitutionalist-legalist tradition of the Chilean elites—led the democratic government to pre-empt popular mobilization of the Uruguayan kind and the long term catharsis of the Argentine kind, both directed against the military of the respective countries. The opposition's acceptance of the rules of the game set by the military implied a basic understanding that the precedents of Argentina and Uruguay would not be re-enacted in Chile.

The Legal-Constitutionalist Angle

During the processes of redemocratization, the constitutionalist and legal traditions functioned in various ways in the three countries. In Chile, once the 1980 Constitution was recognized by Pinochet's opposition as the basis for future democracy, the tradition of respect for the rule of law brought almost all sectors to adhere to the legal established framework for settling political differences. Human-rights violations were treated within this framework. Whereas during military rule the courts and the rule of law were ineffective in protecting citizens against abuses by the state, a situation harshly criticized in the Rettig Report and in Aylwin's address of 4 March 1991, in the democratic period the government was able to restore trust in the law. While trying to characterize the differences between Argentina and Chile in this area, Jacobo Timerman, himself a victim of repression in Argentina, defined Chile in 1987 as a singular case in Latin America because of its 'permanent state of legality':

Politically, he said, it is set apart by its almost 'permanent state of legality', a reference to its having had the longest periods of constitutional rule in the region, with only occasional interruptions. 'Even today,' he said, 'one is struck by how, under a dictatorship of 14 years, Chileans still turn to the judges.'

Repeating the frequently heard description of the Chilean army as 'the last Prussian army in the world', he said it meant that the Chilean military 'never acts unless all act'. 'The character of the Chilean Army continues being the same,' he said. 'Before, it had a rigid structure and, with few exceptions, did not intervene in politics. Even now, no one can introduce into the army any authentic debate over the political situation.'[17]

The armed forces' spirit of legalism was clear from the onset of military rule in 1973, when the *de facto* government issued more than 100 decree-laws in less than three months. In its first two decrees, the junta composed of the commanding officers of the army, navy, air force, and Carabineros promised to guarantee the workings of the judicial system and to respect the constitution and laws of the country, 'inasmuch as the situation will allow them to do so', and assumed legislative functions. Through issuing these decrees, the junta attempted to reconstruct Chilean institutionality and regulate public life through a framework of authoritarian legality.[18]

   This spirit of legalism and constitutionalism was reflected in the transition to democracy and in the subsequent formal relations between the President and the commander-in-chief of the armed forces.

On his relations with the General [Pinochet], President Aylwin said: 'The day I took office he said, You are my boss; I obey you, but no one else.' They also agreed that neither General Pinochet nor any members of the armed forces would engage in political debate and statements.[19]

Even on the human-rights front, where Chile was severely criticized internationally and where the armed forces rejected those criticisms, the latter still attempted to rely upon criteria of legality in their search for legitimation. Following the legal commitment, there was popular consultation over the human-rights policies of the government already in 1978, and in the ensuing decade and a half many high-ranking officers professed their strict adherence to constitutionalism and to the legality of their institutions, even when the issue of human-rights abuses was at the fore.

A psychological campaign that touched the emotional inner fibres of people has been waged around the issue of the disappeared. This has reached the point of an absolute conspiracy against the authorities and, in this sense, Chile had to support pressures that were as unjust as discriminatory. The only important thing to keep in mind about the number of denunciations is the existence of the sincere intention [of the administration] to investigate any legitimately grounded claim by relatives of the disappeared.[20]

In November 1991, following the parliamentary decisions on minor constitutional reforms, navy commander Admiral Jorge Martínez Busch supported the opinion of General Ramón Vega, commander of the air force, that 'From a technical point of view, the armed forces cannot be politicized in any case.'[21]

The issue of the human-rights legacy was the main point of discord between civilian and military sectors. Chilean legalism enabled both sectors to look for solutions in the legal arena and to accept compromises if needed. In the early 1990s, the issue was squarely back in the courts, but under the shadow of military pressure. Judicial reform as intended by Aylwin and Justice Minister Cumplido had failed to receive legislative approval. In order to change the composition of the Supreme Court, the government offered tempting financial incentives for retirement to the members nominated under Pinochet, but only one accepted.[22] The same judicial structure and nearly the same judges who, according to the Rettig Report, had failed to alleviate the past situation of human-rights abuses were dealing with that grim heritage under democratic rule. In the background, all concerned actors—the victims, the NGOs, the opposition, the government, and the military— waited to see the results and react. The role of the courts was also extremely uncomfortable since their previous record had been publicly condemned by the highest authority of the country, and the proceedings they were carrying out in the human-rights cases placed them in the position of sending to jail members of the armed forces with whom many in the judiciary had cooperated until 1990.

These evaluations and attitudes were completely consistent with Chile's traditional legalism and constitutionalism. In this period, the latter were reinforced by the army because of the armed forces' vested interest in the institutional framework they had elaborated and transferred through fair electoral processes into Chile's limited democracy.

In Argentina, the legal and judicial tracks were also very prominent in the first stages of redemocratization, but they were eventually subordinated to political decisions generated under military pressures. Pressures and clashes with the military produced the regressive trend discussed above, which pursued the legal track of laws that limited and finally closed the treatment of human-rights violations. This regressive trend had a highly detrimental effect in the public sphere, since it recreated distrust and a gap between the declared commitment to human rights and the use of the law to carry out the regression. During the military period legal protection (e.g. in the form of habeas corpus rights) had been ineffective, and the progressive legal policies of the democratic administration created high expectations and popular enthusiasm around the application of the rule of law as a central criterion for Argentina. As the legal track entered its regressive stage, the lack of social trust in the role and rule of law that existed before democratization was reinforced once again. The full circle is completed with the pardons granted to the military leaders in 1990. Although this highly political move resulted in the real subordination of the armed forces to the civilian authorities, a major step in the democratization of Argentina, it decreased the public confidence in the rule of law.

As in Argentina and Chile, the legalist tradition of Uruguay could not preclude the infringement of basic human and civil rights during the military period. Nonetheless, the military in Uruguay refrained from adopting extra-legal killings and disappearances as their main tools of repression, favouring long-term imprisonment, torture, and quasi-totalitarian control of civil society and of the public sphere. When asked about military repression three days before the 1989 referendum, one of main military leaders, General Hugo Medina, reflected on the specificities of the Uruguayan experience:

We do not reject the accusation that we used force. Because we used force. But if we had done what was done in other cases—this is a reflection of mine— if we had employed other forms of repression, then of the 5,000 prisoners that we had in this country, 4,000 would have been dead. [When asked if some of the commanders favoured the Argentine style of repression, he added:] There were many opinions. What is important is what was done.[23]

The military leadership tried to institutionalize their rule into a legitimate regime by calling in November 1980 a referendum over the constitutional reforms they had initiated. Whereas in Chile such an initiative in September 1980 resulted in popular approval of the 1980 Constitution, through a referendum which was highly controlled by the military, in Uruguay the military's constitution was rejected by popular vote. The legalist position of the Uruguayan military commands was reflected in their acceptance of the results, which subsequently led to political opening and the Club Naval Pact.

The Role of Civil Mobilization

Following the line of national reconciliation, the Colorado government of President Sanguinetti tackled the issue by legislating the liberation of political prisoners in 1985 and the Law of Expiry in 1986. But the redemocratized state refused to carry out a direct policy towards those who were responsible for human-rights violations under military rule.

The Uruguayan state is the one that least recognized human-rights violations. Here [in Uruguay] there is no official list of disappeared, no list of dead people, nothing, the government recognizes nothing. It did not erect a single monument.

It did not make any public declaration of remorse. Only a law to close the issue . . .[24]

In Uruguay the moves of a particracy, traditionally able to solve conflicts through legislation and political manœuvring, met the initiative of sectors of a civil society committed to human rights and capable of precipitating massive mobilization. The concerned civilian sectors also used a constitutional mechanism to challenge governmental legislation. The tension between the particratic path and the civilian mobilization path found a channel of resolution in the use of constitutional mechanisms interpreted in the traditions of Uruguayan civility, that is, consensual and legal resolutions. Following the 1989 referendum, all sectors accepted the results of this institutional path and the primacy of the rule of law as central to Uruguayan life and civility.

By contrast, both in Argentina and in Chile, the political classes dominated the institutional treatment of the issue, precluding mass participation beyond the symbolic level (as in Chile) or failing to channel mass mobilization to counteract pressures on the part of the military that led to the regression of official policies (as in Argentina). Moreover, resulting from periods of intensive mobilization, Argentine citizens have been reluctant to engage in further mobilization around issues of human rights:

Confronting the human-rights issue, people do not take anymore to the streets but are still very sensitive about the subject. There is passive receptivity. They will not participate in public demonstrations. At most, 500 of us demonstrate. Others stay at home. But, you know, many more stand behind us. This has been a democracy that exhausted its citizens through numerous protests. Groups called time and time again to gather and demonstrate, without taking into account that people have limits and that there are moments in which they cannot or do not have the time and energy to engage in new protests. The events of Semana Santa were highly disappointing and discouraging. . . . Worst of all was that the President negotiated with the military and hid his steps from the public, acting as if absolutely nothing had happened, as if he [and democracy] had won. A historic opportunity was lost.[25]

Conclusion: Paths and Performances

In making the crimes of repression known, a process of social catharsis began, which was more impressive the more that broad sectors of the population ignored or claimed to have ignored their extent. In Argentina, the early authoritative endorsement of the CONADEP report and its mirroring of the horrors of military repression aroused great emotional fervour, prompting wide cathartic debates in the redemocratized public sphere, and raising expectations for forthcoming justice concerning those responsible for human-rights violations. Expectations ranged from due respect for legality and accountability to retributive justice and vengeance. Chile also established an official commission for Truth and Reconciliation, whose mandate was limited by considerations of political contingency. The results of the Rettig Commission were announced by the President in a highly emotional address to the nation, in which he assumed institutional responsibility vis-à-vis the victims. This recognition of past evils by the state as well as the political decision to control truth (by limiting it to assassinations by both the military and political extremist groups) was aimed to preserve political steering concerning the past. Motivated by the same political will, Uruguayan democratic rulers and the political class opted to avoid establishing any official commission of truth. Only the SERPAJ would, years after the return to democracy, prepare a partial report of very limited scope and impact. In Uruguay, it was the mobilization of civil society which contested the policy path taken by the particracy that enabled broad, national discussion of the legacy of authoritarianism.

The demands for accountability clashed with the pressures for recognizing immunity (or as seen by the critics, impunity) for those involved in repression. The legalist-constitutionalist path of Chile, though constrained by the terms of limited democracy, provided a clear-cut avenue for possible punishment only in those cases not covered by an amnesty law dating from military times. Sensitivity to the issue and its implicit threat to the stability of the system led to passing the buck from one institutional arena to another (from the executive to the judiciary to the Parliament and back again). In Uruguay, the elites faced the dilemma of political contingency by attempting to close the legal channels for demanding accountability through the cancellation of any state attempt to forward trials. The challenge of substantial sectors of civil society willing to impose principles of public accountability, though failing to reach the envisioned goal, granted relatively high legitimacy to the formal closure of the issue, since it was done within the agreed-upon mechanisms of voting recognized by Uruguay's constitution. Argentina is the country in which expectations of comprehensive justice were raised the highest, in connection with the trials of the military commands and the autonomy that the judiciary showed initially in following through with these cases. But as the cathartic expectations shifted to wider circles in the security forces, the pressures of the latter and the increasingly reduced political steering of the executive in the midst of an economic crisis led to a regression with regard to policies about the past and to a sense of generalized distrust of the system that was unable to live up to its own professed intentions and previous initiatives.

Very few of those who were involved in repression even partially acknowledged their deeds or asked for expiation. Besides President Aylwin's surrogate role in asking for forgiveness, and General Balza's vow of commitment to democracy and the condemnation of excesses, no major acts of institutional contrition or official excusation have been made. Only a few individuals expressed regrets about past deeds. As Barry Schwartz analysed in a pioneer article, forgiveness can promote social integration when it is considered just by others and when they are convinced of the offender's regret, guilt, and commitment to the shared values of society. In the Southern Cone, such forgiveness has been highly unlikely as the polarized visions of the past persisted under democracy.

The unforgivable transgression is one which, by the manner or circumstances in which it is carried out, betrays the perpetrator's contempt for the values he has violated. It reveals his insincerity, his essential disloyalty and lack of devotion to the basic ideals of his society. . . . But society could not long survive if this rare, genuinely psychopathic, occurrence were encountered more frequently than it is.[26]

In all three cases, the political leaderships favoured national reconciliation, as a systemic necessity, even announcing the celebration of social reunion. But interpreting the past in polar terms, different sectors have initiated a politics of memory and oblivion, while intellectuals have debated the reconstruction of their countries' collective identities. These interpretive efforts both reflected the experience of human-rights violations and contributed to shaping collective memory and identity in light of that experience.

Official reparations and compensations for the victims and their relatives have been incorporated in different forms by all three countries. Some affected groups such as the Madres de Plaza de Mayo have fought this limited treatment of the problem and continue demanding comprehensive truth, acknowledgement, and justice before accepting the concrete measures taken by the democratic governments. The parallel unwillingness of these relatives in Argentina to erect *lieux de mémoire* for the victims of repression, in sharp contrast with the demands of the Uruguayan association and with the collaboration of Chilean associations in erecting the impressive public memorial in Santiago, reflects the unsatisfactory way of closing the issue in the Argentine scene. Although reduced in scope, 'popular violence' against past repressors and collaborators of the military regime has occurred in Chile and Argentina, thus indicating again that polarized visions have been more salient there than in Uruguay, which seems to have endorsed its earlier civilist ethos.

Beyond the paths taken for confronting acts of repression committed under the military, all three countries since the return to democracy have been enmeshed in debates that concern the ways of relating to and mastering the past and the lessons that these societies should learn from the grim period of authoritarianism and its legacy.

Oblivion and Memory in the Redemocratized Southern Cone

This chapter analyses the politics of oblivion and memory of human-rights violations after redemocratization. The memory of human-rights violations during military rule has continued to haunt the Southern Cone societies following the transition to democracy. Along with the institutional mechanisms elaborated for treating these violations, a politics of oblivion and memory was generated, which involved contrasting attempts to diffuse or preserve the memory of the past, while reapproaching past experiences and their varied interpretations in traditional and novel ways. We analyse the role played by different individual and institutional actors, especially the executive, the political forces, the past repressors, the intellectuals, and the relatives of the victims, in these dynamics of symbolic struggle over the shaping of collective memory and its institutional implications.

The Heritage of Authoritarianism

During military rule attempts were made in each country to impose consensus around the official historiographical versions, which were predicated on a vision of national salvation through 'wars' won by the armed forces and waged against the 'evil forces of subversion'. Through control of the public sphere, the educational systems, and information policies, the ruling juntas curtailed alternative visions and conceptions. During the military dictatorships, the international community condemned the wide range of human-rights abuses, especially in Chile and Argentina; the military governments responded by speaking of national dignity and reaffirming the path each government had taken. When facing international criticism about the local treatment of human rights, Lt.-Gen. Jorge Rafael Videla's administration retorted by adopting proudly the slogan: We Argentinians are upright and humane ('Los argentinos somos derechos y humanos'). Under similar circumstances, Pinochet announced on 21 December 1977 that the government was calling a 'consultation' of the whole population, so that

> every man, every woman, and every youth in this country will have to decide in the secrecy of his/her conscience, whether s/he supports the President in his defense of the dignity of Chile, and reaffirms the legitimacy of the government of the Republic . . . or whether, in contrast, he/she supports the resolution of the United Nations and its pretensions to impose upon us from abroad our future destiny.[1]

In the consultation, held on 4 January 1978, an absolute majority of Chileans voted for the military government's position and supported its policies.[2] In this period, a politics of selective construction of memory was implemented, which hid the modus operandi of the military from public eye.

These policies created among many citizens a feeling of scepticism about stories stressing the extent and depth of human-rights abuses that circulated in each of these societies despite censorship. Informal mechanisms of denial, disbelief, and rationalization abounded, which stressed that if acts of violence had been committed, reasons probably existed for such use of 'reactive violence' by the security forces.[3] Similarly, the common view was projected that the notices about the disappearance of detainees were unfounded rumours spread by radicals who had gone underground and by exiles who had fled their country. As Jorge Luis Borges admitted in August 1985,

> We lived in the period of Rosas [Argentine autocratic leader of the nineteenth century], without being aware of it. I was deceived concerning what happened. Some conservative friends made me believe that people had been freed and left the country. But we have been able to attest, through the public trial of the commanders, that terrible things occurred.[4]

The policies of misinformation and shaping of collective consciousness had a long-lasting impact among the supporters of the military regime and also among broad sectors of public opinion not affected directly by physical repression.

Following political openings and redemocratization, a rediscovery of the full extent and magnitude of the problem was projected into the public sphere, and intense debates were initiated on the institutional and extra-institutional mechanisms necessary for dealing with the legacies of authoritarianism. The reshaping of the public sphere—and the ensuing disclosure and institutional treatment of past human-rights violations—did not, however, generate an interpretation of past experiences and deeds, shared by both victims and victimizers or by the different institutional actors. For years the military opposed any opening of the issue of human rights, threatening to destabilize the democratic polity. Nor did they acknowledge responsibility for the abuses of human rights committed during their rule. Only years after the transition to democracy have a few members of the armed and security forces begun to confess or recognize the deeds of the past, albeit mostly in terms that follow the military's traditional thesis that they acted properly given the state of internal war that prevailed when they took power.

Built-in tensions were imprinted in each case by the partial character of the solutions to the human-rights violations legacy; by the limited substantial judicial results; and especially by the lack of knowledge about the victims' fate and the lack of military acknowledgement about their responsibility for violations. The partiality of the institutional treatment and the subsequent crises, analysed above, have projected the unresolved issues into the realm of symbolic and cultural confrontation, through which various social sectors and forces have attempted to gain hegemonic status for their own vision of the past and its implications.

Through the politics of oblivion and memory, the various visions of the past were transposed to a symbolically imbued struggle, in which each sector tries to make its vision hegemonic in the public sphere. The most involved sectors, that is, the victims and the military, related to the human-rights issue in opposite ways. The victims attempted to centralize it in the public sphere and the military to relativize and marginalize it. Other social actors as well have been enmeshed in the debate, approaching the issue with differing agendas and visions. The resulting politics of oblivion and memory is thus refracted at multiple angles, shaping a pluralistic but tension-ridden public agenda. Rather than disappearing, the issue of human-rights violations acquires crucial and renewed implications for the reshaping of these societies' collective memory and identity as time passes.

At the same time, the theme of human rights entered these societies as the correlate of deep internal crises, characterized by high levels of violence, and boosted by the connection of local political autonomy through an international discourse rooted in Western Europe and North America. In spite of the real suffering of the victims of authoritarianism and the universal validity of the concerns with human dignity voiced beyond Latin America, the terms of the discourse of human rights were perceived by large sectors of the citizenry as alien to local conditions and constraints. With redemocratization, the discourse of human rights became central, but as the new political systems face ongoing political pressures and/or economic hardship, different actors are willing to compromise, marginalize, or instrumentalize the legacy of human-rights violations to consolidate democracy, each one according to its vision and interests.

Hence, the universal validity that the discourse of human rights seemingly acquired during the democratic openings was seriously eroded later on. Each of the individual and institutional actors has developed an attitude to memory and oblivion, which reflected the tension between its professed principled visions and its pragmatic strategies. Each of the individual and institutional actors has operated selective mechanisms of oblivion and memory as he or she tried to affect the public sphere.

With the passing of time, and as the issue of human-rights violations reverberated occasionally at the centre of the public agenda, all major actors developed structured and unstructured strategies to deal with a range of problems for which the redemocratized societies have hardly found comprehensive solutions. The range of these problems can be clearly seen in Chilean author Ariel Dorfman's afterword to his work *La doncella y la muerte* (Death and the Maiden):

How can the repressors and the repressed live in the same land, share the same table? How to heal a country that has been traumatized by fear if that same fear continues to do its silent work? And how to reach truth when we have become used to lying? Can we keep the past alive without becoming its prisoners? And can we forget that past without risking its future replication? Is it legitimate to sacrifice truth to assure peace? And what are the consequences for the community if the voices of that past are suppressed? Is it possible that a community should search for justice and equality if the threat of military intervention persists forever? And, given these circumstances, how can violence be avoided? In what sense are we all responsible in part for the suffering of others, for the great errors that led to such a terrible clash? And perhaps the most tremendous dilemma of all: in what ways should these questions be confronted without destroying the national consensus, which is the basis of any democratic stability?[5]

These problems can be approached from various vantage points. From the vantage point of the individuals affected by repression, violence, and torture, the events and institutional crises that projected anew the issue of human-rights violations to the centre of the public agenda have prompted new personal confrontations with painful experiences and memories. For the victims, public debate and struggle often imply reopening sealed—but only partially sealed—memories and mechanisms of selective oblivion. Among the most well-known works that brought this forced re-encounter are *La doncella y la muerte* and Lita Stantic's 1993 film *Un muro de silencio* (A Wall of Silence), an Argentinian-Mexican-English co-production. Both works show how difficult, if not impossible, it is for the victims of repression to heal their personal wounds, even on the background of general normalization. The casual encounter between a victim and her torturer, as in Dorfman's piece, or the attempt by a film director to recreate the past experience of a victim, as in Stantic's film, trigger an uncontrollable outburst of feelings. Even though Dorfman's play was celebrated worldwide, being translated, staged successfully in different locations, and made into a film, it had a cool reception when put on stage in Chile. It could not fill the small hall of the Teatro de la Esquina (Theatre of the Corner) in which it was staged for a short period in 1991, and was ignored by most critics, probably due to its explicitness.[6] Similarly, in Argentina, Stantic's film was also considered too blunt in its treatment and did not become a success, despite being considered by intellectuals as a major contribution to the aesthetization of the persisting personal traumatization of society following the experience of repression.[7] Only in a more stylized, allegorical, and collectively oriented vein—as in Argentine Fernando Solanas's film *Sur*—or in the form of written factual testimonies did the wide public welcome such painful confrontation with the memory of the past.

In general, Chilean theatre—and its foremost figures, such as Gustavo Meza, Marco A. de la Parra, and Juan Radrigan—had played an important role in expressing anti-dictatorial trends after 1973, when political parties and other organizations were proscribed and/or unable to do this; but, following redemocratization, playwrights and directors lessened their direct political commitment and shifted to a wide spectrum of mundane issues.[8] But while this was true in Chile, in Argentina democratization opened the stage for pieces dealing with the legacy of human-rights violations and the society's collective expiation of that society. One of the most representative theatre plays of this period is *Knepp*, by Jorge Goldenberg. In this play, Goldenberg deals with the memory of the *desaparecidos*, through the persistent anxiety and expectations of a woman who is waiting for the—real or imagined—telephone calls of her disappeared fiancé. These calls are coupled with the unavoidable intrusion of a representative of the repressive apparatus, who is willing to negotiate oblivion with her, and with the pressing urge of her new sweetheart, who is willing to move beyond the memories of the past.[9]

While oblivion allowed many of the affected individuals to seemingly move ahead, remembrance—particularly that remembrance which is forced by the unexpected declarations of a former repressor or by the accidental encounter with the physical and metonymical presence of the past—often implies a return to the past experience, which may be no less painful than past torture and abuses themselves:

I lived with the repressors, I lived with the *Turco Julián*, with his [phono-graphic] records of Hitler, with his beatings, with all that brutality which I lived through again after 18 years as I heard him [on TV] tell his feats with total impunity, with irony, with sarcasm, without any sign of remorse and with complete ease say that he 'would do it again'. And I ask why, with what right does he have to introduce terror into me, with what right he does enter my home, the houses of everybody, with what right can he frighten through the screen those who did not come to know him in person . . . with what right? With all the right that grants him the impunity in which we live, with the right of the law that lets him go free and that allows him today to tell his crimes, with the right of a people that hesitates to shout ENOUGH, with the right of a government that allowed them to live free among us, the victims, within society, within a People that once said NEVER AGAIN, a NEVER AGAIN that is not fulfilled, that does not exist.[10]

If when I was set free someone had asked me: did they torture you a lot? I would have replied: Yes, for the whole of the three months . . . If I were asked the same question today, I would say that I've now lived through seven years of torture.[11]

Fear is not only a feeling we suffered during the dictatorship. We know already that fear leaves a trace for years and years. And, in addition, what occurs in our America is not a source of peace and the implict or explicit threat is present in different ways.[12]

We, as many others, are aware of the deep human individual wounds left open by the experience of the military rule.[13] Disappearances, for example, subvert the process of gradual mourning and coming to terms with the loss of the beloved. Depression, memories frozen in time, and anger are stressful and persisting schemata of those affected by the repression.[14] From a sociological perspective, these feelings and coping strategies also bear important collective implications, as they are channelled into the politics of oblivion and memory carried out in redemocratized Argentina, Chile, and Uruguay. We explore these collective dimensions, trying to trace the intricate relationships of the various strategies of oblivion and memory in these societies under redemocratization, as well as their implications for shaping the public spheres in the Southern Cone.

The question is what do we do with memory. Shall we exile it into oblivion? Transform it into a 'past', bearing the loss we suffered without forgetting it? Or discover the real face of our society in order to understand what we must let be forgotten.[15]

A certain oblivion of events (coming after posing the problem from a distance and not through the instantaneous passions) is a step towards symbolic memory. Such a memory is only able to admit the unchanging nature of the vacuum, the irreversibility of violent death, to the extent that it reduces

oblivion to a rational decision and a sustained ethics of value. This stresses
the collective dimension of memory which constitutes a stage in social consciousness, against erasing [the events] automatically (and negating justice)
. . . By stressing that dimension, that of a memory that intends to be shared
by all, the problem of historization of the past becomes that of consolidating
an ethical tradition able to institutionalize what should not be forgotten.[16]

In the Southern Cone, a politics of oblivion and memory began already
under the military and especially following the political transition to
democracy. This politics conditioned the ways in which the Southern
Cone societies have been able to move beyond the experience of past
repression towards the reformulation of their collective imagery and
identities.

The Politics of Oblivion and Memory

The analysis of collective memory has become a burgeoning focus of
theoretical inquiry in different disciplines, from sociology and anthropology to history and cultural studies. Most of the studies in this
analytical line follow the seminal distinction between history and memory developed among others by Pierre Nora. Whereas the concept of
history implies an image of the past clearly distinguished from the
present, the concept of memory places the past within the present, as
an integral and continuously reformulated part of it.[17]

Usually, contemporary studies attribute to political actors a motiva-
tion to transform history into memory, that is, to make the past a
living force for present orientations, in order to gain legitimacy and
public presence. Historical events are often transformed into mobilizing myths and myths of origin, which award legitimacy to contemporary ideological positions and/or political actions.[18]

In the countries of the Southern Cone, these strategies of oblivion
and memory have taken restrictive forms during periods of military
rule, and a plural physiognomy in their wake. During such rule, the
anti-mobilization trend restricted the use of mobilizing myths to initiatives focused in nationalist directions. Historical myths stressing
epic-military images were used by these rulers to emphasize their own
role as builders of the respective nations, and in contemporary settings, as 'saviours' of national integrity and the heritage of the founding fathers. In their eyes and their supporters', legitimacy derived
from this historical mission redefined in contemporary terms. The military rulers were motivated to re-enact the glories of the past. In a
sense, they too were transforming history into a living force of a clearly
nationalist and conservative character, upholding the same values that

were traditionally perceived to belong to the epic story of the founding of the nation. While many movements attempt to gain broad hegemony through such strategies, the military rulers had the full control of the state and the censored control of the public sphere to implement these strategies and shape collective memory from above. When democratization reopened the public sphere to free debate, the centrality of the legacy of human-rights violations coupled with the tension generated between pragmatic considerations and principled commitments brought the most affected actors to state their plight in polar ways, which the political class has attempted to ameliorate and mediate.

Due to the polarized visions of the former military rulers and the victims, as well as to the possible repercussions of any official statement on the issue of human-rights violations for the viability of democracy, no official version of the 'history' of the military period could be elaborated in the first years of redemocratization. The military period remained a black hole that was opened and reopened in the public domain, in direct correlation with the crises that developed over the issue of human-rights violations. Referring to her country, Graciela Scheines sums up the persistent hold and explosive potential of the past in the following terms:

Argentine history is a time bomb, always ready to explode, a tiger ready to attack, a heavy load that is a living burden and produces sorrow and anguish . . . As in Borges' short stories and in the tangos, what happened once continues to be remembered obsessively as if it was the only thing lived through. It destroys the totality of time, it appears like an avalanche against the stream. It flows upstream until it emcompasses all present and explodes there . . . Our history stirs, gets out of its skin, and returns unexpectedly, because the dead dominate the living and the past is stronger than the present.[19]

Whereas the governments endorsed the view that historical writing and discourse are valuable means for portraying the past in a contained form distinct from the present, they were mostly unable or unwilling to implement policies that would have transformed the memory of suffering and the victims' scars into history. The different actors continually resort to the politics of oblivion and memory as a major instrument for dealing with this inconclusive state of affairs.

By following a politics of oblivion and selective memory, the leading political forces tried to objectivize a certain version of history.[20] This selective politics of memory was contested by alternative patterns of oblivion and remembrance, which embedded images of the past—about which there was no consensus—within the present, as meaningful factors that shaped current visions and decisions. This could precipitate a repeated return to these issues, which has indeed characterized the developments in the 1990s. Due to the opening of a symbolic struggle between carriers of contesting visions of the past, these Southern Cone societies went, in Pierre Nora's terms, 'from a history sought in the continuity of memory to a memory cast in the discontinuity of history'.[21]

The Politics of Oblivion and Memory in Redemocratized Argentina

The trials and the parallel avenues of inquiry and public disclosure of the past experience touched upon questions crucial for reshaping collective identity under democracy.

Foremost were questions regarding collective and individual involvement in the context that triggered the military policy of repression and human-rights violations. Was this involvement part of a secluded style of command typical of the military, or was it grounded in the public culture and expectations of wider sectors of the population? What had been the 'correct' path during the military governments: exile or 'insile'?[22] These questions deeply divided civil society from the beginning of the redemocratization process.

The divisiveness in the ranks of intellectuals was paradigmatic. In December 1983, shortly after the inauguration of Alfonsín, Argentine-born University of Maryland Professor Saúl Sosnowski contacted Argentine intellectuals and suggested organizing a seminar on Argentine culture during the PRN period.

The answer was surprisingly unanimous. On the one hand, they told me, there were more urgent needs. On the other, they would not sit around the same table with those who had defied [the military regime] with their words and actions from far away, beyond boulevards, rivers and oceans. The return to democracy was therefore not auspicious enough to sustain a dialogue on differences [and discrepancies].[23]

When Sosnowski arranged a meeting in Washington, he finally managed to bring together a wide range of participants: a sociologist, a journalist, a philosopher, a theatre critic, four literary critics, four writers, a politician, and two historians. The agenda was ample and, yet, the theme that dominated it was that of personal accountability, focusing on the opposition of the exiles vs. those who had remained in the country during the military government.

In engaging in this debate figures such as Beatriz Sarlo, Noe Jitrik, Luis Gregorich, Liliana Heker, and Osvaldo Bayer faced, among other issues, the role played by the heroes of established culture, such as

Jorge Luis Borges and Ernesto Sábato. Sábato was a renowned writer, some of whose books became best-sellers in the period preceding the military takeover. In one of these books, *Abbadón el exterminador*, published in 1974, before the onset of military rule, Sábato touches upon the relationship between torturer and tortured. With a sense of premonition, he brings victimizer and victim to interact in an open and straightforward—or perhaps naive—way, something that would be impossible following the experiences of secluded victimization under military rule. In general, his work is characterized by a profound pessimism, a sense of veiled conspiracy, and a vision leading sometimes towards apocalypse. In December 1983, Sábato was nominated to the CONADEP commission and elected chair by the other members of the commission. According to Beatriz Sarlo,

This was a moment when Sábato's apocalyptic style met an apocalypse. A style that had been always misplaced, because it was a bit overstated ('no era para tanto'). It was like saying: OK, Sábato, do not worry so much about things! Right then [when he was nominated to head the CONADEP], he found himself really opening the gates of Hell. It is then that Sábato found a real meeting point between his style and reality. From then onward, he figured well at the centre of the [public] stage.[24]

Sábato's role as a renowned figure of Argentine letters and as president of the CONADEP had crucial effects on the commission's work and in the conception behind the CONADEP's report.[25] The thematic structure of the report, its use of selected quotations of the victims' testimonies, and the specific ways of systematizing the tens of thousands of files were clearly intended to create a comprehensive picture of the machinery, scope, and especially of the horrendous character of the repression. This structure, along with the trials against the military leaders, was key in creating a collective emotional experience among Argentine citizens in 1984 and 1985.

In spite of Sábato's central role in the fight for human rights, both he and Borges supported the military government of General Videla in its initial phases, thus emblematically representing the wide sectors of Argentinian society that accepted military rule as a needed step to put an end to the generalized atmosphere of anarchy that had developed during Isabel Martínez de Perón's presidency.

The counter-experience was that of the exiles, who after realizing the impossibility of carrying out internal opposition to the military in power and to save their lives, left the country and declared a total war against the military rule. The new exiles joined other Argentinians residing abroad. Among the latter was Julio Cortázar, who in 1978 claimed that the Argentine cultural domain had been squelched during the PRN, and that the only real possibility of opposition lay abroad. Liliana Heker, who stayed in Argentina, replied that, provided Cortázar was right at that moment, the role of those who stayed in the country was even more valuable. Moreover, Heker considered that Argentina was far from having turned into 'Zombie-land' and that an authentic commitment to its people meant contributing to their culture while living with them. Therefore, it was wrong to refer to the intellectuals who stayed as aides of the military government. Those who went into exile failed, according to Heker, to live through the experience that the Argentine people bore during those years.[26]

A rift was reopened as Argentines had to rethink their past role and status in connection with the collective experience of the PRN. The relationship to one another was expressed in terms of what they considered the expected commitment of any political activist and intellectual to the fate of their co-nationals ('el pueblo'). The distinctive place of the exiles vis-à-vis those who opted to stay in Argentina during the military period was the basis of the opposition between both sectors. Exiles considered that those who stayed had muted their voices as they had to compromise principled positions.

Moved by an unwillingness to tamper with principles and by their commitment to the people, political activists and intellectuals who went into exile paid the price of detachment from their natural source of inspiration and creativity. Being uprooted, they were able nonetheless to retain their integrity in the struggle against the military dictatorship. Their principled campaign against the military government and in favour of the tortured and the missing (*los desaparecidos*) was heard worldwide, at the very moment when local colleagues opted to maintain a cautious silence on human-rights violations.

By contrast, those who had stayed considered that they had paid the greatest personal price during the PRN. They were not able to develop international connections as the exiles did. They had to bear the full extent of fear and the external or self-inflicted restraint that impaired their creativity. Moreover, during the democratic transition, they found many of the job openings filled by returnees who could boast of well-developed curriculum vitae. They felt that their suffering as 'insiles' should not be underestimated.

The idyllic vision of the collectivity, the 'people', and the suffering of all insiles (internal exiles), was called into question by some of those who had moved abroad. Osvaldo Bayer, for instance, referred to the issue of widespread collaboration with the regime:

What kind of people is this, whose passive tolerance and, in fact, whose criminal agreement made possible the emergence of such perverse powers? . . . [A]ll this was possible due to a civil society that accompanied and enthusiastically supported [the military government], that maintained a cooperating silence, or that led a 'constructive opposition' (all that tamed demoniacal zoological set of those who know how to circumvent the situation with ambiguous phrases . . . only to reaccommodate the load and be alert to any change in order to shift the route taken . . .) The press attempted to be as 'pluralist' as possible. Hence, the best aides of the dictatorship were not the spokespersons of the military power but those who expressed themselves 'with moderation', those who knew how to leave a delicate line of criticism. It was good as an indicator of the [supposed] 'pluralism'.[27]

In a polemical exchange with Ernesto Sábato, Bayer accused the president of the CONADEP commission of adopting such collaborationist attitudes himself, asking rhetorically:

Why should we expect something different from Sábato? Sábato is the legitimate representative intellectual of our middle class. Today he is the hero because our middle class sees itself reflected in him—with its ghosts, its fears, its escapism, its search for awards, its lack of contrition, its incapacity for remorse. The middle class moves happily and unproblematically, without having shed a tear, from the most tragic dictatorship to a land of freedoms.[28]

In the realm of the arts, the same issues were kindled by Fernando Solanas's successful film *Tangos: el exilio de Gardel* (Tangos: Gardel's exile).[29] The film focused on the experience of exiled Argentinians, fostering debates on the centrality of exile as compared with the experience of political repression. Relatives of the missing victims considered that any account of the dictatorship had a duty to portray victims of repression in a pivotal role. Luis Bilbao, for example, criticized the film, arguing that 'the author neither wants to touch the real victims of the repression nor [to deal with] the factors that led to the repression'. According to Bilbao, through such selective treatment, Solanas marginalizes from the cultural construction of memory those who were militant protagonists in a social struggle. 'This is exactly what the government wants to do at the political level.'[30]

No shared vision of the past could be elaborated at this stage, which could have been a starting point in a dialogic move towards the future. On the contrary, a reading of the debates conducted during the democratic period reveals an atmosphere of mutual projection of blame. Rather than conducting a dynamic exchange of positions and ideas, the interlocutors seem to be trying to demonstrate that their own position was correct and to point out the misjudgement of the other side. This diviseness projected into the future the same divergence of visions of the Argentine experience characteristic of earlier periods, which had triggered the disarticulation of civil order, leading to the military takeovers.

Nonetheless, there was a major shift in this pattern of constructing memory following the work of the CONADEP, the publication of the *Nunca más* report and the *Diario del juicio*, which followed the testimonies of the victims at the trials of the commanders. Political activists were fully aware of this shift. Graciela Fernández Meijide observed in 1989, at the round table at which the Uruguay *Nunca más* was presented:

I do not delude myself. I know that history advances and recedes. But I also know that, fortunately, the history of the period has been written, not in what is pejoratively called the official history of the victor, but as history written by the victims. Whoever honestly wants to know what really happened in these countries in that period . . . can make use of these books to know deeply and be immunized [against authoritarianism].[31]

For the first time in the history of violence and turmoil of Argentina, the story told by victims and from the perspective of the victims was published with an official seal.

No less important in composing a complex picture of the experience of the PRN were a series of unofficial testimonies, which impacted the public sphere. The first years of redemocratization witnessed the re-emergence of testimonial literature, a genre which was able to convey the horrors of repression in unmediated ways, while standing close to the events. In this genre, which enjoyed a wide reception by the readers, Miguel Bonasso's *Recuerdo de la muerte* stands out, as it relates the story of incarceration, torture, and escape of political activists under the military; the book apparently sold over 100,000 copies.[32] Influential as well, in generating international pressures more than on the local scene, was Jacobo Timerman's *Preso sin nombre, celda sin número*.[33] Alipio Paoletti, a contributor to the journal of the Madres de Plaza de Mayo, published in 1987 a comprehensive book detailing the detention centres of Argentina and the names of the repressors identified by the victims.[34]

As we have seen, the events that followed the trials of the members of the military juntas (the rebellions of sectors of the armed forces, the laws of Full Stop and Due Obedience, the Tablada attack, hyperinflation and the economic deterioration, and finally the amnesties by Menem) put an end to the initial expectations and signalled that the issue of human-rights violations had lost centrality.

The most severe consequence of these moves, and especially of the presidential pardons, was the impairment of the symbolic-cultural premises of democracy which had become one of the foci of the redemocratization process. This broke the most important aspect of the political will, to construct democracy around events that functioned as mirrors of that period, as figures shaping collective identity and memory.[35]

If, as Yerushalmi indicates, what we call oblivion in the collective sense emerges when human groups fail to transmit to posterity what they have learned from the past and they transmit those events that they consider formative of the sense of identity and destiny of a people, the trial affected the foundations of our collective identity by retrieving from oblivion something forgotten in order to make it subject of our memory. [Following the pardons] a great part of this history is marginalized from the memory of a society that has not yet posed the crucial question of its own protagonism in the period that the government is trying to bury. In this respect, the pardons—even if repudiated in principle—meet the will present in society to close [the issue], so that the revision of the past risks the possibility of becoming an accomplished fact.[36]

The failure to implement effectively the 'ethical model' of democracy envisioned during the first period of democratic rule prepared the ground for another model of democracy. This later model is less attentive to the demands of civil society and more concentrated at the level of decision-makers, along the lines of what Guillermo O'Donnell calls 'delegative democracy'.[37]

Concerning the legacy of the past, in the latter model institutional stability has prevailed over normative principles. Indeed, vis-à-vis the treatment of human-rights violations, the pardons projected a discourse intended to construct forgetfulness. As leader of the nation, President Menem opposed any divisive claim, even if such a claim concerned the demand for justice and equality before the law. He advised Argentinians to remain above partisan considerations and to follow the dictates of national reconciliation. By reconciliation he meant refraining from confronting divisive issues and from attributing significance to the issue of past human-rights violations.[38] 'Argentina will not be possible if we continue opening the old wounds, if we continue fostering hatred, distrust among co-nationals, on the basis of the false grounds of discord.'[39]

As he carried out these policies, Menem's administration has been accused of shaping a distortive view of the past in popular memory, a view that manipulates memory to prevent mobilization and to marginalize popular demands:

'Remember in order to prevent repetition' [of historical processes]. As this slogan is used by the ruler, it is a threat. As when Menem admonishes: Beware of having new Mothers of Plaza de Mayo . . .[40]

The construction of oblivion and selective use of memory signalled the highest peak in the regressive treatment of past human-rights violations. In a poll conducted in late 1994, people were asked about the most striking event in the last twenty years. While 23 per cent considered that the 1976 dictatorship was the most influential event they recalled (more than the 18 per cent recalling the Malvinas war or 16 per cent recalling the recent bombings of the AMIA building and the Israeli Embassy in Buenos Aires), only 4 per cent considered the disappearances and the Dirty War to be the most striking events of the last two decades.[41]

This trend involved not only the retreat of civil institutions before the military's pressures, but also the hollowing out (*vaciamiento*) of the democratizing principle of equal justice before the law. As put graphically by Mariano Grondona: 'You can imagine the indignation and outrage of those affected [by the violent repression] as they faced the impunity and the double standard of legality. . . . If a citizen steals a chicken he goes to jail. If a member of the armed forces serially kills he stays home.'[42] Expectations from the government and from politics in general were reduced as Argentina entered a hyperinflationary stage and following the pardons. Most people concerned and the human-rights groups were unable to oppose the anticlimatic phase of regressive policies initiated in the late 1980s. They were also unable to prevent the shift from principles to pragmatic considerations that became acute as hyperinflation convinced most Argentinians about the primacy of the need for stabilization. When asked in 1994 what they most remembered from Alfonsín's administration, 46 per cent of the sample mentioned hyperinflation and only 17 per cent redemocratization.[43] Opinion polls show that almost three-fourths of the representative samples interviewed were primarily concerned with socio-economic issues in 1995: problems such as unemployment, economic recession, and low salaries carried percentages of 58, 7, and 6 per cent, respectively.[44] Still, in 1994, the figure of Ernesto Sábato was considered by 79.6 per cent of interviewed Argentinians as the foremost model of moral authority, thus dissociating current concerns from ideals.[45]

Within the framework of Argentine political history since 1930, civil–military relations were perceived as one of the central factors creating stability and instability. Military moves, petitions, public statements, interventions, and *coups d'état* determined the political and economic direction of the country for decades. Menem's inauguration as president took place in the midst of Argentina's worst economic crisis and followed a period of highly tense relationships between the civilian government and the military over planned reforms of the armed forces and over human-rights issues. Menem decided to disarm the traditional role of the armed forces as a major destabilizing factor. Doing so involved mass pardons for the military, which completed the regressive policies initiated under Alfonsín. During his administration, these policies were shaped under the mounting pressures of the armed and security forces; under Menem the initiative was rooted in a presidential decision. As President Menem carried out radical neoliberal policies of macroeconomic stabilization, he decided to neutralize military unrest by trading mass pardons for substantial subordination of the military to civilian rule.

The completion of the regressive trends in the treatment of human-rights violations was launched from above, against the background of a civil society traumatized by the experiences of economic catastrophe and discouragement of public expectations that had characterized the late 1980s.

While in Buenos Aires I went to a demonstration against the pardons. I still remember the feeling. It made me recall a character from Chekhov's work. As death comes to take him, he says: 'I'll go but I protest.' So clear was the futility of acting against an irreversible official decision. We did not feel anymore as agents of change. We began to internalize a world devoid of alternatives to established power . . . Whenever one indulges herself, oblivion promises peace of mind.[46]

Despite the shifts in policies since the initial stages of redemocratization, some groups and associations of civil society carried out sustained efforts that channelled the frustrated hopes for justice to the struggle over the politics of oblivion and memory. Several NGOs played an important role in the struggle for human rights in Argentina. Outstanding are the Centro de Estudios Legales y Sociales (CELS), led by Emilio Fermín Mignone, which operates an important documentation centre; the APDH; the Comisión de Familiares de Desaparecidos por Razones Políticas; the Liga Argentina por los Derechos del Hombre, the Movimiento Ecuménico por los Derechos Humanos (MEDH) and the Movimiento Judío por los Derechos Humanos, led by the late Rabbi Dr Marshall Meyer.

One of the most impressive and influential NGOs in this domain, the Madres de Plaza de Mayo, began with a group of fourteen mothers whose children had been abducted and had disappeared, and whose efforts to locate them had failed. The Mothers began marching every Thursday beginning in March 1977 in Plaza de Mayo, the square in front of Casa Rosada, seat of the Argentine presidency, demanding from the military authorities information and accountability about the whereabouts of their children.

Day after day, Thursday after Thursday we stayed in the Plaza. They called us madwomen, but we kept returning. To struggle and fight it is important to be a little crazy . . . The loss of our children united us. We socialized motherhood. We changed from me to us and from my child to our children. Ours is a collective fight. We know they tortured and executed them. We will never accept their death while their murderers are free. We march in the Plaza for all, not just for our children. For all those who died unjustly in Latin America.[47]

Throughout this period and even more emphatically in later years, the Madres de Plaza de Mayo maintained a continuous claim for comprehensive justice:

We the mothers are a permanent memory; nobody can deceive us, and nobody will be able to prevent our painful march towards the continuation of justice.[48]

Oblivion and pardon cannot be attained by laws and decrees. They cannot be imposed, they cannot be demanded. The people do not forget or forgive. And one form of memory is contempt, the contempt that will fall on their own children [the children of the military repressors], even when they are adults and have to bear the stigma of having a genocidal father.[49]

As long as the bureaucrats in office plan 'final points', amnesties and reconciliations, in secretive and elaborate ways, the Mothers weave with patience the tapestry of collective memory. And they do it in daylight, before everybody's eyes. They have nothing to hide. And nothing to lose either.[50]

Due to the traditional role of motherhood in this society and to their courage and determination, the Mothers (and the Grandmothers— Abuelas de Plaza de Mayo) were able to become the first and most persistent challenger of the military. Their white scarves became an Argentine symbol of demand for freedom and justice, internationally recognized.[51]

Following redemocratization, the Mothers continued to challenge the democratic rulers by resolutely demanding complete truth and justice. However, disagreements emerged within the group concerning the strategy to adopt. The radical political style and stance of Hebe de Bonafini, leader of the group, created a split in 1986 when a group of a dozen mothers formed the Madres-Línea Fundadora (Mothers-Founding Line). The latter, among whom were María Adela Antokoletz and Renée Epelbaum, were determined to work in more pragmatic ways within the political system.

Their members disagreed with Bonafini's intransigent position against exhumations, memorials, and later on reparations. Instead, they favoured a more pluralistic acceptance of concrete mechanisms of compensation, reparation, and perpetuation of the victims' memory, advanced either by the official authorities or by public and private initiatives.[52]

In contrast, struggling over the memory of the victims has meant for Bonafini's organization fighting as well the confinement of memory to ritual *lieux de mémoire*.

[We say] No to the [law of] Final Point, no to impunity, no to the repressive apparatus that remained intact, no to the military men [los milicos] . . . We are not going to allow what we hear often—that they should make a monument [to the missing]. Brick by brick the mothers will tear it apart, since our children do not want monuments. . . . We don't want the topic Human Rights to be taught at school, as long as education is not changed radically, from its base. We cannot teach Human Rights since human rights are to be practised and as long as there is governmental repression, as long as a government beats a student, there is no sense in placing a teacher to teach Human Rights. We are those who practise human rights, everyone of us, day by day, with solidarity towards our brothers, which is the only valuable one, since from there emerge these children who come to these grounds (*plaza*), who accompany us, who understand us in the difficult path we, the Mothers, have chosen. We do not struggle for power or for political space, we fight only for life, for life until death.[53]

Others have shared some of these ethical preoccupations as central to the reconstruction of Argentine collective memory as a whole:

It is necessary to insist on the extreme cruelty and inhumanity of the proceeding: the disappeared were assassinated twice. A planned symbolic death is added to biological death. It was the demented drive of omnipotence of a power that believed it could erase any trace of memory of thousands of human beings: they left no remains, they did not clarify nor tell what happened. The moral crime of discarding human remains as if they were inanimate material, without memory, transforms this tragedy in something particularly unbearable, an ethical hole that must be elaborated and healed collectively.[54]

Consistent with this approach, the Mothers rejected the idea of material reparations of any kind, as compensation for long imprisonment, torture, and disappearance:

We feel anger and shame for those people (whom we cannot call *compañeros* anymore) who have decided to accept that this corrupt government, which has pardoned the genocides, should put a price on horror.

There is no money that can pay for torture, for death, for the forced disappearance of people, for the kidnapping of children, for the destruction, for state terrorism.

The Mothers of Plaza de Mayo regret that there are men and women selling their conscience to those who were (and still are) executioners of their own people.[55]

Their aim is to construct a never-ending sense of elaboration, both rational and ethical, a writing of the past inserted into a shared dimension of knowledge.[56]

Eduardo Rabossi and other figures concerned with the defence of human rights also contemplated a different approach to justice, which takes into consideration the impossibility of totally applying Kant's principle of justice.

Talking with Hebe de Bonafini, I said to her: You are a Kantian. Crime should be punished, I agree. That would make the world better. Theoretically a state could totally assure the lack of theft, by creating an extremely large police force and controlling each step of its citizens. But we would not like to live in such society, and we prefer the risk of theft to the risk of living under such totalitarian control of our lives. . . . In general, the state does not follow the design of total penal control, especially in those cases in which there are substantial political implications and where, as in Argentina, the civilian administration must deal with the power of the military.[57]

The mothers have developed a wide range of activities. Among these, of particular importance is the educational labour they developed by giving talks in secondary schools and universities and by leading workshops in history, philosophy, and politics. Bonafini's organization publishes the monthly *Madres de Plaza de Mayo*, and has published different books and publications. Both organizations cooperate with other NGOs and have taken an active interest in presenting their case through all media channels and other avenues in Argentina and abroad.[58]

In recent years, the CELS has taken a novel approach, shifting from contestatory militancy to professional work in the realm of human rights. This shift, which took place around 1994, implied partially changing the focus of its activities away from the concern with the legacy of past human-rights violations towards current concerns such as police brutality, discrimination of vulnerable groups such as immigrants, access to justice, and training of judges in the protection of human rights. At the current stage, the CELS added to its denunciation of human-rights violations other dimensions, principally changes in the attitudes of power holders and in the institutional links with state agencies. These changes are geared to lessening the confrontational positions of NGOs and the state in recent years and to creating cooperative ventures with the latter, without renouncing being one of the 'external' watchdogs of the state in the field of human rights. As the CELS organized workshops (e.g. on the conditions of imprisonment in Argentina), it discovered the antagonistic reactions of both human-rights activists and state officials to meeting and discussing jointly issues of common concern.[59]

This way of redefining the practice of the NGOs is geared to adopting steps that would incorporate the values and commitment to human rights into the core of Argentine state and society, in a non-ideological way. Such change is hard to be accepted by those who have witnessed what they consider a failure of post-dictatorial justice under democracy. For these sectors, it is still impossible to create a relationship of cooperation with a state that granted impunity to the military repressors and tolerates new infringements of personal and collective rights. Bonafini's Mothers make efforts to preserve the memory of the missing sons and daughters by adopting the ideological banners of the fallen. This ideological position has brought them to fight not only for the discovery of the whole truth about the disappearance of their children, but also for the cause of human rights in its widest interpretation in Argentina, Latin America, and the whole world. This interpretation included the civil, political, and socio-economic dimensions of human rights in a manner ideologically close to Marxist, libertarian, and Third-Worldist ideological positions, like those whose heyday was in the 1960s and 1970s. In their journal, there are numerous articles dealing with social justice, international solidarity, and many issues and causes presented from a radical point of view. The Mothers took staunch positions against Apartheid in South Africa, US intervention in Libya and Iraq, regarding Israeli-Palestinian relations, the defence of Cuba, and against the role of the USA in Central and South America. They adopted a combined strategy that looks backwards and forwards, towards the attainment of the ideals of their beloveds who died in the hands of repressors:

The Fight of our Children continues: The ideology and the fight for redistribution, equality and socialization will not die out, in spite of the advances of the right wing and the trying period that Socialism is living through today. The counter-revolutionaries, in redoubled steps, learned to gallop above the problems and difficulties, riding on the errors, defeatism and crimes of the bureaucrats who, with arrogance and scoffing at the democratic and participatory capacity of the peoples, talked falsely in the name of socialism. . . . The challenge will be to stop this counter-revolution that attempts to free markets and enslave the peoples as they take advantage of the uneasiness of a great part of the European leftist leaderships and rank and file. This is the challenge of the socialists (and revolutionaries) that strive, as our children strove, to build a more just society for the future.[60]

As a result of this strategy that looks backwards and forwards at the same time, symbolically brought together in their public campaign for the accomplishment of their missing children's ideals, the Mothers are trying to preserve the memory of the *desaparecidos* as a living one with current significance. Sectors of the population react to their activities with distaste and feelings of unease, in the same way in which they resent and try to avoid books, films, plays, and other artistic creations bringing back the spectre of the Dirty War. These reactions spring from both a process of social disaggregation and from the saturation of the public sphere with human-rights issues.[61]

Struggling over the memory of the victims has meant, for the relatives of the victims, making efforts to obtain public acknowledgement, to inscribe pain and the deeds of the repressors within the collective memory of the nation. The last page of the monthly *Madres de Plaza de Mayo* is illustrative, as it presents monthly cases composing a 'Gallery of Repressors'. Readers are advised to cut and keep the articles, which are framed within dotted lines, with the accompanying phrase 'Cut the oblivion, keep the memory.'[62]

Paradigmatic to the official resistance to grant public space to the memory of victims has been the recent case of high school No. 1 of the 16th educational district of Buenos Aires. For more than five months pupils, teachers, and parents had been discussing different proposals for naming the school and chose Rodolfo Walsh, the well-known writer and spokesman of the Peronist left slain during the Dirty War, as their designated name. As the proposal reached the Secretariat of Education of the municipality, it was rejected on the grounds that 'the date of Walsh's death is uncertain,' and as an alternative the name of the pilot and writer Antoine de Saint-Exupéry was suggested. A rapid check revealed that the author of *Le Petit Prince* had also disappeared during a flight in 1944 and the date of his death is uncertain too. FREPASO representatives at the council intend to carry on with the original project in the near future.[63]

In the media, it was the daily *Página/12*, and specifically journalist HoracioVerbitsky, that systematically kept public attention focused on the issue of human-rights violations, even when interest waned after the government's regressive policy turn (e.g. pardons) and the macroeconomic situation came to dominate public concern.[64] Verbitsky's prestige as an honest journalist, who sticks to the facts and verifies them thoroughly, gave his research notes and articles added impact, as they from time to time revealed new facets of the legacy of authoritarianism. The most pronounced impact in this work was that raised by Scilingo's confessions in March 1995 (see Chapter 3).

Following Scilingo's revelations and around the twentieth anniversary of the 1976 military coup, a new generation that came to age after the period of the trials and the public coverage of human-rights violations in the mid-1980s heard of the atrocities of the military period. The young people had not known or had been largely unconcerned about that legacy, a fact reflected in numerous panels, polls, and interviews in the Argentine media.

For us, all that, the 'disappeared' and the dirty war was more a story than something real . . . Do you know what? Those youngsters [the radical leftists of the 1960s and 1970s] were totally wrong, but at least they had ideals. We do not have political ideals since we think that everyone lies and therefore we are not interested in the past.[65]

The new generations that grew up under democracy couldn't believe the Scilingo story. For him [Scilingo] and his generation, that was the history they lived through; they had lived the series of developments that took place in a violent society, a society in which violence increased constantly. For the others, it was like showing them how the country was twenty years earlier. I do not say we understand what happened, but we were used to living in the midst of violence. For the youngsters aged 15 or 20, the collective spirit exposed [by the revelations] seemed even more horrendous the further we moved from the events.[66]

Some of the younger sectors, especially the children of the victims, organized themselves into an association of Children for Identity and Justice and against Oblivion and Silence (HIJOS, the Spanish word for children), which began collaborating with the Mothers and participated actively in their actions. This association grew as the new generation, which had not been affected directly, heard about the horrors of the repression and was shocked, thus beginning among some of the youngsters a process of collective learning about the past. This process of social learning recreated links among young people in general and among some of the most active groups struggling to maintain the memory of the past.

We are the children of men and women who disappeared, who were assassinated, who were political prisoners or went to exile. Our commitment is multiplied by the necessity of demanding justice, of bringing the assassins and their collaborators to jail, of reconstructing individual and collective history, [of maintaining] the memory of a generation that fought for the country of all, for a better country.

We are alive and face a reality that attempts to silence us, demobilize us . . . . To be together is to recover the spirit of fight, to challenge power and its mandate of 'don't get involved', to challenge those who try to convince us that it is better to be resigned than to fight for a better country for all. Those who believed in the victory of death were wrong. Twenty years later we stand to say we are here. Thanks to the old ladies and to those who dug trenches in this *plaza* in order to keep the memory. The living faces of our parents escort us.[67]

Scilingo's declarations reopened the debate, which spread to wide circles, involving the political class, the military, concerned NGOs, intellectuals, the Church, and the public in general. The ensuing statements by General Balza received significant civilian support, although some human-rights activists demanded an even more critical stance.

The revelations also emboldened the ongoing debates concerning the attitudes and guilt for what happened in Argentina between 1976 and

1983. In the Church, the claims for self-criticism led to only partial and qualified recognition. No institutional responsibility was acknowledged, in spite of the new revelations that clearly proved that the Church had provided spiritual support to both the heads of the juntas and to the military personnel charged with repression. These debates were replicated within the armed forces. General Balza indicated that, although large sectors of society had supported and even demanded a military intervention in 1976, 'we are now 20 years after an event that we all condemn, some more, some less, but we all condemn it, and you will find nobody in the army, sorry, almost nobody, who defends the thesis of the coup d'état. We are building the army of the future and I am interested in the army's youth.'[68] But General Mario Cándido Díaz, the commander of the joint staff of the armed forces, declared, in an act commemorating the fourteenth anniversary of the Argentine military landing in the Malvinas Islands, that he rejected each and every criticism directed against the armed and security forces, one of the 'fundamental institutions of the fatherland', criticism which he claimed caused malaise in governmental and public circles.[69]

The twentieth anniversary of the 1976 coup was commemorated with a series of symbolic mass meetings in most major cities. In Buenos Aires, the Committee for Memory, Truth, and Justice organized the closing act for March 24 in Plaza de Mayo. The organizers managed to convince the judiciary, against the government's wishes, that they themselves would keep the peace and not the police, who in an earlier gathering of students in the city of La Plata had resorted to violence. The major political force, the Partido Justicialista, did not take part in the act, reinforcing its contestary character. An estimated 50,000 to 100,000 participants repudiated the coup and professed their commitment to democracy.[70]

In parallel, a series of events demonstrated the vitality of the willingness to remember. Teachers' unions and educational authorities organized classes of commemoration in several provincial school systems. Secondary schools organized special activities. In one case, a school filmed a video-reminder as a generational homage to the thousands of adolescents assassinated during the 1970s. Another school performed a historical re-enactment of the period through role playing of military and guerrilla figures and through inquiries to real actors who had lived through the PRN.[71] The Argentine Soccer Association agreed to the players' union's demand to maintain a minute's silence in the stadiums before the games.[72] All these events constituted, according to an observer, 'live scenarios for the exercise of memory'.[73] Around the twentieth anniversary various testimonial works were published about the experiences lived through by Argentinians under military rule, together with cultural creations that addressed the problem of the past, such as the films *Cazadores de utopías* by David Blaustein and *Montoneros* by Andrés Di Tella.[74] The anniversaries of specific acts of repression, for example against students, are being commemorated with massive participations in contemporary Argentina.[75]

On 22 March 1996, the Mothers and Grandmothers of Plaza de Mayo petitioned the judicial system, asking that a number of judges (including a member of the Supreme Court, Augusto Belluscio) be fired and tried for their involvement in violations. The Mothers argued that these judges, having sworn allegiance to the statutes of the military juntas, were partly responsible for acts such as homicide, torture, and illegal deprivation of liberty. On 24 March around 100 habeas corpus petitions were presented by a delegation of HIJOS.[76]

Not less important were the activities led by the Grandmothers of Plaza de Mayo aimed at locating children born in captivity to political prisioners or abducted with or without their persecuted parents, many of them adopted by military couples or others. Since 1983 the Grandmothers composed a list of 230 children taken by force from their parents during the dictatorship. They succeeded in identifying 59 of them, of which 31 were brought back to their natural relatives, 14 remained with the adoptive families after good faith in the adoption was proved, 8 were murdered, and the remaining 6 stayed with the substitute families in spite of the circumstances of their adoption. The other 171 are still among the disappeared.[77] In early June 1998 the former head of the first military junta, Lt.-Gen. Videla, was detained following a decision of federal judge Roberto Marquevich in a case concerning the 'theft' of five babies born to political prisoners in captivity. The decision took all major parties concerned by surprise.[78] Although Videla was condemned for life and later on freed following the 1990 pardons, local jurisprudence has considered—albeit not unanimously—that the crimes of child abduction and forgery of identity can neither be prescribed nor covered by the granted pardons. The Grandmothers of Plaza de Mayo expressed satisfaction, although they were unaware of this development in a judicial case they had initiated in 1985. For the executive, the judge's decision came as a source of immediate worry for its possible impact on the format of civilian–military relationships, as retired and acting military officers voiced their concern vis-à-vis what they defined as 'a wave of vengeance' (*revanchismo*).[79] On a different plane, the autonomy shown by the judiciary in human rights-related cases could well serve as an argument for President Menem to relieve the international pressure put on Argentina by the pending cases of human-rights violations being heard in Europe.[80]

In the 1990s locales of memory remained foci of dissent. In March 1996 political activists, backed by the municipality of Buenos Aires, tried to create a pictorial mural in the victims' memory on the grounds of a former detention centre. That centre, however, currently functions as a police office, and the police prevented the installation of the mural.[81] In January 1998 President Menem issued a decree sanctioning the demolition of the ESMA buildings in order to use the grounds for public purposes and as a sign of national reconciliation. Following a legal appeal by NGOs and parliamentarians of the FREPASO, the decree 8/98 was suspended by a federal judge. The decision was based on the claim that the demolition of one of the major centres of torture and assassination 'would erase proofs concerning the destiny of thousands of forced disappeared'.[82]

The politics of oblivion and memory is open to the persistence of contrasting visions of the past. Over two decades after the beginning of the PRN, there are those who remember 'the crimes committed by the torturers'; others remember 'the tragic errors of the radical youth'; still others, 'the military victory over subversion'; and finally, there are those such as Interior Minister Carlos Corach, who professes to remember the importance of 'national reconciliation'. But has the past been superseded? The reactions connected with the politics of memory have recently turned violent in the form of attacks against perpetrators of human-rights violations. The attacks against Astiz and Bergés (see Chapter 3 above) and the recentring of the scars of the past in the public agenda should be interpreted as a recurrent reaction against the policies of oblivion. The divided visions of the past die hard.

The Politics of Oblivion and Memory in Redemocratized Uruguay

In Uruguay, in contrast with Argentina, citizenship was historically based on a series of shared understandings and views of the nation. The experience of military dictatorship partly shattered these visions of Uruguay as a civilian and civil nation. But the shared ground of that experience provided a basis for elaboration following the transition to democracy. Thus, for example, when Uruguayans met in 1986 for a round of discussions on the recent experience of their country and the prospects of democracy, they seemed to share a basic consensual view of their country's past. Saúl Sosnowski, the workshop convener, discerned in the meetings the existence of an essential base that justified 'variants' of regimes, but not —or at least not yet—a radical transformation that would demand the final abandonment of something so dear to national mythification . . . The initial drive was to protect the 'fragile democracy' from any attack, even of the threat of a divisive debate . . . Maintaining the best segments of liberalism is seen as the rescue ladder in a historic moment of seeming initial recuperation. Basic questioning is therefore an uneasy task . . . that eradicates the rotten or failing base without replacing it with other myths that do not meet with the fragrant warmth of nostalgia and the recovery of utopia.[83]

Disagreements were not lacking, but there was a basic agreement on the importance of redemocratization, which reinforced the willingness to focus on the common interest rather than to open debate around 'turbulent disagreements'.

Meanwhile, although a similar tension existed between exiles and 'insiles', the theme did not enter the agenda as a focus of dissent and debate, as in Argentina, but rather as two positions in a joint bridging experience.

The very creation of the term 'insile' to identify the rejection of the [military] regime and the marginalization [of the intellectuals] in the country as equivalent to the experience of the exiles, served to soften the identification of national borders as the only demarcating line of attitudes facing the dictatorship.[84]

The military regime was seen as a sort of catastrophe that fell on Uruguayan society as a whole. Those launching the dictatorship were depicted as standing outside the basic understandings and value parameters shared by the whole Uruguayan society. Eduardo Galeano put it as follows:

During the twelve years of military dictatorship Liberty was only the name of a prison . . . One out of every eighty Uruguayans suffered from torture (his head covered with a hood). But invisible hoods were placed also upon all other Uruguayans, as they were confined and could not communicate with the outside world, even though they escaped torture . . . The armed forces acted as if they were an occupation army in their own countries . . . The guerrilla threat served as an excuse for the terrorism of the State.[85]

During the transition and after 1985, the thriving media, especially the press, was instrumental in keeping the debate alive in the public sphere concerning the legacy of human-rights violations. As in Chile, substantial parts of the Uruguayan press were closely identified with different political orientations and took clear positions in dealing with the legacy of authoritarianism. The weekly *Opinar*, which began publication in 1983 under the editorship of Enrique Tarigo (who would become Vice-President in redemocratized Uruguay), served as a forum for discussing the issue under military rule and reported Pérez

Aguirre's and SERPAJ's denunciations of continuing torture during the political negotiations leading to the transition. The press, spearheaded by *Jaque*, under the editorship of Manuel Flores Silva, made public the blatant case of torture and police murder of physician Vladimir Roslik on 15 April 1984, which constituted one of the most flagrant cases of human-rights violations, and tilted the negotiations during the political opening in a new direction.[86] Prominent on the left side of the media was *La hora*, with Communist ties; *Mate amargo*, identified with the MLN-Tupamaros movement for the return to democracy; and *Brecha*, associated with Frente Amplio and covering the human-rights issue consistently. The ideas of the National (Blanco) party were reflected in *La democracia*, while *La república* supported the green vote since 1988 (see Chapter 2). This debate was very important in the process of consolidating various versions of public opinion that became crucial for the later incorporation of memory.[87] Testimonial literature appeared, which presented in highly emotional terms the texture of life in prison of those political activists who suffered torture and reclusion for years, beginning in the early 1970s. Probably the most influential testimonies of this kind are Ernesto González Bermejo's *Las manos en el fuego*, which relates the experiences of David Cámpora who lived in various prisons between April 1972 and December 1980, and Mauricio Rosencof and Eleuterio Fernández Huidobro's reminiscences of the long periods they, as Tupamaros activists, shared in Uruguayan prisons (where they served thirteen and fifteen years, respectively).[88] At the same time, testimonies were published with the explicit aim of precluding oblivion and maintaining the memory of resistance to the military rule.[89]

The legal/institutional solution advanced by the civilian politicians won the 1989 referendum by a narrow margin. In spite of the narrow margin, however, this solution was widely accepted and served, in following years, as a basis for the political leaders' repeated claims that the debate had been definitively closed (in contrast to Argentina).[90] This closure projected the legacy of human-rights violations into the realm of oblivion and memory.

But even in this realm, the potential actors interested in conducting a politics of memory around the victims lacked the protagonism that characterized similar organizations in Argentina and to lesser extent in Chile. The role played by the Association of Mothers and Relatives of Detainees-Disappeared in Uruguay has been illustrative. This forum was informally established around 1978 by people who were looking for their missing loved ones. Since the majority of missing Uruguayans disappeared in Argentina, it was largely there that the relatives demonstrated, joining the activities of the Argentine

Madres. In the mobilization for the referendum, between 1986 and 1989, they were active, joining the Comisión Nacional Pro-Referendum. Subsequently, this group did not play a leading role. It reacted mostly to the initiatives of the political class and was increasingly marginalized in the public sphere.

It was evident that the Association of Relatives of Detainees-Disappeared was weak as a social agent, as it lacked its own frame of reference, which would be a source of identity, capable of playing a role in the democratic dynamic. The fact that they sustained a specific mandate as the sole base of collective effort ['núcleo'] not only conditioned the movement's continuity, but also established precise limits on its capacity to incorporate new members.[91]

At present, the group attempts to influence the government in legislation (e.g. that the figure of the missing should be recognized in law) but is mostly concerned with the issue of memory. In a 1995 interview, the Uruguayan Mothers complained about the lack of public space devoted to the memory of the missing. Until the late 1990s, the municipality of Montevideo, dominated by the left-wing Frente Amplio, refrained from full-fledged allocation of space for establishing a public monument in memory of the victims of repression. It only devoted a bronze plaque in a small square 'to the [undifferentiated] memory of the detained-disappeared in America', in Montevideo. In a clear-cut contrast with the Chilean official initiative, the locale did not indicate the names and dates of the disappearance of victims. The spirit of the project was of a more general and diffuse character, envisioning it as

a contribution to collective memory, with the purpose of opening demands in favour of human dignity, not only for those who have suffered personally by not ignoring it [i.e. ignoring human dignity], but also for the benefit of future generations. . . . In the framework of human-rights violations, the forcible disappearance of people is, undoubtedly, a paradigmatic case, a crime, not only of the past, but also a current crime . . .[92]

Only in February 1999, a project was chosen for finally launching the construction of a public monument in memory of the disappeared, in a part in the Cerro of Montevideo. The Uruguayan Mothers, in contrast with the Argentine Mothers, are trying to expand this localization of memory, as their way of 'honouring the missing by dedicating [to their memory] a medical clinic or a kindergarten'.[93] The group has also devoted efforts to clarifying the whereabouts of the abducted children of the victims and has published two booklets, one of a general nature and one describing the successful restoration of a child to her biological family.[94]

Despite the claims that the issue of past human-rights violations was closed after the referendum, the legacies of the dictatorship have remained an open issue on the sideline of the public agenda, 'un tema pendiente', as Carlos Demasi recently indicated.[95] Still ahead lies the search of conscience and deep questioning. Catholic priest Father Pérez Aguirre—speaking about the missing memory of the detained-disappeared in Uruguay—reflected on the inconclusiveness of the Uruguayan path. He emphasized that in societies in which impunity triumphs, state institutions promote collective forgetfulness of violations of human rights. It has to be understood, he said, that oblivion and impunity go hand in hand. He concluded: 'You don't remember, you don't judge the past only to punish or to condemn, but in order to learn too. Oblivion must be fought with energy, because it impedes the kind of historical learning vital to recomposing the identity of the people and to facing the future.'[96] The process of reflection may challenge Uruguay's self-image and foundational myths. The breakdown of democracy has often been portrayed in Uruguay as the product of actions of elements external to the nation's true 'spirit'. But the armed forces were not the only ones responsible for bringing society to the verge of violence and self-destruction. Different social sectors and individuals pushed or at least supported the military as they took increasing power and finally replaced the civilian government in the early 1970s. The collective involvement in and support for the *coup d'état* was recognized during redemocratization, but this problem has been addressed mainly through mutual criticisms of one sector against another; that is, it has been enmeshed in partisan considerations and political moves. Thus, while the central political forces ignored the issue, both the right wing and the left wing accused each other of conniving with the military. The MLN accused bankers, entrepreneurs, the Colorado Party, and the US-oriented political class of contributing to the military coup, while the rightist forces denounced leftist agitation and destabilization as the triggers of the coup.

As time passed and as the institutional paths seem closed, individuals began calling for reflection about past deeds (i.e. about the role they and other sectors of civil society played in the past) as a necessary step in shaping a democratic public culture. Hugo Achugar has been the most explicit in calling Uruguayans to a review of conscience that would facilitate recovering the democratic narrative of the nation. Achugar has noted that the twin processes of forgetting and remembering are fundamental poles central to the construction of a collective identity. In this connection, he pointed out that societies emerging from repressive authoritarian rule should make a conscious distinction between two forms of oblivion. One is an imposed mechanism that signals the inability of a society to confront thorny issues such as the roles played by various social forces in the processes leading to the military takeover. The other is a voluntary mechanism, instrumental in selecting themes to remain in the public domain and in the continuous shaping of collective identity.[97]

After the military period, there was a radical change in the rules of the game and in the self-perception of Uruguayans. The inhabitants of the Banda Oriental could no longer assume that they were a distinct, European-like society, rather than a Latin American society with recurrent crises. Even though in the 1960s and 1970s such claims were voiced by intellectuals, they were largely dismissed due to the leftist characterization of the latter. Following the 1973–85 experience, the dictatorship entered into the category of the imaginable, of the plausible, as a widely expressed notion in the Uruguayan scene. As other countries in the region, the democratic 'soul' of the nation could no longer be taken for granted (see also Chapter 7, below).

Historical debates interacted with unexpected developments, like Tróccoli's declarations, and with attempts made by politicians and concerned sectors to reopen the issue of memory and of the place to be awarded to the experience of past human-rights violations in the reconstituted identity of the country.

The central figure in leading this trend has been Senator Rafael Michelini, the son of assassinated Colorado Senator Zelmar Michelini. He was invited to give a lecture at the academy of CALEN (Centro de Altos Estudios Nacionales de las Fuerzas Armadas). In that lecture, on 15 May 1996, Rafael Michelini stated that the armed forces were responsible for assassinating his father in the framework of the political repression. These declarations generated much unease within the military and tensions between them and the Minister of Defence, Raúl Iturria.[98]

On 18 May the members of the armed forces commemorated the Day of the Fallen in Defence of the Institutions, previously known as the Day of Commemoration of those Fallen in the Fight against Subversion. In the main speech, the commander-in-chief of the armed forces harshly criticized the wave of revisionism 'that is trying to damage the [military] institution'.[99] Michelini, who was conducting a public campaign to force the government to acknowledge past human-rights violations and to provide information concerning victims, called for a massive march in homage to the *desaparecidos*. The march—known as the March for Truth, Memory and Never Again, or as the March of Silence—was planned for 20 May 1996, on the twentieth anniversary of the killing of Colorado Senator Zelmar Michelini and Speaker of the Chamber of Deputies Héctor Gutiérrez Ruiz of the National Party. The initiative, supported by some politicians and by trade unionists, religious and social organizations, human-rights groups, and the families of the missing and the victims of military repression, was planned to exclude speeches. People were encouraged to carry Uruguayan flags and to lay a rose at the Monument of Liberty, in memory of the missing. The march was attended by between 30,000 and 50,000 individuals and was conducted in almost complete silence. When some of the participants attempted to sing a phrase stating that the military deserved the death penalty rather than pardons, they were silenced by the multitudes. Similarly, when the military march used during 1973–85 was heard from a house overlooking the march, the massive reaction was to cover its music by singing the national anthem.[100]

The march was accompanied in the Uruguayan Parliament by an act of homage to the murdered parliamentarians, preceded by a compromise between the major political forces not to mention the armed forces' involvement in the assassination of Michelini and Gutiérrez Ruiz. The commemorations were thus characterized by the silence that surrounded both the march and the parliamentary act. This silence reflected the tacit agreement of major political forces and the military not to reopen the debate closed by the 1989 referendum. Rafael Michelini's New Space Party and the Encuentro Progresista block (composed by the left-wing Frente Amplio and dissident sectors of the National Party), which together have over 30 per cent of the national vote, would welcome such an opening. However, they too are committed to national reconciliation. Beyond tactical considerations, the use of silence in the march carried deep symbolic meanings, intended to convey deep pain, sorrow, and solemnity. No justice was demanded but rather the attainment of full truth. In evaluating the effects of the march, Rafael Michelini considered:

Up to the day of the march, there were those who used to say that the Law of Expiry—which had solved the legal and penal aspects—had also obviated the other problems, such as the theme of reconciliation. The march showed that there are things that remain unsolved. . . . There are very deep and profound fibres of Uruguayan society that were touched and that are trying to find an equilibrium that would enable reconciliation again. Without a doubt there is the issue of the missing and the fact that the state did not provide answers. . . . Reconciliation will have to come through the truth, through memory and through guarantees—in the conscience of every one—that this will not occur anymore. . . . The state must assume the responsibility of recognizing that this happened, that there were people who were responsible for those deeds, and that the victims deserved a just treatment . . . irrespective of their affiliation or lack of affiliation with an illegal or armed organization.

We demand a change of perspective. . . . We demand the obvious, to bury the dead.[101]

In spite of a wide consensus about the institutional closure of issue, feelings of inconclusiveness and a sense of disorientation remain, which even the leftist journal *Brecha* poignantly conveyed on its front page the day after the 1996 march: 'And now what?'

In March 1997 Michelini asked the courts to inquire about the possible existence of buried corps of detainees-disappeared in the grounds of military camps. The courts tried to carry out this request without success, due to the explicit opposition of Lt.-Gen. Raúl Mermot, commander-general of the armed forces, who issued an order of non-compliance to his subordinates.[102] In May 1997 a second March of Silence took place, with the explicit support of the Church, which offered its services to get confidential information from the military about the fate and place of burial of the forced disappeared and transmit it to the relatives, without revealing the source.[103] In December 1997 Pedro Sclofsky, president of the Central Jewish Committee of Uruguay, reopened public debate on human-rights violations as he declared that 'it is an inalienable right to know the burial place of one's kin.'[104] The incomplete treatment of past human-rights violations continues to haunt the Uruguayan public sphere.

The Politics of Oblivion and Memory in Redemocratized Chile

For years, in protests and street demonstrations we heard the cry: 'Tell us where they are'. They were mostly women, bearing on their bodies a photograph (and some, more than one) of their beloved father, brother, husband. They became living memories, reminding us of a history that was being secluded. I still remember with shock the father who, in the style of a *bonze*, immolated himself in flames in an act of impotence because he was not told where his children were being held . . . The years of the dictatorship reflect a traumatic experience, encoded in the polarity between collective and personal memory, and in the dynamics between memory and oblivion, which each person has internalized in a different way. We are loaded down with memories that we must still make room in the family album . . .[105]

The constraints on Chilean redemocratization implied that the disparate visions held by the military and their supporters did not disappear once the forces of the Concertación reached power under democracy. Even though democracy began operating around a common agreement about the need for national reconciliation, each of the sides interpreted reconciliation differently and retained varied visions of memory.

The political path adopted by President Patricio Aylwin's administration forced a redefinition of these positions by establishing an official truth through the work of the Rettig Commission and the President's presentation of its report to the wide public. Aylwin was asked in 1995 if the virtual impunity granted to most perpetrators of human-rights violations had imbued Chile's political culture with the idea that, in a future (hypothetical) situation verging on civil war, gross abuses would again be justified to 'save the nation'; Aylwin replied:

I do not believe that, if situations of conflict develop in Chile in another 50 to 100 years, what happened now would determine the paths of action and the conscience of the actors then. An exemplary punishment would be undoubtedly better from that point of view. [But] I believe that, as the report of the Commission of Truth and Reconciliation states, to create in the country a culture of respect for human rights is far more important than punishing past deeds. . . . The truth is that what happened was so brutal that it exceeds the imaginable. It is only comparable with the Holocaust, not in magnitude but in terms of analogous procedures, absolutely barbaric. [What is important is] the simple moral horror vis-à-vis the past, which generates a culture of respect for human life.[106]

The symbolic acts undertaken by the democratic government from the beginning of its tenure in March 1990 led to a process of creating physically defined *lieux de mémoire*. On 4 September 1990, the Chilean civilian government carried out a public ceremony for the reburial of former President Salvador Allende's remains, which had been located in an anonymous grave in Viña del Mar, where he had been buried by the military when they took power in September 1973. Exactly twenty years after Allende was elected as President of Chile, the government of Patricio Aylwin decided to honour his memory and bring him to rest in the General Cemetery of Santiago, where most former heads of state are buried. The tomb became a focus of commemoration and every year, on 11 September, Leftist activists pay homage to Allende's memory.

Similarly, on 26 February 1994 a public monument was inaugurated in memory of the detained-disappeared victims and those executed for political reasons. The monument was erected by the *Memoria* Foundation, presided over by the Subsecretary of the Interior, Belisario Velasco, with contributions from private and public sources. It was located near the main entrance in the General Cemetery of Santiago, and consists of a 30-metre-long 4-metre-high marble wall, in which the names of more than 4,000 victims of repression were engraved. The wall is surrounded by four huge heads in marble, intended to represent the absent dead 'who wait to recover their dignity in the remembrance of all the people'.[107] The memorial was symbolically inaugurated by the pouring of an eternal fountain of water brought by the relatives of the victims from all the regions of the country. The act, as well as the verse by the poet Raúl Zurita that crowns the names of the victims ('all my love is here and has remained close to the rocks, the sea, and the mountains') aimed to transform the memorial into an icon of Chile, anchoring the memory of the victims in the context of its primordial landscape. The monument gave the public a focus for remembering and honouring the memory of those who died in the most flagrant cases of human-rights violations.[108]

The establishment of such locales of collective memory did not put an end to the competition among interpretations of the past. Rather, a symbolic struggle over public hegemony was re-enacted. The public ceremony of relocating Allende's remains was preceded by a Te Deum mass at the Santiago Metropolitan Cathedral and a funeral procession, in which tens of thousands of Chileans mourned Allende publicly, for the first time since his death in 1973. The ceremony was attended by the highest civilian authorities, led by President Aylwin, by Hortensia Bussi (widow of Allende), by the French Prime Minister Michel Rocard, by a Cuban delegation, and other foreign dignitaries. An MIR deputy, Patricio Rivas, voiced the opinion of the extreme left, praising the civilian administration's effort 'to preserve an example of real reconciliation' through this funeral. Right-wing politicians and the military, led by General Augusto Pinochet, boycotted the ceremony, declaring that Allende's presidency had produced social and economic chaos and that he had planned to establish a Marxist dictatorship. During the funeral, seven bombs exploded in Santiago, and the Carabineros conducted mass arrests. Unrest was reported from other Chilean cities as well.[109]

Struggle over the interpretation of recent history and symbols has been re-enacted periodically whenever the 11th of September, the date of Pinochet's coup, approaches. During military rule the 11th of September was declared a national holiday. Following redemocratization in 1990, as the public sphere opened to debate, clashes concerning interpretations of recent Chilean history have centred around the meaning of the 11th of September. Surveys have traced these disparate interpretations and views. In 1993, those who supported the military's thesis of having liberated Chile from Marxism were 30 per cent of the sample, being older, wealthier, and of higher status than those who supported the alternative argument that the military had created a repressive dictatorship, who amounted to 53.9 per cent. Those who had no opinion, did not answer, or were uncertain constituted 16.1 per cent of the sample and up to 25 per cent of those were from higher socioeconomic strata.[110]

On every anniversary of the 1973 events, both sides have commemorated publicly those events in diametrically opposed ways. On that date, the different military branches commemorate with pride their public intervention and mourn those among their comrades in arms who lost their lives defending their public vision. Participating in masses of remembrance, using national flags, singing the anthem, and giving patriotic speeches, the active and retired members of the armed and security forces pledge allegiance to national values. Following democratization, every commemoration of the 1973 coup has been marked by Pinochet's and other generals' claim that the issue of human rights is used by civilian politicians in a Machiavellian way. According to the military leaders, those political forces that created the chaos leading to the military takeover in 1973 are still trying to affect the status and role of the armed forces by attacking them on the human-rights front.

Anniversaries have been marked by new public scandals involving the military. In 1990 the *Valmoval* case and the fate of the Lo Curro presidential residence (built by Pinochet in the 1980s) produced fresh controversies; in 1992 revelations concerning the military's spying on right-wing politicians drew public outcries. On 11 September 1991, Pinochet presented the second volume of his memoirs, *Camino recorrido: memorias de un soldado*, in which he developed a defence of his policies. The UDI, the right-wing political party closest to the military, centred its annual event around the memory of assassinated senator Jaime Guzmán, awarding a medal to General Pinochet.[111] In 1995, in the midst of the Contreras-Espinoza crisis and along with Pinochet's incursion into politics to block the proposed constitutional and legal reforms of President Frei, sectors of the right suggested the establishment of a Fundación Presidente Augusto Pinochet as an educational organization. This foundation was conceived as a way for the military and their supporters to advance their interests during their struggle for hegemony in the Chilean public sphere.[112]

The 11th of September has continued to provoke troublesome memories for those who opposed military rule, especially for the most heavily persecuted sectors in the extreme left. While the government and the Church used that date to call for national reconciliation, the sectors discussed above have opted to demonstrate publicly and even violently against impunity for past repressors and against the current policies of the civilian administration. In 1992 clashes erupted when leftist demonstrators tried to extinguish the eternal flame in a monument to military men killed in action in front of La Moneda presidential palace in downtown Santiago. Earlier in the day, as hundreds of Pinochet's supporters rallied to his residence to celebrate the coup, he declared that the action taken on 11 September 1973 'was not a mission assigned by the armed forces, but rather the people of Chile requested it to free them from Marxist aggression'.[113] The most acute confrontations took place on the 1993 and 1995 anniversaries. In 1993, on the twentieth anniversary of the military coup, violence resulted in two deaths as thousands of demonstrators called for punishment of human-rights abusers under Pinochet and tried to break through security barriers in downtown Santiago. For the first time, the media showed harsh documentaries and extensively discussed the 1973 events around the *coup d'état*. Pinochet's supporters organized memorial events and marches and an all-night vigil in support of their leader outside the General's home in Santiago.[114] During that week, in the aristocratic Union Club, Pinochet rejected various accusations:

Every so often, the issue of human rights comes up. Good, and so you weigh it in the balance. Everything we did, you weigh it in the balance. The other day, a woman journalist told me, 'Listen to the poor mothers, who lost their sons, who were taken to prison and never returned.' Yes, they were bandits. They were nothing else but bandits. We did not move against disarmed people, against unprepared or innocent people. Here in Chile there were 15,000 guerrillas.[115]

General Pinochet has preached reconciliation via oblivion. In September 1995, in the midst of the Contreras crisis and the political negotiations around constitutional reform and human-rights violations, he explained his views:

People talk about reconciliation, but they attack the army commander, they accuse him and they harass him, but when he responds, they accuse him of opposing the unity of Chile . . . Both sides should forget. We must continue working for Chile, for our republic; we should not look back. Let's not allow this country to become a third-class nation but a second- or first-class one if possible. But to achieve that it is necessary to be intelligent, capable, and to have the ability to forget. . . . Gentlemen, the only alternative is to forget. This is not achieved by reopening court cases and by throwing people in jail. No, forget is the word.[116]

Since the late 1970s and 1980s, and into the democratic period, a substantial sector of those who had supported the military have suggested oblivion when new revelations about past and present atrocities reached the media. Although these sectors had not been involved directly in repression and were shocked by its extent and severity, they were the principal beneficiaries of the Pinochet administration's economic policies and of the latter's endorsement of what they perceived as their legitimate social privileges. These social sectors, with some exceptions, strongly opposed any politics of memory centred on events involving human-rights violations, as depicted among others by Isabel Allende in her novel *De amor y de sombra*. In this book, centred around the discovery in a Lonquén mine in 1978 of the bodies of fifteen individuals assassinated in 1973, Allende develops two parallel histories. One is the official history of order, stability, and prosperity, sustained by the military and their supporters, and the alternative history is that of coercion, repression, and poverty. As perceived by the beneficiaries of military rule, there is no sense in reopening inquiries about the past: 'The best is to forget the past and build the future . . . Not to talk anymore of the disappeared. . . . Why the eagerness to identify those bodies of the mine and look for the guilty? That happened years ago, those are musty dead.'[117] Other sectors of Chilean society have tried to reinforce the memory of the repression, irrespective of the passing of time. National polls done in 1993 showed that 53.4 per cent of those sampled supported policies of clarifying human-rights violations and their punishment and an additional 18.5 per cent supported only clarification, while only 17.4 per cent thought it necessary to leave the past behind.[118]

On 11 September 1995 groups publicly displaying—for the first time since military rule—the flags of the Movimiento de Izquierda Revolucionaria (MIR) took to Santiago's streets and blocked the city's main thoroughfares, violently clashing with the police. Demonstrations took place in different parts of the city, while the security forces were ordered to show restraint, due to the charged symbolic atmosphere and significance of the 11th of September. Some of the demonstrators vandalized and looted shops, barricaded streets, stoned public buildings, and fired on police vehicles, in the capital, in peripheral working-class neighbourhoods, and in Concepción. One of their main actions was the takeover of the Monument of the Detained-Disappeared in the General Cemetery. Unwilling to accept the possibility of a legal closure of the human-rights issue as a trade-off for constitutional reform, the protesters reacted, according to a Communist leader, to the lack of an ethical attitude which may have been the example to be followed. When Pinochet is able to express himself without acknowledging his responsibility in the human-rights violations, [the young generation] feels insulted on the grounds of the moral values it strives to attain.'[119] Jorge Inzunsa alluded to the basic line of argumentation of General Pinochet and the military, which was reflected in the five volumes of Pinochet's memoirs, published by the Instituto Geográfico Militar del Ejército. Following the publication of the fifth volume, Jaime Castillo Velasco, the co-founder with Máximo Pacheco of the Chilean Commission of Human Rights, published a book in which he took issue with Pinochet's line, by using the latter's own arguments and judicial testimonies before civilian courts.[120]

The parties to the debate are struggling to promote or deny hegemonic status to each other's interpretations; to promote or avoid the canonization of the victims; and to attain some specific structuration of (historical) time, embedding the past within the present and projecting their visions into the future. Periodicals of different political orientations and affiliations have produced a flurry of original journalistic research, interviews with leading political figures, and analyses of human-rights violations in the democratic period.[121]

One of the major arenas in which such struggle has taken place is that of testimonial literature and journalism. During the years of military rule, a large number of books appeared, focusing on different issues and experiences relating to the policies carried out from 1973. Some related the daily experiences in detention camps.[122] Others, such as Patricia Politzer's book of collected interviews, *Fear in Chile*, reflected the impact of polarization and repression in different sectors of Chilean society.[123] Patricia Verdugo's books brought the tragedy of detainees-disappeared to public attention.[124] Her book *Los zarpazos del Puma* (1989), which describes the massacre of seventy-two prisoners in October 1973 by a military special commission that travelled around the country in a Puma helicopter, became a major editorial success, and was reproduced in numerous 'pirate' editions, selling thousands of copies on the streets.[125] Similar in focus were books such as *Los secretos del comando conjunto*, *Operación Siglo XX*, and *Manuel Contreras: la historia de un intocable*.[126]

By far the most important journalistic work on the military period is *La historia oculta del régimen militar*, published in Santiago by the publisher of the opposition's newspaper, *La Epoca*, in 1988. The book is a detailed chronological and thematic account of the development of military rule in Chile.[127] In February 1991, weeks before the publication of the Rettig Report, the leftist weekly *Apsi* published a special issue dedicated to the problem of human-rights violations during military rule, presenting a comprehensive account of the repressive apparatus (DINA, CNI) and a list of 877 cases of forced disappearances. This kind of combative press activity attempted to uncover the mechanisms of repression. Without having to accept the limitations placed on the Rettig Commission, *Apsi* published the full names of officers and perpetrators of human-rights violations together with a detailed account of their crimes.[128]

In contrast to the above reports and visions of the period are testimonial works authored or inspired by General Pinochet,[129] by Senator Jaime Guzmán,[130] and by leading figures of the military administration such as Generals Medina, Toro, Baez, and Danús (collected by Sergio Marras in *Palabra de soldado*).[131]

Another important, albeit more elitist arena for the re-enactment of memory has been that of the visual arts. Works such as Osvaldo Peña's sculpture *El vigía de la espera* (polyester, 1989), Patricia Israel's painting *La negra noche de América* (oil, 1987), Ernesto Banderas's work *Angelus* (paper, 1989), and the whole portfolio of painter Roser Bru have been interpreted as reflecting in a subtle way a refusal to accept the criteria of cultural homogeneity imposed during the military period.[132] Alberto Madrid described the impact of Roser Bru's paintings in the following terms:

I get near the paintings of Roser Bru as an observer who finds in his images the obsessions of the period he lived through. Scenes of violence, of phantasmagoric presences, who look at us inquisitively, searching for peace. His characters remind us of a collective memory . . . After seeing an exhibition by Roser Bru, we are moved. His characters look back at us, as if pleading. Shaking our indifference, sounding echoes of an unsolved history in our memory, they seem to say: Have you forgotten us? Their histories and pains are ours . . . They are part of the mourning that we have not yet accomplished.[133]

Reflecting on the ongoing politics of oblivion and memory, former President Patricio Aylwin pondered that 'Oblivion cannot be imposed by law. Besides, it is no good that nations should forget these tragedies! On the contrary: They should not be forgotten, in order that they should never be repeated.'[134]

Conclusion: Confinement and Expansion of Collective Memories

John Davis distinguished between societies that follow the principle of 'never again' and those that follow the principle of 'always so'. He claimed that, while pre-modern societies tend to be based upon tradition and hence to follow some vision of immutable patterns (what Davis defined as a state of 'always so'), modern societies tend to be near the pole of 'never again', of progressive moves in an undifferentiated schedule towards an undefined future.[135] While we basically agree with Davis in this primary distinction, there is a huge secondary difference between two sorts of modern, future-oriented societies. Some societies 'move into the future' following a path of progressive and unreflective disengagement from the past, while others, following conflict, disruption, and acute pain, either cling to the past or consciously attempt to leave the past behind. Both types face their past and reflect upon it, but the latter must, in addition, elaborate mechanisms to enable forgetting, so as to move beyond past experiences and their varied interpretations.[136]

Uruguay, Chile, and Argentina have moved to different extents and in different paths to elaborate such mechanisms, through a conflict-ridden process of reinterpreting the past experiences and contexts of violence. They share the general process, but each society has elaborated visions of the recent past in different ways. After closing the progressive-regressive cycle of policy-making, Argentina's vision is unclear, as the country faces the challenging task of reconstructing public values as part of its democratic imagery. Following the mobilization of civil society and the results of the 1989 referendum, Uruguay is also disoriented and has not yet really begun its public discussion concerning the recent past; on the other hand, the country has confidence in the strength of its democratic institutions. In Chile, in spite of its institutional approach and its creation of official *lieux de mémoire*, there are sectors that strongly invoke different interpretations of the historical context of the violence that occurred during military rule. Comparing Argentina, Chile, and Uruguay indicates how, within a shared cultural and sociodemographic background, the politics of oblivion and memory can take distinctive turns according to the nations' different collective visions and the different role social actors played in reconstructing collective identities under democratic rule.

The discourse of the dictatorships was a prototypical one of organic national integration and homogenization. The return to democracy has been marked by a distrust of any such discourse of nationalization and of similar strategies of constructing a unitary collective identity. A retreat into social multiplicity and heterogeneity and to individual pursuits could be perceived in the late 1980s and early 1990s. This trend was reinforced by neoliberal economic policies and the intellectual ambiance concerning the global arena, which was very critical of any discourse that essentializes 'the' nation.[137]

But these societies still face a collective endeavour, i.e. the need to get to grips with their past. 'To do so, people must forget, but to forget they should first remember.'[138] They must choose to close a painful chapter in their recent political history by consciously facing it, by commemorating and willingly forgetting but not by ignoring it. The task may take several generations. It will be rephrased time and again according to the challenges of the ever-changing context.

A major trend in the elaboration of the experience of human-rights violations has been the almost complete absence of physical *lieux de mémoire* in these societies. This poses a challenge for those who are trying to sustain the memory of their loved ones; it also poses problems for society at large. The existence of specific and contained *lieux de mémoire* could help encapsulate and frame the past. Their absence is extremely painful for the relatives of those missing victims whose burial sites are unknown. It prompts some of the relatives (and particularly the Argentine Mothers and other associations of victims' relatives) to claim an ever-present role as a living collective memory and ethical collective consciousness. For society at large, the absence of *lieux de mémoire* keeps the memory of the past very much alive; the basic disagreements about the past can thus become crises in the public sphere. The structuring of time—with the ever-recurring anniversaries of the onset of military rule and the like—becomes the predominant path of struggle over signification.

A physical presence (in the form of tombs, mausoleums, or public sculpture) could focus the nostalgia for the dead. In principle, their physical presence could enable the evocation of the past into the present. However, in the countries under consideration, creating physically defined *lieux de mémoire* could also establish boundaries between the places designated for commemoration and the spaces in which social sectors and individuals live their daily lives.

Disagreement about the past has precluded in most cases the confinement of memory. As analysed above, only in Chile was the construction of a public memorial for the disappeared officially completed by the authorities in the 1990s; in Uruguay, a similar project was conceived in early 1999 in the Cerro of Montevideo. Far away from the Southern Cone, in Israel, victims of military repression and families of the disappeared, who had found shelter in that country, founded Memoria, an association to keep alive the memory of their beloved and of all the victims. Among its educational and remembrance activities, this association undertook between 1989 and 1992 the planting of a forest in memory of the victims, symbolically near the San Martín, O'Higgins, and Artigas forests.[139]

The dearth of places for commemoration contributes to interweaving the experience of past human-rights violations within everyday life and routine. It indicates that there is no institutionalization of a shared or widely recognized interpretation of the past, and that information and full acknowledgement of the legacy of human-rights violations under military rule is still partial. This is not to say that there are no interpretations of the past. On the contrary, as analysed in this chapter, there are many opposing sectors struggling to promote or deny hegemonic status to each other's interpretations; to promote or avoid the canonization of the victims; and to attain some specific structuration of time by embedding the present within the past or the future.

Following the establishment of locales of collective memory, the variety of interpretations of the past does not necessarily come to an end. The process is twofold. On the one hand, there is a search for the definition of new *milieux de mémoire*, as in the efforts of active associations of victims' relatives to collectivize the memory of the younger generations within the visions and patterns set by an older generation. On the other hand, there is an ongoing process of redefining existing locales, such as that of the Plaza de Mayo in Buenos Aires or the Estadio Nacional in Santiago, a process related to the politics of oblivion and memory. Both are dynamic processes that focus the political struggle of those who promote varied visions and interpretations of the past experience of human-rights violations.

In the passage from generation to generation, these issues are necessarily reopened and reinterpreted. At any given moment, struggles may be launched over the signification of these issues, especially concerning the past. As Arjun Appadurai has indicated, the past is a scarce resource, and its appropriation has political and cultural importance.[140] In the context of societies confronting the unsolved legacy of past human-rights violations, representing the past, either through collective memory or history, turns into a political achievement, a practical accomplishment. We can expect that the question of who is entitled to use the past and how, as part of his or her claims and agenda, will remain a critical factor in the politics of oblivion and memory of the Southern Cone.

The Transformation of Collective Identities and Public Life in Argentina, Chile, and Uruguay

The unprecedented magnitude, depth, and violence of human-rights violations affected the core bases of collective life in Argentina, Chile, and Uruguay. They affected the basic elements of routine institutional and legal procedures; they changed the character of participation and restricted possibilities for autonomous organization and mobilization; they narrowed pluralism through depolitization and the control of public arenas; they curtailed individual rights and suppressed opinions for the sake of the 'common good', as defined by the military rulers; they imposed a 'truth' which citizens could not challenge and for which no accountability could be demanded, a truth that eventually and to different extents proved to be tainted by lies, especially in the area of human rights.

Following redemocratization, this legacy of human-rights violations was confronted on institutional grounds, with different policies and results, as analysed in previous chapters. Most political and social actors had to face that legacy. Some did it in a reactive way, in so far as current pressures and crises forced them to do so. Others, led by political will or social commitment, worked in an active way to centralize the issue of human rights in the process of reshaping collective identity. As for the political leaderships in the newly democratized settings, their main concern was to preserve stability and attain a certain level of democracy, a level which differed from case to case according to what they perceived as 'possible' given the framework of the civil–military relationships inherited from the previous period.

When facing such crises of democratic rule, these individuals and social actors reflected on them in terms of democratic consolidation in a broader sense. Some attempted to reformulate the format of legal and basic constitutional principles of democracy. Others suggested reforms that would address the major problems left open in these societies as they returned to democracy, problems related to participation in public life, to distribution, institutional flexibility, and the creation of novel forms of citizenship. Among those who adopted a long-term perspective to national self-understanding, some reached back into the roots of the process of forming collective identities and their institutional and cultural transformations throughout the centuries.

Reshaping Collective Identities after the Crises

Societies undergoing deep institutional crises are forced to reflect on the roots of such crises in connection with the ways in which their collective tenets were constructed. Throughout history there has been a continuous process of construction and human agency in the shaping of collective identities and public life. As emphasized by Shmuel N. Eisenstadt and Berhard Giesen, collective identities have changed constantly under the impact of contextual transformations and through the agency of social actors, collective and individual.[1] But while in routine times this process is overlooked and taken for granted, in times of crisis different social sectors assume reflexivity as they attempt to identify the axes through which such identities have been constructed along with the structuring of public arenas and struggling over them.[2]

The patterns and criteria that evolve in different societies as they create and recreate these domains are usually related to basic value orientations of the hegemonic culture, the components of its unity, perceptions of 'the other(s)', the dynamics of the relationship of individuals to the state and society, the patterns of inclusion into and exclusion from the political framework. All these dimensions come together in the shaping of public spheres, in which individual and institutional actors encounter one another and the political centre, as they redefine their sectorial and more comprehensive identities.

Collective identities are not uniform and monolithic. In any society, as homogeneous as its inhabitants may want to 'imagine' it (in Benedict Anderson's sense[3]) different worlds of values coexist. Even in those countries in which the population is rather homogeneous, no homogeneous visions of history, society, and culture should be expected. Different collective identities are projected and represented, sometimes converging and sometimes diverging.

In the countries of the Southern Cone, struggles have taken place over the shaping of public spheres in ways that, while emphasizing formal universalistic rules of access, were often compounded by the prevailing patterns of construction of such public spheres and by the expectations shaped by the prevailing definitions of collective identity.

In their relations to the centre and to one another, different sectors in these societies maintained tense relationships over the definitions, dimensions, and interpretations of membership. In their struggle over the continuous reformulation of collective identity and public life, they stressed some elements and dimensions and downplayed others.

Membership in political communities seems to be connected to cultural programmes that define in distinctive ways the prevailing modes of access to public spheres and to the centre, and of interaction between individuals, institutions, and groups. These models, which define the external as well as the internal 'others' in a hegemonic way, have varied both historically and geographically, in connection with differences in the format of ethnic and demographic composition, the criteria of collective identity and representation articulated by different elites. In Latin America such models were explicitly authoritarian (in Juan J. Linz's terms), populist-corporatist (as analysed by Philippe Schmitter or Ruth Collier and David Collier) and bureaucratic-authoritarian (as defined by Guillermo O'Donnell).[4] The configuration of these models implied a close connection with social agents and cultural actors articulating them in reflexive ways.

This has been especially salient in the Southern Cone, where there has been a close relationship and intermingling between the political and intellectual domains.

On many occasions, politicians have tried to expand their role as creators of collective attitudes and identity, through the elaboration of public visions defining both the modes of access to public spheres and to the political centre and patterns of social and cultural interaction. In parallel, intellectuals found it difficult to seclude themselves from politics. Rather than conceiving their role exclusively in terms of cultural production, they have envisioned culture as a wide framework from which they addressed political and social issues. In social settings besieged by extreme inequalities and dilemmas of modernization, such role assumptions have pushed them towards the political centre, which they have regarded with ambivalence. On the one hand, many of them could not survive without state resources channelled into the areas of cultural creation. On the other hand, many of them tried to influence public decisions by entering the political arena or by using their public image, often by adopting critical stands towards the state and current politics.[5]

The intermingling of politicians and intellectuals has contributed in these countries to a dynamic and often conflict-ridden confrontation over the construction of collective identities and shaping of public spheres.

The construction of collective identities is crucial for any society as it affects: the boundaries of inclusion and exclusion and the images of the other; how political and social systems and collectivities organize membership and refer to outside and inside referents; and the processes through which a public sphere is constituted and the consequent forms of incorporation and granting of entitlements as well as delineation of the limits of exclusion from such participation and entitlement.

The processes of constituting and selecting collective identities crystallize through debate, interpretation, confrontation, imposition, and struggle, led by specific social and cultural carriers who shape and condition the various trends of configuration.

Whenever a society undergoes a serious process of reconstitution, its impact is projected onto the reformulation of its basic tenets of self-definition and collective identity, with effects on the construction of membership, the patterns of inclusion and exclusion, and the shaping of entitlements. Crises such as those undergone by the Southern Cone countries during the breakdown of democracies in the early 1970s, the military rule of the late 1970s and 1980s, and redemocratization in the 1980s and 1990s, have left a profound mark in their subsequent development, imprinting the character of the ensuing problematique. A leading role in this respect was played particularly by those cultural creators, politicians, public figures, and professionals who were active in the attempts to rethink and reshape the public agenda following redemocratization.

In the following sections, we study some of the major trends of such social actors' agency in redefining collective identities in Argentina, Chile, and Uruguay in the wake of redemocratization. We bring examples of the lines of thought and debate through which these different social actors attempted to come to grips with what (in their interpretation) the experience of the military period revealed about the kind of society they were part of and about the prospects of future change. We would like to stress emphatically that, although many of the works mentioned below are important contributions to this problematique, they are by no means the only ones and they are far from a complete representation of the cultural domain in these societies. Our concern is to open—not to close—analysis on the broad impact of the experiences of the military period on the meaning-making process of collective self-understanding and reshaping of identities and public life in Argentina, Chile, and Uruguay.

History and Identity: Societies Pervaded by violence?

During the initial period of democracy, the political leaderships faced the legacy of human-rights violations by looking for ways to reach 'national reconciliation'. Parts of the politicians, the intellectuals, and public and professional circles began to address that legacy and the emerging policies by questioning the basic forms of each society's identity and self-representation, in historical and cultural terms. These individuals suggested that the problem that became identified with the military could not be comprehensively addressed by restricting the issue to the problems of the 1970s and 1980s. Instead, they suggested looking far back in history, to previous periods and even to the very foundation of these societies. The European conquest, the colonial period, the struggle for independence, the ensuing civil wars, and the processes of modernization: all should be questioned in terms of their connections to a particular pattern of social formation and shaping of collective identity. They claimed that, on the eve of the military dictatorships, the Southern Cone societies slipped once again into a pattern that already existed of repressions, violence, destruction of individual life, demobilization of the masses, monistic ideals, and other exclusionary practices.

Honestly, we cannot say 'how did this happened to us?' It keeps happening to us since our birth as a nation. Argentina is a saga of massacres (and we seem not to have learned the lessons from past massacres). Even in a century in which mass media allowed access to information, most of the Argentine people did not know in depth the events of the Rebellion in Patagonia [1921], did not know thoroughly what happened at the massacre of Trelew; did not know how the massacre of Ezeiza occurred [upon Perón's return to Argentina in 1973]; neither did they know about the bombing of Plaza de Mayo in 1955. None of these events was thorough analysed. Their knowledge was the patrimony of some enlightened sector, more concerned with the event.[6]

No other single issue could have more effectively forced these societies to confront their historical heritage and collective identity. This re-evaluation of identity is painful, and its results uncertain. Tulio Halperin Donghi, one of the leading contemporary historians of Argentina, analysed the difficulties inherent in incorporating the military dictatorship into national history, and its potential force for changing the views of the country:

As the recent decade of violence and tyranny slowly recedes into the past, few signs have yet emerged that Argentines are making headway in coming to terms with this troubled heritage. . . . Yet, one cannot deny that to incorporate the recent episode of terror into the body of Argentine history requires modifying some of the basic assumptions on which the historical image of the country has been built, as well as modifying the image relied on instinctively by Argentines in negotiating their daily lives.[7]

Alternative, critical visions emerged already in the past throughout the Southern Cone, alongside the official and conservative versions of history, in both cases carried out by intellectuals and professional historians. In particular, alternative arts and letters and historical criticism flourished from the 1950s to the early 1970s. Many films, novels, theatre plays, visual arts, and music pieces presented in those years different versions that reinforced existing lines of social and political polarization. In Argentina, for example, several historical visions crystallized, which represented different political ideologies, such as official conservative liberalism and revisionist nationalism, right-wing and left-wing Peronist views, the social democratic vision linked with the Unión Cívica Radical, and a series of radical leftist (Marxist and non-Marxist) visions. These contrasted visions, in their extreme forms, supported various streams of 'revolutionary violence', which were confronted by counter-violence among parts of the extreme right and by the 'imposition of order' by the armed forces, resulting in the Dirty War.[8]

Similarly, there were historical interpretations of Chile that followed nationalist and corporatist orientations, and which vied with the historical visions of various leftist sectors on the one hand, and, on the other, the visions of Social and Christian Democracy.[9] Intellectual life prior to 1973 was described by José Joaquín Brunner as structured around three axes: the struggle for revolution and refoundation of society, the supression of the past and elaboration of utopias, and the centrality of politics and the state. Along the first axis, Social Christian and leftist intellectuals analysed the social crisis from different points of view, proposing a series of alternative models to the existing order. Ideologically, this created the central ideological cleavage between left and right, strengthening the sense of menace among the liberal-conservative right, especially since the alternative model was posed in terms of total change. On the second axis,

The local ideological universe functioned until 1973 by producing a permanent 'escape towards the future'. The utopian contents prevailed over the organic contents of reality. History came to be perceived as the pure terrain of ideological struggle, not as the locus of sedimentation of traditions. The past was the crisis manifest in the present, which accordingly had to be overcome. The density of the accumulated experiences was continuously deprived of value as a function of proposals that promised a better future. The intellectual culture of the *intelligentsia*, with the exception of a small part of the rightist intellectuals, focused its attention almost exclusively on the present and towards the future, suppressing the past as a conservative weight or inertia.[10]

In Uruguay the socio-economic crisis of the 1960s and early 1970s led to the questioning of the basic models and images of self-representation, found in the official history of the country. The public sphere was increasingly dominated by labour conflicts, the application of a state of emergency and internal security measures, the creation in 1971 of the left-wing Frente Amplio, and the parallel emergence of armed resistance movements such as the MLN (Tupamaros), the OPR-33, and the MRO.[11] Meanwhile, the view of Uruguay as a cultured nation was increasingly challenged in that period: 'Montevideo was called the Athens of the [Río de la] Plata as it was earlier called the New Troy; Uruguay was called the Switzerland of the Americas. But today, the institutional order, the [social] order and the image of our democracy are conserved by importing CIA procedures and by replicating the system of searches, captures, and tortures used in Vietnam.'[12] A literary boom took place in this period, associated with the 'Generation of '45', also known as the 'critical generation' which included, to name only a few representative individuals, Mario Benedetti, Juan Carlos Onetti, Eduardo Galeano, Arturo Ardao, Emir Rodríguez Monegal, and Angel Rama. The writers in this generation were critical of social reality and of the traditional portrayals of the Uruguayan nation, and they assumed a distanced but concerned mode of critical consciousness:

Critical consciousness cannot be validly measured except through its confrontation with dominant values . . . Against the attempt to celebrate, which . . . transformed everything into a perfect rose, it counterpoised the disintegrating analysis that sees the thorns, the withering of colour, the expiry of forms, as well as the grotesque celebratory impulse. Against idealism, stubbornly and fraudulently anchored in the future, it posed the insertion in time, the flow of life, the history as obsession, the recuperation of the past as a need for inquiry about roots, the feeling of insecurity and the precariousness of existence.[13]

Basically identified with the left, members of the 'critical generation' tried to inscribe Uruguay within the Latin American context, disengaging it from its image as a European nation. One of the main representative works of this line is Mario Benedetti's *El país de la cola de paja*, in which the author coined what would become a famous counter-definition of his country's identity:

If my intention were to paint this chapter with a satirical colour, I would begin by saying that Uruguay is the only office in the world that had reached the category of a republic. I do not know how right it is to make a joke out of one of the most pitifully dramatic aspects of our national life. Let us state it seriously: Uruguay is a country of office clerks. It is unimportant that there are also some waiters, a few cowhands in the *estancias*, some stevedores in the port, some shy smugglers. What is really important is the mental style of the Uruguayan, and that style is the style of an office-clerk.[14]

In 1964 Benedetti could write sarcastically on 'That Anaesthesia Called Soccer', a line followed by Fernando Andatch, who recently claimed that the victory of the Uruguayan team over Brazil in Maracaná in

1950 symbolized the religion of mediocrity rooted in the Uruguayan imagination.[15]

These intellectuals tried to transform their culture from an official 'universalist' (Western) culture to one that is less structured and more open to participation: a popular culture. In this line, cultural manifestations associated with the hinterland were no longer depicted as indigenous folklore, but were contextualized within Uruguayan and Latin American culture, and were perceived as a vehicle for expressing social injustices and demands. Illustrative of this trend are the pop-rock folk groups Los Olimareños, Larbanois y Carrero, and El Sabalero. The journal *Marcha* became the main vehicle for expressing these views.

The critical and committed line of thought was prominent in the Southern Cone in the period before the military takeovers. As Jean Franco thoroughly analysed it in *The Modern Culture of Latin America* (1967), Latin American art had traditionally been 'much more concerned with social phenomena and social ideals . . . with that form of love which the Greeks called *agape* or love for one's fellow men . . . Here lies the true originality of Latin American art: it has kept alive the vision of a more just and humane form of society and it continues to emphasize those emotions and relationships which are wider than the purely personal.'[16] One of the most widely read books in the Southern Cone and in other Latin American countries in the early 1970s, Eduardo Galeano's *Las venas abiertas de América Latina*, epitomized this deep supra-individual commitment, which was constitutive of the self-image of the Latin American intellectuals in that period.

There is much rottenness to be thrown to the sea in the way to the reconstruction of Latin America. The deprived, the humiliated, the damned, they have this task in their hands. The Latin American national cause is, before anything else, a social cause: In order that Latin America should be reborn, there is a need to throw down the lords of the land, country by country. Times of rebellion and change are beginning. There are those who believe that destiny rests on the knees of the gods, but the truth is that it works, as a constant challenge, in the conscience of men.[17]

The potential for violence was imbued in the ideologically polarized character of many of the works of that period. For the left, the 1960s were

years of 'exercise of criteria' in the social sciences: the theory of dependency as opposed to 'desarrollismo' [developmentalism], criticism and counter-criticism, a dialogue with the Africans who were emerging from their process of decolonization. Years of strengthening of popular organizations; the times of the Cuban Revolution; of a significant dynamics of Latin American and Caribbean integration; of a resurgence of anti-imperialist feelings; of the germination of Liberation Theology; of minorities' revindication at the international level; of the emergence of feminism.[18]

The messages contained in the elaborations of these thinkers were rejected by others who held diametrically opposed visions of their society, and who were no less passionate in their views and positions. As one sympathetic observer and member of the right wing in Chile commented in 1966: 'The political passion of the Right, sometimes suicidal and often disguised as doctrine . . . converge on the same result: that it [the Right] is not able to be an alternative power in Chile.'[19] The very principled positions of these circles and the semi-sacredness with which they cognitively structured and evaluated the forces of society contributed to the clash that tore apart these societies in the period prior to the military takeovers. Works such as those of Chilean Antonio Skármeta retrace in fictionalized terms the violence in the lives of concrete individuals, for whom neutrality becomes a non-option in the early 1970s.[20] Once the results of the confrontation in the 1970s became visible with the onslaught of the military rulers, many would doubt their conviction about the formative force of violence.

Violence and coercion constituted a major characteristic of military rule in the 1970s and 1980s in the Southern Cone. The military dictatorships were one more episode in a long series of states of emergency that most Latin American countries experienced throughout the twentieth century. With relative ease, the military took power, either following the request of civilians and/or according to their own schemes and plans. Once in power, the military rulers concentrated time and again all constitutional powers in their hands, on the basis of the 'National Emergency' which propelled them into power.[21] This situation became more complicated in the 1970s and 1980s, when the Southern Cone military rulers attempted to establish a new political order. They found an ideological justification for coercion and violence in the doctrines of National Security, which assumed the existence of a widespread Communist menace.

With the return to democracy, all sectors of civil society and the political class rejected the manichean violence linked to the traumatic experience of breakdown of democracy and the military period. The image of violence was focused on its political origins and the ensuing repression. As politicians intended democracy to be antithetical to military rule, they professed to avoid violence and polarization in political confrontations. National reconciliation was endorsed, in this sense, as the basis for avoiding any recurrence of polarization and violence. In the semi-official version of Argentine Radicalism, *La república perdida* (a 1984 film by Miguel Pérez), this vision achieved pristine clarity. Tracing the developments that led to the PRN, the narrator indicates that 'To our regret, after many frustrations and unfulfilled promises, important juvenile groups resorted to weapons, renegading from the slow and patient effort of democracy. The violent ones who wanted to change everything would become the accomplices of the violent others who wanted to keep everything the same.' All this would change following the foundational vision of the new civilian government:

On 10 December 1983 Raúl Alfonsín assumes the presidency and we return to life under the protection of the Constitution and the three representative powers. We remain alert to defend ourselves from the gangs of white gloves, from the oligarchical minorities, from the terrorist bands, from the military putschists who claim to represent us but rule in solitude. Here we are [and the image on the screen focuses on Alfonsín's inauguration and presidential address at the Plaza de Mayo, while the accompanying music moves the audience to emotion], brothers in pain and joy, children of a recovered Fatherland!!!!!![22]

During Alfonsín's administration the cultural 'theory of the two demons'—i.e. of the terrorist left and of the military repressors—was diffused through the cultural media and the educational system, as a kind of 'psychological artifact' that identified violence with small, marginal sectors.[23] The explanations encoded in the 'theory of the two demons' for the violence and for the efforts towards reconciliation were plausible following redemocratization; it was most plausible to those who had been affected by military violence and to those who took seriously the disclosures concerning the extent of the violence. This interpretation, however, relied on the equation violence equals specific institutional violence and human-rights violations. The partiality of this view has been highlighted by Halperin Donghi:

Thanks to the [CONADEP] report's impact and the ensuing trial of the commanders in chief, a new consensus emerged that recognized the savage repression begun in 1976 as an unforgivable crime. But precisely because it had been categorized under such a satisfying label, many Argentineans felt ready to lay the matter to rest and to address more pressing concerns. While understandable, this reaction did not represent any genuine coming to terms with the complex developments that fostered military terror . . . Such condemnation was not necessarily unfair but it tended to dismiss the deepest crisis in Argentine history as merely a succession of meaningless episodes in which the country had been victimized by rival gangs of kidnappers and killers coming apparently from nowhere.[24]

The line of interpretation that endorsed the 'theory of the two demons' stressed the need to control and marginalize social forces that were capable of violence, such as the radical left and the military. Leaders of the guerrilla movements such as Firmenich were mentioned as bearing the same public reponsibility for the spiral of violence as military leaders such as Videla and Massera. By conducting their trial in parallel, the democratic administration was trying to go beyond the mere punishment of proven crimes. The parallel trials were to be geared to a vision of Argentina freed from the demons of the past, a country returning to 'normal life'. Learning from the experience of breakdown of democracy and military rule, the civilian government launched several reforms, including civil–military relationships and the introduction of the theme of human rights into the educational curricula.

Opposing this line of interpretation were all those who considered that the military experience of human-rights violations was linked to the attempt to preclude any change in the imbalanced socio-economic structure of society. These sectors, mainly composed of former leftist activists, felt that violence should indeed be beyond the pale, but they still rejected the thesis of a return to 'previous normality' and constitutional orderliness. For them, such a 'normality' had bred polarization and political violence in the 1960s and 1970s. Rejecting both the 'theory of the two demons' as well as violence as means of social change, the new left has raised demands of deep political change and reform through social agreement. Some of these sectors have created new political organizations. Such was the case of the twenty-nine intellectuals close to Peronism, who, after returning from exile, left the Partido Justicialista in 1985, since they became disappointed with its positions, and in 1990 joined leader 'Chacho' Alvarez and the 'Group of 8' to found the Frente Grande and five years later, the FREPASO, that became the third major political force in Argentina.

For a core of cultural creators, professionals and politicians, the experience of military rule opened a period of self-reflection and deep questioning into the 'narratives' that structured their own vision of their country. As Jeffrey Alexander and Philip Smith have remarked:

People, groups, and nations understand their progress through time in terms of stories, plots which have beginnings, middles, and ends, heroes and anti-heroes, epiphanies and denouements, dramatic, comic and tragic forms. This mythical dimension of even the most secular societies has been vastly underestimated . . .[25]

As individuals have internalized many of these elements and codes, often their symbolic and evaluative logic goes unquestioned in society. It is during identity crises such as those which followed public revelations of the deeds of the military regimes that deep questioning begins.

In the Southern Cone, this questioning revolved around the responsibility of different sectors for contributing to the onset of military rule and the ensuing massive human-rights violations: How aware were we of what eventually occurred? What did we do? How do we confront that legacy?

Illustrative is the Chilean 'narrative of *mea culpa*', which follows in an introspective style the feelings of different individuals and social sectors towards personal and collective history. *Los convidados de piedra* (allegorically, the muted/absent guests) by Jorge Edwards, for example, shows the encounter of a group of young people from the high bourgeoisie for a birthday celebration one month after the fall of Allende. The individuals recall their childhood and youth experiences, and the reader perceives how the upper class participated in—and perhaps contributed to—the events leading to the military takeover and the disappearances of many young people.[26] *La secreta obscenidad de cada día* by Marco De la Parra and *La contienda humana* by Juan Radrigan follow the same introspective line. The latter focuses on two sexual criminals who constantly change identities, from torturers to victims, from revolutionaries to housewives. The former deals with the remorse of an individual who did not protect his wife and child from their kidnappers.[27] Diamela Eltit's *El cuarto mundo* brings together fragmentation, violence, and exploitation into a very personalized, introspective, and intimate account of the conception and life of twins as they jostle for space in the womb and maintain close and tense relationships in a family consumed by illness, obsession, and insanity, in what critics read as a metaphor of Chilean social and political crisis in the 1970s.[28]

All these works raise the question of personal responsibility in terms that go beyond the dualism of the state as repressor versus the citizens as victims to a more complex domain, in which each person carries with himself or herself the dichotomy repression/subversion. Nobody, according to this view, is completely free from responsibility and guilt.

In some circles, this questioning was expressed in explicit collective terms, as a questioning of the basic tenets of collective identity, the relationship of representations of identity to political order and democracy, the assessment of the kind of democracy that developed in these societies, and an inquiry about how such identities have been affected and transformed by the harsh experiences lived under military rule.

David Viñas' novel *Cuerpo a cuerpo* and Enrique Medina's *Las muecas del miedo* describe in crude terms the visceral violence that, according to the authors, pervades all human relationships in Argentina, as they are structured by power and inequality.[29] In a very aggressive narrative and language, Medina portrays in brutal terms a series of interpersonal, sexual, and sectorially violent situations as an overall, sometimes literal and sometimes allegorical, picture of the country.[30] In his book, Viñas returns to one of the main axes of his earlier work, the issue of violence as an instrument of domination. Viñas has written works of historical fiction, such as *Indios, ejército y frontera* and *Los dueños de la tierra*, in which he forces the reader to confront the extremely violent pattern of rule of Argentine elites and the recurrent attempts of official history to overlook it. Violence is the thread that runs through *Cuerpo a cuerpo* too, starting with General Ce Mendiburu's monologue as he hurts his son's testicles and ending with his murder at the hands of his daughter. This fearless, cruel, despotic, and morbid character accompanies all acts of violence (against opponents, subordinates, relatives, and lovers) with excerpts from Argentine historical wisdom and cultural background. 'El Payo', as he is known, emerges as a representative of the Argentine elites and rulers (cited in the text). These elites, indicates Viñas, aimed to negate the 'other', be it the Indian, the rural worker, or the leftist, through domination, exclusion, and repression, in terms of a civilizatory symbology and brutal practice.[31] In his characterization of Viñas's work, Ricardo Piglia— one of the authors currently at the forefront of Argentine literature— identifies this pattern in the existence of 'Coercion that not only appears on the surface during moments of systemic crisis, but also in its peculiar silencing capacity for negating the violence which underlies the establishment of the liberal state. Also, in its exercise of censorship when it confronts the problems relating to its own origins.'[32] According to Piglia, Viñas shows how the ruling forces have 'animalized' their enemies and how, by declining to recognize their humanity, have treated them in ways that no human being deserves.

[In a society in which] there were no grey areas, only friends and enemies existed. Whoever divides the world between friends and enemies may conclude that the best enemy is a dead enemy, and act accordingly. [To kill and make disappear under such circumstances] is a great leap forward but only a leap.[33]

The issue of past violence brought authors to raise questions that have led to historical revisionism. Piglia himself described the violence inherent in the hierarchical (oligarchical) mode of domination typical of the Argentine 'Golden Age'. In *Respiración artificial*, a book written originally in 1980 (during the military rule) and which became a best-seller of Argentine letters under democracy, Piglia describes the tendency toward violence among the upper classes:

Because in reality these gentlemen, these lords discovered (vis-à-vis others and *with* others) that they needed to prove who was the Slave. They discovered, said the Senator, that they had another way of proving their manliness and chivalry, and that they could still live facing death without the need to kill each other. Rather, they would *unite themselves* in order to kill those that did not resign themselves to recognizing their condition of Lords and Masters. For instance, he said, the immigrants, the gauchos and the Indians.[34]

Similarly, through the years, the *Madres de Plaza de Mayo* contributed varied evidence about the violence inherent from the start in the shaping of Argentine identity:

A year after the dark death of Moreno, in 1812, the revolutionary Juan José Castelli suffered the same fate: he was tried, tortured and his tongue was cut off. These facts are not taught in our schools, of course. Perhaps his crime was to understand, in the 'Inka' North of Argentina, that the Indian masses were more interested in recovering their lands and freeing themselves from the racist and feudal yokes, than in changing the Spanish gallows for those of a Creole landlord.

The classes of exploiters of their own people would incorporate to their military 'tutelary' and policy role, repression of other, neighbouring peoples . . . Thus, General Bartolomé Mitre carried out in 1864–1870 the genocide of the people of Paraguay, together with the regimes of Brazil and Uruguay, united from London, angered by Paraguay's economic independent stand. Similarly, the last genocidal military dictatorship (1976–1983) made Chileans, Uruguayans, Paraguayans, Bolivians and other patriots of our America disappear, surrendering them to their 'sister' military dictatorships, this time with Washington's blessing.[35]

In these portrayals, violence emerges as one of the most continuous and tragic threads of Argentine history. In some of these analyses, the source of violence is projected onto an outside enemy—represented either by imperialism and its allies or by the local upper classes and the military. In others, there is a realization that the more widespread character of violence is a part of the structure of local interests, decisions, and coalitions, although some of these authors too still project the blame onto others.

Throughout these works, there are incipient signs of a search, either literal or metaphorical, for the deeper sources of violence, a search that involves introspection into the collective history of Argentina, which is highly consternating, as the following imaginative piece suggests:

Yesterday evening, when I sunk my right hand in the coffer in which I keep my papers, the bugs climbed onto my forearm, they stirred their little legs, their antennas, trying to reach fresh air. These insects that crawl over my skin each time I decide to sink my hand in the past cause me an infinite sense of repugnance, but I know that the scaly friction of their legs is the price I must pay each time I want to find out who I have been.[36]

In Uruguay, the breakdown of democracy produced a materialization of the criticisms raised already in the 1960s and 1970s by intellectuals who criticized the image of Uruguay as the most civil, educated, developed, and peaceful society in the Americas. These foundational myths, critically analysed by intellectuals and professionals such as Carina Perelli, Juan Rial, and Gerardo Caetano, proved ineffectual in stopping violence and military coercion.[37] During the transition and following the restoration of democracy, though still far from returning to the mythical image of 'Uruguay, the Land of the Merry' (*el Uruguay feliz*), some components of this social imagery were reappraised as necessary elements of the return to 'normality'. Civility and consensual mechanisms of conflict resolution became cherished in the new setting, especially for confronting potentially explosive issues such as the legacy of human-rights violations. In this sense, parts of the social imagery of the foundational myths were recovered as a means for reconstructing collective identity.[38]

Following the above imagery, on the eve of the transition to democracy, some intellectuals, politicians, and public opinion leaders reflected on the mechanisms necessary to close the stage of war in which their society was immersed during the last decade and a half. Manuel Flores Mora, a columnist for *Jaque*, looked back in history in his search for a local model of reconciliation. He reminded Uruguayans of the phrase used by the military to justify their fight as part of a project to end subversion: 'the peoples who forget their pasts are doomed to live it again'. However, for Mora, the current sense would be to achieve reconciliation through pardoning political prisoners. According to Mora, this pattern was encoded in the wake of Uruguayan civil wars:

I belong to a tradition, perhaps somewhat harsh, of people who could kill each other with spears, but when the battle was over, they stretched their hands to help the fallen in rising up. I am part of the Oriental [Uruguayan] nationality. But not of those Uruguayans of 9 February [1973], but rather of those Uruguayans of Cagancha.[39]

The model cited by Flores Mora is that of President Battle y Ordóñez in 1904. On that occasion, according to the author, the President—who had led his forces to victory—gave a speech honouring the memory of the fallen on both sides of the civil war. During the victory parade, the batallions marched by the presidential podium and, as soon as they finished the track, they dissolved and went back home:

Farewell to arms. And to the uniform. Back to the homeland dressed in a shirt, in overalls, in *bombachas* [rider's trousers]. Back to the pickaxe, to the shovel, to the inkwell, or to the counter in the office or in the shop. Back to peace and work.

... Like someone who puts a flower over a tomb, I only want to say: The death of the fighter was not in vain, because the war has ended. The war has ended.[40]

Around this period, it was common to hear calls for national reconciliation, drawing on historical examples and images. Lawyer and researcher Patricio Rodé's statement is illustrative:

'Clemency for the defeated', demanded Artigas [the father of Uruguayan independence] after the battle. Our confrontations should be solved in freedom, without offence or fear, without any wishes for revenge, by facing reality and learning from past experience.[41]

In spite of the persistent effort to reconstruct the unity and soul of the Uruguayan collectivity according to the pre-dictatorship models (a thread seen in the calls to cling to the Uruguayan pattern of reconciliation), the military period brought about a radical change in the self-perception of many Uruguayans. The experience of 1973–85 prompted questioning about the social and political conditions that led to the breakdown of democracy. It had as well a demystifying effect on social thought about what constitutes 'the nation'. It has implied that the self-image of Uruguayans as a country based on codes of citizenship and civility—with almost no primordial referents, to an extent unknown in most other Latin American countries — has been deeply affected.

These countries [Uruguay and Argentina] are deeply embedded in Borbonic authoritarian culture. It is not easy to deal with the military spectre, even though there are constraints around the army, generated by a global climate of respect for democracy, of rejection of that authoritarian background that we *rioplatenses* possess. But this climate includes both a rejection of the military legacy together with preoccupying trends of departing from involvement in public affairs, of closing oneself in the public sphere, of depolitization, all these phenomena not only typical of Uruguay but are of global dimensions.[42]

One of the central works in deepening the trend of historical revisionism has been the novel by Tomás de Mattos, *Bernabé! Bernabé!*, which became a best-seller in 1989, following its publication in 1988. Through fictitious letters about Bernabé Rivera, the book deals with a dark chapter in the history of the 'civilist country'. In 1830 Bernabé Rivera, half-brother of one of Artigas's generals, Fructuoso Rivera (who would later become president of the country) commanded the forces that massacred the last Uruguayan Indians in an ambush in Salsipuedes and in other locations.[43] Mattos presents an image of the forefathers of the Republic which stands in contrast to the epic, plural images of the previous historical interpretations of Uruguay. In the 1960s and 1970s, each of the political forces approached the image of the founding fathers (primarily that of José Gervasio Artigas) from varied points of view, but always as heroes, as incarnations of *virtus*. The various political forces incorporated different images of the heroes, by emphasizing and reclaiming as their own some facets of the latter's polychromatic image. Thus, for instance, the Unión de Trabajadores Azucareros de Artigas (UTAA, the trade union of sugar-cane workers), led by Tupamaro leader Raúl Sendic, stated that 'This is not the country for which Artigas fought. If, to reach it, we have to take out the arms with which the Leader of the Orientals, Don José Gervasio Artigas, fought to attain happiness for the poor of the land ['la criollada pobre']—we will do it.'[44] The parliamentary left also had its own Artigas. Liber Seregni, leader of the Frente Amplio, declared in March 1971 that

The Frente Amplio will be a third great unifying block of the Oriental People: Yesterday, Artigas; afterwards Lavalleja, Oribe y Rivera together, and today, the Frente Amplio. . . . Since we are on the side of Artigas, Artigas is ours. We are and we want to be the renovation of Artigism, a return to the best tradition of the country, in order to confront this menacing hour and open the future of Uruguay, giving all that we have to the struggle.[45]

The armed forces projected an image of tutelary nationalism, as reflected in Rear-Admiral Francisco Sanjurjo's words: 'The armed forces, heirs of the Artigist ideals, will protect their people and will never allow the return of times of loss and disarray. No one will dare to depart from the right road.'[46] According to Abril Trigo, for the armed forces 'Artigas was a *caudillo* of Hispanic and Christian roots, herald of a "pragmatic methodology", completely contrary to the subversive and Jacobine "imported doctrines" that were threatening and disturbing the Western Civilization of the nineteenth century.'[47] In redemocratized Uruguay, Mattos presents a more complex and polyfaceted image of the heroes of the wars of independence, an image that touches on the grim dimensions of the forefathers and their deeds. The tensions between patriotic ideals and their cruel and violent implementation turned, after the attainment of independence, towards the road of constructing the nation. In this phase, the forms of heroic violence used previously to fight for freedom were recast in the form of a war of extermination against the aboriginal population. Fructuoso Rivera and the landlords decided to kill their former allies in the Wars of Independence, the *Charrúa* Indians. Bernabé Rivera, the heroic colonel of Sarandí (scene of a battle against Brazil), fulfils the mission. Mattos poses the question to the reader:

. . . What Bernabé should we remember? That of Sarandí or that of Salsipuedes? The idol of Misiones or the repressor of San José del Uruguay? The one who loved Manuela, or the other, whom Venado [the Indian chieftain, who thought him a friend] never really knew? Or the one he could have been if he had not stubbornly sought to die at Yacaré-Cururú? The commander or the servant? The repressor or the victim?[48]

Even if placed in the past, *Bernabé, Bernabé!* discloses the thread of destructive violence which was ostensibly inimical to Uruguay since its birth as a nation. Is that violence to be read in a historical key that contextualizes it and restricts it to the nineteenth century, or is it a metaphor basic to Uruguayan identity, which has been rediscovered as part of the perspective shaped by the experiences of the last military period? In a debate with historian Washington Lockhart, Hugo Achugar defended the metaphorical reading of the novel as an allegory of the dictatorship period. While Lockhart claimed that the novel should be contextualized in the nineteenth century, Achugar argued that anyone reading the novel after the military government would have to take into account the resurgence of violence in Uruguay in the second half of the twentieth century.[49] And that the experiences of military rule are prompting such rereading and interest for historical materials: 'I think that to turn the gaze back to the 19th century at this end of century is not an empty exercise of the Academy; I think that the fracturing of memory led by the Southern Cone dictatorships has much to do with this backward look.'[50] Similarly, Carlos Demassi has attempted to contextualize in a recent article[51] the shift prompted by the last military government. According to Demassi, since the early twentieth century until the collapse of the Batllist model in the 1960s, a vision of the past was institutionalized which projected the image of Uruguayans as a white, almost European nation, composed of peaceful and profoundly democratic citizens, with high levels of education. The historical discourse that accompanied the Batllist model emphasized those elements of the historical past that might contribute to reinforcing this image of 'being Uruguayan': national heroes, foremost José Gervasio Artigas, were portrayed as 'proto'-Batllists; the Indians were described as proud defenders of national independence; and the gauchos were depicted as freedom fighters.

This endeavour implied overlooking the foggy origins of the state, the lengthy civil wars, the genocide of the Indians, the military dictatorships of the nineteenth century, and the violence that was a dominant feature for almost the entire nineteenth century and which did not disappear in the twentieth century. The canonical historized version of the past, sustained by the Colorado Party, was tolerant enough to provide a place of merit for the contending Blanco party as a partner in the construction of Uruguayan democracy. Uruguayans were socialized in this mode of historical discourse through the system of public education founded by José Pedro Varela in the 1870s. During its heyday, other sources which pointed at an alternative vision of the past were discredited as merely anecdotal and marginal.

This construction of collective identity was successful at the cognitive level yet entered into crisis with the re-emergence of violence and repression. With the decay and collapse of the Batllist model, a review of the discourse that supported the myth of Uruguay as the Switzerland of America took place. With the wave of violence generated since the 1960s, intellectuals 'rediscovered' the heritage of violence, repression, and intolerance that was long ignored in the school books. Nonetheless, in the 1960s and 1970s, this revisionist line also fell into a manichean categorization of heroes and villains. The same dichotomous view of the old model was evident in the search for 'good' and 'bad' characters, thus obscuring the ambivalence and multiplicity of interpretations of the past. Interestingly enough, according to Demassi, the same manichean tendency to think in terms of the 'good' and the 'bad guys of history' was reinforced from a totally different angle through the historical discourse of the military, which glorified the past in its own way.

With the return to democratic rule, Uruguayans could not avoid reflecting upon the genesis and impact of the military dictatorship. At the most general level, the military interregnum was conceived as a phenomenon of cataclysmic character that was imposed upon Uruguayan society 'from the outside' and which 'victimized' that society as a whole.

This view was placed in doubt once the results of the 1989 referendum were known, and the public learned that over half of the Uruguayan citizenry opted to support the Law of Expiry. These results and the terms of the debate that preceded them call for a different understanding of the dictatorship. Demassi suggests that the military government is an integral part of Uruguayan history, as it preserved many of the features of the country's political life, while making explicit the parallel tradition of violence and repression that the hegemonic historical discourse attempted to relegate to oblivion.[52]

There are many different views on the dictatorship. Considering these varied accounts is instructive in two respects. It will possibly help overcome the manichean discourse that dominated the Uruguayan public sphere, and it may contribute as well to reopening public debate, thus leaving behind the public silence that followed the 1989 referendum. As a result, the pluralism inherent in full democracy would be reinforced in Uruguay. In turn, by opening such a public debate, Uruguayans would reconsider whether the dictatorship was a radical altering structure that victimized them from the outside or, rather, whether it was an integral part of the socio-economic, political, and cultural framework of their society. Only then, concludes Demassi, will the experience of that period be incorporated as part of the generalized vision of the past, and will its impact be fully assessed and put in perspective.

Several works contributing to this project stand out: *Uruguay: cuentas pendientes* and *Identidad uruguaya: mito, crisis o afirmación*, and Juan Rial and Carina Perelli's *De mitos y memorias políticas*.[53] A reminder of the open state in this society's pattern of elaborating the past took the shape of a new wave of artistic production in 1996 which, once again, touched upon the issues raised by military rule, coercion, and human-rights violations. In the realm of theatre, Alvaro Ahunchain produced the play 'Where were you on 27 June 1973?'[54] Alfonso Lessa, a well-known journalist, recently published a book of interviews with the main military and civilian participants of the dictatorial period, under the name *El estado de guerra* (The State of War); the book has become a best-seller. Journalist Graziano Pascale has published his experiences in prison in *Los años sin alma* (The Years without Soul). Two young historians, Vania Markarián and Isabella Cosse are about to publish *1975: año de la Orientalidad. La historia en la escena dictatorial* (1975: Year of Orientality. History in the Dictatorial Scene), which will contain the results of their research on the cultural policies of the military and the texts elaborated in the period. The Roslik case is analysed anew by Luis Udaquiola, who in *El país de los domingos* sums up, on the basis of interviews, all the known data about the case. The motivations of these various authors are different but converge on a renewed concern with the break from previous institutional patterns and identities. Lessa was surprised by how little people knew about the period, even though most of the protagonists are still alive. The experience of Makarián's parents prompted her to carry out documentary research on the period of military rule. Udaquiola worked on the idea, formulated by Roslik's widow, about the need to write a book to make the truth known. Ahunchain was more interested in the affective and aesthetic aspects of the problem and by his deep impression that theatre circles were reluctant to touch upon the onset of authoritarianism in Uruguay. 'We need to perform Neil Simon or Noel Coward—they claimed. The dictatorship is *passé*. People have already forgotten it.' Lessa had the opposite experience: his interviewees claimed that it was too early to talk. Pascale wanted to explore the absurdity of being tried, when he was 23 years old, for assisting the subversion and for expressing 'scorn to the armed forces' in his work, which stands halfway between fiction and testimony. Cosse points out the fact that different views of history are being elaborated in direct relation to the contemporary positions and interests of social actors. For Pascale, who compared the experiences of post-fascist Italy with post-dictatorial Uruguay, the latter is still haunted by its past but lacks a common vision of it. While many profess to cherish the value of democracy after the authoritarian interregnum, there are other figures, who—though marginal—still dream about strong rule and order.[55]

In Chile, with the transition to democracy, the dual character of the model followed by Pinochet—with its coercive and developmental traits—was amply recognized, albeit interpreted from contrasting perspectives. The perception of Chile as a highly stable society since the 1830s, a democratic exception in a continent marked by civil wars, anarchy, *caudillismo*, and oligarchical authoritarianism, has been prominent in the visions of Chilean nationalists and military rulers in the 1970s.

The existence of a President of the Republic according to the Portalian vision (1831–1891) coincides with the most brilliant period of the History of Chile. There is stability and progress in the economic domain; well-known advances in the cultural and educational realms; two highly difficult international wars were won; the Land of the Araucanians was pacified and colonized; nitrate was exploited; order and social peace dominated in the whole country. The coincidence between the period of the Portalian presidents and Chilean prosperity is not accidental. This zenith is due precisely to the existence of a central authority that always watched out for the whole country and [worked] for the common interests of the members of Nation.[56]

The model inspired by Diego Portales in the 1830s was characterized by a strong and centralized government, led by public figures who were portrayed as examples of prudence, dignity, and strength. Portales imposed an impersonal system of government, founded on respect for an abstract authority: this reinforced the stability of the system of rule, regardless of which individuals held power (as long as the latter functioned within the framework of the constitution and the law). Presidential rule was paramount and conferred a strongly authoritarian but legal character to Chilean democracy in the nineteenth century. The Portalian model was a guiding light for later Chilean nationalists and was portrayed as antithetical to 'decadent' liberal democracy. 'This explains that after the catastrophe of the Marxist administration of President Allende, which looked like the final shipwreck of the spirit and work of Portales, the latter would inspire the [Pinochet] government . . .'[57] The alternative visions of Chile's past attributed the high levels of stability to the authoritarian character of the local pattern of rule. Within the democratic pattern of Chile, the elites did not hesitate to use force when it fit their political objectives, as in the case of the challenge posed by President Balmaceda in the 1890s. A parallel and extreme example of authoritarian repression and violence is commonly depicted through the interaction of the Chilean state and its Indian minorities, especially the Araucarians.

This is a history of intolerance. Of a society that does not tolerate the existence of different people. Of a Spanish-Creole-European Christian Western country calling itself civilized and trying to exterminate the barbarians, the savages, the men who freely transit the *pampas* and the mountain ridges of the south of the continent. They [the Araucarians or *mapuches*] defended themselves from civilized savagery, did what they could, fought to the end and finally died, vanquished by progress . . . This senseless war, which our glorious Republican armies began in the second half of the last century, was guided by intolerance: the right to fight barbarianism on the part of he who believes himself civilized, in the name of flags and saints, crowned by the mythologies of human progress.[58]

This view, writ large and antithetical to the Portalian ideals, depicted the Chilean state and society as imbued by repression and violence, especially against the Indians, the mobilized lower classes, and any group perceived as a threat to social order, stability, and progress (as interpreted by the ruling classes).

Allende's period was perceived by the right-wing forces as a challenge to the established order and to institutional stability. While recognizing the violence experienced during military rule, the right-wing forces contextualized differently the roots of this violence. Jaime Guzmán, one of the legal minds behind the 1980 Constitution, and founder and leader of the UDI party, was one of the intellectuals who most persistently defended the claims that contextualized the actions of the security forces:

. . . We, Chileans, owe an imperishable debt of gratitude to the armed forces and forces of order, not only because on 11 September they freed us from Communism . . . [Also for] winning first and assuring afterwards social peace. This social peace, which some people despectively call the 'tranquility of cemeteries', is one without which those who express themselves in such a manner would probably be buried in a cemetery, without being able to pour out their resentment or display their presumptuous arrogance.

Order . . . certainly comprehends and requires justice, but it relies on social peace. The tranquility that sophisticated people hold in contempt, but which the common people enjoy as they are able to go to work and come home, send their children to schools or perform home chores, without fearing violent aggression. A reality that we could appreciate fully only when we experienced some years ago the anguish of losing it.

. . . In Chile today, social peace should not be taken for granted. It is the result of a daily combat against a permanent and audacious subversion, fed by ideologues and material executors, solely responsible for the common doctrine of hatred and immorality, which inspires them. A subversion, whose victims are usually ignored by the solicitous international defenders of human rights.[59]

Guzmán differentiated between human-rights violations by commission and by omission. While states are responsible for such violations when they limit and affect individual liberties beyond what is required by the social and political situation, he said, international organizations and hypocritical individuals often ignore the fact that states and institutions are also responsible for human-rights violations if they refrain from intervening in a situation in which human rights are being affected by acts of terrorism, subversion, and social disruption, such as those that characterized the Chilean scene before the 1973 military takeover. If by intervening in the public spheres some rights are restricted, this may be necessary to preclude the victory of subversion, which enjoys existing liberties but will eventually abolish them.[60] To accuse Pinochet and his administration of human-rights violations and violence involves a distortion of reality:

If one is shown two photographs of a person, one in which he happily enjoys an afternoon in the countryside and one in which he is shown on the operation table, nobody would doubt that the first situation is more pleasant. But if the photograph is turned into a movie and it happens that a nearby tree falls on the person in the countryside, killing him, whereas the person who underwent surgery recovers, the comparison will be radically reversed . . . A country on the verge of falling prey to totalitarianism can display a context of personal rights and liberties more flattering than one submitted to restrictions necessary to minimize that threat. But that would change diametrically once the totalitarian regime takes hold of the country. The respect for any human right will then suddenly and brutally end, bringing the country to a far more disadvantaged situation . . . With the perspective of its evolutionary trend, this could be neatly perceived before it would become reality. Only the superficiality of the static, photographic approach never realized it.[61]

Most of Chile's political forces and intellectual circles emerged from the period of military rule sharing a total rejection of the senseless use of violence in politics. They still differed in their interpretation of the origins, causes, and historical depth of violence in Chilean society. They also disagreed about the ways to contain or eliminate violence, and about the political and legal format of institutions that would enable the country to move beyond violence. On the twenty-fifth anniversary of Allende's electoral victory, a series of debates were maintained on the significance and implications of that event, rekindling public attention on the basic disagreements that persist concerning the past. While the left commemorated a happy era 'without disappearance', right politicians and intellectuals assessed the dangers of armed Socialism and insurrection.[62] Beyond the traditional polarization between right and left, the recent debates opened incipient signs of historical revisionism in each camp. On the left, Tomás Moulian defined the Popular

Unity project of the 1970s as unviable, since it attempted to move through democratic means towards a Soviet-Cuban model, which was unacceptable for substantial sectors of Chilean society. Reassessing the situation in the 1970s, Moulian suggests that the only viable path would have been for Allende to deepen the reforms initiated by the Christian Democracy through a pragmatic coalition with sectors of the latter. Regretfully, this path was foreclosed by the ideological promises and exacerbated rhetorics of the leftist coalition.[63] On the right, political scientist Oscar Godoy, who had supported Pinochet and turned liberal, has suggested that the coup, which was prompted by the political impasse and authority vacuum of Allende's last months in power, were preceded by hopes of restoration of democracy, while *de facto* the military slipped into authorian rule after 1973.[64]

Despite these initial signs of historical revisionism, the contrasting and confrontational positions still dominate the visions of the recent past. Against this background some intellectuals in the 1980s voiced deep concerns about the possibility of ending the cycle of violence which was rooted in the past and which would eventually be projected into the future, unless some effort were made to enact a radical break with violence. Isabel Allende's *La casa de los espíritus* raised these questions, in direct relation to the social structure of Chile. She implied that violence is imprinted in the pattern of domination, hatred, and fear that has traditionally separated the high and lower strata. Once initiated, the cycle of violence is difficult to halt. In this novel, the granddaughter of landlord and right-wing Senator Esteban Trueba, Alba, meditates on the cycle of violence, after suffering torture by Colonel Esteban García, the illegitimate grandchild of her grandfather:

When I was in the doghouse [where Alba was imprisoned] I wrote in my mind that one day Colonel García would stand before me in defeat and that I would avenge myself on all those who need to be avenged. But now I have begun to question my own hatred. Within a few short weeks, ever since I returned to the house, it seems to have become diluted, to have lost its sharp edge. I am beginning to suspect that nothing that happened is fortuitous, that it all corresponds to a fate laid down before my birth, and that Esteban García is part of the design. It is a crude, twisted line, but no brushstroke is in vain. The day my grandfather tumbled his grandmother, Pancha García, among the rushes of the riverbank, he added another link to the chain of events that had to complete itself. Afterward the grandson of the woman who was raped repeats the gesture with the granddaughter of the rapist, and perhaps forty years from now my grandson will knock García's granddaughter down among the rushes, and so on down through the centuries in an unending tale of sorrow, blood and love.[65]

Despite the grim prospect of bringing violence to an end, Allende makes Alba reflect on a way out of the trap of confrontation and violence, by learning from history, by accepting what cannot be changed, and by being willing to understand the other's feelings and perspectives:

> And now I seek my hatred and cannot seem to find it. I feel its flame going out as I come to understand the existence of Colonel García and the others like him, as I understand my grandfather and piece things together from Clara's notebooks of Clara, my mother's letters, the ledgers of *Tres Marías,* and the many other documents spread before me on the table. It would be very difficult for me to avenge all those who should be avenged, because my revenge would be just another part of the same inexorable rite. I have to break that terrible chain. I want to think that my task is life and that my mission is not to prolong hatred but simply to fill these pages . . .[66]

The implications of the attempt to understand violence as a component of collective identity and public life are ambiguous. The violent polarization of the 1960s and early 1970s, which led to the violent repression of the 1970s, caused many to think that ideological projects with a collectivist character have reached a catastrophic end. Since the attempts of the leftist forces to counteract violence (the violence of the system and the rulers) were phrased in the same language of violence, resistance to the military could be interpreted in the sequel of military rule as a source of mounting bloodshed, which made no positive contribution.

Perhaps the widest message implicit in the continuous reminders of historical violence has been, for the broad public, to renounce violence altogether as a force shaping history. But can violence be eradicated? On what grounds? It might be a herculean task, if political violence is basically rooted in, or reinforced by, the struggles evolving around the patterns of domination and the socio-economic structures in these countries.

Even if the 'old' forms of violence, which were ideologically oriented, have been marginalized, what seems to be replacing violence as a whole? Is it the endorsement of an institutionalized pattern of autonomous participation and conflict resolution in the framework of democracy, or is it a wave of public apathy and discouragement, in which violence remains submerged and/or sectorialized against those defined as marginal figures and criminals?

Inclusion and Exclusion, Demobilization and Social Disaggregation

Central to the shaping of any collective identity are the criteria defining citizenship, the criteria and arena of inclusion and exclusion, the patterning of membership in primordial, civil, or other terms, and the shaping of public spheres and access to them, as well as the connections between these aspects of social life. In societies such as Argentina, Chile, and Uruguay, collective identities and public life were shaped around republican, civil ideas, endowed with the ideals of the struggle for independence and the spirit of state building as the basis of nation building. A strong participatory element was imprinted in these tenets of identity, which were combined from early on with strong regulative, authoritarian patterns of rule. This duality of possible mobilization (a potential generator of autonomy) and of demobilization and control was played out time and again according to the changing historical and social contexts. Its dynamic was enacted by different social, political, individual, and corporate forces, which claimed to represent and project various visions of their imagined collectivity. These visions implied varied forms and avenues of inclusion and exclusion, which in the twentieth century revolved around concepts such as the Nation and the People ('Pueblo').

The military governments that took power in the 1970s in the Southern Cone reformulated the criteria of inclusion and exclusion according to their own ideological tenets. From the start, they created whole categories of individuals and institutions to be excluded from the collectivity, as alien to the nation, its spirit, tradition, well-being, and future. Marxism, Leninism, Socialism, Communism, and whoever promoted these ideologies or merely sympathized with them had to be marginalized and/or eliminated due to the threat posed to the nation and its 'values'. The doctrine of National Security determined clear-cut criteria of inclusion and exclusion.

These criteria were applied with varying degrees of autonomy of interpretation by the different apparatuses of repression, that is, in a more controlled and hierarchical manner in Chile and Uruguay and in a more decentralized and chaotic manner in Argentina. Nonetheless, and despite differences in the patterns of repression, in all three cases the enemies were marked from the start. They included such varied targets as a professor who taught Marxism or other 'alien doctrines'; trade union leaders and members who fought for greater benefits; high-school students who contested the established authorities in their demand for reduced fares for public transportation; a priest who defended the poor in his parish; a lawyer committed to the cause of human rights; a security official who refused to shoot students in a demonstration; some academic disciplines, especially in the social sciences and humanities, such as psychology, sociology, and political science, and—in Argentina briefly—even modern mathematics, which was perceived as critical of the established order, institutions, and traditions; artists and forms of art that expressed protest against social injustice and oppression; and all types of organizations—from political parties to professional to neighbourhood associations—that were committed to 'anti-national', anti-Western, anti-Christian ideas. Various degrees of exclusion were applied in each of the countries, finding expression in the intervention into academic life, the destruction of several professional career tracks, the proscription and sometimes burning of 'dangerous' books and artistic creations, the prohibition against broadcasting and even possessing recordings of such music as the Nueva Canción Chilena and the Uruguayan Canto Popular.[67]

Exclusion involved many degrees and forms, which were reflected in the cultural realm of the 1970s and following decades.[68] One form was social ostracism, reflected in testimonial literature. Another form was *relegación*, that is, judicial banishment and internal exile, as illustrated in the Chilean film *La frontera*. Imprisonment and torture were also common and found their cultural reflection in such varied works as the Argentine films *Sur* and *La noche de los lápices*, Timerman's book, Chilean books such as *Isla 10*, *Anatomía de un golpe de estado*, Uruguayan works such as González Bermejo's *Las manos en el fuego*, Rosencof and Fernández Huidobro's *Memorias del calabozo*.[69]

Among the most influential early depictions of torture in Uruguayan fiction of the 1970s are Nelson Marra's *El guardaspalda* and Mario Benedetti's *Pedro y el capitán*. In Benedetti's work, the relationship between tortured and torturer is explicitly fictionalized, introducing the issue of military rule with its violent implications.[70] Marra's story tells, in a first person account, the life and death of an officer of the 'political police'. Written in 1973 for a literary contest organized by the leftist journal *Marcha*, it was read as alluding in rather explicit terms to the ambush and heavy wounding of Intelligence Police Chief, Moran Charquero (allegedly the leader of the Death Squads) by the MLN-Tupamaros in 1970. The close reference to a real figure turned the story into a highly explosive piece. Following the first prize award and its subsequent publication in the journal, the military justice ordered the arrest of the panel of judges as well of Marra himself who spent four years in prison, leaving the country for exile in 1978.[71] The main character starts as a petty burglar in a shantytown (*cantegril*), who kills people according to the whims of a traditional party politician and is promoted to be his bodyguard, is given a position in the police, and finally enters the 'political force'. One morning, as he drives to the headquarters, he is ambushed and shot by 'subversives'. From the hospital bed, he recalls his life, without sparing fully detailed accounts of violence and of the torture methods that the main character employs against a wide range of figures, from childhood friends (to whom he is disloyal), his wife and daughter, to, obviously, his enemies. Sex appears associated with violence. In this connection, probably the passage that most alarmed official censorship was the description of the bodyguard having homosexual relations with his political patron. As in other Latin American novels, such sexual relationships were read as allegories of the relationships between the political elites and the marginal thugs who served them.[72]

Particularly dramatic in terms of exclusion and often ignored was the situation of the *exonerados*, those public employees, from the highest to the lowest ranks, who were expelled from their employment, or imprisoned and marginalized. The personal costs these individuals paid (during military rule but also after the return to democracy) is illustrated by the case of Horacio Ciafardini, as described by his widow, María Inés Olivella, in an interview:

Horacio was an intellectual, an economist who studied in Europe. Back home he taught economics in various universities and worked also at the Federal Council for Investments. They detained him in his work place, at the Council, in 1976, before the military coup. We knew it before. Some colleagues had been detained, others managed to go away. Horacio decided to stay in Argentina. Once in prison, under the legal procedure of state arrest (PEN—which explains he was not affected by the secretive system of repression), they gave him the unusual chance of being liberated if he agreed to leave the country, and this without any request on his part. He decided to stay in prison, and they kept him for five and a half years . . . He was a neat prisoner of conscience, imprisoned for his ideological views. He had no connections with the guerrillas and was not involved in violence. . . . The years in prison were extremely difficult for me, for him, and for our little daughter. But, once he was liberated in October 1982, during the transition, life became no less difficult. . . . He could not find a job. The ordeal continued. He, who had suffered for his convictions, once free, found that spaces at the Council and the universities were closed for him. Finally, after two years of unemployment, the director of the academic centre for economic research offered him a job as teaching assistant, not the professional position he occupied in the past. On the very day he went to campus to receive the position, he collapsed at the corner of the school, and died. To tell the truth, I believe this was the outcome of the democratic torture.[73]

Uruguayan emigré Fernando Aínsa perceptively referred to such tragic human exclusions in his book of aphorisms, *De aquí y de allá*:

One discovers the inner exile of those who stayed. . . . There are those who do not talk (because they are not able), do not act (because others do not let them), only stay alive in marginal activities. They are the exiles of a time devoured by another time. They have no right to history, only to remember and repeat themselves in the hope that does not abandon them. One should remember them. Don't you think so?[74]

Exclusion also involved the experiences of tens and hundreds of thousands of emigrés and exiles, who fled to other Latin American countries, to North America, and to Europe. Emigrés and exiles included famous creators such as Onetti, Benedetti, Carlos Martínez Moreno, and Eduardo Galeano (Uruguay); Osvaldo Bayer, Fernando Solanas, Juan Gelman, David Viñas, Manuel Puig, Osvaldo Soriano, Juan Carlos Martini (Argentina); Antonio Skármeta, Poli Délano, Jorge Edwards, Isabel Allende, Hernán Lavín Cerda, Miguel Littín (Chile); and many others. Works that reflect such experiences include Fernando Aínsa's *Con acento extranjero* and *De aquí y de allá*, Patricia Politzer's *Altamirano*, Solanas's *Tangos: el exilio de Gardel*, and José Rodríguez Elizondo's *La pasión de Iñaki*.[75] The experiences of exile comprise the problems of involvement, absorption, and development of new identities among exiles and their families in the host countries. While many of the exiles maintain signs of uprootedness, even after years of residence, their children develop ambivalent attitudes which sometimes involve being part of the new societies but also related to their parents' nostalgias, their own vision of the country of origin, and their secluded or hyphenated identity.[76]

Exclusion reached its peak in the disappearances, in covert or open assassinations of those excluded from the 'National Being', and in the abduction of the young children of the victims and their adoption by families of those involved in the apparatus of repression. Luis Puenzo's film *La historia oficial* (1985) brought this tragic chapter to the attention of the Argentine and the world public. The forceful presence—and struggle for renewed inclusion—of those excluded by the violence of the system can be traced in numerous works of fiction; Alicia Steimberg's sensitive short story of 'Cecilia's Last Will and Testament', in which, after reading over a document left by her friend years ago, the narrator realizes:

> But I don't know why I'm talking about Cecilia as if she were dead. It's that eccentricity of hers that drove her to make out this will.
> I will take these pages with me. They have no legal value and Cecilia won't be able to be buried as she wishes until we find the . . . [probably, the body] But this has to be handled delicately. It doesn't seem particularly nice to hurry things along where a case like this is concerned. Besides, I don't know when I'll see her next, since she says she's not coming back. But I know she'll be back. As long as I live, Cecilia will be back.[77]

One of the main issues highlighted by the period of military dictatorship was that of the demobilization of the masses. In Argentina, this issue has been historically centred on the role played by Peronism in Argentine politics since 1955. Many works have been dedicated to this issue.[78] The corpus of works by Tomás Eloy Martínez since 1985 (*La novela de Perón, Santa Evita,* and *Las memorias del General*) is especially relevant in trying to understand how Argentina entered, in Tulio Halperin Donghi's words, the period of 'present horror' in which massive human-rights violations were committed. Argentine military dictatorships tried consistently to deal with the inclusionary and mobilizatory trends that Peronism placed at the centre of Argentine politics in various ways (though with scant results). In this framework, the PRN constituted the last episode in this concatenation of attempts to demobilize the masses. In his work, Tomás Eloy Martínez addressed the major 'absent presence' in Argentine politics—the populist inclusionary project of Peronism:

By using Perón as the link between the Argentine past and present, *La novela de Perón* succeeds where many scholarly studies have failed. It draws a map of Argentine contemporary history, in which Peronism has finally found its proper place—not as an aberration, not as a new beginning, but as yet another thread in the complex web of continuity and change in which even the recent catastrophe will finally find its place.[79]

The problem of inclusion through massive mobilization, as shown by Peronism among the working classes (and by Hipólito Yrigoyen before, among the middle and lower-middle classes), reaches its tragic zenith with the return of General Perón to Argentina on 20 June 1973, after eighteen years of exile. In the largest gathering of masses in Argentine modern history, over a million persons poured into the area around the Ezeiza international airport to welcome the 'Leader'. The scenes of this event, the meeting point of the three narrative threads developed in the book, constituted an inchoate climax of joy and tragedy, an epitome of Argentine history. As a mass movement, Peronism brought together the politically instrumental but irreconcilable right and left sectors under the populist wings of Perón's leadership. Each of the Peronist poles interpreted the Leader's mandate in their own ideological terms and, as they flowed to Ezeiza, the script of mutual bloodshed was unavoidable, almost like a Greek tragedy.[80]

The Ezeiza mobilization was only the beginning of the descent into guerrilla violence and military repression that served as a prelude to the PRN. In the context of Argentine social and political history, mobilization threatened to bring about radical change. Even though tamed by the Peronist leader, mass mobilization was perceived as a critical danger by the upper classes and the security forces. As in the other societies of the Southern Cone, the elites and middle classes of Argentina were ready to sacrifice democracy and individual freedoms for the sake of social order and demobilization.

Looking back, from the post-1983 stage, and from the perspectives of those who participated in the mobilizations that preceded the military coup, the benefit of political activism is questionable. This trend is illustrated by the release from prison and return of Floreal, the main character of *Sur*, a 1988 film by Fernando Solanas. In one of the (real or imagined) encounters with his father (a trade union activist and leader of many strikes), Floreal rejects the latter's recrimination of his inactivity and questions his father's militant activity during his childhood years:

But stop with that, papa! . . . Stop with that, I beg you! . . . How many times are you going to repeat that! I do not attend [the trade union activities] because they depress me. O.K. . . . I don't go because I remember the kind of life we lived! . . . I don't go for the [many] times we had to come for you at the police . . . Because we had no money! . . . Because mama was always protesting . . . That is why I don't go . . . I don't care . . . Nothing else . . .[81]

This scene prompts the mother to defend the purist stand of the militant father, who kept dignity and pride intact, the only cherishable treasure available for somebody of the working class. Nonetheless, the general ambience is one of discouragement, as in one of the closing dialogues of the film, between Floreal and *El negro*, a former friend assassinated by the security forces who walks the streets as one of Floreal's alter egos:

Floreal: I'm going . . . I'm going forever . . . Listen! . . . Peregrino is right . . . We live in a River of Shit . . .
El negro: Where are you going with all that rancor? . . .
Floreal: Hah! Hah! Five years . . . [in prison] Five years for what? . . . To come here . . . To continue picking trash and shit . . .
El negro: And if we don't pick it, who will do it?
Floreal: Not me! . . .
El negro: Who will fight for what's yours? Who, besides you, will defend what you dreamed about?
El negro: Look at you! Look at you! You are a waste! . . . Look at your face! . . . You don't see? You seem a mess, Floreal . . . Take yourself less seriously . . .
Floreal: What's going on with you, Negro? . . .
El negro: I want to forget . . . It is impossible to live knowing everything . . . Nothing is of value for me . . . I don't want anything . . . I know everything . . . I'm finished. Like this movie . . . I am dead . . .
Floreal: Ease up, Negro [*Vamos Negro* . . .].[82]

In Argentina, in addition to the issue of the inclusion of the popular and working classes, a major role was played by the consolidation of a middle class as constitutive of collective identity and a major participant in public life. Particularly since the 1930s, many writers and intellectuals have practised, in Alberto Ciria's words, some sort of middle-class self-analysis of collective identity and its frustrations.[83] One of the central tenets of this literature is the failure of externally oriented social actors to play a protagonist role in their country's history. Writing in the 1980s, playwright Roberto Cossa follows this line. Cossa shows, for instance in *Los compadritos*, that the changes that apparently modernize his country are mere reflections of a mimetic incorporation of outside models. This is typically symbolized in the metamorphoses of the Quilmes bar in which he locates the scenes, and which becomes successively a German beer bar, a vernacular *parrillada*, a stockyard, and an American bar. Moreover, beneath modernization there are strong authoritarian traits, which imply a constant return to patterns that developed in the past, as shown by Alfonso's drive for control and order and by the submissiveness of most of his characters to authority. The past remains present, as well as the dependence on external centres and forms of thinking.[84]

Similarly harsh in its view of a society of middle classes and of the intellectuals in particular is Roberto Piglia. In *Respiración artificial*, Piglia shows how externally oriented Argentina and its intellectuals have been, as the latter go astray after the fanfare of second-rate European philosophers, whose major virtue is that they can speak several languages and shift with elegance from one to the other.[85]

Individuals contributed to the polarization and ideologization of debate in the 1960s and 1970s, finding themselves in the midst of an increasingly radicalized polity, in which widespread mobilization took place. Santucho, one of the active participants in the process of polarization, characterized the almost messianic feeling of the activists in those years: 'We believed ourselves to be among the chosen to carry out revolution. We believed we were a generation born to transform the world. By adopting Leninism we acquired the dogmatic aspect of the vanguard and cadres' party. Today this can be seen as messianic.'[86] The impact of the ensuing repression cut across the spectrum of social forces mobilized in this period. The Mothers of Plaza de Mayo and other NGOs became foci of resistance against repression and, with the passing of time, extended and radicalized their aims far beyond the search for the *desaparecidos*. They took upon themselves a deeper questioning of the patterns of exclusion of their society. They addressed authoritarian patterns of control and violence in the framework of social injustice, economic inequality, imperialism, and corruption. In the period of redemocratization, the civilian administration acceded to power amidst a generalized expectation of radical redefinition of the Argentine public sphere. Alfonsín and the UCR envisioned not only a formal return to democracy but also promised to instil real substance into democratic practice. This foundational approach opened wide the gates of inclusion and participation for all the sectors that had been marginalized under military rule. The rising expectations of post-dictatorial justice and the initial bold steps adopted towards its attainment framed the events of 1984–6 with cathartic overtones. The subsequent institutional obstacles and the economic crisis led to an undermining of the foundational promises and to a reversal in the treatment of past human-rights violations. The spontaneous mobilization of parts of the civil society, which had accompanied all major developments since 1983, proved futile and found no institutional channels after the military uprising of Semana Santa in 1987, thus failing to prevent a full shift into the regressive policy path. When Menem implemented his twin policies of military and economic restructuring, the experience of the late 1980s weighed heavily on behalf of enhancing his capability to rule by presidential decrees, while largely disregarding public opinion and overruling parliamentary opposition. Under Menem, formal criteria of inclusion and participation have been incorporated through the reformed constitution of 1994. At the same time, the neoliberal policies of stabilization and adjustment have increased the magnitude of unemployment, pauperization, social marginalization, and crime. However, in contrast with the situation in the 1960s and 1970s, the reactive capacity of the most affected sectors seems severely reduced, partly due to the lack of appeal of positions that could challenge the decision-making capability of an executive power that had managed to stabilize the economy and halt hyperinflation. When groups such as the Mothers, who have achieved a high moral status, have demanded a radical restructuring of society to incorporate popular interests and social commitments, in contrast to current macroeconomic trends, their position has been criticized. The political establishment has tried to discredit such positions as those of a marginal and unrepresentative sector motivated by deep grief and sorrow to take positions which are no longer relevant. Moreover, vast sectors of the population, overwhelmed by personal hardships and a difficult economic situation, place the concern for survival far above collective solidarity and thoughts about structural socio-economic reform.

A perceptive observer of his home society, Tomás Eloy Martínez portrayed the change, as the exiles returned to Argentina, in the following terms:

Buenos Aires—and the country at large—appeared to be preoccupied only with the state of the economy, interest rates, the party primaries and power games in the trade unions. Argentina was becoming myopic. Critical intellectual discussion had virtually disappeared. . . . There is the impression that history is on the run. Last week's 'eternal values' are interred tomorrow. Yesterday's joys and sadnesses had been taken by the wind. Nobody grasps how it is possible to live with dignity in such a volatile country.[87]

In Chile, the model of social and economic change imposed by the military led to substantial rates of growth and development (after the economic crises of the mid-1970s and early 1980s). As in Argentina and Uruguay, the Chilean version of the Doctrine of National Security aimed to exclude leftists from participating in politics, the economy, culture, and the public spheres. This implied not only the personal persecution of leftist activists, but also the dismantling of the institutions perceived by the military rulers as likely to become a basis for the re-emergence of ideas and actions of this kind. The dual character of the project pursued by Pinochet prompted debate which focused accordingly on the significance of the modernizing and foundational drive of the military in the history of the country, and of its human and structural costs. General Pinochet stated time and again the foundational contribution of the armed forces:

It will never be enough to recall the state of spiritual and material violence, of administrative corruption and economic chaos, in which we found the country; as it will not be tiresome to insist that [we attacked] all that destroyed our shared life and democratic constitutionality to the point of making impossible its simple restoration, in the terms in which we knew it. . . . Succinctly, it could be claimed that the whole institutional 'status' built along 160 years of independent life was shaken to its foundations in order to destroy it and to build in its stead the new Socialist, Marxist-Leninist State, symbol of tyranny and oppression of the human being.[88]

Today order in the different fields of national life has been re-established. The revolutionary purpose designed to establish a Marxist-Leninist government at that time and the violent and generalized politization of national life had produced in September 1973 a profound breakdown of shared life not only among Chileans, but even at the base of family life. . . . The principal achievements of this Government have been the multiple advances in the process of materialization of the new institutionality.[89]

It cannot be denied that, beginning with the heroic feats of September 11, 1973, the foundational deeds and the administration by the military and the forces of order have been synonymous with rectifications and with substantial progress in the existence of the Chilean nation. In the same way, they have produced profound transformations in the whole spectrum of political and juridical institutions, in the modes of shared life, in the personal and social projects and conceptions, and even in the ways of behaviour of the Chileans. [We rejoice] upon the commemoration of an historical moment as transcendental as the recovery of freedom, of the historical and cultural identity and dignity of the Chilean people. There is an idea that sums up all my message to the country: The armed forces and the forces of order of Chile have reconstructed authentic democracy![90]

The economist Joaquín Lavín, current mayor of Las Condes (one of the elegant quarters of Santiago) and a member of the UDI, has characteristically emphasized the structural transformation of the country under the aegis of Pinochet towards an open, non-violent, and entrepreneurial society. In his book, *Chile: revolución silenciosa* (Chile: The Quiet Revolution) he analyses the many facets of this transformation: the worldwide integration of the Chilean economy, the modernization of agriculture, the new directions of Chilean industrial development, the emergence of high-tech and open access to information, the growing efficiency of Chilean firms, the client-oriented emphasis of consumer markets, the entrepreneurial trends of the new professional and economic circles, the professionalization of the fight against poverty, the emergence of new leaderships, and the enhancement of marketing options and of choices in general. These are changes that, according to Lavín, are already part of the present.

Chileans begin progressively to live with many more options than in the past. The society of 'this or the other', of a maximum of two or three alternatives, has been superseded by a new society of 'multiple options', among which it is possible to make the most diverse choices. . . . These trends form part of present-day Chile. They are part of a reality that does not require numbers, projections, or theories. Everybody can appreciate them by only opening a window, by strolling the streets, by travelling on public transport, by working in an office, by turning on the TV set, by talking with young children.[91]

This popularized vision of modernization followed the more principled approach towards modernization, which was defined since the mid-1970s by the government as leading to 'seven modernizations' geared toward the enhancement of individual freedoms, equality of opportunities and social justice, and efficiency and rationality in decision-making processes.[92] This model was ideologically antithetical to the one promoted by the Popular Unity government in 1970–3. From the point of view of the inclusion-exclusion parameters, this model enshrined limited democracy in Pinochet's 1980 Constitution, which defined clear-cut criteria of access to the public spheres, as typified in article 8. Article 8 defined in ideological terms (e.g. 'class warfare') those actions which were considered to be illegal and contrary to the institutional code of the Republic.[93]

   The sectors that opposed Pinochet and the military administration could not avoid debating these issues on the terms that the latter had imprinted in public discourse. They could not ignore the deep impact of the military project upon the reconstitution of Chilean society, although they emphasized the violent dimensions of changes and interpreted the project in the terms of the left. 'Pinochet wants to pass into history as the man who modernized Chile, the great Jefferson of Chile. We want to say that the bloody period was not a positive thing.'[94] In these circles, the general analysis of the Chilean model in terms of modernization and the application of neoliberal economic policies were harshly criticized for their authoritarian overtones, implicitly supporting coercion.

> . . . An economic liberalism of this nature, which lacks links to liberty, to social justice and democracy, does not include conceptual elements that, on the basis of ethical principles, can award legitimacy to a strongly authoritarian and exclusionary political model.[95]

Despite the persistence of disparate visions of the historical process and of the effects of military rule, following redemocratization the debate has been mostly confined to the political arena. Besides electoral participation, Chileans are mostly concerned with the pragmatic aspects of economic and social life. With an emphasis on economic growth and higher standards of living, the image of the jaguar emerged as the parallel to the East Asian economic tigers, as the basic image of Chile's reshaped identity. By Aylwin's mid-term, around 1992, large circles of Chilean society—led by the President himself—considered that Chile had successfully ended its transition to democracy. This sense was rooted in the unwillingness of many to dwell on the past, as required when looking in detail into the legacy of human-rights violations. This historical debate, which would be reopened during the public aftershocks of the mid-1990s, when avoided, makes it difficult to recreate collective identity.

> To reopen that debate is uncomfortable for various groups. It is uncomfortable for those who openly promoted military intervention. It is uncomfortable for those who openly promoted violence and the Cubanization of Chile. It is uncomfortable for those who tried to renovate the Left. . . . It is a historical debate that many in this country thought was over. But they discovered it blew up with enormous strength in the face of all and that nobody can escape being trapped in this situation. This is a country that told itself the story that it can concentrate on developing itself, as the transition is over, and that suddenly discovers that the past is part of its current life. It is like a wall that does not move aside, unless you scale it.[96]

The image of development has taken the lead, nonetheless. The public aftershocks have been confronted in terms of realpolitik, largely secluded from the developmental ethos of the New Chile. However, the 'leap forward' has been largely secluded from other dimensions of membership. For instance, the model encompasses a varied degree of inclusion and exclusion of different social sectors: some of them are totally included and identified with the Chilean economic miracle, while others are excluded from its benefits and lack voice and the technical know-how to be heard and taken into consideration in the drafting of economic policies.[97]

There is a high degree of social passivity produced by the decay of political parties, the rise of individualism, and the constraints of insertion in the markets. There is a feeling that rights and duties, which formerly were subject to political debates, are currently determined by the market, lessening the power and relevance of political actors. There is also a sense of fatigue of a generation that, for 17 years, lived in a state of [political and social] activism. This generation has been replaced by another, which is linked to business. There is also the premature death of NGOs, which I must confess surprised me.[98]

The effects of military rule and of neoliberalism weighed similarly in the Uruguayan situation: a disaggregation of collective commitments occurred, even though Uruguayans still talk of their society's civility, especially after the substantial effort of mobilization against the Expiry Law (December 1986–April 1989).

During military rule many of these cultural elites fell silent or, hoping to remain critical, opted for exile.[99] The officially approved authors worked in this period within a logic of a 'refounding' of culture, seeking to create a literature that would be understood widely by the common person ('comprensible para el lector medio'), that is, a literature signalled by previsibility, routine, and conventionalism. The government tried, mostly unsuccessfully, through official support and contests, to encourage the emergence of this 'new literature'. There was a shift in the directions of cultural creation in this period, albeit not in the direction encouraged by the rulers. What can be perceived is the rise of an intimate, personal literature, somewhat dissociated from a collective perspective and focused more on reflections, philosophical positions, 'magical realism' *à la* García Márquez, lyrical and feminist turns, with a substantial increase in poetry at the expense of prose.[100] Teresa Porzecanski and others consider that the narrative of imagination encouraged a revision of the solemn and realistic views in which the military rulers had vested interests.[101] As the printed word suffered from high levels of censorship, the burden of protest was taken over by music. In the late 1970s there was a resurgence of 'Canto Popular', which had earlier roots in a tradition of protest and popular styles in the pre-dictatorial period (Viglietti, Zitarrosa). In its new versions, this genre developed in small pubs and theatres, at first stressing personal motives and reflections. The main group in this period was Los que Iban Cantando. Towards the 1980s, in tandem with the weakening of military rule, the contents of 'Canto Popular' slowly became more political and social-collective.[102]

With the return to democracy, there was a resurgence of collectivist, political, and social themes and concerns. Sanguinetti's administration itself fostered the idea of a 'restoration' of the cultural splendour of the 1950s, though it provided only meagre public resources for that purpose. But the line of the '45 Generation was criticized and displaced by younger writers and composers, who adopted alternative approaches at the end of the military rule. Notorious among them was the 1985–87 movement of 'National Rock'. Dozens of youth groups succeeded in attracting thousands to live concerts, and their hits were broadcast widely. The main examples of this trend were the Los Estómagos, Los Tontos, Neoh-23, Zero, La Chancha Francisca, Tabaré Riverock Band, and Los Traidores. Many of these groups moved from criticizing the repression to disengaging from any connection with the traditional ways of interpreting the collectivity and, in some cases, even to nihilistic trends, such as the line of Los Traidores, whose main song was 'Put Flowers on my Tomb'.[103]

The prospects of recreating pre-dictatorial culture, desired by the Sanguinetti administration, proved short-lived.

They [the older intellectuals] thought that the country had preserved its ideological spectrum. . . . The University was reconstructed, the silenced or exiled intellectuals and politicians began expressing themselves again, cultural and editorial enterprises began operations. There was a return to democratic practice, to civilization, to being very European and much less Latin American . . . The illusion lasted only a short time. The re-encounter with Uruguayan society and culture was much more traumatic than many had thought.[104]

Related to the generational tensions, a gradual marginalization of the collectivist perspective occurred. In music, while high levels of professionalism have become the norm, there is both a renewed interest in tango, candombe, tropical music, and folklore, as well as pop music. Jaime Roos, the main pop figure, launched in 1992 one of his most popular hits, 'El hombre de la calle' (The Man in the Street), which expressed a clear-cut rejection of politics:

The man in the street suddenly changes frequency,
He knows that he will never see that man [the politician] at his home
Neither will he share with him bread and wine . . .[105]

Similarly, the Cuarteto de Nos, an outgrowth of the Canto Popular (Popular Song, a genre that emphasized struggle and resistance) and one of the central groups of National Rock in the 1990s caused great public commotion when the lyrics of some of its recent songs were distributed. In one of them, 'The Day Artigas Got Drunk', the figure of the founding father of the nation is ridiculed, as he shapes the colours of the national flag thinking of the wine he drinks and the wind he has passed. Artigas is portrayed as misleading his army and as driven by hormones in a promiscuous way that did not distinguish between women and his black male aide, which caused an uproar among the black community of Uruguay.[106]

Hugo Achugar sums up these shifts towards a greater privatization in the themes and concerns of Uruguayan culture:

In the 1960s and especially toward the end of the decade, social and political messages were explicit and were almost hegemonic in the 'writing' of the discourses. In the 1970s, suggestion and symbolism are preferred. In the democratic period, after the initial outburst, there seems to be a saturation with social and political issues, and a passage towards the intimate and the imaginative.[107]

The fragmentation of Uruguayan society and, as a result, of its culture, even though it always existed, seems to have surfaced in the public conscience after the traumatic experience of the dictatorship and the worsening of the economic crisis or the questioning of the country's viability.[108]

A similar line has been raised concerning Argentina by David Viñas. In an interview, Viñas characterized the democratic period in his home country as one in which the critical intellectual is out of place, as he or she becomes a barbarian. When the general norm is one of intellectual domestication, Viñas considers—looking back at the former experience of such inquisitive intellectuals as the slain writer Rodolfo Walsh—that society has moved to a stage in which nobody seems willing to talk about death and the real problems of society. Passion for collective deeds and injustice seems *passé*.

It seems to be that todays' slogan is 'let's calm ourselves'. A cooling of passion, of exasperation, [a weaning] of the dramatic character that predominated over the social space and the domain of culture in the 1970s. There is a whole process of folklorization, of trivialization, of a clear-cut wearing out of what evidently could be disturbing and uncomfortable.[109]

These trends are reflected in shifts in cultural styles, as an acute analyst of Argentine theatre has observed:

Between 1983 and 1985 very few satirical works were produced. Tragedy and comedy predominated [then], two genres that, according to Frederic Jameson and Hayden White, look for reconciliation and synthesis. One, in a pessimistic way, through catastrophe, and the other, in an optimistic way, with a happy end. . . . The theatrical production of the last decade is geared to atomization. National 'disappointment' has generated its theatrical counterpart: the satirical play. Beating humour, conscious deformation of characters, monologues, sketches and scripts prevail. . . . In contemporary Argentine theatre there is an authoritarian epistema, both individual and social, guided by oblivion, de-politicization and carnivalistic mocking.[110]

Along the same line, and with the entire Latin American region in mind, Jean Franco refers to the social correlate of the privatization of interests: the displacement and, in some cases, the marginalization of the intelligentsia that had traditionally played a central role in the shaping of public spheres and in the previous—often utopian—struggle over the definition of the collective identity of these societies:

The displacement of the intelligentsia from its hegemonic position [in the 1960s] by the technocrats has marginalized the one group that, in the past, took upon themselves to 'imagine' the nation. This marginalization has been intensified by the market forces which have undermined the legitimation narratives which had justified the literary intelligentsia as a disinterested group that, precisely because of their disinterestedness, could claim to represent truth. In her recent book, *Escenas de la vida posmoderna*, Beatriz Sarlo laments the fact that the claim of modernist literature to challenge the status quo has not only been weakened, but the public sphere of debate is itself deprived of any intellectual voice . . .[111]

In the period that preceded the last wave of military rule, the public sphere was characterized by the presence of ideological projects related to various ethical interpretations of reality, charged with utopian views for reshaping collective identities and the material basis of social life. After the experience of life under the military, most of these ideals faded away. Contemporary public spheres in the Southern Cone seem to be dominated by debates of a more pragmatic and immediate character. Renowned actor Miguel Angel Solá explains:

Poor us, poor society, what a folly. A thinking and living society. A stirring society. A society that was going to revolt. And through that revolution, it was going to evolve. I'm not talking about weapons. I'm talking about thoughts. I'm talking about feelings. And it turned into this. A society focused on profit. A faint-hearted society. A society where money talks.[112]

Even the protagonists of the radical movements of the 1960s and 1970s have rejected the ideals and hopes that led them to be politically active then. As Lautaro Murúa in the role of the veteran leftist writer explained in *El muro de silencio* to Vanessa Redgrave, who played the role of the English film director who thought of interviewing the surviving victims in her attempt to understand what motivated the thousands of young people who took to the streets to demonstrate for social justice and against imperialism and repression in Argentina:

'I don't understand at all, what did these young people think? They were all crazy . . .'
'They were thousands and thousands of heedless people . . .'
'There is no way I can ask Julio [the 'disappeared', whose story was to be represented in the film], but I can ask Ana [the surviving spouse and mother of Julio's daughter].'

'You are candid . . . Do you think that nowadays you would find them defending the same ideals . . . ?' [and he shook his head from side to side, indicating that the answer was negative][113]

These trends are related to the structuring of the legacy of human-rights violations as containing messages of discouragement of the old styles of political action and of ideological commitments and public engagement, which were portrayed as leading to the catastrophe. Low-intensity fear became internalized as a 'second nature' in these societies, with disaggregating and demobilizing effects. While redemocratization formally opened the criteria of inclusion and generalized the citizens' access to the public spheres, wide sectors have been unable to materialize such an access due to socio-economic hardship, while others feel insecure or unwilling to develop public involvement. Paradoxically, it has been under democracy that the demobilizing effect of the military repression is fully felt. León Rozitchner has recently drawn attention to these roots of the changing cultural landscape:

Negated in the public sphere, terror undermines from within the subjectivity of Argentines. The system fails to address the same terror it creates: Terror of death . . . terror of unemployment, bankruptcy, and poverty in the economy; terror of the use of power in the armed forces. We are supposed to believe it does not exist . . . to save ourselves from its constant hold. . . . Military terror curtailed what civil society had gained as collective experience. Its destructive fury ended social ties and confined us to the individual dreading body. Since then, . . . any attempt of expansion . . . has to overcome and live with that silent dread, installed in the unconsciousness of everybody. We feel it but do not know [that it turned into] a new trait of the Argentine character.[114]

Rozitchner claims that the public sphere has become dominated by a search for stability as an ontological category, while sociability has been reduced to limitations imposed by the market, democracy failed to connect politics to popular demands, and a monolithic discourse dominates the media. Intellectuals, he stresses, have abandoned their ability to analyse reality and understand it. They have been defeated by the force of reality.

In spite of this characterization, all along this chapter we have seen that there is an ample and sophisticated debate on the tenets of collective identity, which was triggered by reflection on the legacy of human-rights violations and repressive military rule. What has changed is the resonance of this debate and the capacity of ideologies and ideas to generate mobilization among wide social strata. In tandem with this, much of the public attention has been displaced from the written word to the electronic media, in which a more segmented pattern of paying attention to information and culture develops. This relativizes the impact of the artistic and especially literary production that reflected the impact of military rule in the societies of the Southern Cone. Although many more books and uncensored works were published after the demise of military rule than during the latter period, economic constraints and the new patterning of the cultural industry and cultural consumption markedly diminished the effect of some of the more principled debates in these societies.[115]

Conclusion: Evaluating the Trends of Change

Societies traumatized by deep violence and human-rights violations are forced to revise their constitutive premises and visions of identity. The countries of the Southern Cone were pressed into such reflection and debate by the unprecedented magnitude of human-rights violations under military rule. Some of the lines of reflection analysed in this chapter are reminiscent of axes of debate opened in recent years in the *Historikerstreit* around the place of the Third Reich and the singularity of the Holocaust in history, with two major differences.

Like Germany's Second World War experiences, the experiences of the military period forced Southern Cone societies to face issues connected with their history and identity, their humanity and attitudes towards the other, their policies of inclusion and exclusion, and their patterns of social and cultural reconstruction.

But while revisionism emerged as a potent voice for some consensual interpretation and vision shaped in post-war Germany, in the Southern Cone it was the lack of consensus and, moreover, the disaggregation of the public arena that dominated the public sphere. And whereas Ernst Nolte and other revisionist historians compared Nazi Germany to other modern regimes of terror, this 'horizontal' focus of comparison was rather minor in these societies' concern with such phenomena beyond the Southern Cone. True enough, in a broader sphere, political and social actors evinced some conscience of parallelism with other Latin American countries, and some individuals looked at the Jewish plight as a landmark from which to address the disruption of archetypes and paradigms on which discussion and representation of human experience is based.

[Some] attempted to normalize what happened then in Argentina, showing that it happened before and that in fact it is not a totally novel and distinct phenomenon. Some made use of the metaphor of the Holocaust, suggesting that what happened was something unrelated to previous historical precedents, something radically different, which left us completely disarmed and unprotected.[116]

By and large, however, the controversy was more inward-looking, raising 'vertical' comparisons, more in the line of Martin Broszat in the *Historikerstreit,* about the path of violence and repression that goes back in time in these societies. Similar to the controversy raised by the work of David Goldenhagen on Germany, a parallel and related dimension of debate raised in the Southern Cone touched the role of the 'bystanders', without which, it was claimed, no full understanding of the repression could be attained. Recent works have also called to reflect on the prospects of reformulating the collective ethos by incorporating the past, 'mastering' it by grappling with and understanding its context and implications, instead of shifting unreflectively to the realm of macroeconomics and realpolitik.[117]

Finally, while in democracy the actions and spirit of the military regime were condemned, the message that the old forms of mobilization and collective solidarity can destroy the social fabric and are therefore to be avoided seems to have been internalized. Together with a worldwide trend of decline of ideologies and collectivism, the public spheres of these societies have crystallized into a more individualistic or sectorial form of participation, very different from the trends of the 1960s and 1970s. These trends reflect a global shift in the approach to universal values, under the strong influence of neo-liberal economic policies. Societies that tolerate the parallel emergence of new groups of 'super-rich' people and high levels of exclusion rooted in unemployment and pauperization seem to have abandoned commitments usually identified with ideas of social justice and/or collective welfare.

If the new democracies are unable to provide law and order, as expected widely in these societies, the temptation of authoritarianism may raise sharply. As collective identities disintegrate and social tensions mount, fewer mechanisms of containment may be found to prevent such authoritarian temptation. As Ralf Dahrendorf has suggested recently, the model of Singapore becomes the dream of the disintegrating middle classes: social order and cohesion with economic efficiency and competitiveness, even at the cost of sacrificing political liberties.[118] The problem of enhancing the defence of human rights may thus become once more an integral part of the defence of democratic institutions in the 21st century.

·················
Conclusions
·················

This work supports the claim that the complex interplay between the changing public agenda of these societies following redemocratization and the confrontation with the lingering contrasting visions of the past has been constructed as a long-term issue due to the inconclusive treatment of the legacy of human-rights violations. Confronting and interpreting this legacy of repression and violence has meant facing a multiplicity of issues simultaneously; namely, how to achieve thorough knowledge about the past experience and some agreed-upon version of truth; how to deal with issues of accountability and impunity; what to do in terms of acknowledging wrongs, expiation, official apologies, and requests of forgiveness addressed to the victims; how to tackle the issue of reparations and compensations; how to move beyond the problem of past human-rights violations, by shaping oblivion and/or incorporating the memory of the experience of repression and violence; how to use policy to restructure the realm of human rights, by reforming old visions (e.g. through education), curtailing undemocratic enclaves of power, and reducing new forms of violations of human rights committed under democracy. In analysing how these societies confronted the legacy of human-rights violations, we followed an approach that stressed the multifaceted nature of these issues in which conflicting moral values and views, different perspectives and interests, concessions and compromises interacted as part of the democratic game.

We also examined the choices made by different social actors at critical junctures, from a myriad of possible lines of action and policies. While making these choices under constraints, decisions were taken under conditions of relative open-endedness. The decisions taken were the product of ideas, interests, and interactions between social actors. As we have analysed these choices, we could reflect on the impact of these decisions not only in shaping immediate outcomes but also in conditioning long-range developments and processes, particularly in their implications for the format of relationships between human rights, legality, and democracy in each of these societies.

It seems that in the cases of Argentina, Uruguay, and Chile, the main problem in incorporating a commitment to human rights did not exist on the level of formal adoption of principles but rather in their practical implementation. Despite serious attempts at restructuring the framework of human rights in the Southern Cone societies, we found many indications that past trends have been re-enacted: namely, basic disjunctures between the formal organizational principles of these polities and the informal workings of their institutions; between decision-making and policy enforcement; and between the rhetorical projection of new models in the public sphere and the actual practices of social life. The manner of adoption of the discourse of human rights and the rejection of human-rights violations, closely connected with a political project and its ethical message, was not inconsequential. The discourse of human rights entered these societies as a main theme in the opposition to military rule. It provided at that time a minimal set of agreed principles around which all sectors opposed to the military could rally and raise a banner of ideals antithetical to the projects based on the doctrines of national security. As in other settings during periods of political transition from authoritarian and totalitarian rule, the cry for truth and justice—spearheaded by the movement of human-rights activists—became the intense and yet minimalist battle banners of the anti-authoritarian forces of the Southern Cone. As Michael Walzer has emphasized in connection with his observations of Prague's Velvet Revolution, moral minimalism acquires under such circumstances an intensity that can be self-evident:

It is a picture of people marching in the streets of Prague; they carry signs, some of which say, simply, 'Truth' and others 'Justice.' When I saw the picture, I knew immediately what the signs meant, and so did everyone else who saw the picture. Not only that: I also recognized and acknowledged the values that the marchers were defending—and so did (almost) everyone else. . . . There isn't much that is more important than 'truth' and 'justice,' minimally understood. The minimal demands that we make on one another are, when denied, repeated with passionate insistence. In moral discourse, thinness and intensity go together.[1]

In the Southern Cone, the thinness of the discourse of human rights proved to be of great political leverage in the short—transitional—term but revealed itself more fragile in the long term, especially as the democracies faced consolidation. As long as the thin elements prevailed, this discourse, as a major demand in the path towards democracy, while intense, bracketed a myriad of political and ideological positions and views that, if stressed, would have broken apart the anti-authoritarian coalitions.

The opening of the public sphere enabled the thickening of a range of alternative discourses, favouring disagreement and eventually eroding the minimal understanding on human rights that had prevailed during the transition. The attempts to thicken the discourse of human rights following redemocratization turned such thick versions into the property of more restricted sectors of the political spectrum. While parts of these societies fundamentally accepted this discourse, for many it was more a rhetorical than a real commitment, and for others it was politically tainted with adversarial intent and as such unacceptable. For many political actors, it had to be balanced with more general needs and constraints at the centre of the public agenda. Under these circumstances, the problems of implementation were revealed following redemocratization, when the civilian governments had to confront the legacy of repression in terms defined by the discourse of human rights, accountability, and justice. In this context, the governments often proved too weak to resist the demands of political contingency. In turn, this recreated in new forms the traditional gaps between the normative dimension and the effective implementation of human-rights principles.

A sense of inconclusiveness has been generated by the policies of institutional closure in the treatment of past human-rights violations. This has been manifest through the intermittent presence and reverberations of that legacy whenever attention was triggered once again at the centre of the public spheres of redemocratized Argentina, Chile, and Uruguay to the horrors experienced by these societies under military rule. Under these circumstances, the politics of oblivion and memory—which had begun already under military rule—have acquired increasing relevance in the Southern Cone. These politics of oblivion and memory have incorporated contrasting views of the past within the present as factors in shaping current visions and decisions. Sharp disagreements about the past have precluded in most cases the confinement of memory, while the apathy of the majority has at the same time allowed for the marginalization of the issue. From time to time, the inconclusive resolution of the legacy of past human-rights violations has been shown to be a source of tension, as during the recurrent aftershocks that took place in the 1990s regarding events of the 1970s and 1980s as well as new cases of human-rights violations in democracy. The recurrent confrontation with past human-rights violations has also triggered historical-political debate about the violent character of public life in these societies; their trends of exclusion; the patterns of mobilization and demobilization; of control and political participation; of social disaggregation and solidarity; and of the very nature of the collective identities of Argentina, Chile, and Uruguay.

Looking from the late 1990s, an appraisal can be made on the long-term effects of the last wave of military rule and repression on the societies of the Southern Cone. On a psychosocial dimension, the revealed horrors have installed various forms of low-intensity fears, based on the precedent of social inability to safeguard basic rights and human life. On another plane, the socio-economic models upheld by the military, while sometimes ineffective in the short term, eventually became entrenched under democracy, with both positive and negative results. Finally, the policies of control of the public spheres have waned under democracy, but a basic trend of demobilization and the shifting of concerns from the public to the private spheres has remained into the 1980s and 1990s.

Under the effects of the military policies, these societies have echoed, in their own terms, the international move toward de-emphasizing ideologies as a correlate of the fall of communism, the disintegration of the Soviet Union, and the end of the Cold War. Resulting from these trends, majoritarian sectors in these societies have adopted positions of apathy regarding the marginalization of social and political issues, shifting toward concerns of a more private nature. Accordingly, the 'thick' visions of human rights, which retain a convergence of political and of moral-ethical concerns, have been marginalized, despite the institutionalized formal adoption of the discourse of human rights. This re-enacts a long-term characteristic of institutional life in these societies; namely, the disjuncture between the formal leanings and the working of institutions. It is in the existing gap between the letter and the deed that human-rights violations of new kind occur, while the irresolution of the legacy of past human-rights violations persists.

The manner in which the legacy of human-rights violations has been treated in the framework of the political game seems to have impaired the scope and strength of democratic institutions. Principles such as the lack of accountability, impunity, the lack of investigation, and non-prosecution of publicly known crimes, and lack of equality before the law, which are inimical to modern constitutional democracy, have been projected nonetheless through the treatment of the legacy of human-rights violations into the Southern Cone societies in the period of redemocratization. As these democratic systems consolidate, the presence of these features may discredit their institutional premises. Nobel Peace Prize recipient Adolfo Pérez Esquivel has reflected on these dynamics in the case of Argentina:

The consequences of impunity, not only about crimes committed under the dictatorship, but also that of corruption of public employees that enjoy total impunity, produce a crisis of credibility of politics, of institutions.

People say that today we live in democracies. But in practice these are more formal than real. Events provide evidence about easy trigger practices of the police, repressive actions, basically against the youth, but also to face social explosions rooted in unemployment and in rising marginality affecting two-thirds of the population . . .[2]

Throughout the treatment of the legacy of human-rights violations, individuals and social organizations made efforts to take the lead in shaping the public agenda. The dynamics of redemocratization brought political parties and state administrations to try to manage and control the disruptive potential of the human-rights issue. Through a series of decisions, even when contested, the core political class and the state apparatus acquired a persistent centrality in determining the public agenda. The statist élan of presidential steering was, in the framework of the historical path of these societies, the key to stabilization and the move towards normality. Presidential steering proved a highly instrumental factor in this sense in the short and medium range. In Argentina the state used it as leverage for reforming the format of civil–military relationships, in Uruguay it achieved approval for the institutional closure through referendum, and in Chile it geared the closure of the human-rights violations issue to attempts to achieve constitutional reform. However, the appropriation of the banners of human rights by the state instrumentalized the issue in political terms and relegated it to the sidelines of the public agenda.

The groups and NGOs that opposed the military governments over human-rights violations (such as the Vicaría de la Solidaridad, SERPAJ, the Madres, AFDD, CELS, and many others), became core organizations of civil society as they embodied the moral opposition to authoritarian rule. They carried out this role in a forceful manner as the public spheres reopened in the transition to democracy. These self-managed organizations, autonomous from the state and linked to institutional networks, played a central role in forwarding human-rights issues and demands. Moreover, they provided through their mobilization 'from below', a model of organization and participation that was relatively novel in the context of the Southern Cone. Despite their marginalization in recent years, their example has provided a long-term counter-legacy favouring the creation of a democratic culture rooted in society and the establishment of mechanisms of pluralistic control of the state.

Notes

INTRODUCTION

1. Hannah Arendt, *Between Past and Future* (New York: Viking Press, 1961 (c.1954)), 7.
2. This has been stressed recently by Richard A. Wilson: 'Local interpretations of human rights doctrine, draw on personal biographies, community histories, and on expressions of power relations between interest groups. Their relationship to formal, legal versions has to be discovered, not assumed.' ('Human Rights, Culture and Context: An Introduction', in id. (ed.), *Human Rights, Culture and Context: Anthropological Perspectives* (London: Pluto, 1997), 12.

CHAPTER 1

1. Batia B. Siebzehner, *La universidad americana y la ilustración: autoridad y conocimiento en Nueva España y el Río de la Plata* (Madrid: MAPFRE, 1994).
2. See among others Juan Carlos Chiaramonte, *Formas de sociedad y economía en Hispanoamérica* (Mexico: Grijalbo, 1983); Alberto Edwards, *La fronda aristocrática en Chile* (Santiago: Editorial Universitaria, 1982) (c.1928); and a general discussion in Roderic A. Camp (ed.), *Democracy in Latin America: Patterns and Cycles* (Wilmington, Del.: Scholarly Resources, 1996), especially the chapters by Glen Caudill Dealy, Mitchell A. Seligson and Alan Angel, María D'Alva Kinzo and Diego Urbaneja, 49–66, 67–90, and 183–206 respectively.
3. On populism see Gino Germani, *Política y sociedad en una época de transición: de la sociedad tradicional a la sociedad de masas* (Buenos Aires: Paidós, 1966); Gino Germani, Torcuato Di Tella, and Octavio Ianni, *Populismo y contradicciones de clase en Latinoamérica* (Mexico: ERA, 1977); Enzo Faletto and Fernando Henrique Cardoso, *Dependency and Development in Latin America* (Berkeley and Los Angeles: University of California Press, 1979). On populism in general see Ghitta Ionescu and Ernest Gellner, *Populism: Its Meanings and National Characteristics* (London: Weidenfeld & Nicolson, 1969).

4. The political parties have played a central role in modern Uruguay, to the point that its political system has been described as a 'particracy'. See Gerardo Caetano et al., *De la tradición a la crisis: pasado y presente de nuestro sistema de partidos* (Montevideo: CLAEH and Ediciones de la Banda Oriental, 1985); Edy Kaufman, 'El rol de los partidos políticos en la redemocratización del Uruguay', in Saúl Sosnowski (ed.), *Represión, exilio y democracia: la cultura uruguaya* (Montevideo: Ediciones de la Banda Oriental, 1987), 25–62; and Luis E. González, *Estructuras políticas y democracia en Uruguay* (Montevideo: Fundación de Cultura Universitaria, 1993).

5. See Alain Touraine, *Vida y muerte del Chile popular* (Mexico: Siglo XXI, 1974); Manuel Antonio Garretón, *The Chilean Political Process* (Boston: Unwin Hyman, 1989), 18–42; The increasing governance crisis of Allende can be traced, among others, in Arturo Valenzuela, *The Breakdown of Democratic Regimes: Chile* (Baltimore: Johns Hopkins University Press, 1978). See also Salvador Allende's statements in *Chile's Road to Socialism* (Harmondsworth: Penguin, 1973).

6. There is a vast literature on these topics. See for instance Samuel Huntington, Michel Crozier, and Joji Wataniki, *The Crisis of Democracy: Report on the Governability of Democracies to the Trilateral Commission* (New York: New York University Press, 1975); Juan J. Linz, *The Breakdown of Democratic Regimes* (Baltimore: Johns Hopkins University Press, 1978); and Abraham Loewenthal and Samuel Fitch (eds.), *Armies and Politics in Latin America* (New York: Holmes & Meier, 1986). See also Juan J. Linz, 'Totalitarian and Authoritarian Regimes', in Fred Greenstein and Nelson Polsby (eds.), *Handbook of Political Science* (Reading, Mass.: Addison-Wesley, 1975), vol. iii. For references on the countries under consideration see below.

7. With the emergence of the leftist coalition of the Frente Amplio, the political system of Uruguay became a three-party system. The Colorados divided their allegiance between several candidates. Bordaberry was elected with the lowest percentage of votes obtained ever by a winning presidential candidate. The Colorado Party won the elections, but the opposition received a larger percentage of votes, when counted together. The disaggregation of the political class weakened the civilian capacity to withstand military intervention. A comprehensive analysis can be found in Silvia Dutrénit, 'Del margen al centro del sistema político: los partidos uruguayos durante la dictadura', in id. (ed.), *Diversidad partidaria y dictaduras: Argentina, Brazil y Uruguay* (Mexico: Instituto Mora, 1996), 235–317.

8. Luis E. González, *Political Structures and Democracy in Uruguay* (Notre Dame, Ind.: University of Notre Dame Press, 1991), 43.

9. Edy Kaufman, *Uruguay in Transition: From Civilian to Military Rule* (New Brunswick, NJ: Transaction, 1979), 11.

10. Charles Guy Gillespie, *Negotiating Democracy: Politicians and Generals in Uruguay* (Cambridge: Cambridge University Press, 1991), 55. Gillespie mentions the existence of parallel trends of development, such as Colonel Bolentini's idea of founding a new party controlled by the military, and

the unfulfilled political ambitions of General Alvarez to become an elected president within the framework of a Uruguayan limited democracy, ibid. 66–70.

11. In 1936, a bloody confrontation with the Nazis enabled Alessandri to gather parliamentary support for his proposal of the Law of State Internal Security, which was systematically enforced against the Communists. The Communist Party was outlawed between 1948 and 1958 by the Law for the Permanent Defence of Democracy (Law 8987). Brian Loveman, *Chile: The Legacy of Hispanic Capitalism* (New York: Oxford University Press, 1988), 254.

12. Allende received 36.2% of the total vote, slightly over the 34.9% of Alessandri and ahead of Christian Democrat Radomiro Tomic, who obtained 27.8%. Cesar N. Caviedes, *Elections in Chile* (Boulder, Colo.: Lynne Rienner, 1991), 16–17.

13. On the increasing governance crisis in that period see also Edy Kaufman, *Crisis in Allende's Chile: New Perspectives* (New York: Praeger, 1988); Ricardo Israel Zipper, *Politics and Ideology in Allende's Chile* (Tempe: Center for Latin American Studies, Arizona State University, 1989), and Mark Falcoff, *Modern Chile, 1970–1989: A Critical History* (New Brunswick, NJ: Transaction, 1989).

14. Alexandra Barahona de Brito, 'The Politics of Memory' (manuscript), 43. This work served as basis for id., *Human Rights and Democratization in Latin America: Uruguay and Chile* (Oxford: Oxford University Press, 1997).

15. Hugo Frühling, 'Determinants of Gross Human Rights Violations: The Case of Chile' (Santiago: manuscript 1995), 59 and 63. A very detailed account of the process can be found in Carlos Prats González, *Memorias: testimonio de un soldado* (Santiago: Pehuén, 3rd edn. 1987), 403–546.

16. Disagreements existed among the members of the junta about the goals and timing of military rule, primarily between Pinochet and General Gustavo Leigh Guzmán, commader of the air force, who had opposed the former's presidentialism. On July 1978 Leigh Guzmán and eight senior officers in line were forced to resign. Pinochet thus completed his presidential enthronement over the junta, a process initiated in 1974. For detailed analyses see J. Samuel Valenzuela and Arturo Valenzuela (eds.), *Military Rule in Chile* (Baltimore: Johns Hopkins University Press, 1986); and Genaro Arriagada, *Pinochet: The Politics of Power* (Boston: Unwin Hyman, 1988).

17. Guillermo O'Donnell, *El estado burocrático-autoritario, 1966–1973* (Buenos Aires: Editorial de Belgrano, 1982).

18. During the years of political proscription, the divide inside Peronism had grown. When Perón arrived in Buenos Aires on June 1973, different Peronist factions with left and right leanings fought a fierce gun battle, on the outskirts of the Ezeiza airport, causing many deaths and injuries. Robert D. Crassweller, *Perón and the Enigmas of Argentina* (New York: W. W. Norton, 1987), esp. 357–8. For an outstanding literary description see Tomás Eloy Martínez, *La novela de Perón* (Buenos Aires: Planeta, 1991), 332–53.

19. Decrees No. 261 (5 Feb. 1975) and No. 2772 (10 Oct. 1975). The latter ordered 'to carry out the needed military and security operations in order to annihilate the capacity of the subversive elements in the whole territory of

the country'. Prudencio García, *El drama de la autonomía militar* (Madrid: Alianza, 1995), 189–90. On the Triple A see ibid. 58–65 and 437–42.

20. See David Pion-Berlin, *The Ideology of State Terror* (Boulder, Colo.: Lynne Rienner, 1989), 104–23.

21. Alyson Brysk, *The Politics of Human Rights in Argentina* (Stanford, Calif.: Stanford University Press, 1994), 52–3.

22. Jorge Antonio Tapia, *National Security: The Dual State and the Role of Deception* (Rotterdam: By the author, 1989).

23. Garretón, *The Chilean Political Process*, 70. See also the declarations of Colonel Juan Diechler Guzmán in Patricia Politzer (ed.), *Fear in Chile: Lives under Pinochet* (New York: Pantheon Books, 1989), 20–39.

24. Mario Sznajder, 'Entre autoritarismo y democracia: el legado de violaciones de derechos humanos', in Leonardo Senkman and Mario Sznajder (eds.) (in cooperation with Edy Kaufman), *El legado del autoritarismo: derechos humanos y antisemitismo en la Argentina contemporánea* (Buenos Aires: Grupo Editor Latinoamericano, 1995), 16–17; Luis Roniger, 'Sociedad civil y derechos humanos: una aproximación teórica en base a la experiencia argentina', ibid. 37–54.

25. Emilio F. Mignone, *Witness to the Truth: The Complicity of the Church and Dictatorship in Argentina, 1976–1983* (Maryknoll, NY: Orbis, 1988), 95.

26. See Pamela Lowden, *Moral Opposition to Authoritarian Rule in Chile, 1973–1990* (New York: St Martin's Press, 1996), 19–25.

27. Sznajder, 'Entre autoritarismo y democracia', 18–20; and an interview with Sergio Kiernan, a leading journalist, Buenos Aires, 4 July 1995. In an interview, Graciela Fernández Meijide stressed the need to distinguish between the decentralized character of the repressive apparatus and the overall systematic design of the system of repression, which was decided upon at high levels of command. Interview in Buenos Aires, 7 July 1995.

28. John Simpson and Jana Bennett, *The Disappeared: Voices from a Secret War* (London: Robson Books, 1985), 66.

29. See Comisión Nacional sobre la Desaparición de Personas (CONADEP), *Nunca más* (Buenos Aires: EUDEBA, 1984). On the basis of her research experience in Guatemala, and referring to Scheper-Hughes's work among Brazilian poor, Linda Green observes that in such settings, 'whisperings, innuendos, and rumors of death lists circulating would put everyone on edge . . . As Nancy Scheper-Hughes has noted: "The intolerableness of the situation is increased by its ambiguity." ' Linda Green, 'Fear as a Way of Life', *Cultural Anthropology*, 19/2 (1994), 231. See also Nancy Scheper-Hughes, *Death without Weeping* (Berkeley and Los Angeles: University of California Press, 1992).

30. Mignone, *Witness to the Truth*, 71.

31. Servicio de Paz y Justicia, *Uruguay: Nunca más. Informe sobre la violación de derechos humanos (1972–1985)* (Montevideo: SERPAJ, 1989), esp. 111–15 and 425–30.

32. According to some reports, 300,000 individuals left the country from the early 1970s, although it is impossible to assess how many were mainly political exiles (William Rowe and Teresa Whitfield, 'Thresholds of Identity:

Literature and Exile in Latin America', *Third World Quarterly*, 9/1 (1987), 230–1.

33. Interview with Gerardo Caetano, director of the Institute of Political Studies of the University of La República, Montevideo, 12 July 1995.

34. Juan Rial, 'Los militares en tanto "partido político sustituto" frente a la redemocratización en Uruguay', in Augusto Varas (ed.), *La autonomía militar en América Latina* (Caracas: Editorial Nueva Sociedad, 1988), 197–229.

35. Interview with Carina Perelli, Uruguayan political scientist and international consultant, Jerusalem, 10 Nov. 1995.

36. Juan Rial, 'Makers and Guardians of Fear: Control Terror in Uruguay', in Juan E. Corradi, Patricia Weiss Fagen, and Manuel Antonio Garretón (eds.), *Fear at the Edge: State Terror and Resistance in Latin America* (Berkeley and Los Angeles: University of California Press, 1992), 90–103.

37. *Informe de la Comisión Nacional de Verdad y Reconciliación* (Santiago: Secretaría de Comunicación y Cultura, Ministerio Secretaría General de Gobierno, 1991), ii. 883–7; US Department of State, *Chile Country Report on Human Rights Practices for 1996* (http://www/issues/human_rights/1996_hrp_report/chile.html). See also Elías Padilla Ballesteros, *La memoria y el olvido: detenidos desaparecidos en Chile* (Santiago: Ediciones Orígenes, 1995).

38. The DINA seems to have begun operating *de facto* already in November 1973, but was legally established on 14 June 1974. Ascanio Cavallo, Manuel Salazar, and Oscar Sepúlveda, *La historia oculta del régimen militar* (Santiago: Ediciones La Epoca, 1988), 32–5; Arriagada, *Pinochet: The Politics of Power*, 17–18.

39. By 1978 over 100,000 people had been forced to live outside the country. In mid-1986 the Comité Pro-Retorno in Chile estimated the numbers of exiles at between 100,000 and 200,000. The military government published lists of individuals not allowed to return, in the range of between 3,700 and 4,600. Alan Angell and Susan Cartairs, 'The Exile Question in Chilean Politics', *Third World Quarterly*, 9/1 (1987), 148–67.

40. In addition to the tables above, see also the detailed analysis of Edy Kaufman, 'Análisis de los patrones represivos en el cono sur: los regímenes militares argentinos 1976–1983', 55–78 in Senkman and Sznajder, with Kaufman, *El legado del autoritarismo*.

41. Corradi et al., *Fear at the Edge*.

42. Pion-Berlin, *The Ideology of State Terror*.

43. D. Becker, E. Lira, M. I. Castillo, E. Gómez, and J. Kovalsky, 'Therapy with Victims of Political Repression in Chile: The Challenge of Social Reparation', *Journal of Social Issues*, 46/3 (1990), 133–49. See also Marcelo Suárez-Orozco, 'Speaking of the Unspeakable: Toward a Psychosocial Understanding of Responses to Terror', *Ethos*, 18/3 (1990), 353–83.

44. Marcelo Suárez-Orozco, 'A Grammar of Terror: Psychocultural Responses to State Terrorism in Dirty War and Post-Dirty War Argentina', in Carolyn Nordstrom and Jo Ann Martin (eds.), *The Paths to Domination, Resistance and Terror* (Berkeley and Los Angeles: University of California Press, 1992), 219–59, quote from p. 222.

45. Salvador Schelotto, 'La "nueva objetividad" tramposa del terrorismo de Estado', *Brecha* (htpp://www.chasque.apc.org/n566/debate.html), 17 Oct. 1996.
46. Alicia Kozameh, 'El encuentro: pájaros'. Los Angeles, Nov. 1994, manuscript, 27–8. In the same style are also id., 'Dos días en la relación de mi cuñada Inés con este mundo perentorio', *Confluencia* (fall 1995), 230–40; and id., *Pasos bajo el agua* (Buenos Aires: Contrapunto, 1987) (English translation: *Steps under Water* Berkeley and Los Angeles: University of California Press, 1996)).
47. Marguerite Feitlowitz, 'Códigos del terror: Argentina y los legados de la tortura', in Senkman and Sznajder, with Kaufman, *El legado del autoritarismo*, 79–94; quote from p. 92.
48. Juan E. Corradi, 'Towards Societies without Fear', 267–92 in Corradi et al., *Fear at the Edge*, and Manuel Antonio Garretón, 'Fear in Military Regimes', ibid. 24–5. The apprehensions and subconscious fears are most evident in dreaming and chronic disease. See Marcelo Viñar and Maren Viñar, *Fracturas de la memoria* (Montevideo: Trilce, 1993); and Green, 'Fear as a Way of Life', 227–57.
49. Suárez-Orozco, 'A Grammar of Terror'.
50. Electric prod, an instrument of torture.
51. Frank Graziano, *Divine Violence: Spectacle, Psychosexuality and Radical Christianity in the Argentine Dirty War* (Boulder, Colo.: Westview, 1992), 164–5; René Girard, *Violence and the Sacred* (Baltimore: Johns Hopkins University Press, 1977), esp. 49.
52. Fictional reflections of these drives can be found in works dealing with these experiences, for instance in Héctor Olivera's Argentinian film *La noche de los lápices*, in which the repressor declares his omnipotence: 'Here [in prison]', he says, 'we are God.'
53. Declarations by Montonero leader Mario Eduardo Firmenich, in *Historia Argentina 1976–1983*, videofilm directed by Felipe Pigna (Buenos Aires: Universidad Nacional de Buenos Aires and Diana Producciones, 1996).
54. *Malajunta 76: a veinte años del golpe militar. La memoria de pie*, videofilm directed by Eduardo Aliverti, Pablo Milstein, and Javier Rubel (Buenos Aires: Crears Producciones, 1996).
55. Suárez-Orozco, 'A Grammar of Terror', 232.
56. Cavallo, Salazar, and Sepúlveda, *La historia oculta del régimen militar*, 25–30.
57. Felipe Agüero, 'Autonomía de las fuerzas armadas en el autoritarismo y la democracia en Chile', in Varas, *La autonomía militar en América Latina*, 174; García, *El drama de la autonomía militar*, 78–9.
58. Alain Rouquié, 'Hegemonía militar, estado y dominación', in *Argentina hoy* (Mexico: Siglo XXI, 1982), 18.
59. The only previous case of military control of public life occurred during the dictatorship of Gabriel Terra in the 1930s.
60. See Gerardo Caetano and J. P. Rilla, 'Breve historia de la dictadura', in Gerardo Caetano and M. Alfaro, *Historia del Uruguay contemporáneo* (Montevideo: Fundación de Cultura Universitaria, 1995), 297–300.

61. On the increasing involvement of the military in Chilean public affairs see Prats González, *Memorias: Testimonio de un soldado*, esp. 312–75 and 459–512; Agüero, 'Autonomía de las fuerzas armadas', 171–3.

62. Arriagada, *Pinochet: The Politics of Power, passim* and esp. 33; Agüero, 'Autonomía de las fuerzas armadas', 180–1.

63. Jeffrey C. Alexander, 'Citizen and Enemy as Symbolic Classification: On the Polarizing Discourse of Civil Society', in Michèle Lamont and Marcel Fournier (eds.), *Cultivating Differences: Symbolic Boundaries and the Making of Inequality* (Chicago: University of Chicago Press 1992), 289–308. Alexander's cultural approach has universal validity; nonetheless, we would like to note that the terms of any such discourse are locally inflected, and thus may differ from those of liberty and repression alluded to in this text.

64. Ricardo Piglia, 'Los pensadores ventrílocuos', in Raquel Angel, *Rebeldes y domesticados* (Buenos Aires: Ediciones el Cielo por Asalto, 1992), 32. See also Frederick Nunn, 'The South American Military and (Re)Democratization: Professional Thought and Self Perception', *Journal of Interamerican Studies and World Affairs*, 37/2 (1995), 7–9.

65. Interview with Hermógenes Pérez de Arce, Chilean lawyer and political analyst, Santiago, 17 July 1995.

66. On the impact of international treaties and other non-treaty sources on states' obligation to investigate, prosecute, and provide redress see Naomi Roth-Arriaza's contribution in id. (ed.), *Impunity and Human Rights in International Law and Practice* (New York: Oxford University Press, 1995), 24–56.

67. Richard Pierre Claude and Burns H. Weston (eds.), *Human Rights in the World Community* (Philadelphia: University of Pennsylvania Press, 1989), 10, and 1–44 for a comprehensive analysis of international human rights.

68. An example may be found in the CGT Labour Federation's reluctance to participate in protests organized by human rights NGOs, not only during the military rule, but even after redemocratization. On 7 Sep. 1985, the *Buenos Aires Herald* reported that the CGT took part for the first time in such a demonstration, along with other political and student organizations, and that the Mothers of the Plaza de Mayo, while supporting the march, refused to take part if the CGT did, since 'they never did a single thing for the missing'. *FBIS-LAT-85*, 10 Sep. 1985, Argentina, B3.

69. See Alfred Stepan, *Estado, corporatismo e autoritarismo* (Rio de Janeiro: Paz e Terra, 1980), 51–84.

70. Edward Shils, 'Center and Periphery', and 'Society and Societies: The Macrosociological View', in *Center and Periphery* (Chicago: University of Chicago Press, 1975), 3–11.

71. It is worth noting that the interpretation of the Bill of Rights has not been as radical as might have been expected. The judiciary has been conservative and it opposed the radicalization of the rights discourse. See Michelle Falardeau-Ramsay, 'The Changing Face of Human Rights in Canada', *Constitutional Forum*, 4/3 (1993), 61–6; Alan C. Cairns, 'Reflections on the

Political Purposes of the Charter: The First Decade', 163–91 in Gerald-A. Beaudoin (ed.), *The Charter: Ten Years Later* (Quebec: Les Éditions Yvon Blais, 1992); M. Mandel, *The Charter of Rights and the Legalization of Politics in Canada* (Toronto: Thompson Educational Publishing Co., 1992); and P. M. Macklem et al. (eds.), *Canadian Constitutional Law* (Toronto: Montgomery, 1994).

72. On the USA see in particular Mary A. Glendon, *Rights Talk* (New York: Free Press, 1991); and Robert Post, *Constitutional Domains* (Cambridge, Mass.: Harvard University Press, 1995). We would suggest that in the USA such an implementation has occurred in a very selective manner, e.g. with speech being highly valued while other claims have been less so.

73. Interview with Isaac Frenkel, lawyer and former president of the CREJ, representative committee of Chilean Jewish organizations. Santiago de Chile, 17 July 1995.

74. Interview with Fr. Luis Pérez Aguirre. Montevideo, 14 July 1995.

75. John Rawls, 'The Law of Peoples', in Stephen Shute and Susan Hurley (eds.), *On Human Rights: The Oxford Amnesty Lectures, 1993* (Oxford: Oxford University Press, 1993), 41–82; and id., 'Justice as Fairness: Political, not Metaphysical', *Philosophy and Public Affairs*, 14 (1985), 225–30.

76. See for instance the criticisms raised by Sandel in his long-lasting debate with Rawls. See, in addition to his books, Michael J. Sandel's 'The Procedural Republic and the Unencumbered Self', *Political Theory*, 12/1 (1984), 81–96, which develops the argument, also found in Glendon's *Rights Talk*, that, despite its claim to universality, this vision reflects notions of rights embedded in the American framework.

77. Thomas M. Franck, *The Power of Legitimacy among Nations* (Oxford: Oxford University Press, 1990), 208–46.

78. María Pura Sánchez, 'Postfoundationalism, Human Rights and Diversity of Cultures', paper presented at the Conference on Collective Identities and Symbolic Representation, Paris, FNSP, 3–6 July 1996; H. Pogge, *Realizing Rawls* (Ithaca, NY: Cornell University Press, 1989).

79. Sandel, 'The Procedural Republic', 81. For an analysis of this tension in the US context see Neal Milner, 'The Denigration of Rights and the Persistence of Rights Talk', *Law and Social Inquiry*, 14/4 (1989), 631–75. See also Carlos S. Nino, 'The Communitarian Challenge to Liberal Rights', in id., *Rights* (Aldershot: Dartmouth, 1992), 309–24.

80. Richard Rorty, *Objectivity, Relativism, and Truth* (Cambridge: Cambridge University Press, 1991), 175–210; id., 'Human Rights, Rationality and Sentimentality', in *On Human Rights: The Oxford Amnesty Lectures*, 111–34.

81. Rorty, *Objectivity, Relativism, and Truth*, 210.

82. Sánchez, 'Postfoundationalism, Human Rights and Diversity of Cultures', 7.

83. Alison Dundes Renteln, *International Human Rights: Universalism versus Relativism* (London: Sage, 1990).

84. Abdullahi Ahmed An-Na'im, 'Toward a Cross-cultural Approach to Defining International Standards of Human Rights: The Meaning of Cruel, Inhuman, or Degrading Treatment or Punishment', in id. (ed.), *Human*

Rights in Cross-cultural Perspectives: A Quest for Consensus (Philadelphia: University of Pennsylvania Press, 1992), 19–20.

85. Abdullahi An-Na'im, 'Toward a Cross-cultural Approach'; id., 'Problems and Prospects of Universal Cultural Legitimacy for Human Rights', in An-Na'im and Francis Mading Deng (eds.), *Human Rights in Africa* (Washington: Brookings Institution, 1990), 331–67.
86. Among these early works see Clodomiro Bravo Michell and Nissim Sharim Paz, *Restricciones a las libertades públicas* (Santiago: Editorial Jurídica de Chile, 1958); and Carlos A. Zubillaga Barrera, *Artigas y los derechos humanos* (Montevideo: Comité Central Israelita del Uruguay, 1966).
87. Paul J. Di Maggio and Walter W. Powell, 'The Iron Cage Revisited: Institutional Isomorphism and Collective Rationality in Organizational Field'. *American Sociological Review*, 48 (1983), 147–60.
88. Ian Guest, *Behind the Disappearances: Argentina's Dirty War against Human Rights and the United Nations* (Philadelphia: University of Pennsylvania Press, 1990), 86. Guest's book is essential reading on the international dimensions analysed in this section. On the European dimensions see Jean Grugel, 'External Support for Democratization in Latin America: European Political Parties and the Southern Cone', *Estudios interdisciplinarios de América Latina y el Caribe*, 4/2 (1993), 53–68.

CHAPTER 2

1. Jürgen Habermas, *The Structural Transformation of the Public Sphere* (Cambridge: MIT Press, 1989), 27.
2. Nancy Fraser, 'Rethinking the Public Sphere: A Contribution to the Critic of Actually Existing Democracy', in Craig Calhoun (ed.), *Habermas and the Public Sphere* (Cambridge: MIT Press, 1992), 110. See also Habermas's work, in particular *The Structural Transformation of the Public Sphere*.
3. On its elaboration from a Western perspective see Craig Calhoun, 'Civil Society and the Public Sphere', *Public Culture*, 5 (1993), 267–80. For its applicability beyond the West see for instance Robert P. Hymes and Conrad Schirokauer (eds.), *Ordering the World: Approaches to State and Society in Sung China* (Berkeley and Los Angeles: University of California Press, 1993), esp. 1–58 and 255–79; Frederick Wakeman, 'The Civil Society and Public Sphere Debate: Western Reflections on China's Political Culture', *Modern China*, 19/2 (1993), 108–38; and Michael Watts, 'Islamic Modernities? Citizenship, Civil Society and Islamism in a Nigerian City', *Public Culture*, 8 (1996), 251–89.
4. Robert Dahl, *Polyarchy* (New Haven: Yale University Press, 1971), 1–15.
5. See Steven R. Ratner and Jason S. Abrams, *Accountability for Human Rights Atrocities in International Law: Beyond the Nuremberg Legacy* (Oxford: Clarendon Press, 1997), 133–8.

6. See Ronaldo Munck, 'Democratization and Demilitarization in Argentina, 1982–1985', *Bulletin of Latin American Research*, 4/2 (1985), 85–93.

7. On the *sui generis* character of democratization in the area important contributions have been made also, among others, by Laurence Whitehead, Terry Lynn Karl, Brian Loveman, Guillermo O'Donnell, Philippe C. Schmitter, Manuel Antonio Garretón, James Petras, Bolivar Lamounier, and Helgio Trindade. See for instance Guillermo O'Donnell, Philippe Schmitter, and Laurence Whitehead, *Transitions from Authoritarian Rule* (Baltimore: Johns Hopkins University Press, 1986), esp. vols. i and iii; Manuel A. Garretón, 'Problems of Democracy in Latin America: On the Processes of Transition and Consolidation', *International Journal*, 43 (1988), 357–77; Laurence Whitehead, 'The Alternatives to "Liberal Democracy": A Latin American Perspective', *Political Studies*, 40 (1992), 146–59; Terry Lynn Karl, 'Dilemmas of Democratization in Latin America', *Comparative Politics*, 23/1 (1990), 1–21; James Petras and Steve Vieux, 'The Transition to Authoritarian Electoral Regimes in Latin America', *Latin American Perspectives*, 21 (1994), 5–20; Brian Loveman, 'Protected Democracies and Military Guardianship: Political Transitions in Latin America, 1978–1983', *Journal of Interamerican Studies*, 36 (1994), 105–90; Guillermo O'Donnell, 'Delegative Democracy', *Journal of Democracy*, 5/1 (1994), 55–69. See also the readers by James M. Malloy and Mitchell Seligson (eds.), *Authoritarians and Democrats: Regime Transition in Latina America* (Pittsburgh: University of Pittsburgh Press, 1987); Paul W. Drake and Eduardo Silva (eds.), *Elections and Democratization in Latin America 1980–1985* (La Jolla: UCSD Center of Iberian and Latin American Studies, 1986); Larry J. Diamond, Juan J. Linz and Martin S. Lipset (eds.), *Democracies in Developing Countries* (Boulder, Colo.: Lynne Rienner, 1989); and Enrique A. Baylora (ed.), *Comparing New Democracies: Transition and Consolidation in Mediterranean Europe and the Southern Cone* (Boulder, Colo.: Westview, 1987).

8. Mónica Peralta Ramos and Carlos Waisman (eds.), *From Military Rule to Liberal Rule in Argentina* (Boulder, Colo.: Westview, 1987).

9. The deterioration of the socio-economic conditions of the country and the huge external debt narrowed the range of possible macroeconomic policies that the democratic government could adopt. 'By June 1985, inflation was up to 6,900% per year, the GNP was rapidly declining (the output of the manufacturing sector was 13.2% below that of the year before), unemployment had increased by 30%, real wages had declined 20%, and investment was down 15%' (D. Erro, *Resolving the Argentine Paradox: Politics and Development, 1966–1992* (Boulder, Colo.: Lynne Rienner, 1993), 137.

10. *Por qué, doctor Alfonsín? Conversaciones con Pablo Giussani* (Buenos Aires: Sudamericana-Planeta, 1987), 200–5.

11. *Ex-post factum*, Alfonsín's initial policies of punishment dealing with human-rights violations can be framed within the denunciation theory and victim-centred retribution, which 'require punishment as one of an array of measures designed to provide redress for victims and to establish

the force of societal norms'. Naomi Roth-Arriaza, *Impunity and Human Rights in International Law and Practice* (New York: Oxford University Press, 1995), 23. See also Jaime Malamud-Goti, 'Punishing Human Rights Abuses in Fledgling Democracies: The Case of Argentina', ibid. 161–6.

12. Law 22924 of self-amnesty was emblematically called by the military the 'Law of National Pacification'. Following redemocratization, tribunals either largely ignored it or declared it to be unconstitutional.

13. An analysis of the different approaches to this issue can be found in Carlos H. Acuña y Catalina Smulovitz, 'Militares en la transición argentina: del gobierno a la subordinación constitucional', in Carlos H. Acuña et al., *Juicio, castigos y memorias: derechos humanos y justicia en la política argentina* (Buenos Aires: Ediciones Nueva Visión, 1995), 19–100, esp. 48–9.

14. David Pion-Berlin, 'To Prosecute or to Pardon? Human Rights Decisions in the Latin American Southern Cone', *Human Rights Quarterly*, 15 (1993), 101–30.

15. In his speech before both houses of Congress, one day after becoming President, Alfonsín stressed the need to investigate the whereabouts of the disappeared, modernize the armed forces, and replace the National Security Doctrine with a new national defence doctrine. *La nación*, 12 Dec. 1983.

16. On the spectrum of NGOs in Argentina and their role in the process of redemocratization see Elizabeth Jelin, 'The Politics of Memory: The Human Rights Movement and the Construction of Democracy in Argentina', *Latin American Perspectives*, 21/2 (1994), 38–58 and also below, in this chapter and in Ch. 6. See also Carina Perelli, 'Settling Accounts with Blood Memory: The Case of Argentina', *Social Research*, 59/2 (1992), 415–51.

17. Interview with Dr Eduardo Rabossi, member of CONADEP, Professor of Human Rights, School of Law, University of Buenos Aires, and first Subsecretary of Human Rights, Ministry of Interior, Buenos Aires, 6 July 1995. See also: 'Se juzga a los hombres y no a las instituciones: lo afirmó el Dr. Jaunarena respecto de los militares', *La nación*, 21 Mar. 1985.

18. Decree No. 158/83 ordered the arrest and prosecution of the members of the military juntas that ruled the country from 1976 until 1983. Decree No. 157/83, issued the same day, ordered the arrest of the main leaders of the terrorist groups during the 1970s. Less than a month later, both houses of Congress approved almost unanimously Law 23040, annulling the law of self-amnesty enacted by the military. For the full text of Law 23040 and of Alfonsín's message to the Congress on this issue, see República Argentina, *El gobierno democrático y los derechos humanos* (Buenos Aires: Imprenta del Congreso de la Nación, 1985), 13–15.

19. In December 1986 Camps was found guilty on 73 charges of illegal torture between the years 1975 and 1979 and was sentenced to twenty-five years in prison. See Kathryn Lee Crawford, 'Due Obedience and the Rights of Victims: Argentina's Transition to Democracy', *Human Rights Quarterly*, 12 (1990), 28–31.

20. The CONADEP commission was composed, in addition to Ernesto Sábato, of journalist Magdalena Ruiz Guiñazú, Professor Gregorio Klimovsky, lawyer Ricardo Colombres, surgeon René Favaloro (who resigned), Professor Hilario Fernández Long, Carlos T. Gattinoni, Rabbi Marshall T. Meyer (of the Jewish Movement for Human Rights and the Ecumenical Movement for Human Rights—MEDH), Bishop Jaime F. de Nevares (of MEDH), human-rights activist Eduardo Rabossi, and members of Congress Santiago M. López, Hugo D. Piucill, and Horacio H. Huarte. The work of the CONADEP was coordinated through five divisions headed by Graciela Fernández Meijide (of the Permanent Assembly for Human Rights—APDH), Daniel Salvador, Raúl Aragón, Alberto Mansur, and Leopoldo Silgueira.

21. *Por qué, doctor Alfonsín?*, 238–40.

22. This ambivalence prompted debates in both scholarly and popular circles. See for instance the legal debate in the *Yale Journal of International Law*, 100 (1991), 2537–643: Diane F. Orentlichter, 'Settling Accounts: The Duty to Prosecute Human Rights Violations of a Prior Regime'; Carlos S. Nino, 'The Duty to Punish Past Abuses of Human Rights Put into Context: The Case of Argentina'; D. Orentlichter, 'A Reply to Profesor Nino'; and C. Nino, 'The Human Rights Policy of the Argentine Constitutional Government: A Reply', ibid. 217–30.

23. Interview with Dr Eduardo Rabossi, Buenos Aires, 6 July 1995.

24. Augusto Varas, 'Democratización y reforma militar en Argentina', in id. (ed.), *La autonomía militar en América Latina* (Caracas: Nueva Sociedad, 1988), 73.

25. Massera repeated and elaborated those arguments again and again, as in a 1995 interview with the magazine *Gente*: 'This society is like a chameleon. When things are working out in the right direction, many walk along with you. But when they turn bad, everyone retreats. It is a hypocritical society. The people who protest today and are horrified by the things that happened are the very same that in those years used to tell me: Admiral, please go on and kill them all. Follow them to their den and destroy them. And what did they believe that it was all about? It was a war. And in the war—the little Jesus should forgive me—you must kill to remain alive. So, why must we nine men alone express remorse? They persecute us as if we alone were responsible for what happened, and the other 30 millions are not involved at all and can sleep with their consciences at peace? What an injustice!' (Emilio Massera, 'Yo llevo a Dios sobre mi hombro', *Página/12* (27 July 1995), 7. The original interview was published in *Gente* and quoted by *Página/12*). See also: 'Nadie tiene que defenderse por haber ganado una guerra justa', *La Nación*, 7 Oct. 1985.

26. 'Severas críticas de Arguindegui', published by *Clarín*, 27 Mar. 1985.

27. A statement by Julio César Strassera in the documentary film *Malajunta 76* (1996).

28. Ibid.

29. A few days before the opening of the public trial, the National Council of the Peronist Party issued a press declaration against the idea of 'Due Obedience'. 'El peronismo frente a los derechos humanos', *La Voz*, 17 Apr. 1985. Some of the Peronist leaders continued, however, to endorse the view that the military actions against subversion were justified. See M. Osiel, 'The Making of Human Rights Policy in Argentina: The Impact of Ideas and Interests on a Legal Conflict', *Journal of Latin American Studies*, 18/1 (1986), 144.

30. David Pion-Berlin, 'Between Confrontation and Accommodation: Military and Government Policy in Democratic Argentina', *Journal of Latin American Studies*, 23/3 (1991), 552–60.

31. See for instance: 'Advierten sobre el proceso público a jefes castrenses', *La Nación*, 1 Apr. 1985; and 'Sombrío vaticinio de Isaac Rojas', *La Razón*, 21 Apr. 1985.

32. The APDH handed a list of 6,500 detainees-disappeared to the CONADEP. During the latter's work, the number of disappeared grew to 8,960, mainly due to the testimonies of relatives of victims, many of them assembled during visits of the commission representatives from different parts of the country. The CONADEP estimated that the number of the victims was probably three times as large. This estimate was based on the fact that the commission did not reach many distant places and that many relatives did not testify. Americas Watch and CELS, *Verdad y justicia en la Argentina* (Buenos Aires: AW and CELS, 1991), 33.

33. Ibid. 34.

34. This confidential list was made public later on in the pages of the weekly *El periodista de Buenos Aires* (3–9 Nov. 1984, Special supplement to issue No. 8).

35. The report was made public both in book format and in a television documentary film and had great impact on public opinion. Since its first edition in November 1984 and including its 20th edition, in May 1995, the report of the CONADEP has been printed in 256,000 copies. Data extracted from the 20th edition of *Nunca más: Informe de la Comisión Nacional sobre la Desaparición de Personas* (Buenos Aires: EUDEBA, 1995). The book has been translated into six languages, most recently —in June 1998—into Hebrew. This report was published once again in 1995 by the newspaper *Página /12* in weekly supplements, selling over 1,000 copies per week especially among youngsters and university students. Interview with Cristina Leveratto, at the Subsecretariat for Human and Social Rights, Ministry of the Interior, Buenos Aires, 4 July 1995.

36. It was subsequently incorporated into the Ministry of Interior Affairs.

37. Elizabeth Jelin, 'La política de la memoria: el movimiento de derechos humanos y la construcción democrática en la Argentina', 101–46 in Acuña et al., *Juicio, castigos y memorias*.

38. Rama Argentina de la Asociación Americana de Juristas, *Argentina juicio a los militares: documentos secretos, decretos-leyes, jurisprudencia*

(Buenos Aires, 1988), 34, quoted in Acuña and Smulovitz, 'Militares en la transición argentina', 55.

39. Guillermo A. C. Ledesma, 'La responsibilidad de los comandantes por las violaciones de derechos humanos', in Leonardo Senkman and Mario Sznajder with Edy Kaufman (eds.), *El legado del autoritarismo* (Buenos Aires: Grupo Editor Latinoamericano, 1995), 121–9; Jorge A. Valerga-Aráoz, 'Los juicios a los militares argentinos: significación jurídico-penal', ibid. 143–6.

40. Interview with Dr Eduardo Rabossi, Buenos Aires, 6 July 1995.

41. Three former commanders presented formal requests of dismissal against prosecutor Strassera on the grounds that the latter's declarations to the press revealed his hatred and animosity towards the military. 'Videla y Agosti recusaron al fiscal Strassera', *La Razón*, 12 Jan. 1985; 'Recusa Lambruschini al fiscal Strassera', *Clarín*, 5 Feb. 1985; Human-rights groups condemned the tactics of the military and supported Strassera: 'El CELS acusa a los ex-comandantes: apoyo al fiscal Strassera', *La Razón*, 16 Jan. 1985. As a consequence of this decision some of the former members of the Juntas began a boycott against the trial, which created wide public consternation.

42. Agosti accepted charges in only eight of those cases, hinting that the army bore principal responsibility for the majority of the cases (R. Felice, 'Agosti descargó en el Ejército responsabilidades por la represión', *La Razón*, 1 Mar. 1985. Brigadier-General Omar Graffigna, a member of the second Junta, adopted Agosti's defence strategy. 'Declaró Omar Graffigna', *La Razón*, 14 Mar. 1985). As the opening of the public phase of the trial got closer, Agosti assumed political responsibility for the deeds of the Junta, but maintained that the actual character of the anti-subversive war was the responsibility of each commander in his area of command and was not decided by the Junta as a whole; Valerga-Aráoz, 'Los juicios a los militares', 145–6; Another high-ranking officer of the army, General Luciano B. Menéndez, adopted a stand similar to that of Videla, when he was brought to testify in front of a civilian judge in a different trial.

43. Hugo Vezzeti, 'El juicio: un ritual de la memoria', *Punto de vista* (Aug.–Oct. 1985), 4. Terms which abounded in the references to the trial were 'ceremony', 'ritual', 'liturgy', 'dramatization of an ethical conflict reaching to the society at whole', 'ethical affirmation of knowledge', 'moral staging', etc. For a comprehensive discussion of the trial as drama, with its potentiality and shortcomings, see Mark J. Osiel, 'Ever Again: Legal Remembrance of Administrative Massacre', *University of Pennsylvania Law Review*, 144/2 (1995), 683–91.

44. 'El fiscal desestima un "Juicio de Nuremberg"', *Clarín*, 18 Mar. 1985; 'Opina la Asamblea Permanente por los Derechos Humanos', *La Prensa*, 4 Mar. 1985.

45. *El diario del juicio* (Buenos Aires: Editorial Perfil, 1985–6). The motto of the journal read: 'History is the prologue to the world that our children will inherit.'

46. Carlos Cabeza Miñarro, 'Qué pasa cuando se pregunta a un testigo si era subversivo', *El diario del juicio*, 2 (June 1985), 4.
47. On the legal strategy of the attorneys of the accused see Osiel, 'The Making of Human Rights Policy', 168–75; and Rubén Felice, 'Estrategias del fiscal y de los defensores', *La Razón*, 20 Apr. 1985.
48. Interview with José Luis D'Andrea Mohr, retired military captain, writer, and journalist, of the Centre for Democratic Military Officers, Buenos Aires, 10 July 1995.
49. Life sentences were given to General Jorge R. Videla and Admiral Emilio E. Massera; General Roberto E. Viola was sentenced to seventeen years' imprisonment; Admiral Armando Lambruschini to eight years; Brigadier Orlando R. Agosti to four years. Admiral Jorge I. Anaya, General Leopoldo F. Galtieri, Brigadier Omar R. Graffigna, and Brigadier Basilio Lami Dozo were liberated. For analyses of the verdicts, see *El diario del juicio*, 29–36 (Dec. 1985–Jan. 1986). The full text of the verdicts appears in Nos. 33–6. A detailed analysis of these and subsequent verdicts is found in a statistical annex to the Report to the European Parliament (http://www.derechos.org/nizkor/arg/parlamento/an3.html), Madrid, Oct. 1996.
50. The disapprobation they expressed was not shared by human-rights groups outside Argentina.
51. See Mark Osiel, *Mass Atrocity, Collective Memory and the Law* (New Brunswick, NJ: Transaction Books, 1997).
52. Carlos Cabeza Miñarro, 'Los jueces dijeron no al punto final', *El diario del juicio*, 29 (Dec. 1985), 3.
53. The commander-in-chief of the armed forces, General Ríos Ereñú, declared years later that he received an explicit promise from the government that every officer convicted would be pardoned before the administration came to an end. See Acuña and Smulovitz, 'Militares en la transición argentina', 59.
54. Varas, 'Democratización y reforma militar en Argentina'. Interior Minister Antonio Tróccoli declared at the National Congress that although a new wave of subversion was not expected, 'the people that have stolen the country and denied the right to life, are the very same that today want to teach us a moral lesson in politics, beginning a systematic campaign to create an image of chaos and national dissolution' ('Tróccoli negó que haya un rebrote subversivo', *La Nación* (3 June 1985), 8).
55. Americas Watch and CELS, *Verdad y justicia en la Argentina*, 37–40.
56. As a consequence of this incident, one of the members of the Federal Court (Jorge Torlasco) resigned from the court. See Acuña and Smulovitz, 'Militares en la transición argentina', 60–1. The Supreme Council of the armed forces interpreted these Instructions in the broadest sense; in only two cases it reached verdicts and in both it absolved the accused. One was the absolution of General Luciano B. Menéndez for the assassination of María Amelia Inzaurralde, a teacher with Communist leanings. The second was the absolution on technical grounds of navy captain Alfredo Astiz for the murder of 17-year-old Swedish citizen Dagmar Hagelin,

abducted and wounded in 1976 in Buenos Aires and seen alive in the School of Mechanics of the Navy (ESMA). Astiz was also accused of infiltrating the group of Madres de Plaza de Mayo and of leading the capture and assassination of fourteen of its leading activists.

57. Law No. 23492 (22 Dec. 1986). For discussions on the enactment of the law, see Crawford, 'Due Obedience', 25–6; and Alison Brysk, *The Politics of Human Rights in Argentina* (Stanford: Stanford University Press, 1994), 81–4.

58. *Verdad y justicia en la Argentina*, 66–7.

59. 'Incidentes al finalizar la marcha de reprobación al punto final', *La nación*, 22 Dec. 1986; 'Punto final: duro ataque de Alfonsín a los extremismos', ibid.

60. According to Deborah Norden, in early 1987, the number of military men who were being prosecuted for human-rights violations had climbed to about 450. 'Democratic Consolidation and Military Professionalism: Argentina in the 1980s'. *Journal of Interamerican Studies and World Affairs*, 32/3 (1990), 166–7.

61. Quoted by Emilio F. Mignone, 'The Catholic Church and the Argentine Democratic Transition', in Edward C. Epstein (ed.), *The New Argentine Democracy* (Westport, Conn.: Praeger, 1992), 160.

62. Arosa's declarations are discussed in Carlos A. González Gartland, '¿Desobediencia o apología?', *Madres de Plaza de Mayo*, 29 (Apr. 1987), 5. On FAMUS, see R. Angel, 'Las misas de FAMUS', ibid. 25 (Dec. 1986), 11. On the Military Circle see Brysk, *The Politics of Human Rights in Argentina*, 97–8. On Ríos Ereñú's declarations and their impact see Ernesto Garzón Valdés, 'La democracia argentina actual: problemas eticopolíticos de la transición', in E. Garzón Valdés, Manfred Mols, and Arnold Spita (eds.), *La nueva democracia argentina (1983–1986)* (Buenos Aires: Editorial Sudamericana, 1988), 240. See also Carlos Rodríguez, 'El falso demócrata Ríos Ereñú', *Madres de Plaza Mayo*, 19 (June 1986), 7, which lists the declarations of General Ríos Ereñú since 1976.

63. Interview with José Luis D'Andrea Mohr, 10 July 1995; Acuña and Smulovitz, 'Militares en la transición argentina', 62–6.

64. Brysk, *The Politics of Human Rights in Argentina*, 130–1.

65. Interview with Liliana de Riz, political scientist and director of graduate programmes at the Faculty of Social Sciences, University of Buenos Aires, 5 July 1996.

66. Diego R. Guelar, *Crónicas de la transición*, vol. ii: *El pueblo nunca se equivoca (los dirigentes a veces sí)* (Buenos Aires: Editorial Sudamericana, 1988), 231.

67. Ibid.

68. Brysk, *The Politics of Human Rights in Argentina*, 83. See also Crawford, 'Due Obedience'.

69. Interview with Emilio Mignone, President of the Centre for Legal and Social Studies (CELS) and father of a disappeared daughter, Buenos Aires, 6 July 1995.

70. Guelar, *Crónicas de la transición*, 237–8.

71. Ten human-rights organizations published a book in 1988 with the names of all those military and police officers who were exonerated either by the Supreme Court, the Punto Final Law, or the Due Obedience Law. The book was based on information gathered mainly by the Centre for Documentation of the CELS. *Culpables para la sociedad, impunes por la ley* (Buenos Aires: Abuelas de Plaza de Mayo et al., 1988).

72. Brysk, *The Politics of Human Rights in Argentina*, 102–3.

73. Pardons covered 217 cases. At the same time, Menem used his presidential prerogatives to grant pardons to 64 left-wing guerrillas, not including Montonero leader Mario Firmenich.

74. A letter addressed to Menem, rejecting the pardons, was signed by nearly one million citizens.

75. Emilio Mignone, 'Los decretos de indulto en la República Argentina' (http://www.derechos.org/lidlip/indultos.html), 7 Dec. 1996.

76. E. Robinson, 'Freed Argentine General Unrepentant', *Washington Post*, 3 Jan. 1991. On the popular reaction to the pardons see Ian Katz, 'Analysts: Pardons May Hurt Menem's Image Abroad', *Miami Herald*, 2 Jan. 1991.

77. Paul W. Zagorski, 'Civil–Military Relations and Argentine Democracy: The Armed Forces under the Menem Government', *Armed Forces and Society*, 20/3 (1994), 431–3.

78. Carlos E. Rodríguez, 'Cebados por la impunidad', and 'Carrasco y las atrocidades de las fuerzas armadas', 2 and 23, in *Madres de Plaza de Mayo*, 108 (May 1994). In August 1996 the authorities indicted two army officers charged with the covering up of Carrasco's murder.

79. Vicente Palermo, 'Argentine: Réformes de structures et régime politique, 1989–1994', *Problèmes d'Amérique Latine*, 20 (1996), 61–80; and Delia Ferreira Rubio and Matteo Goretti, 'Cuando el Presidente gobierna solo: Menem y los decretos de necesidad y vigencia hasta la reforma constitucional (julio 1989–agosto 1994)', *Desarrollo económico*, 36/141 (1996), 443–74.

80. Isidoro Cheresky, 'Argentina, una democracia a la búsqueda de su institución', *European Review of Latin American and Caribbean Studies*, 53 (1992), 38.

81. Silvia Sigal, 'Argentine, 1992–1995: une société en mutation', *Problèmes d'Amérique Latine*, 20 (1996), 3–24; and Liliana de Riz, 'Argentine: les élections de 1991 à 1995', ibid. 25–40.

82. David Lehmann, *Democracy and Development in Latin America* (Cambridge: Polity Press, 1990), 148–85.

83. Interview with Fr. Luis Pérez Aguirre. Montevideo, 14 July 1995. SERPAJ was instrumental in establishing the Instituto de Estudios Legales y Sociales (IELSUR), which undertook the task of legal advice and representation of the victims of repression; and the Servicio de Rehabiliación Social (SERSOC), charged with providing medical, psychological, and social assistance to the prisoners and their families. SERPAJ was also in touch with parallel organizations in Brazil and Chile.

84. Manuel Flores Silva, 'Un hombre clausurado para siempre: un canal clausurado por tres días', *Jaque* (11 May 1984), 24; and Carina Perelli

and Juan Rial, *De mitos y memorias políticas* (Montevideo: Ediciones de la Banda Oriental, 1986), 72–86.

85. Wilson Ferreira Aldunate, one of the leaders of the National Party and himself a victim of repression, declared years later that the armed forces had enabled the democratic opening in exchange for a compromise, on the part of civilian political leaders, not to bring the military to trial. Ferreira Aldunate's declarations, made in Kiyú on 10 Jan. 1987, were published by *Brecha* (16 Jan. 1987).

86. Ley de amnistía 15737, published in *Diario oficial*, 22 Mar. 1985.

87. See Ch. 4.

88. J. Barreiro, 'Derechos humanos: crónica en tres actos', *Cuadernos de marcha* (Montevideo), 12/8 (Nov. 1986), 16. See also 'Se acabó el tiempo de la capucha: los partidos y los delitos de lesa humanidad', *Brecha* (Montevideo) (10 Oct. 1986), 7.

89. Interview with Gerardo Caetano, director of the Institute of Political Studies, University of La República, Montevideo, 12 July 1995.

90. On the popular mobilization see 'Para una crónica de las jornadas en que se perpetuó la tristeza', *Brecha* (26 Dec. 1986), 6–8.

91. Eventually, an NGO, the Service of Peace and Justice (SERPAJ) elaborated an unofficial report published in 1989. See below.

92. Law 15848 carries the title, in its literal wording, of the 'Law of Cancellation of the Punitive Pretension of the State'.

93. Instituto Interamericano de Derechos Humanos, *El referéndum uruguayo del 16 de abril de 1989: disposiciones legales* (San José de Costa Rica: IIDH, 1989), 62.

94. The full text of the law can be found in Centro Uruguay Independiente, *Referéndum* (Montevideo: CUI, 1987), 42–8.

95. On the role of the political parties see Gerardo Caetano et al., *De la tradición a la crisis; pasado y presente de nuestro sistema de partidos* (Montevideo: CLAEH and Ediciones de la Banda Oriental, 1985); Edy Kaufman, 'El rol de los partidos políticos en la redemocratización del Uruguay', 25–62 in Sosnowski (ed.), *Represión, exilio y democracia: la cultura uruguaya* (Montevideo: Ediciones de la Banda Oriental, 1987) (the English version appeared in Sosnowski and L. Popkin (eds.), *Repression, Exile and Democracy: Uruguayan Culture* (Durham, NC: Duke University Press, 1992)); and Luis E. González, *Estructuras políticas y democracia en Uruguay* (Montevideo: Fundación de Cultura Universitaria, 1993).

96. For the text of the call of the CNP see 'El llamamiento', *Brecha*, 66 (30 Jan. 1987), 2. For English reports on the campaign see Jo-Marie Burt, *El pueblo decide: A Brief History of the Referendum against the 'Impunity Law' in Uruguay* (Montevideo: SERPAJ, 1989) and Americas Watch Committee, *Challenging Impunity: The Ley of Caducidad and the Referendum Campaign in Uruguay* (New York: Americas Watch, 1989).

97. 'Yo firmo (Yo firmo con alegría) para que el pueblo decida'.

98. Most of the written propaganda included statements and portraits of national leaders, e.g. Artigas, Batlle Ordóñez, and Aparicio Saravia, whom Uruguayans consider the founding fathers of modern Uruguay.

References to the images of the illustrious past and to the role of history abound in the flyers of the Comisión Nacional Pro-Referendum—CNP (e.g. the flyer 'La historia confirma que la justicia es patrimonio irrenunciable de todos los uruguayos'). The CNP reaffirmed in its campaign the commitment to strengthening Uruguayan democratic institutions. Illustrative is the following flyer: 'By signing, the people strengthen the institutions and democracy'; 'Who promotes the Referendum? An integrated Commission which is above all party interests. What is the goal of the Referendum? To enable the people to decide if they do or do not want this Law of Caducity; What is achieved by signing? A popular decision is made possible. If the people reject the Law, would an institutional crisis then take place? No. The expression of our will does not endanger the institutions, but, on the contrary, defends and consolidates them' (From the flyer 'Sr. vecino, sabe que es el Referendum?' by the Comisión Pro-Referendum of Malvín).

99. See Roger Rodríguez, 'Las brigadas verdes, puerta a puerta: el Referendum llama dos veces', *Brecha* (24 Feb. 1989), 5. The following is typical of the tenor of the campaign: 'Dear Neighbour: We invite you to share the afternoon of the 4th of April with: Puppets; Antimurga BCG, the First Actor, Alberto Candeau, the actress Jebele Sand, Los del Yerbal and more . . . ; I sign with happiness for the people to decide. Sponsors: Pro-Referendum Neighbours' Commission, Millan y Raffo corner. Free admission' (SERPAJ Documentation Centre's Archives, Document No. E05/59/002.111/1987.04.04).

100. See as an example the text of the following flyer: 'Change now!! For the victory of the Referendum'; 'We believe that is time to change the orientation of the campaign 180 degrees in order to assure the success of the Referendum campaign, a success that the Workers' and Popular Movement needs very much'; 'We have to stress the importance of keeping the autonomy of the Neighbours' Commissions in order to provide the Campaign with an authoritative orientation. This is the only guarantee to achieve our goal: TRIAL AND PUNISHMENT FOR THE GUILTY' Coordinadora de Comisiones Barriales (SERPAJ Documentation Centre's Archives, Document No. 35/009.111/1987.04.00). This slogan, adopted by the local commissions, reminiscent of the Argentine experience, was not endorsed by the national CNP.

101. The following analysis relies on flyers, brochures, and other campaign materials, reviewed at the documentation centre of the SERPAJ in Montevideo, as well as on secondary sources. See Madres y Familiares de Detenidos Desaparecidos, *El referéndum desde familiares* (Montevideo: MFDDU, 1990).

102. See the declarations of President Julio María Sanguinetti: 'The other way (annulling the Law of Caducity) creates a climate of confrontation, a climate of strife and drama . . . The issue at stake is whether we leave this theme in the past or whether we enter a long, risky, unstable, dramatic period.' *El Día* (23 Dec. 1988), 8–9. See also Lacalle: 'Voto Amarillo clausura el pasado y abre las puertas al porvenir', *El País*, 13 Apr. 1989.

103. Jorge Gamarra, 'Las oscuridades del Presidente: el voto verde y claro del 16', *Brecha* (24 February 1989), 2–4.

104. 'Lo que dijo el Presidente durante los 844 días que duró la campaña por el referendum', *La República* (17 Apr. 1989), 4.

105. Ibid.

106. 'El pueblo dijo que no al agravio a las instituciones', *El soldado* (Montevideo), 122 (May–June 1989), 1, and 'Todos iguales ante la ley? Eso sí que es cuento', *El soldado*, 121 (Jan.–Apr. 1989), 2 and 8.

107. The referendum on the Law of Expiry prompted legal discussions among politicians with a juridical background. The positions of Dr Martín Sturla, Dr Gros Espiell, Dr Juan R. Ramírez, Dr Gonzalo Aguirre, Dr Julio César Espinola, Dr Miguel Semino, Dr Horacio Casinelli Muñoz, and Dr José Korseniak, appear in IIDH-CAPEL, *El referéndum uruguayo del 16 de abril de 1989* (San José de Costa Rica: Instituto Interamericano de Derechos Humanos, 1989).

108. 'Tarigo no aceptaría el desafío de Matilde: "Solo con presidenciables"', *La república* (3 Apr. 1989), 3; 'Cuatro presidenciables rehusaron polemizar con Matilde', *La República* (5 Apr. 1989), 3.

109. See Juan Rial, 'El referéndum del 16 de abril de 1989 en Uruguay', in IIDH-CAPEL, *El referéndum uruguayo*, 15–58, esp. 19–24.

110. 'Por la Patria no pedirá a sus simpatizantes votar amarillo', *La república* (9 Apr. 1989), 1; 'García Costa: la Ley de Caducidad coopera a mantener paz y democracia'. *El país* (24 Dec. 1988), 2; Héctor Rodríguez, 'El largo silencio de Zumarán y Lacalle', *Brecha* (7 Apr. 1989), 6.

111. *Los montevideanos y el referéndum: la irreductibilidad de las posiciones*, poll of Equipos Consultores for *Búsqueda*, 3 Apr. 1989.

112. The results of the referendum and their statistical analysis appeared in *Búsqueda* (Montevideo) (20 Apr. 1989), 4–5. On the results of the Montevideo area see Alvaro Portillo and Enrique Gallicchio, *Montevideo: Geografía electoral 2* (Montevideo: Centro Uruguay Independiente, 1989).

113. *La república* (17 Apr. 1989), 5. From an interview with Sanguinetti published in Madrid: 'You have declared that with the referendum, the transition in Uruguay has reached an end; what do you mean by that? Sanguinetti: It means that Uruguay has resolved all the problems of the past. The debate about the dictatorship period is over. The country is facing its future.' *El país* (19 Apr. 1989), 6.

114. The expression 'neither vanquished nor victors' ('ni vencidos ni vencedores') is an allusion to the pact signed by the Blanco and the Colorado caudillos on 8 Oct. 1850, to put an end to the decades-long civil war, known as the Guerra Grande.

115. *Búsqueda* (20 Apr. 1989), 8.

116. 'Que tristeza . . . Vencieron, pero no convencieron', *La hora* (Montevideo, organ of the PCU) (17 Apr. 1989), 1; 'Los militares no irán ante el juez: el juicio lo hará la historia', *La república* (17 Apr. 1989), 1; 'Que la lucha continúe', *Mate amargo* (Montevideo, organ of the MLN-T), 20 Apr. 1989.

117. Francisco Bustamante, 'La verdad no puede destruirse', part of a round table for the presentation of the 'Uruguay Nunca Más', *Paz y justicia*,

Año IV, No. 17, p. 26. For the report see Servicio de Paz y Justicia, *Uruguay: Nunca más* (Montevideo: SERPAJ, 1989).

118. Mario Sznajder, 'Transition in South America: Models of Limited Democracy', *Democratization*, 3/3 (1996), 336–9.

119. Manuel A. Garretón, *Hacia una nueva era política* (Santiago: Fondo de Cultura Económica, 1995), 161; Carlos A. González, *Ley de partidos políticos y votaciones populares (leyes No. 18,603 y 18,700)* (Santiago: Ediciones Publiley, 1995), 90–1.

120. Fifty-four reforms to the 1980 Constitution were negotiated between the military government and the opposition before the democratic elections, and approved by popular referendum in July 1989. These reforms, while retaining the basic framework of limited democracy, opened the political system beyond the extent envisaged by Pinochet. Carlos A. González Moya (ed.), *54 reformas a la constitución política de Chile* (Santiago: Editora Jurídica Publiley, 1989).

121. Pamela Lowden, *Moral Opposition to Authoritarian Rule in Chile, 1973–1990*. The Vicaría was closely related to Catholic forces in Chile and abroad, and was protected by the Catholic Church as part of its plural structure.

122. The Academia was created following Cardinal Raúl Silva Henríquez's initiative in November 1975, with a staff integrated by many former employees of the Catholic University and other institutions, who had been dismissed after the coup. See Hugo Frühling (ed.), *Derechos humanos y democracia* (Santiago: Instituto Interamericano de Derechos Humanos, 1991), 33–50; and Lowden, *Moral Opposition*, 54.

123. Barahona de Brito, *Human Rights and Democratization in Latin America, Uruguay and Chile* (Oxford: Oxford University Press, 1997), 112–13.

124. For an analysis of the Christian Democratic model see Brian Loveman, *Chile: The Legacy of Hispanic Capitalism* (New York: Oxford University Press, 1988), esp. 280–90. See also Michael Fleet, *The Rise and Fall of Chilean Christian Democracy* (Princeton: Princeton University Press, 1985), 68 and 80.

125. Patricio Aylwin spoke of repaying the 'social debt of Chile', by which he meant redressing the social regression caused by the stern application under military rule of neoliberal economic programmes. These programmes, of 'social market economy', though successful from a macroeconomic point of view, at the same time widened the already broad socio-economic gaps of Chilean society, increasing poverty among some of the lower strata. See David E. Hojman, 'Chile after Pinochet: Aylwin's Christian Democrat Economic Policies for the 1990s', *Bulletin of Latin American Research*, 9/1 (1990), 25–47; Roberto Espíndola, 'Democracy and Redistribution: The Problems of Governance in Chile', in David Hojman (ed.), *Neo-Liberalism with a Human Face: The Politics and Economics of the Chilean Model*, Monograph Series No. 20 (Liverpool: Institute of Latin American Studies, 1995), 64–70.

126. The extreme left, primarily the Communists and some of the Socialists, demanded full justice and punishment as well as the revocation of the

amnesty law issued by the military. See Alan Angell and Benny Pollack, 'The Chilean Elections of 1989 and the Politics of the Transition to Democracy', *Bulletin of Latin American Research*, 9/1 (1990), 1–23.

127. The Amnesty Law was applicable to all human-rights violations prior to 1978, with the exception of the *Letelier* case. The Ley Orgánica Constitucional de las Fuerzas Armadas (Organic Law of the Armed Forces— No. 18948) was approved in January 1990. It ensured military budgetary autonomy by setting the 1989 defence budget as the minimum standard of military expenditure, its indexation, a share of copper sales by CODELCO—the state copper company—for military expenditure, and control over promotions and retirements. It even sanctioned the financing by the state of the costs of implementing 'regimes of exception'. See Loveman, ' "Protected Democracies" and Military Guardianship: Political Transitions in Latin America, 1978–1993' Anthony H. O'Malley, 'Chile's Constitution, Chile's Congress', *Canadian Review of Latin American Studies*, 15 (1990), 85–112. David Pion-Berlin, 'Military Autonomy and Emerging Democracies in South America', *Comparative Politics*, 25/1 (1992), 83–102; Mario Sznajder, 'Limited Democracy: A Comparative Approach', in Roberto Espíndola (ed.), *Problems of Democracy in Latin America* (Stockholm: Institute of Latin American Studies, Stockholm University, 1996), esp. 67–71.

128. In an interview with José Zalaquett, he confirmed that the Chilean leadership followed closely the developments in Argentina and Uruguay, trying to learn from these experiences which steps to avoid and how to proceed within the constraints of Chile, which were tighter than in Argentina's initial situation (Santiago, 20 July 1995). For general analyses of the institutional dilemmas in these nations see José Zalaquett, 'Balancing Ethical Imperatives and Political Constraints: The Dilemma of New Democracies Confronting Past Human Rights Violations', *Hasting Law Journal*, 43 (1992), 1425–38; Pion-Berlin, 'To Prosecute or to Pardon? Human Rights Decisions in the Latin American Southern Cone', and Manuel Antonio Garretón, 'Human Rights in Processes of Democratization', *Journal of Latin American Studies*, 26 (1994), 221–34.

129. During the interview with Patricio Aylwin, he quoted from his speech at the National Stadium on 12 Mar. 1990. Interview with Patricio Aylwin, Santiago, 18 July 1995.

130. These senators were appointed for different periods rather than elected as representatives. Ex-presidents that have served for at least six years could decide to become senators for life. Ex-commanders of the army, navy, air force, and Carabineros—one for each branch—and former judges of the Supreme Court (2), one former Comptroller of the Republic, one former rector of a state university, and one former minister of state could be appointed for a period of eight years. Artículo 45, *Constitución política de la República de Chile*, 1980 (Santiago: Publiley, n.d.), 38.

131. 'The Armed Forces . . . exist for the defense of the fatherland, are essential for national security and guarantee the institutional order of the Republic. . . . The Armed Forces and the Armed Police . . . are essentially

obedient and not deliberating bodies. In addition, . . . [they] are professional, hierarchic and disciplined.' *Political Constitution of the Republic of Chile* (translated by the official translator), ch. 10, art. 90.

132. We follow here Manuel Antonio Garretón's conceptualization of the authoritarian enclaves. See his *Hacia una nueva era política*, 161; and id., 'Human Rights in Processes of Democratization', 222–5. The other three enclaves defined by Garretón are: the institutional enclave that frames limited democracy, according to the rules of the 1980 Constitution; the presence of authoritarian actors, military and civilians, that do not fully integrate into democracy and may conspire against it; and a set of values and attitudes that constitute the authoritarian mentality.

133. On the problem of public spheres in connection with the shaping of collective identities see S. N. Eisenstadt, *Trust, Meaning and Power* (Chicago: University of Chicago Press, 1995); and S. N. Eisenstadt and B. Giesen, 'The Construction of Collective Identity', *Archives européennes de sociologie*, 36 (1995), 72–102.

134. These activities are detailed in the annual reports (*Resumen de actividades*) by the Agrupación de Familiares de Detenidos-Desaparecidos published in Santiago. See also 'Carta abierta a los miembros de las fuerzas armadas', *La epoca* (30 July 1995), 19.

135. According to Myriam Krawczyk, a sociologist in ECLA, this was part of a weakening of the NGOs after redemocratization. Funds coming from international sources dried up. The government was willing to implement part of their political demands. These processes transferred the main thrust of many NGOs' leaders from articulating social movements to articulating policies. Interview in Santiago, 20 July 1995.

136. The commission was created by a presidential decree: Decreto Supremo No. 355, 25 Apr. 1990, in *Informe de la Comisión Nacional de Verdad y Reconciliación* (Santiago: Secretaría de Comunicación y Cultura. Ministerio Secretaría General de Gobierno, 1991), vol. i, pp. vii–x. On the problem of knowledge in situations of transitions see the theoretical analysis in Stanley Cohen, 'State Crimes of Previous Regimes: Knowledge, Accountability and the Policing of the Past', *Law and Social Inquiry*, 20/1 (1995), 12–22. On the experience of truth commissions in Chile and other Latin American countries see also Margaret Popkin and Naomi Roth-Arriaza, 'Truth as Justice: Investigatory Commissions in Latin America', ibid. 79–116.

137. *Informe de la Comisión Nacional*, p. viii.

138. See Jorge Mera, 'Chile: Truth and Justice under the Democratic Government', in Roth-Arriaza, *Impunity and Human Rights*, 171–84.

139. Article 1, sections (*a*) to (*d*) of Supreme Decree No. 355.

140. The list of organizations that forwarded information and lists of victims of human-rights violations resulting in death to the Rettig Commission is impressive and reflects the dense organizational network of human-rights associations of civil society, in addition to state organs. They included: seven professional associations, the army, the navy, the air force,

Carabineros, and the civilian police (*Investigaciones*), the Socialist and the Communist parties, the Movimiento de Izquierda Revolucionaria (MIR), the Vicariate of Solidarity, the Chilean Commission for Human Rights, the Fundación de Ayuda Social de Iglesias (FASIC), the Committee for the Defence of People's Rights (CODEPU), the Pastoral de Derechos Humanos de la Octava Región, the Movement against Torture Sebastián Acevedo, the National Corporation for the Defence of Peace (CORPAZ), the National Front of Autonomous Organizations (FRENAO), the Agrupación de Familiares de Detenidos Desaparecidos, the Agrupación de Familiares de Ejecutados Políticos, the Central Única de Trabajadores (CUT), and the Comisión Nacional de Juntas de Vecinos. *Informe de la Comisión Nacional de Verdad y Reconciliación*, 5.

141. Barahona de Brito, *Human Rights and Democratization in Latin America*, 159.
142. 'Discurso de Su Excelencia el Presidente de la República, Don Patricio Aylwin Azócar', recording of the TV broadcast, Santiago, 4 Mar. 1991.
143. Ibid.
144. Ibid.
145. The organization was led by Alejandro González, who had served as chief lawyer of the Vicaría de la Solidaridad.
146. 'Discurso de Su Excelencia el Presidente de la República', ibid.
147. Here we agree with the division established by Garretón between ethical-symbolic and state-political factors. Still we have to observe that the respect of human-rights is a *sine qua non* of democratic institutionality which is not ensured by the mere existence of a democratic administration but requires legal and institutional substance. In this sense, the resolution of the unsolved cases becomes paradigmatic not only for the issue of human-rights but also for democratic practice in general. See Garretón, *Hacia una nueva era política*, 162–3.
148. Article 9, Political Constitution of the Republic of Chile (Santiago, 1986).
149. For a detailed account see Barahona de Brito, *Human Rights and Democratization in Latin America*, 167–72.
150. Augusto Pinochet's declarations to Raquel Correa and Elizabeth Subercaseaux in *Ego sum Pinochet* (Santiago: Zig-zag, 1989), 110–11. See also 112–22.
151. 'Pinochet Assails Rights Report', *Facts on File, 1991* (New York: Facts on File Publications, 1991), 248.
152. Interview with José Zalaquett, Santiago, 20 July 1995.
153. Jaime Guzmán, 'A raíz del informe Rettig', in *Jaime Guzmán: su legado humano y político* (Santiago: Ercilla, 1991), 126–7.
154. Interview with Jose Zalaquett, Santiago, 20 July 1995.
155. 'Respuesta de las Fuerzas Armadas y de Orden al Informe de la Comisión Nacional de Verdad y Reconciliación', *Estudios políticos*, 41 (1991), 449–504. The armed forces' replies, as presented to the National Security Council by the commanders of the army, the navy, the air force, and Carabineros, ranged from a 22-page document by the army to a 3-page document by the air force. The document of the army contained a

quotation from a statement made by Patricio Aylwin on 19 Oct. 1973, in which he justified the military coup. Aylwin never claimed to have sympathized with Allende, but this did not justify human-rights violations, as he clearly indicated with the passing of time. Ibid. 470.

156. UDI gave unqualified support of the army and navy's rejection of the Rettig Report; RN claimed that the armed forces' reaction did not endanger national reconciliation; Christian Democracy called to support national reconciliation by accepting the report; left-wing parties (PPD; the Socialist Party) and national trade unions (CUT; ANEF) condemned the position of the army. 'Military Responses to Rettig Report Viewed'. *FBIS-LAT-91-062* (1 Apr. 1991), 33–4.

157. Rosario Guzmán Errázuriz, *Mi hermano Jaime* (Santiago: Editorial VER, 1991), 13–22; 'Guzmán murder kills Rettig Report', *Latin American Weekly Report* (8 May 1991), 4.

158. 'Army, Pinochet View Murder'; 'Air Force Expresses Regret', 'Carabineros Denounce Murder'. *FBIS-LAT-91-064* (3 Apr. 1991), 26–8. Following the mass in memory of Guzmán, UDI members heckled the government representatives and especially Enrique Correa, secretary-general of the presidency (who served as secretary to the Rettig Commission). Pro-government demonstrators outside the church confronted the UDI sympathizers and Carabineros were caught in the middle. 'Confrontation at Guzman's Mass', ibid. 28.

159. In an interview (18 July 1995), Patricio Aylwin told us that Mónica Madariaga, who was Minister of Justice under Pinochet, supported the idea that investigation of the cases liable to be covered by the Amnesty law of 1978 was to be completed, including the establishment of personal responsibility. Aylwin himself thought that civil and criminal matters were to be prosecuted separately, and that therefore in the criminal proceedings there was no need to establish personal guilt.

160. Interview with Patricio Aylwin.

161. In contrast to Wendy Hunter's thesis about the increasing capacity of democratic actors to diminish the military's political influence—what she calls the 'electoral dynamic argument'—this analysis indicates that the combined effects of authoritarian enclaves and military power succeeds in blocking attempts of democratic reform in Chile. See Hunter, 'Civil-Military Relations in Argentina, Chile and Peru', *Political Science Quarterly*, 112/3 (1997), esp. 453–63.

CHAPTER 3

1. *El Día* (Montevideo), 1 Mar. 1988.
2. Interview with Sanguinetti published in Madrid's *El País* (19 Apr. 1989), 6.

3. *Latin American Daily Report*, 15 Mar. 1991.
4. *Informe de la Comisión Nacional de Verdad y Reconciliación* (Santiago: Secretaría de Comunicación y Cultura, Secretaría General del Gobierno, 1991), 13.
5. José Zalaquett, 'Introduction', *Report of the Chilean Commission on Truth and Reconciliation* (English translation) (South Bend, Ind.: University of Notre Dame Press, 1993).
6. 'Nueva evangelización para Chile: orientaciones pastorales 1991–1994' (Santiago: Conferencia Episcopal de Chile, 1990), 23. See also Hannah Stewart-Gambino, 'Redefining the Changes and Politics in Chile', in Edward L. Cleary and Hannah Stewart-Gambino (eds.), *Conflict and Competition: The Latin American Church in a Changing Environment* (Boulder, Colo.: Lynne Rienner, 1992), 21–44.
7. ' "Tedeum Evangélico": gobierno debe hacer prioritaria la reconciliación', *El mercurio* (Santiago) (18 Sept. 1995), 1.
8. *Página/12* (12 July 1995), 10–11.
9. *El soldado* (Montevideo) (May–June 1989), 35.
10. Interview by Emiliano Cotelo on Radio El Espectador (24 May 1996), 9.10 a.m.
11. Interview with Emilio Mignone, Buenos Aires, 6 July 1995.
12. Horacio Verbitsky, 'Fuerzas armadas y sociedad civil', *Página/12* (16 July 1995), 10–11, from an interview for *Time* magazine.
13. In a survey published in November 1994, 84% of teenage students had little or no knowledge about the meaning of the *Nunca más* report, 56% did not know who Jorge Rafael Videla was, and 74% did not know how Mrs Perón's administration came to an end. It should be noted that the survey was based on a random sample of 50 students. See 'Cómo se enseña a olvidar la historia', *La maga* (Buenos Aires), 147 (Nov. 1994), 1 and 44–7.
14. Horacio Verbitsky, *El vuelo* (Buenos Aires: Planeta, 1995). For an English review see *Newsweek* (27 Mar. 1995), 23.
15. Samuel Blixen, 'Por supuesto que no me voy a callar', *Brecha* (Montevideo) (7 May 1996).
16. Mariano Grondona's TV talk show *Hora Clave*, Channel 9, 2 Mar. 1995. The newspaper *Página/12* published the interview that Scilingo gave to Horacio Verbitsky, 'La solución final', on 3 Mar. 1995. The Mothers and Grandmothers of Plaza de Mayo published a special issue on the Scilingo confessions (*Madres de Plaza de Mayo*, 118, Apr. 1995). Scilingo's declarations were followed by the statements of soldier Pedro Caraballo and Sergeant Víctor Armando Ibáñez, who declared they had been involved in human-rights violations. They expressed remorse and provided new details on the throwing of prisoners into the sea. See 'Las revelaciones de un ex gendarme', *Clarín* (1 July 1995), 12.; Fernando Almirón, 'Arrojó desaparecidos al mar y está arrepentido', *La Prensa* (24 Apr. 1995), 14; 'La caída de un muro (de silencio)', *Página/12* (28 Apr. 1995), 2–5. At the same time, 'El Turco Julián', an officer involved in torturing detainees, appeared on TV, expressing no remorse and stating that, if required, he 'would do it again' (*Página/12* (3 May 1995), 6).

17. A detail of the events triggered by the declarations is found in 'Cronología periodística de los hechos ocurridos a raíz de las declaraciones del ex-Capitán de Corbeta (R) Adolfo Francisco Scilingo', in CELS, *Informe anual sobre la situación de los derechos humanos en la Argentina* (Buenos Aires: CELS, 1996), 123–45.

18. General Balza made his speech on live television, 25 Apr. 1995 ('Tiempo Nuevo' hosted by Bernardo Neustadt). The text of his speech was published the following day by Argentinian newspaper *Página/12*, 1–3, and prompted the demand that other institutions that participated in the 'Dirty War' should take a similar, self-critical stand. The navy and the air force did that on 3 May; the Federal Police on 5 May. The leadership of the guerrilla groups did not remain indifferent to the new reality, as shown in the reactions by ex-Montonero leader Firmenich, who was interviewed in the same talk show. Reactions appeared by other ex-guerrilla leaders such as Fernando Vaca Narvaja, of the Montoneros (*La nación*, 3 May 1995); Arnold Kremer of the ERP (*Clarín* (7 May 1995), 16); and Enrique Gorriarán Merlo of the ERP (*Página/12* (5 May 1995), 4). See also *Ambito financiero* (4 May 1995), 1 and 5–6.

19. 'Histórico reconocimiento por la represión ilegal: el mea culpa del ejército argentino', *El observador* (htpp://www.zfm.com/observdiario), 27 Apr. 1995.

20. Olga Wornat, 'Increíble pero cierto: las confesiones de Massera', *Gente* (Buenos Aires) (27 July 1995), 48–56, and *Página/12* (13 Aug. 1995), 11. For Díaz's declarations see *Página/12* (5 May 1995), 5. Other reactions can be traced in the following publications: *Ambito financiero* (27 Apr. 1995), 2–3; *Página/12* (7 May 1995), 10; *Clarín* (28 Apr. 1995), 4; and *La prensa* (6 May 1995), 3. In October 1996, General (R.) Carlos Suárez Mason, who commanded the 1st Army Corps in Buenos Aires, the area of the harshest kind of repression during the Dirty War, gave his first interview and denied that any crimes were committed. Darío Gallo, 'Suárez Mason, "Nunca fui blando" ', *Noticias* (Buenos Aires) (5 Oct. 1996), 26–32.

21. The letter appeared in *Clarín* (htpp://www.clarin.com/), 27 Apr. 1995.

22. Bonafini was referring to the case of soldier Omar Carrasco, slain by his colleagues and officers in a military camp a few months before Balza's statement. Other NGOs reacted with moderate optimism (e.g. CELS) or even expressed strong support for Balza's action (e.g. the Permanent Assembly of Human Rights—APDH). The disparate positions of the NGOs can be found in *Página/12* (27 Apr. 1995), 1–7; (6 May 1995), 32; *Clarín* (27 Apr. 1995), 1–10; (28 Apr. 1995), 17; and *La prensa* (27 Apr. 1995), 1–5. Atilio Borón and Sergio Kiernan, analysing Balza's positions from different angles, saw it as a significant step forward in the process of the armed forces' adopting criteria of accountability (interviews in Buenos Aires, 10 July and 4 July, respectively).

23. Hesayne accused the Episcopal Conference of not regretting 'having had meals with the torturers at the same time that they did not receive the mothers of the disappeared'. See in particular Horacio Verbitsky. 'Una lluvia de recuerdos', *Página/12* (16 Apr. 1995), 1–3.

24. *Clarín* (8 Mar., 1–12 Apr., and 29 Apr. 1995).

25. See the declarations of Emilo Mignone, Adolfo Pérez Esquivel, Nora Cortinas, and Domingo Quarracino in 'Culpas que debe asumir la Iglesia', *Página/12* (25 Apr. 1995); Ruben Dri, 'La Iglesia es santa, algunos de sus hijos, pecadores', *Madres de Plaza de Mayo* (June 1996), 12–13.
26. The Federal Police subsequently provided Astiz with personal security. In May 1995, Astiz—a notorious young officer involved in repression during the dictatorship—was at the centre of a heated diplomatic incident between the French ambassador and the Argentinian authorities around his involvement in the killing of French nuns and a public debate as civil associations reacted strongly to navy commander Enrique Molina Pico's attempt to promote Astiz, claiming him to be the possessor of the required 'moral qualities' for the prospective role. In January 1998, and stemming from bold press declarations by Astiz to the journal *Tres puntos*, in which he threatened politicians and journalists and suggested the possibility of a military uprising if pressure on human-rights issues continued, the new command of the navy incarcerated him for six months and demoted him to the rank of private. He stood trial for the above threats and for this 'apology for crimes committed.' On the latter developments see 'Procesan a Astiz por amenazas', *Clarín digital* (http://www.clarin.com.ar/diario/98-05-08/t-02101d.htm), 8 May 1998.
27. Conspiracy theories abounded, with observers on the right and on the left speculating about the forces behind this little-known revolutionary group. See reports in *Clarín* (6 Apr. 1996), 12–13 and *Brecha* (20 Apr. 1996), 31.
28. On the operations of the DINA in Argentina and its cooperation with the security authorities of that country see Manuel Salazar, *Contreras: historia de un intocable* (Santiago: Grijalbo, 1995), 111–20. On Arancibia see Roberto Ortiz, 'Los secretos de Arancibia Clavel', *Punto final* (Santiago) (17–30 Mar. 1996), 4–6; Graciela Deco, 'Arancibia Clavel: Dime quién te defiende', *Mate amargo* (Montevideo) (15 Feb. 1996), 23.
29. Salazar, *Contreras*, 182–8.
30. 'Fallo del Caso Letelier: texto completo', *La segunda* (31 May 1995), 19–30.
31. On the military reactions to the verdict see José Rodríguez Elizondo, *La ley es más fuerte* (Buenos Aires: Grupo Editorial Zeta, 1995), 31–9.
32. *La tercera* (Santiago) (21 Oct. 1995), 8–10. In another wing of the Punta Peuco prison the Carabineros found guilty in the *Degollados* case served their terms, together with those convicted on the cases of Carlos Godoy Echegoyen, Quemados, Mario Fernández López, and Nelson Carrasco Bascuñán, a total of thirteen inmates. See 'Detenidos en la cárcel de Punta Peuco', *Informe de la Vicaría de la Solidaridad* (http://www. derechos. org/nizkor/chile/vicaria/presos.html), 10 Dec. 1996. Due to the nature of the prisoners, Punta Peuco is heavily guarded by three rings of security, composed by Gendarmería (the corps of the prison system), Boinas negras (elite troops of the army), and Carabineros, who watch the prison and surrounding hills (Juan Pablo Moreno <jmoreno@eclac.cl> Más antecedentes, 14 Oct. 1996).

33. Mónica González, 'Buscan en Chile más restos de presuntos desaparecidos', *Clarín* (16 Dec. 1995), 36.
34. 'Revelaría la suerte de un millar de desaparecidos: un represor tiene en vilo a Chile', *Clarín* (10 Aug. 1995), 30.
35. '36 años de "Dignidad" en Chile', *La segunda* (10 July 1997), 1–20.
36. The Uruguayan NGO's report on human-rights violations indicates at least 157 Uruguayans 'disappeared' and 95 political prisoners were killed, died from illness, or committed suicide in detention centres between 1972 and 1985. Out of the 157 disappeared persons, 117 disappeared in Argentina. See SERPAJ, *Uruguay: Nunca más* (Monterideo: SERPAJ, 1989), 111–15, 425–30.
37. Carlos Rodolfo De Luccia, son of Yolanda Iris Casco and Julio César D'Elia, was adopted illegally by Lieutenant (R.) Federico de Luccia and his wife Marta Elvira Leiro, who received the baby from Dr Bergés. The kidnapped child was identified in 1995, when he was 17 years old. The arrest of the three was ordered by Judge Roberto Marquevich in 16 June 1995 (*Página /12* (17 June 1995), 2–3; *Clarín* (22 June 1995); (24 June 1995), 11). This is only one of a series of heart-breaking attempts to identify the kidnapped children and restore their original identity, which in many cases is an impossible task, due to the time lag and the psychological burden for all involved. See for instance Guillermo González, 'Dónde está Simón?', *Brecha*, 16 June 1996.
38. 'Some people in Uruguay look with envy at the other shore [of the River Plate, i.e. Argentina] and ask themselves why Uruguayan civil society did nothing similar in 1993 when it was the 20th anniversary of "our" military coup' (Daniel Gatti, 'Ejercicios de la memoria', *Brecha* (22 Mar. 1996), 31).
39. The anonymous declaration appeared in *Posdata* (Montevideo) (26 Apr. 1996). In the interview they describe the practices of torture and the dismantling of the underground Uruguayan Communist Party. León Lev, leader of the Communist underground in the 1970s, suggested that these declarations, rather than being an expression of remorse, are the result of manœuvres of Military Intelligence as a way to restore the deterring power of the army (interview by Daniel Schwartz, Montevideo, Aug. 1995).
40. Jorge Tróccoli, 'Yo asumo . . . yo acuso', *Brecha* (htpp://www.chasque. apc.org/brecha), 10 May 1996. Tróccoli's letter generated a wide range of reactions, which Radio El Espectador from Montevideo distributed through the internet, 7 May and 17 May 1996. In one of these reactions, former Tupamaro leader and MP for the MPP José Mujica observed that his movement would not apologize, since 'speaking at such an early stage would not contribute to the building of a slow but firm collective trust' (htpp://www.zfm.com/espectador), 17 May 1996.
41. Jorge Néstor Tróccoli, *La ira de Leviatán* (Montevideo: Caelum, 1996).
42. Interview with Senator Rafael Michelini, 'Las fuerzas armadas tienen que dar la cara', *Brecha* (htpp://www.chasque.apc.org/brecha/n566/politica/ html), 10 Oct. 1996.
43. 'Con Oscar Lebel: no hubo guerra sino carnicería', *Brecha* (27 Sept. 1996), 5.

44. Guillermo Waksman, 'Los imperdonables', *Brecha* (27 Sept. 1996), 7; and María Urruzola, 'La mentira de Leviatán', *Brecha* (http://www.chasque.apc.org/brecha/n565/tapa.html), 17 Oct. 1996.
45. Interview with Eleuterio Fernández Huidobro, 'Ellos siguen enfermos', *Brecha* (18 Sept. 1996), 10–11.
46. For an account on the Condor Operation see Keith M. Slack, 'Operation Condor and Human Rights: A Report from Paraguay's Archive of Terror', *Human Rights Quarterly*, 18 (1996), 492–506. See also 'Más plumas del cóndor: quién mató a Juan José Torres?', *Brecha* (http://www.chasque.apc.org/brecha), 31 May 1996. For details of fourteen Uruguayans who disappeared in Argentina, and about whom testimonies existed already in 1976 see *Report of an Amnesty International Mission to Argentina*, 6–15 Nov. 1976, appendix 3–4, pp. 56–72. According to information gathered by Chilean journalist and researcher Juan Pablo Moreno, seventy-nine Chileans were abducted and assassinated in Argentina between 1973 and 1981 (<jmoreno@eclac.cl> Más antecedentes, 14 Oct. 1996). See also *Más allá de las fronteras: estudio sobre las personas ejecutadas o desaparecidas fuera de Chile (1973–1990)* (Santiago: CODEPU-DIT-T, 1996). In the framework of the Condor Operation, a policy of disinformation was launched through 'the appearance of bodies of disappeared Chileans' in Argentina. Under the code name of Operation Colombo, the DINA and Argentinian elements spread the interpretation of an internecine war among Chilean exiles, members of the Movimiento de Izquierda Revolucionario (MIR). The bodies, with counterfeited documents, proved not to belong to the disappeared Chilean victims. See *La gran mentira: el caso de las 'listas de los 119'* (Santiago: CODEPU-DIT-T, 1994), 15–22.
47. Quoted from Hugo Frühling, 'Determinants of Gross Human Rights Violations: The Case of Chile' (Santiago: unpublished manuscript, 1995), 136.
48. 'Proponen en el Brazil crear un "Mercosur de los desaparecidos" ', *Clarín* (7 Aug. 1995), 29. This suggestion had a precedent in the Mothers of Plaza de Mayo being granted access to police archives in Brazil. See 'Madres accederá dentro de pocos días a los archivos de la policía política brasileña', *Madres de Plaza de Mayo*, 84 (Mar. 1992), 21. At the level of governments, there have also been follow-ups, such as the Uruguayan government's request from the Argentinian government for information about 114 Uruguayan nationals who disappeared in Argentina under the PRN ('Uruguay interesó al gobierno argentino por sus desaparacidos', *La nación* (6 May 1995), 4). Similarly, three Argentinian *desaparecidos* were included in an official 1995 document of the Brazilian government detailing 136 disappeared and granting their relatives material reparations of $US100,000 to $US15,000 (Adriana La Rotta, 'Piden que Brazil admita muertes de argentinos', *La Nación* (13 Aug. 1995)).
49. 'Paraguay entregó sus archivos secretos al gobierno argentino', and 'La Operación Cóndor', *Clarín* (15 July 1996), 13. Due to the decades-long anti-Communist position of General Alfredo Stroessner, Paraguay was a locus of this international network of political repression. See also

Esteban Cuyas, 'La operación Cóndor: el terrorismo de estado de alcance internacional' (http://www.derechos.org/koaga/vii/2/cuya.html).

50. Observers have indicated that it was more than coincidence that the Chilean cable systems expunged the programmes of the Argentinian TV station that was to broadcast the trial around the *Prats* case. 'El "Caso Prats" hizo volar a Telefé de Chile', *Página/12* (14 June 1997), 7.

51. Samuel Blixen, 'El avestruz levanta la cabeza', *Brecha* (http://www.chasque.apc.org/brecha), 28 Jan. 1996; and ibid. 28 May 1995.

52. Even General Balza stated time and again that the army has no list of the victims of repression between 1976 and 1983. See *La nación* (1 Apr. 1995), 12.

53. 'Sin comentarios en ambas cancillerías', and 'El ejército chequea capacidad de reacción de sus efectivos', *Búsqueda* (2 Mar. 1987), 7.

54. Polls in *El observador* (21 Oct. 1992), 7; (15 Mar. 1995), 26–7.

55. Interviews with Helios Sartou, senator and university professor of Labour Legislation, 13 July 1995, and Felipe Michelini, member of the lower chamber of Congress, 14 July 1995; personal communication by political scientist Alberto Spektorowski, Montevideo, 14 Aug. 1997. See 'Acuerdo programático del encuentro progresista' (Programme of the Frente Amplio), Montevideo, Aug. 1994; 'El Uruguay entre todos: el Programa 2,000 del Foro Battlista' (Colorado Party) (Montevideo, n.d.); Volonté-Ramos, 'Manos a la obra: cómo hacerlo' (programme of the main *lema* of the Blanco Party), Oct. 1994.

56. Plataforma electoral de la Unión Cívica Radical, Buenos Aires, 1995; Secretaría de Medios y Comunicación, Presidencia de la Nación, 'Aún queda mucho por hacer . . .' (Buenos Aires, 1996); FREPASO, 'Buenos Aires Autónoma, empecemos bien: proyecto de Constitución para la Ciudad Autónoma de Buenos Aires' (Buenos Aires, 1994); id., 'Propuesta de los equipos programáticos' (Buenos Aires, May 1995).

57. Bases programáticas del Segundo Gobierno de la Concertación, 'Un gobierno para los nuevos tiempos' (Santiago, n.d.), 13–16. The latter initiative has not been carried out, prompting the condemnation of Chile by the Interamerican Commission of Human Rights, which demanded swift resolutions of pending cases and the adaptation of local legislation to the American Convention on Human Rights. See 'Informe del Departamento Jurídico de la Fundación de Ayuda Social de las Iglesias Cristianas—FASIC—sobre la Resolución 34/96 de la Comisión Interamericana de Derechos Humanos de la OEA. Santiago, 20 March 1997' (http://www.dereechos.org/nizkor/Chile/fasic/cidh1.html).

58. Revonación Nacional, 'Declaración de principios' (Santiago, n.d.); Unión Democrática Independiente, 'Un programa de gobierno para Chile' (Santiago, Jan. 1993); Partido Unión de Centro Centro, 'fundamentos de la UCC', (Santiago, n.d.); 'Declaración de principios del Partido Demócrata Cristiano de Chile' (Santiago, n.d.); 'Declaración de principios del Partido Social-Demócrata' (Santiago, n.d.); Partido por la Democracia, 'Declaración de principios' (Santiago, Serie Documentos Oficiales, Apr. 1993); 'Resolución del 25 Congreso del Partido Socialista de Chile: agenda programática',

Cuadernos del avión rojo, 4 (autumn 1997), 91–115; 'Programa del Partido Comunista de Chile: XX Congreso Nacional' (Santiago, Aug. 1995).

59. Samuel Blixen, 'Menem y Sanguinetti: las culpas en la nuca', *Brecha*, 17 May 1996 (http://www.derechos.org/nizkor/uruguay/blixe1.html).

60. Corte d'appello di Parigi, *Decisione* (http://www.derechos.org/lidlip/grusol/parigi.html).

61. Marlise Simons, 'Unforgiving Spain Pursues Argentine Killers', *New York Times*, 24 Oct. 1996 <argentina-noticias@beau.math.indiana.edu>; 'Juicio en España', *Microsemanario* (gopher://gopher.uba.ar:70/00/microsem), 247.1 (8–14 July 1996); 'Desaparecidos: España podría pedir extradicciones', *Clarín* (3 July 1996), 17.

62. If extradition is not granted, these cases will not be heard in court, since Spanish law does not contemplate trials *in absentia* of the accused. 'Rechazarán el pedido español', *Clarín* (17 Sept. 1996), 12; and Richard Wilson, 'Spanish Criminal Prosecutions Use International Human Rights Law to Battle Impunity in Chile and Argentina' (http://www.derechos.org/koaga/iii/5/wilson.html).

63. Jorge Ithurburu, 'El juicio por los desaparecidos italianos' (http://www.derechos.org/lidlip/j1.html), 16 June 1996 and 12 Sept. 1997; Lega Italiana per i Diritti e la Liberazione dei Popoli, 'Il caso dei desaparecidos italiani' (http://www.derechos.org/lidlip/grusol/), 10 Nov. 1996. The original proceedings are available at the above site.

64. Uki Goñi, 'El precio de la paz: entrevista con Alicia Pierini' (http://ukinet.com/first/espanol/index.html), 20 Oct. 1996.

65. Equipo Nizkor, 'Familias de desaparecidos de origen alemán iniciarán juicio en Alemania con apoyo de la Iglesia Evangélica' (http://www.derechos.org/nizkor), 24 Aug. 1997; Katya Salazar, 'Habrá justicia para los alemanes desaparecidos en Argentina?' (http://www.desaparecidos.org/arg/coalition), 24 June 1998.

66. The case was first made public in June 1993, causing tensions between President Lacalle and the military and police forces. As a result of the disclosure, the police chief of the Department of Canelones was dismissed. In 1996, Berríos's family was considering bringing the case to the Chilean courts, suing the Uruguayan state. This step would imply extradition of the military involved and would complicate Chilean–Uruguayan relations. The developments in this case are reported in COPESA (http://www.copesa.cl), 2 June 1996, and *El observador* (http://www.zfm.com/observdiario), 16 and 28 May 1996. Interestingly enough, the Chilean right has used the *Berríos* case to attack human-rights organizations for ignoring the infringement of individual rights when those affected are not leftists. See Manuel Fuentes, 'Desaparecidos de segunda clase', *Noticias del mundo* (New York), 16 Aug. 1996.

67. José Miguel Barros, 'Casos Prats y Berríos, al menos para perpetua memoria', *La segunda* (7 Mar. 1996), 9; Roberto Ortiz, 'Los secretos de Arancibia Clavel', *Punto final* (Santiago), 364 (17–30 Mar. 1996), 4–6.

68. Graciela Daleo, 'Arancibia Clavel: dime quién te defiende'. *Mate amargo* (Montevideo) (15 Feb. 1996), 23.

69. Gregorio Dionis, 'Caso Leighton', *Arzobispado de Santiago, fundación documentación y archivo de la Vicaría de la Solidaridad* (http://www.derechos.org/nizkor/chile/informain.html), 18 Nov. 1996.

70. Ibid. In Sept. 1996, the Spanish Socialist PSOE proposed a law requesting the extradition of Chilean nationals that had committed human-rights violations against Spanish citizens. See 'El grupo parlamentario socialista pide la extradicción de los responsables de violaciones de derechos humanos en Chile', http://www.derechos.org/nizkor/chile/juicio/extra.html, 18 Nov. 1996.

71. 'Chile rechaza juicio por los desaparecidos', *El Mercurio* (30 May 1997), 1 and A15, and 'ingerencia indebida', ibid. (7 July 1997), A3. High-ranking figures of former administrations have been protected from being subpoenaed by foreign courts through the use of diplomatic passports awarded to them as they travel abroad; interview with political scientist Ricardo Israel, Santiago, 4 July 1997.

72. 'Estados Unidos apoya a España en su juicio contra Pinochet', *Clarín* (26 June 1997), 34.

73. Iván Cabezas, 'La pregunta del millón de dólares', *La nación semanal* (29 Sept. 1996), 17–22; Juan Pablo Moreno e Iván Cabezas, <jmoreno@eclac.cl>, 'Operación Cóndor y caso Soulman-Pessa', 25 Oct. 1996; Dorrit Saietz, 'Ambassadørens chef waren af kuplederne', and 'Jeg vidste intetom overgrebene', *Det fri aktuelt* (25 Oct. 1996), 18–19.

74. Lord Slynn of Hadley, Lord Lloyd of Berwick, Lord Nicholls of Birkenhead, Lord Steyn, and Lord Hoffmann, *Opinions of the Lords of Appeal in the Cause Regina* v. *Bartle and the Commissioner of Police for the Metropolis and Others (Appellants) ex parte Pinochet (Respondent) (On Appeal from the Divisional Court of the Queens Bench Division); Regina* v. *Evans and Another and the Commissioner of Police for the Metropolis and Others (Appellants) ex parte Pinochet (Respondent) (On Appeal from the Divisional Court of the Queen Bench Division*, London, House of Lords, 25 Nov. 1998.

75. The British Home Secretary, Jack Straw, decided to proceed with the Spanish extradition request. Pinochet's lawyers got a second hearing by the Lord of Appeals after succeeding in disqualifying Lord Hoffman's opinion on grounds of his links with Amnesty International.

CHAPTER 4

1. Alexandra Barahona de Brito, *Human Rights and Democratization in Latin America, Uruguay and Chile* (Oxford: Oxford University Press, 1997), 153.

2. Hugo Frühling, 'Determinants of Gross Human Rights Violations: The Case of Chile' (Santiago: unpublished manuscript, 1995), 191.

3. 'Temuco Missing Person's Case', FBIS-LAT 95-244 (21 Dec. 1995), 34; 'Degollados: las otras condenas', *La tercera* (5 Nov. 1995), 12.

4. '20 respuestas sobre ley 24,321 (desaparición forzada), ley 24,411 (beneficio personas desaparecidas y fallecidas durante la dictadura militar

de 1976–1983)' (Buenos Aires: Ministerio del Interior/ Subsecretaría de derechos humanos y sociales). Flyer distributed to the public in 1994–5. Law 24411 was extended by Law 24499 (1995) for five more years (Subsecretaría de Derechos Humanos y Sociales).

5. Comisión Interamericana de Derechos Humanos, 'Informe 28–92: Argentina' (1992), 42–53.

6. 'Desaparecidos: la pista brasileña', *Clarín*, 30 July 1996 (internet edition). These initiatives were linked to the August 1995 law-project of President Cardoso, which recognized the deaths of 136 prisoners as the result of political persecution under military rule and established criteria for compensation.

7. See Reuter's Jason Webb, 'Ruling to Make Ex-Junta Members Pay for Crimes', 18 Nov. 1994 (transmitted by e-mail).

8. 'Ex-presa política demanda al estado argentino por torturas durante la dictadura', *La juventud* (20 June 1995), C3.

9. 'Indemnizaciones por más de 27 millones a perjudicados durante el régimen militar'. *Búsqueda* (9 Feb. 1989), 7.

10. 'Pensión para familiares de desaparecidos', *Brecha* (14 Aug. 1987), 2. Between 1973 and 1978, 32 Uruguayans disappeared in Uruguay; 127 in Argentina; 3 in Chile; and 2 in Paraguay.

11. Barahona de Brito, *Human Rights and Democratization in Latin America*, 153.

12. Marcelo Pereira, 'Punto de encuentro: indemnización por torturas de la dictadura', *Brecha* (23 June 1989), 10.

13. Interview with Jorge Pan, member of IELSUR, broadcast in Radio El Espectador, Montevideo, 20 May 1996 (http://www.zfm.com/espectador/soni-text/ent20052. htm).

14. 'News Briefs: Uruguay', *Latinamerica Press* (20 Sept. 1991), closing page; SERPAJ, *Informe anual de 1991* (Montevideo: SERPAJ, 1991), 18–19.

15. See Brian Loveman, *The Constitution of Tyranny* (Pittsburgh: University of Pittsburgh Press, 1993).

16. In the aftermath of the pardons, an MP pronounced a phrase that would be reiterated decades later by one of the leading politicians of the opposition to military rule, Wilson Ferreira Aldunate: 'Let them take away everything but the tranquillity of the Republic.'

17. Decree Law 2191, issued on 19 Apr. 1978 (*Diario oficial* No. 30042), covered acts committed between 11 Sept. 1973 and 10 Mar. 1978.

18. In 1992, four Socialist senators tried unsuccessfully to promote legislation to repeal the amnesty law of 1978 (Decree Law 2191), on the grounds that it contradicted the international commitments assumed by the democratic government.

19. 'Menem no vetará la abolición de las leyes de punto final que decidió el Senado', *El País* (Madrid), 8 Apr. 1998.

20. Law 15737 shortened the terms of imprisonment and freed prisoners sentenced for political terrorism. Law 15848 extended an all-inclusive amnesty to the military and members of the security forces implicated in human-rights violations.

21. Based on a series of interviews with: Dr Isaak Frenkel, lawyer and president of CREJ, Santiago, 17 July 1995; Dr Israel Creimer, lawyer and jorunalist, Montevideo, 11 July 1995; Dr Eduardo Rabossi, Professor of Human Rights, Faculty of Law, University of Buenos Aires, former member of CONADEP and first Subsecretary of Human Rights, Buenos Aires, 6 July 1995; and Rabbi Daniel Goldman, member of the Argentinian Permanent Assembly of Human Rights (APDH), Buenos Aires, 10 July 1995.

22. Articles 36 and 29. Roberto Dromi and Eduardo Menem, *La constitución reformada* (Buenos Aires: Ediciones Ciudad Argentina, 1994), 102.

23. Ibid. 466.

24. Ibid. 169–70, 496.

25. Martín Abregú, 'La tramitación de las causas judiciales sobre el derecho a la verdad', in CELS, *Informe anual sobre la situación de los derechos humanos en la Argentina, 1995* (Buenos Aires: CELS, 1996), 119.

26. 'Frei Reform Package Soon', *Latin American Weekly Report* (11 Aug. 1994), 6; 'Dupla castigada', *Qué pasa* (19 Aug. 1995), 16–17.

27. 'Constitutional Reform Proposal', FBIS-LAT-95-213 (3 Nov. 1995), 41–2.

28. 'Frei Strikes "Reform" Deal with Allamand', *Latin American Weekly Report* (16 Nov. 1995), 526.

29. The Chilean model of 'all truth and as much justice as possible' was adopted by President Mandela's government in South Africa in 1996, after consultations with Chilean experts such as José Zalaquett and political leaders such as Patricio Aylwin. In South Africa, the public acknowledgement of torture and political assassinations as a preliminary stage to immunity and pardons did not receive popular endorsement. As detailed evidence of gross human-rights violations comes through, large sectors formerly affected by repression raise mounting protest against pardoning criminals responsible for those crimes. See Marcus Mabry, 'Truth or Justice', *Newsweek* (25 Aug. 1997), 18.

30. Interview with political scientist Ricardo Israel, Santiago, 4 July 1997.

31. The characterizations that follow are based on the reports by the Department of State, *Country Reports on Human Rights Practices* and *Amnesty International Annual Reports* in the 1980s and 1990s. The trends under consideration can be found in other settings of the Americas. In Brazil for decades there has been persistent violation of human rights against the lower strata, portrayed as necessary to fight criminality among marginals. Between January 1996 and July 1997, 1,472 cases of extra-judicial killing by the police were referred by the civilian authorities to the military courts for prosecution. Of these, less than a third were granted court hearings. US Department of State, *Brazil Country Report on Human Rights Practices for 1997* (Washington: Bureau of Democracy, Human Rights and Labor, 30 Jan. 1998), 2 (http://www.brazil.com/report98.htm).

32. This argument was voiced by the Minister of Interior, Carlos Vladimiro Corach, in a public lecture on the state of affairs in Argentina at the Hebrew University of Jerusalem, 27 Mar. 1996.

33. Ariel Delgado, *Agresiones a la prensa, 1991–1994* (Buenos Aires: Madres de Plaza de Mayo, 1995).

34. 'Relator de la ONU acusa casos de tortura en Chile', *El Mercurio* (7 Feb. 1996), A1 and A8. At the time Rodley reported his findings, a legislative proposal on detainees' guarantees was under review in Congress. CODEPU has received a growing number of reports of mistreatment and abuse of detainees by the Carabineros and fewer reports about such acts committed by the other branch of the police, *Investigaciones*. The US Department of State Chile Country Report on Human Rights Practices for 1996 mentions 'a study by Diego Portales University [that] indicates that 71% of detainees interrogated had suffered some form of ill treatment. . . . the Government has taken insufficient action to ensure that the activities of the Carabineros are in accord with the law' (http://www/issues/human_rights/1996_ hrp_report/Chile.html).

35. In 1989, a series of human-rights violations by the police was made public. In one of these cases, Delfor Guillermo Machado, a 31-year-old worker, died in police headquarters. This led to demonstrations and strikes. As a result of protest, Minister of the Interior Francisco Forteza resigned in August 1989, and the police suspended *razzias* in poor neighbourhoods. SERPAJ, *Derechos humanos en Uruguay, informe 1989* (Montevideo: SERPAJ, 1990), 13–14.

36. *Microsemanario* (gopher://gopher.uba.ar:70/11/microsem), Nos. 227–8, 19 Jan.–18 Feb. 1996 and 19–25 Feb. 1996. See also Martín Abregú, 'Contra las apologías del "homicidio uniforme": la violencia policial en Argentina', *Nueva sociedad*, 123 (1993), 68–83. Similar cases of police violence were reported and treated in 1996, as indicated in the US Department of State Argentina Country Report released in Washington on 30 Jan. 1997 (http://www.state:gov/www/global/human rights/1996_hrp_report/argentin.html).

37. See SERPAJ, *Derechos humanos en Uruguay: informe 1992* (Montevideo: SERPAJ, 1992), 23–24; SERPAJ, *Derechos humanos en Uruguay: informe 1994* (Montevideo: SERPAJ, 1994), 26–34.

38. 'State of Siege Decree, Related Events Reported', *FBIS-LAT-85* (28 Oct. 1985), B1–B11.

39. *Argentina: The Attack on the Third Infantry Regiment Barracks at La Tablada* (New York: Amnesty International, 1990).

40. Carlos Ernesto Rodríguez, 'Caso Carrasco: un crimen institucional', and 'Colimbas en el cuartel: historias de muerte joven', *Madres de Plaza de Mayo* (May 1994), 23 and 32.

41. 'Frei pidió a la justicia: rapidez, eficiencia y transparencia', *La segunda* (Santiago) (30 May 1997), 20; 'La tumbra del conscripto'. *La tercera* (Santiago) (6 June 1997), 1; 'Crimen con disfraz de suicidio', *Punto final* (13 June 1997), 6.

42. The Chilean reaction has been less emphatic than the Argentinian. For example, in late May 1997, as the radical left-wing journal *Punto final* published a graphic note on current torture training at the Chilean Marines' School in Reñaca, the revelation had little impact. Only the Association of Families of Disappeared-Detainees (AFDD) sent a dramatic letter reacting to the note. See 'Escuela de torturas de la Armada

Nacional', *Punto final* (30 May 1997), 1–5; and 'Clamando en el desierto', ibid. (13 June 1997), 7.

43. For a comprehensive discussion see Stanley Cohen, *Denial and Acknowledgement: The Impact of Information about Human Rights Violations* (Jerusalem: Center for Human Rights, 1995).
44. 'El 46% de los uruguayos dice ser partidario de la pena de muerte', *El observador* (15 Mar. 1995), 1, 27, and 36.
45. Interview with Israel Creimer, lawyer and law professor, Montevideo, 11 July 1995.
46. Interview with Tomás Lynn, editor of *Búsqueda*, Montevideo, 14 July 1995.
47. Centro de Estudios de la Opinión Pública, 21–2 June 1990, N = 300. Sofía Tiscornia of the Programme on Institutional Violence of the CELS has kindly given us access to the poll data quoted in these paragraphs.
48. Centro de Estudios de la Opinión Pública, telephone poll, 23 Aug. 1996, N = 415; reported also in 'Encuesta exclusiva: más del 85% de la gente dice que no se siente protegida', *Clarín* (http://www.clarin.com), 25 Aug. 1996.
49. Polls by Germano and Giacobese, 11–13 Mar. and 11–13 Aug. 1996, N = unavailable (CELS data).
50. Polls by Graciela Romer and Associates, 11–13 May 1996, N = 510 (CELS data).
51. Centro de Estudios de la Opinión Pública, see n. 48 above.
52. Gabriel Fernández, 'Qué es el ser nacional', *Madres de Plaza de Mayo*, 131 (June 1996), 2.
53. Manuel Antonio Garretón, Marta Lagos, and Roberto Méndez, *Los chilenos y la democracia: la opinión pública, 1991–1994*, i: *Informe 1991* (Santiago: Editorial Participa, 1992), 36.
54. 'DIY Justice versus Sending Troops', *Latin American Special Report*, 97-02, p. 8.
55. Garretón et al., *Los chilenos y la democracia*, iii: *Informe 1993* (Santiago: Editorial Participa, 1994), 107. Issues such as increased participation in governmental decisions, anti-inflationary measures, and protecting freedom of expression did not receive more than 23% as major concerns. Paulina Calleja, 'Encuesta condena a la justicia', *La tercera* (27 Mar. 1997), 5.
56. Poll conducted by Desuc-Copesa, N = 1,931, 11 Apr.–12 May 1997. 'Balance de lo que preocupa a los Chilenos', *La tercera* (6 June 1997), 6–7 and 20.
57. Poll conducted by Estudio Adimark, N = 1,545, 7–25 Mar. 1997, in Calleja, 'Encuesta', 5.
58. *Persona—Derechos humanos—Razonamiento moral* (Buenos Aires: Ministerio de Educación, Materiales de trabajo para la elaboración de los borradores de Contenidos Básicos Comunes para la Educación General Básica, 1994), 2.
59. Ibid. 10. The importance of implementing an interdisciplinary approach to human rights in the classroom has been stressed also by the NGOs in their proposals for educational reforms. See e.g. AMSAFE, 'Los derechos humanos: un contentido transversal', Comisión Directiva Provincial—Sección de derechos humanos, 1996/97, 2nd edn., 6–7.

60. On the first two factors see Adriana Puiggrós, 'World Bank Education Policy: Market Liberalism Meets Ideological Conservatism', *International Journal of Health Services*, 27/2 (1997), 217–26.

61. Ministerio de Cultura y Educación de la Nación, Consejo Federal de Cultura y Educación, *Contenidos básicos comunes para la educación general básica* (Buenos Aires: MCE and CFCE, 1994), 290.

62. 'La formación ética y ciudadana en la escuela', *Zona educativa*, 1/8 (Oct. 1996), 20 and 24.

63. Autores varios, *Manual Esencial Santillana, 5* (Buenos Aires: Ediciones Santillana, 1993), 117 (for 11-year-old children); autores varios, *Manual métodos sexto grado, educación general básica* (Buenos Aires: Editorial Métodos, 1995), 258–9 (for 12-year-old children). Other works along the same lines are the following: autores varios, *Manual Aula Taller 7 grado* (Buenos Aires: Angel Estrada y Cia., 1989); autores varios, *Manual Kapelusz Bonaerense* (Buenos Aires: Kapelusz, 1992); autores varios, *5 manual esencial* (Buenos Aires: Santillana, 1994); Herminia Mérega (ed.), *Manual Bonaerense 7* (Buenos Aires: Santillana, 1987); id. (ed.), *7 manual esencial* (Buenos Aires, Santillana, 1990); and Mario Giannoni (ed), *Aula nueva* (Buenos Aires: Kapelusz, 1995).

64. Torcuato S. Di Tella, *Historia Argentina 1830–1992* (Buenos Aires: Editorial Troquel, 1993); *Historia 3: el mundo contemporáneo* (Buenos Aires: Santillana, 1995).

65. Inés Dussel, Silvia Finocchio, and Silvia Gojman, *Haciendo memoria en el país de Nunca más* (Buenos Aires; Eudeba, 1997). In spite of being priced at $15 in mid-1997, the book's first edition of 3,000 copies sold out and a second edition of 5,000 was published a month later.

66. Communication by Leo Vital <avita@econ.uba.ar>, 6 Nov. 1996.

67. Interview with Carlos Monestez, high-school teacher of literature and social communication, at the tent of the hunger-striking teachers in front of the National Congress in Buenos Aires, 30 June 1997.

68. 'Podrán cortar todas las flores pero nunca detendrán la primavera'. A class presentation given by the Liceo Nueve students to the students of Bet-El, Buenos Aires, June 1996.

69. Consejo de Educación Secundaria, *Programa: educación moral y cívica; introducción a la sociología; introducción al derecho* (Montevideo: CES, 1986).

70. Consejo de Educación Secundaria, *Educación social y cívica: programa del ciclo básico único* (Montevideo, 1993).

71. 'Educación y derechos humanos, cuadernos para docentes: reflexiones y experiencias' (Montevideo: SERPAJ, Issue No. 1, Mar. 1988).

72. Francisco Bustamante and María Luisa González, *Derechos humanos en el aula* (Montevideo: SERPAJ, 1992).

73. Interview in Montevideo, 18 Nov. 1996.

74. Benjamín Nahum, *Manual de historia del Uruguay 1903–1990*, vol. ii (Montevideo: Ediciones de la Banda Oriental, 1991).

75. Carlos Zubillaga and Romeo Pérez, *La democracia atacada* (Montevideo: Ediciones de la Banda Oriental, 1988); Gerardo Caetano and José Rilla,

La era militar (Montevideo: EBO, 1989); José Luis Castagnola and Pablo Mieres, *La ideología política de la dictadura* (Montevideo: EBO, 1989); Danilo Astori, *La política económica de la dictadura* (Montevideo: EBO, 1989).

76. The bibliographical list on human rights, elaborated by the Instituto Hebreo Uruguayo Ariel, includes numerous articles of the Courier of UNESCO together with, among others, Erich Fromm's *Fear of Freedom* and *Represión, exilio y democracia*, edited by Saúl Sosnowski.

77. Humberto Nogueira (ed.), *Manual de educación cívica: educación para la democracia* (Santiago: Editorial Andrés Bello, 1991), 22 and 187–8.

78. Among the former stands out Walterio Millar, *Historia de Chile* (Santiago: Zig-zag, 44th edn. 1987; 1st edn. 1955). Among the latter is Julio Maltés and Concha Cruz, *Historia de Chile* (Santiago: Bibliografía Internacional, 1992). Maltés's and Cruz's textbook follows a neutral line as it analyses the 1973–90 events.

79. Luis Emilio Rojas, *Nueva historia de Chile* (Santiago: Gong Ediciones, 1991).

80. *Informe a su Excelencia el Presidente de la República sobre las actividades desarrolladas al 15 de mayo de 1996* (Santiago: Corporación Nacional de Reparación y Reconciliación, 1996).

81. Autores varios, *Ensayos para la reconciliación* (Santiago: Corporación Nacional de Reparación y Reconciliación, 1994); autores varios, *Nuevos acercamientos a los derechos humanos* (Santiago: Corporación Nacional de Reparación y Reconciliación, 1995).

82. The didactic publications include: Corporación Nacional de Reparación y Reconciliación, *Catálogo de material didáctico para la educación en derechos humanos* (Santiago: Trama Color, 1994); *Para recrear la cultura escolar* (Santiago: Trama Color, 1994); *Perfeccionamiento del docente: tarea permanente para la educación en derechos humanos* (Santiago: Trama Color, 1994); Abraham Magendzo and Claudia Dueñas, *La construcción de una nueva práctica educativa* (Mexico: Comisión Nacional de Derechos Humanos, 1994), 79–102; Abraham Magendzo, *Curriculum: educación para la democracia en la modernidad* (Santiago: PIIE, 1996). SERPAJ has published a guide for seminars on peaceful resolution of conflicts: Fernando Aliaga Rojas, *Educación para la paz: módulos y dinámicas en resolución no violenta de los conflictos* (Santiago: SERPAJ, 1996).

83. Interviews with Cristina Leveratto, Buenos Aires, 4 July 1995; Emilio Mignone, Buenos Aires, 6 July 1995; Hugo Frühling, Santiago, 20 July 1995; Ricardo Changala, Montevideo, 12 July 1995.

84. 'A Culture for Democracy in Latin America', University of Maryland at College Park, June 1996.

CHAPTER 5

1. Ricardo Piglia, 'Los pensadores ventrílocuos', in Raquel Angel, *Rebeldes y domesticados* (Buenos Aires: Ediciones el Cielo por Asalto, 1992), 33.

2. Mark Osiel, 'Ever Again', *University of Pennsylvania Law Review*, 144/2 (1995), 690–1.

3. Juan E. Corradi, 'Towards Societies without Fear', in Juan E. Corradi, Patricia Weiss Fagen, and Manuel A. Garretón (eds.), *Fear at the Edge* (Berkeley and Los Angeles: University of California Press, 1992), 285. Corradi elaborates on the analysis of Otto Kirchheimer, *Political Justice: The Use of Legal Procedure for Political Ends* (Princeton: Princeton University Press, 1961).

4. Uruguayan historian Mónica Marona claims that 'there is no political will to touch anything, which ensures peacefulness between the military and the civilian sectors'. Interview by Daniel Schwartz with Mónica Marona, Montevideo, 19 Sept. 1995.

5. Illustrative of the high levels of mutual cooperation and consultation is the participation of leading figures of the human-rights camp in those official acts paradigmatic of the government policies in this domain. In January 1992, on the occasion of the enactment of the Law of Reparations to the relatives of the victims, which was passed following the recommendations of the Rettig Report, the main speakers were President Aylwin; Enrique Correa, Minister Secretary-General of the government and former secretary of the Rettig Commission; and Sola Sierra, president of the Association of Families of the Detained-Disappeared (AFDD). *Reparaciones a los familiares de las víctimas a que se refiere el informe de la Comisión de Verdad y Reconciliación* (Santiago: Secretaría de Comunicación y Cultura, 1992).

6. Hermógenes Pérez de Arce, lawyer, writer, publicist, and prominent right-wing politician. Santiago, 17 July 1995.

7. Ernesto González Bermejo, 'Las singulares opiniones del ciudadano Medina', *Brecha* (27 Mar. 1987), 3.

8. Carlos María Gutiérrez, 'Una solución "a la uruguaya" ', *Brecha* (24 Apr. 1987), 32.

9. Guillermo Chifflet, 'Poder militar o poder popular', *Brecha* (8 May 1987), 3.

10. 'Uruguay interesó al gobierno argentino por sus desaparecidos', *La Nación* (6 May 1995), 4.

11. Zelmar Lissardy, 'La dirigencia política argentina discrepa entre sí sobre el análisis del referendum', *Búsqueda* (20 Apr. 1989), 11.

12. Hugo Frühling, 'Determinants of Gross Human Rights Violations: The Case of Chile' (Santiago: unpublished manuscript), 196–7. Jorge Correa became the executive secretary of the Commission on Truth and Reconciliation.

13. José Zalaquett, 'Balancing Ethical Imperatives and Political Constraints: The Dilemma of New Democracies Confronting Past Human Rights Violations', *Hastings Law Journal*, 43/6 (1992), 1432.

14. Mauricio Carvallo, 'Lo que no debe hacerse', *El Mercurio* (2 Aug. 1995), D2. Chile's transition to democracy resembled the Brazilian path. In both cases, the process was protracted and the military preserved a tutelary position in the restored democracies. In both countries, the armed forces had enacted self-amnesty laws (in Brazil, in 1979). Differences existed in

the patterns of repression. In Brazil, both during military rule and following redemocratization, human-rights violations had a class-demarcated bias and the extent of them carried out on strict political grounds was statistically negligible when compared with the situation in Chile. In Brazil, a country at least ten times demographically as large as Chile, the number of direct victims of politically motivated torture, forced disappearance, and assassination has been reported to be 333 between 1964 and 1981. The different magnitude of political repression seems to have made Brazil less relevant for Chile as a meaningful model for elaborating public policy in the realm of human-rights violations. On these issues in Brazil see among others Thomas Skidmore, *The Politics of Military Rule in Brazil, 1964–1985* (Oxford: Oxford University Press, 1988); and Amanda Sives, 'Elites' Behavior and Corruption in the Consolidation of Democracy in Brazil', *Parliamentary Affairs*, 46/4 (1993), 549–62.

15. Tulio Halperin Donghi, 'Argentina's Unmastered Past', *Latin American Research Review*, 23 (1988), 23.

16. Interview with Patricia Politzer, Santiago, 18 July 1995.

17. Shirley Christian, 'Timerman, Stranger in Two More Strange Lands', *New York Times* (14 Nov. 1987), 4.

18. *100 primeros decretos-leyes dictados por la Junta de gobierno de la República de Chile* (Santiago: Editorial Jurídica de Chile, 1973), 6–9.

19. Nathaniel C. Nash, 'Pinochet is "My Franco", Chile's Chief Says, Going his Own Way (Carefully)', *New York Times* (30 Apr. 1992), A3. The legal profession is prominent in the political classes of the Southern Cone countries. Many of the presidents and political leaders of Argentina, Chile, and Uruguay were members of the bar and law professors. This added to the constitutionalist tradition of the three countries, shaping a political culture embedded with legal formalism.

20. Declarations by General Odlanier Mena in an interview with Raquel Correa, Malú Sierra, and Elizabeth Subercaseaux, in Jaime Castillo Velasco, *Hubo en Chile violaciones a los derechos humanos? Comentario a las memorias del General Pinochet* (Santiago: Editora Nacional de Derechos Humanos, 1995), 69.

21. 'Las FFAA no se pueden politizar, en ningún caso', *El Mercurio* (27 Nov. 1991), C1 and C8.

22. The attempt to reform the judiciary was opposed by the Supreme Court and the right-wing parties which, together with the designated Senators held a blocking parliamentary minority that defeated the proposed legislation in April 1992.

23. Interview by Lawrence Weschler, *Brecha* (13 Apr. 1989), 17.

24. Interview with Ricardo Changala, co-director of SERPAJ, Montevideo, 12 July 1995.

25. Interview with Atilio Borón, Argentinean political scientist, director of EURAL Research Institute, Buenos Aires, 10 July 1995.

26. Barry Schwartz, 'Vengeance and Forgiveness: The Uses of Beneficence in Social Control', *School Review*, 86/4 (1978), 655–68.

CHAPTER 6

1. James R. Whelan, *Out of the Ashes: Life, Death and Transfiguration of Democracy in Chile, 1833–1988* (Washington: Regney Gateway, 1989), 186.
2. Supporting the government 4,177,064 voted 'yes'. Opposing the government—1,131,115 voted 'no'. Over 250,000 were blank or null votes. Supposedly to assist illiterate voters, the yes option was symbolized by a Chilean flag and the no option by a black flag *1979 Book of the Year, Encyclopaedia Britannica* (Chicago: EB, 1979), 24).
3. According to Marcelo Suárez-Orozco, rationalization provides people living in situations of terror and generalized threats with some sense of false security by invoking the (fallacious) theorem that only those who are involved in subversive activities shall be punished; 'I am not involved . . . ; therefore, I shall not be punished, I need not fear the reports.' Marcelo Suárez-Orozco, 'A Grammar of Terror', in Carolyn Nordstrom and Jo Ann Martin (eds.), *The Paths to Domination, Resistance and Terror* (Berkeley and Los Angeles: University of California Press, 1992), 244.
4. 'Borges: hemos estado viviendo en la época de Rosas', *La nación* (international edition) (19 Aug. 1985), 3.
5. Ariel Dorfman, *La doncella y la muerte* (Buenos Aires: Ediciones de la Flor, 1993), 96.
6. Personal communication, Professor Myrna Solotorevsky, Jerusalem, Oct. 1996. See also 'Sección espectáculos', *La epoca*, 20 Jan. 1994, commenting on the success of the piece when staged abroad.
7. Interview with Beatriz Sarlo, writer and editor of *Punto de vista*, a publication in the field of culture in Argentina, Buenos Aires, 6 July 1995.
8. María de la Luz Hurtado, 'Presencia del teatro chileno durante el gobierno militar', *Cuadernos hispanoamericanos*, 482–3 (1990), 158.
9. Jorge Goldenberg, *Knepp*, Buenos Aires: script provided by the author, 1983.
10. Delia Barrera, Buenos Aires, 4 May 1995. E-mail communication of Aug. 1995, The Vanished Gallery (vanished@yendor.com). The latter site is one in a series of sites in the internet that have become major *lieux de mémoire* in recent years, bringing together testimonies and following up the case of the victims and disappeared to current times.
11. Miguel D'Agostino, File No. 3901. The Vanished Gallery (vanished@yendor.com).
12. Daniel Gil, 'Prólogo: Memorias del horror', in Maren and Marcelo Viñar, *Fracturas de la memoria: crónicas para una memoria por venir* (Montevideo: Trilce, 1993), 6.
13. On the psychological and psychoanalytical dimensions of individual treatment of those affected by the repression see Maren and Marcelo Viñar's *Fracturas de la memoria*; Servicio de Rehabilitación Social, *Intercambio* (Montevideo: Productora Gráfica, 1986); David Becker et al., 'Therapy with Victims of Political Repression in Chile: The Challenge of Social Reparation', *Journal of Social Studies*, 46 (1990), 133–49.

14. See Alexander and Margarete Mitscherlicht, *The Inability to Mourn* (New York: Groove Press, 1975), which focuses on the problem in post-Second World War Germany.
15. Alberto Madrid, 'La escena de la memoria', *Cuadernos hispanoamericanos*, 482–3 (1990), 16.
16. Hugo Vezzeti, 'La memoria y los muertos', *Punto de vista* (Aug. 1994), 4.
17. Pierre Nora, 'Between Memory and History: Les Lieux de mémoire', *Representations*, 26 (1989), 7–25. Other important contributions in this domain are: Michael Schudson, 'The Present in the Past versus the Past in the Present', *Communication*, 11 (1989), 105–13; Yosef Hayim Yerushalmi, *Zakhor* (Seattle: University of Washington Press, 1982); Barry Schwartz, 'The Social Context of Commemoration: A Study in Collective Memory', *Social Forces*, 61 (1982), 374–402; Bernard Lewis, *History Remembered, Recovered, Invented* (New York: Simon & Schuster, 1975); and Maurice Halbwachs's work, especially *The Collective Memory* (New York: Harper & Row, 1980 (c.1951)); Arjun Appadurai, 'The Past as a Scarce Resource', *Man*, 16/1 (1981), 201–19; Jonathan Friedman, 'Myth, History, and Political Identity', *Cultural Anthropology*, 7/2 (1992), 194–210; and Popular Memory Group, 'Popular Memory: Theory, Politics, Method', in R. Johnson et al. (eds.), *Making Histories* (London: Hutchinson, 1991), 205–52.
18. See for instance Zeev Sternhell, Mario Sznajder, and Maia Asheri, *The Birth of Fascist Ideology* (Princeton: Princeton University Press, 1994), 75–6, 117, 194.
19. Graciela Scheines, *Las metáforas del fracaso* (Buenos Aires: Sudamericana, 1993), 180.
20. Ernest Renan perceptively suggested this more than a century ago, in his 1882 lecture at the Sorbonne. See *Che cos'è una nazione?* (Rome: Donzelli Editore, 1993), 7–8.
21. Nora, 'Between Memory and History', 17.
22. The term 'insiles' was used to refer to the intellectuals and members of the opposition who stayed in the country under military rule, thus living in a condition of 'internal exile'.
23. Saúl Sosnowski, 'Introduction', in id. (ed.), *Represión y reconstrucción de una cultura: el caso argentino* (Buenos Aires: Universidad de Buenos Aires, 1984), 7.
24. Interview with Beatriz Sarlo, Buenos Aires, 6 July 1995.
25. Interview with Cristina Leveratto, who collaborated with the CONADEP and later became an officer of the Subsecretariaty of Human Rights, currently at the Ministry of the Interior, Buenos Aires, 4 July 1995.
26. Sosnowski, *Represión y reconstrucción*, 221; Luis Gregorich, 'Literatura: una descripción del campo. Narrativa, periodización, ideología', ibid. 123.
27. Osvaldo Bayer, 'Pequeño recordatorio para un país sin memoria', in Sosnowski, *Represión y reconstrucción*, 203.
28. 'La polémica Bayer-Sábato', *Madres de Plaza de Mayo*, 5 (Mar. 1985), 17. Osvaldo Bayer quoted verbatim statements by Sábato, Borges,

Mujica Lainez, Gregorich, Heker, and others, who made highly positive appreciations of Videla's rule in its beginnings and some of whom had talked, even during the heyday of repression, of the victory in the 1978 Mundial (world soccer championship) as the resurgence of national hope and in terms that strongly discredited the critics of the military government. Carlos Waisman has remarked that it may be difficult to define the extent to which the above levels of verbal attack were due more to matters of substance or to the highly polemical style that has characterized great parts of the Argentinian intelligentsia (personal communication, 5 May 1997).

29. *Tangos: el exilio de Gardel*, directed by Fernando Solanas (Buenos Aires, 1985).
30. Luis Bilbao and David Schapces, 'Dos opiniones divergentes sobre la película de Solanas', *Madres de Plaza de Mayo*, 19 (June 1986), 15.
31. Graciela Fernández Meijide, 'La historia escrita por las víctimas', *Paz y justicia*, Año IV, No. 17, 22.
32. Miguel Bonasso, *Recuerdo de la muerte* (Buenos Aires: Editorial Planeta, 1994; 1st pub. 1983). In a later work of fiction, Bonasso traces the whereabouts of an exiled journalist who returns, obsessed with finding out, after eleven years, whether his detained-disappeared wife had confessed under torture details that could have led to his own and others' detention (*La memoria donde ardía* (Buenos Aires: El Juglar Editores, 1990)).
33. Jacobo Timerman's *Preso sin nombre, celda sin número* (New York: Random House, 1981) (the English version was published under the title *Prisoner without a Name, Cell without a Number* (New York: Alfred Knopf, 1981)).
34. Alipio Paoletti, *Como los nazis, como en Vietnam: los campos de concentración en la Argentina* (Buenos Aires: Edición Cañón Oxidado, 1987).
35. José María Gómez, 'La cuestión de los derechos humanos en una democracia no consolidada', *Punto de vista* (Dec. 1989), 5.
36. Hilda Sábato, 'Historia reciente y memoria colectiva', *Punto de vista* (Aug. 1994), 30–5.
37. Guillermo O'Donnell, *Delegative Democracy* (Notre Dame, Ind.: University of Notre Dame Press, 1991).
38. The structure of the presidential addresses indicates that acts such as the repatriation of Rosas's remains were not a gesture aimed at re-opening debate over historically divisive figures and events, but rather a move aimed at building an image of reconciliation, overcoming historical debate, initiating an era 'beyond history'. In the domain of human-rights violations, Menem has accordingly been accused of leading a policy of 'banalization'.
39. So said Menem in his address as the TV screen was showing nineteenth-century liberal President Sarmiento along with nineteenth-century nationalist Caudillo Rosas with a peace dove bringing them together. The President emphasized his willingness to open an era of synthesis without any type of exclusion. See also Hilda Sábato, 'Olvidar la memoria', *Punto de vista* (Dec. 1989), 8.

40. Eduardo Grüner, in the round table 'Políticas de la memoria', *La Gandhi Argentina* (Apr. 1997), 4.
41. 'La encuesta inolvidable', *Página/30* (Dec. 1994), 7.
42. Interview in Buenos Aires, 4 July 1995.
43. 'La encuesta inolvidable', 7; and Mora y Araujo Noguera Asociados, 'Principal problema del país', survey results from March 1987 to May 1995', information provided by Manuel Mora y Araujo, Buenos Aires, 17 July 1995.
44. Poll by Estudio Graciela Romer y Asociados, *Noticias* (9 July 1995), 42.
45. Poll among 500 persons of both sexes, aged 15–65, residents of Buenos Aires, conducted by CEOP (Centro de Estudios de Opinión Pública), published in *La Revista de Clarín* (7 Aug. 1994), 29.
46. Marina Pianca, 'La política de la dislocación (o retorno a la memoria del futuro)', in Adriana J. Bergero and Fernando Reati (eds.), *Memoria colectiva y políticas de olvido* (Rosario: Beatriz Viterbo Editora, 1997), 131. Pianca relies on an analysis by Juan Jorge Fariña about the psychosocial impact of successive regressive policy stages (Fariña, 'Aspectos psicosociales de la amnesia/amnistía en Argentina: los tres tiempos de exculpación', in Horacio Riquelme (ed.), *Otras realidades, vías de acceso* (Caracas: Nueva Sociedad, 1992)).
47. Meredith H. Montgomery, 'Las Madres: No Guns to Argentina', *Golden Gater* (2 Mar. 1995), 2.
48. 'Editorial: la justicia que tenemos', *Madres de Plaza de Mayo*, 14 (Jan. 1986), 3. The reaction followed the indictment of the heads of the military juntas.
49. 'Editorial: no las hagas, no las temas', *Madres de Plaza de Mayo*, 49 (Jan. 1989), 2.
50. Raquel Angel, 'Sexta marcha de la resistencia: una lucha contra el olvido'. *Madres de Plaza de Mayo*, 26 (Jan. 1987), 10.
51. *Historia de las Madres de Plaza de Mayo* (Buenos Aires: Página/12, 1996); and *Historia de las Abuelas de Plaza de Mayo* (Buenos Aires: Página/12, 1996).
52. Marguerite Guzmán Bouvard, *Revolutionizing Motherhood: The Mothers of the Plaza de Mayo* (Wilmington, Del.: Scholarly Resources, 1993).
53. 'Hebe: seguir el camino de la liberación', *Madres de Plaza de Mayo*, 26 (Jan. 1987), 11. The quotation reproduces verbatim part of the speech of Hebe de Bonafini on the occasion of the sixth March of Resistance, following the promulgation of the Law of Final Point. In contrast, the army has established a Museum of Subversion in one of its main bases, in Campo de Mayo, where mementoes of the Dirty War are kept.
54. Hugo Vezzetti, 'Variaciones sobre la memoria social', *Punto de vista* (Dec. 1996), 2.
55. 'No a las repaciones económicas', *Madres de Plaza de Mayo*, 83 (Jan.–Feb. 1992), 1.
56. In an article in *Punto de vista*, Hugo Vezzeti analyses how such construction of collective memory implies in Argentina a struggle over the historicization of the past ('La memoria y los muertos' (Aug. 1994), 1–5). See Sábato, 'Olvidar', 9.

57. Interview with Dr Eduardo Rabossi, Buenos Aires, 6 July 1995.
58. On the human-rights NGOs see among others Elizabeth Jelin, 'The Politics of Memory: The Human Rights Movements and the Construction of Democracy in Argentina', *Latin American Perspectives*, 21/2 (1994), 38–58.
59. Martín Abregú, the executive director of CELS, has provided a first-hand report of these experiences in 'Democratizando la lucha por los derechos humanos: la difícil relación entre el movimiento de derechos humanos y las instituciones republicanas en la Argentina. Una experiencia de trabajo', paper presented to LASA '97, Guadalajara, 17–19 Apr. 1997.
60. 'Socialismo: la lucha de nuestros hijos sigue vigente', lead article in *Madres de Plaza de Mayo*, 79 (Sept. 1991). For a representative selection see the following: L. Bilbao, 'Reagan prepara la guerra contra Nicaragua', ibid. (Jan. 1986), 3; M. Caiati, 'Colombia: sin palacio ni justicia. Antes del volcán, el terrorismo de estado de Betancur', ibid. (Dec. 1985), 11; E. Marroco, 'Sudáfrica: la vejación de un pueblo', ibid. (Nov. 1985), 16; H. Schiller, 'La masacre de los palestinos, crimen de lesa humanidad', ibid. (Mar. 1988), 16; M. Sanjurjo, 'Hacia nuevas opciones, desde nuestra historia: ecología y luchas campesinas en América Latina', ibid. 120 (June 1995), 14–15.
61. A penetrating analysis of such rejection in the realm of theatre, with reference to Griselda Gambaro's plays, can be found in Jean Graham-Jones, 'De la euforia al desencanto y al vacío: la crisis nacional en el teatro argentino de los '80 y los '90', in Bergero and Reati, *Memoria colectiva*, 253–77.
62. A figure appearing prominently in recent issues of the journal is General Martín Balza, who despite his 1995 democratic statements has been accused by the Mothers and their collaborators of promoting criminal officers within the ranks of the armed forces; of covering up cases of brutalization and assassination of soldiers (as in the case of Omar Carrasco, who died from beatings on 6 Apr. 1994); etc. See for instance Carlos E. Rodríguez, 'Mentiras verdaderas', *Madres de Plaza de Mayo*, 110 (Aug. 1994), 24; and id., 'Con el apoyo de Balza', ibid. 122 (Aug. 1995), 24. General Balza presented a perjury claim against Hebe de Bonafini, after she accused him before an international forum of human rights of being 'a murderer and protector of murderers'. See Leopolodo Brizuela, 'Carta abierta a un juez de la Nación', ibid. 122 (Aug. 1995), 12–13.
63. Nora Veiras, 'Walsh, Nombre Vetado' (http://www.pagina12.com/walsh. htm), 14 Aug. 1997.
64. *Página/12* began publication in 1987. It was a publication that adopted the style of investigative journalism, which was adopted in the 1960s and 1970s by Timerman's publications, *Primera Plana*, *La Opinión*, and by 'research journalists' such as Rodolfo Walsh. In a way unconventional for those years, *La Opinión* spread notes and articles on culture throughout its pages, not confining culture to a special section or supplement. This denotes a strategy of diffusion of culture to a wide public, breaking the former elitist pattern. On the changes in the pattern of cultural diffusion see Jorge Warley, 'Revistas culturales de dos décadas (1970–1990)',

Cuadernos hispanoamericanos, 517–19 (1993), 195–207. Among the cultural publications that have stood out since the 1980s is *Punto de vista*, edited by Beatriz Sarlo.

65. 'Desaparecidos, tema ignorado por una mayoría de jóvenes', *La Nación* (6 May 1995), 4; Eduardo Blaustein, 'La encuesta inolvidable', *Página/30* (La revista mensual de Página/12) (Dec. 1994), Año IV No. 53, 5–36.

66. Interview with Mariano Grondona, Buenos Aires, 4 July 1995.

67. 'Débora Villanueva de H.I.J.O.S.: el exterminio no bastó para silenciarnos', *Madres de Plaza de Mayo*, 132 (July 1996), 13.

68. *Clarín*, 24 Mar. 1996.

69. 'Malestar en el gobierno por el discurso de un jefe militar', *Clarín* (3 Apr. 1996), 6.

70. See 'Masivo repudio al golpe', *Clarín* (25 Mar. 1996), 1; and 'Corach fracasó en su intento de prohibir el acto de las Madres en Plaza de Mayo', *Página/12* (23 Mar. 1996), 1.

71. Daniel Gatti, 'Ejercicios de memoria', *Brecha* (http://www.chasque.apc.org/brecha), 22 Mar. 1996.

72. The most popular phrases that people sang in the stadiums were 'Hay que saltar, hay que saltar, el que no salta es militar' (Let's jump, let's jump. Whoever doesn't jump is a military man); 'Paredón, paredón, a todos los milicos que vendieron la nación' (The [execution] wall, the wall for those military men who sold the nation). Diego Armando Maradona, who organized the minute's silence, declared he would not have pardoned the military: 'Videla goes to the church and the people clap hands. I can't understand this. In what kind of country are we living? This is not my country.' See 'El fútbol también lo rechazó', *Clarín* (25 Mar. 1996), 4.

73. Gatti, 'Ejercicios de memoria'.

74. Worth mentioning among the testimonial literature is Susana Falcón's collection, *20 años: memorias de la impunidad y el olvido, Argentina 1976/1996* (Sevilla: Cromoarte, 1997). See also the collection of essays by Bergero and Reati, *Memoria colectiva y políticas de olvido, Argentina y Uruguay, 1970–1990*.

75. 'A 20 años de la noche de los lápices, miles de estudiantes marcharon', *Clarín* (17 Sept. 1996), 12.

76. *Microsemanario* (gopher://gopher.uba.ar:70/00/microsem), 232 (28 Mar. 1996).

77. Pablo Calvo, 'Juicios por derechos humanos: anticipo de la decisión que tomará esta semana el juez Marquevich', *Clarín* (http://www.clarin.com.ar), 28 June 1998.

78. According to local observers, the move could have been motivated by Marquevich's interest in deflating the chances of being implicated in scandalous cases of judicial corruption. This logic would explain why the judge directed his inquiry into Videla as 'mediate author', rather than into those with direct knowledge of the facts, reaching out eventually to the military hierarchy. See 'Videla utilizado por Marquevich', *La Nación* (international edition) (9–15 June 1998), 2; and Joaquín Morales Solá, 'Un país con más sospechas que certezas', ibid. 3.

79. The possible reaction of the armed forces has been mitigated due to a series of transformations that made the situation in the late 1990s radically different from that of the late 1980s. First, generational shifts left fewer officers in active service who had direct involvement in the repression. Second, the international involvement of 1,500 Argentine officers in the framework of UN peace missions has broken the localist perspective of the military, making them more aware than before of the international salience of human-rights concerns. Third, the military themselves have become increasingly aware that the uprisings of the late 1980s affected the public status and image of the armed forces negatively, as they led to institutional restructuring.

80. Gerardo Young, 'Juicio por derechos humanos...', *Clarín* (http://www.clarin.com), 10 June 1998; Calvo, 'Juicios por derechos humanos'.

81. When human-rights activists decided to paint the exterior of the detention camp known as 'El Olimpo', which now houses the Department for the Verification of Automobiles, Adrian Pelachi, the Federal Police chief, strongly opposed the initiative. He declared that such an action would prompt his resignation, as 'the (police) force feels this is an act of provocation. I am strongly pressured from within the ranks.' The municipal counsellors who belonged to the Radical Union and the Frente Grande suggested at the Buenos Aires Council that El Olimpo should be turned into a 'Museum of Memory'. *Página/12* (22 Mar. 1996), 2.

82. Equipo Nizkor y Derechos Humanos, 'La justicia impide a Menem demoler la ESMA' (http://www.derechos.org/nizkor/inf.html), 23 Jan. 1998.

83. Saúl Sosnowski, 'Desde la otra orilla: la cultura uruguaya', in id. (ed.), *Represión, exilio y democracia: la cultura uruguaya* (Montevideo: Maryland University Press and EBO, 1987), 13.

84. Ibid. 16; and see also pp. 15–20.

85. Eduardo Galeano, 'La dictadura y después: las heridas secretas', in Sosnowski, *Represión, exilio*, 107.

86. 'Caso Roslik: Cronología, I–II–III', *Jaque* (4 May 1984), 2; (11 May 1984), 2; (18 May 1984), 3.

87. The role of the broadcast media and television has been less prominent over the issue of past human-rights violations. La Radio (CX-30) was instrumental during the period of debate of the Law of Expiry. Radio Panamericana (CX-44), close to the line of the MLN, served as a voice for human rights in later years.

88. Ernesto González Bermejo, *Las manos en el fuego* (Montevideo: Ediciones de la Banda Oriental, 1985); Mauricio Rosencof and Eleuterio Fernández Huidobro, *Memorias del calabozo* (Navarra: Txalaparta-Argitaletxea, 1993). The latter book was an editorial success. In a communication, Marisa Ruiz of the University of Maryland mentioned another important testimony, still in manuscript form, by a former political prisoner, María Condenanza, titled *La espera* (personal communication, 9 Sept. 1996).

89. Illustrative is Wladimir Turiansky, *Apuntes contra la desmemoria: recuerdos de la resistencia* (Montevideo: Arca, 1988), and Alfonso Lessa, *Estado de guerra: de la gestación del golpe del '73 a la caída de Bordaberry* (Montevideo: Fin de Siglo, 1996).
90. 'Lo que dijo el Presidente durante los 844 días que duró la campaña electoral', *La República* (17 Apr. 1989), 4; 'Uruguay interesó al gobierno argentino por sus desaparecidos', *La Nación* (6 May 1995), 4.
91. C. Midaglia, *Las formas de acción colectivas en Uruguay* (Montevideo: CIESU, 1992), 00.
92. 'Por los que deberían estar', *Carta SERPAJ* (Nov.–Dec. 1994), 9.
93. Interview by Daniel Schwartz, research assistant in this project, with Amalia Pereira, Hortensia González, Marta Pereira, and Julia Vallejo, Montevideo, 28 Aug. 1995. In May 1996, in the week preceding the March of Silence, mourning ceremonies were held daily at the site and the March itself departed from the piazza.
94. Madres y familiares de detenidos-desaparecidos de Uruguay, *María Victoria Moyano Artigas: la alegría de una niña uruguaya recuperada* (Montevideo: MFDDU, n.d.); Santelices y Dinamarca, *Por los chiquitos que vienen . . .* (Montevideo: MFDDU, n.d.).
95. Carlos Demasi, 'La dictadura militar: un tema pendiente', in Alvaro Rico (ed.), *Uruguay: cuentas pendientes* (Montevideo: Trilce, 1995), 29.
96. Luis Pérez Aguirre, 'Memoria de los detenidos desaparecidos', *Carta SERPAJ* (Nov.–Dec. 1994), 8–9.
97. Hugo Achugar, *La balsa de la medusa* (Montevideo: Trilce, 1992), esp. 37–53.
98. 'Invitación a Michelini genera malestar', *El Observador* (http://www.zfm.com/observdiario), 18 May 1996.
99. 'Discurso de Mermot: Malestar en las fuerzas armadas', *El Observador* (http://www.zfm. com/observdiario), 20 May 1996.
100. In 1997 the SERPAJ produced a CD intended to give voice to those struggling to keep alive the memory of the detainees-disappeared. In contrast with the public use of silence, the motto of *Cantares de la memoria* was to sing 'the history and the pain that cannot be forgiven nor silenced'. Among the contributors to this work were some of the most prominent Uruguayan and Latin American composers and interpreters, e.g. Daniel Viglietti, Chico Buarque, Victor Heredia, Jaime Ross, and the late Alfredo Zitarrosa.
101. Interview by Emiliano Cotelo with Rafael Michelini, broadcast on Radio El Espectador, on 24 May 1996 (http://www.zfm.com/espectador/soni-text/ent2405. htm).
102. 'Tensa situación en Uruguay' (http://www.derechos.org/nizkor/uruguay/doc/zanahoria.html), 22 Apr. 1997.
103. '1997, desaparecidos: un reclamo general!!', *Brecha* (http://www.chasque.apc.org/guifont/ddh2.htm), 21–2 May 1997.
104. Equipo Nizkor, 'Uruguay: el gobierno le pide explicaciones al embajador de Israel sobre declaración del Comité Central Israelita relativa a los

desaparecidos' (http://www.derechos.org/nizkor/press.uru1.html), 26 Dec. 1997.
105. Madrid, 'La escena de la memoria', 15.
106. Interview with Patricio Aylwin, Santiago, 18 July 1995. This policy line was reflected in the Rettig Report, which emphasized in its conclusions 'That "never again" implies as well that what was done to us will not be inflicted on others. In juridical and political terms, this means that the respect for the rights of human beings will be enforced as a foundation for coexistence' (Informe de la Comisión de Verdad y Reconciliación, volume I/2, 876).
107. 'Para que Nunca más: memorial del detenido desaparecido y del ejecutado político' (Santiago de Chile: Cementerio General, Nov. 1994).
108. Lautaro Muñoz, 'Memorial del desaparecido: para que nunca más en Chile . . .', *La Nación* (27 Feb. 1994), 2–3; 'Monumento recuerda a detenidos-desaparecidos', *El Mercurio*, 27 Feb. 1994.
109. 'Allende Reburied in Public Ceremony', *Facts on File, 1990* (New York: Facts on File), 664; FBIS-LAT-90-173, 6 Sept. 1990, pp. 37–8.
110. Manuel Antonio Garretón, Marta Lagos, and Roberto Méndez, *Los chilenos y la democracia: La opinión pública, 1991–1994*, iii: *Informe 1993*, 95, Cuadro 46.
111. 'Los otros septiembres', *El Mercurio* (17 Sept. 1995), D16.
112. 'Pinochet: a qué juega el General?', ibid. D1 and D16.
113. William R. Long, 'Protesters, Police Clash as Chile Marks 1973 Coup', *Los Angeles Times*, 12 Sept. 1992.
114. Malcolm Coad, 'Chile Rocked by Violence', *Le Monde/Guardian*, 19 Sept. 1993.
115. Nathaniel C. Nash, '1973 Coup Still Divides Chile after 3 Years of Civilian Rule', *New York Times*, 12 Sept. 1993.
116. 'Pinochet says Reconciliation Entails Forgetting Past', FBIS-LAT-95-178 (14 Sept. 1995), 41 and 'More on Pinochet's Remarks on Reconciliation', FBIS-LAT-95-179 (15 Sept. 1995), 36.
117. Isabel Allende, *De amor y de sombra* (Mexico: Edivisión, 1986), 226 and 227.
118. Garretón et al., *Los Chilenos y la democracia*, iii: *Informe 1993*, 36.
119. 'Explicaciones del P.C.' (Interview with Jorge Inzunsa), ibid. D19. The protests resulted in the death of a youth and several civilians and Carabineros wounded as well as in the detention of over 160 individuals.
120. Jaime Castillo Velasco, *Hubo en Chile violaciones de derechos humanos? Comentarios a las memorias del General Pinochet*. See esp. 9 and 83–9.
121. The main dailies which worked in this line were *La Epoca* (with left-wing orientation); *La Nación* (owned by the government of Chile); and *El Mercurio* (with right-wing orientation). The weeklies *Apsi, Análisis, Hoy, Qué Pasa*, and *Ercilla* reflected, from left to right, most of the political spectrum. The broadcasting media have played an important role, albeit secondary to the written media, in this respect.

122. Among these are Hernán Valdés's *Tejas verdes* (Barcelona: Ariel, 1974); Alejandro Wilker's *Prisión en Chile* (Mexico City: Fondo de Cultura Económica, 1975); and Aníbal Quijada Cerda's *Cerco de púas* (Havana: Casa de las Américas, 1977)—all published outside Chile.

123. Patricia Politzer, *Fear in Chile: Lives under Pinochet* (New York: Pantheon Books, 1989). The Spanish version was published in Santiago by CESOC in the 1980s, and was reprinted in at least seven editions with over 10,000 copies. Her *La ira de Pedro y los otros* (Santiago: Planeta, 1988) reported on popular protest and repression in the marginal suburbs of Santiago.

124. Patricia Verdugo, *Detenidos-desaparecidos: una herida abierta*, was published in 1980. In the same line followed *André de la Victoria* (1985), *Rodrigo y Carmén Gloria* (1986).

125. Information provided by Patricia Politzer, interview in Santiago, 18 July 1995.

126. Mónica González and Héctor Contreras, *Los secretos del comando conjunto* (Santiago: Ornitorrinco, 1991); Patricia Verdugo and Carmen Hertz, *Operación siglo XX* (Santiago: Ornitorrinco, 1990); *Contreras: la historia de un intocable*. Also of interest is José Cayuela's *Laura Soto: una dama de lila y negro* (Santiago: Planeta, 1991) which relates the story of a leftist Senator as a defender of human rights under military rule. The regional commission for human rights of the Province of Linares organized literary competitions on the theme and published some of them in booklet format (*Toda persona tiene derecho a . . . Concurso de poesía y cuento, 1986–1987: obras premiadas* (Comisión regional de derechos humanos de Linares, 1987)).

127. Ascanio Cavallo, Manuel Salazar, and Oscar Sepúlveda, *La historia oculta del régimen militar* (Santiago: La Epoca, 1988).

128. Claudia Lanzarotti, 'Los tentáculos del terror', *Apsi*, special issue on human rights (Feb. 1991), 16–23; Marcela Torrejón, 'CNI: cuando la represión cambió de nombre', ibid. 24–31; '877 casos', ibid. 32–8.

129. Augusto Pinochet, *El día decisivo: 11 de Septiembre de 1973* (Santiago: Empresa periodística La Nación, 1979); *Pinochet: patria y democracia* (Santiago: Editorial Andrés Bello, 2nd edn. 1985); Raquel Correa and Elizabeth Subercaseaux, *Ego sum Pinochet*.

130. Jaime Guzmán Errázuriz, *Escritos personales* (Santiago: Zig-zag, 3rd edn. 1993); Rosario Errázuriz, *Mi hermano Jaime* (Santiago: VER, 1991).

131. Sergio Marras, *Palabra de soldado* (Santiago: Ornitorrinco, 1989).

132. Milan Ivelic, 'Itinerario de las artes visuales', *Cuadernos hispano-americanos*, 482–483 (1990), 205–24.

133. Madrid, 'La escena de la memoria', 14–15.

134. Raquel Correa, 'Aylwin rompe su silencio', *El mercurio* (6 Aug. 1995), D1, D20.

135. John Davis, 'The Social Relations of the Production of History', in E. Tonkin et al. (eds.), *History and Ethnicity* (London: Routledge, 1989), 104–20.

136. See John Shotter, 'The Social Construction of Remembering and Forgetting', in David Middleton and Derek Edwards (eds.), *Collective Remembering* (Sage: London, 1990), 120–38; and Jonathan Boyarin, 'Space, Time and the Politics of Memory' (Center for Studies of Social Change, SSRC/Mac Arthur Foundation, 1991, MS).

137. See among others Sheldon Wolin, 'Postmodern Politics and the Absence of Myth', *Social Research*, 52/2 (1985), 217–39; and Luis Roniger, 'Globalization as Cultural Vision', *Canadian Review of Sociology and Anthropology*, 32/3 (1995), 259–86.

138. Interview with Hugo Achugar in Montevideo, 13 July 1995. See also Achugar's *La balsa de la medusa* (Montevideo: Trilce, 1992).

139. The Memoria association is led by Luis Jaimovich, father of Alejandra ('disappeared'), and José Hojman, brother of Abraham ('disappeared'). 'Primer bosque plantado en memoria de los desaparecidos argentinos', in L. Senkman and M. Sznajder (eds.), *El legado del autoritarismo* (Buenos Aires: Grupo Editor Latinoamericano, 1995), 365–8.

140. Appadurai, 'The Past as a Scarce Resource'.

CHAPTER 7

1. Shmuel Noah Eisenstadt and Bernhard Giesen, 'The Construction of Collective Identity', *Archives européennes de sociologie*, 36 (1995), 72–102. See also Ana María Alonso, 'The Politics of Space, Time and Substance: State Formation, Nationalism, and Ethnicity', *Annual Review of Anthropology*, 23 (1994), 379–405; and Kay B. Warren, 'Transforming Memories and Histories: The Meanings of Ethnic Resurgence for Mayan Indians', in Alfred Stepan (ed.), *Americas: New Interpretive Essays* (Oxford: Oxford University Press, 1992), 189–219.

2. E. Bradford Burns, 'Cultures in Conflict: The Implications of Modernization in the 19th Century', in V. Berhard (ed.), *Elites, Masses and Modernization in Latin America* (Austin: University of Texas Press, 1979); Hilda Sábato, 'Citizenship, Participation, and the Formation of the Public Sphere in Buenos Aires, 1850s–1880s', *Past and Present*, 136 (1992), 139–63; and Francois-Xavier Guerra and Mónica Quijada (eds.), *Imaginar la nación* (Hamburg: LIT Verlag, 1994).

3. Benedict Anderson, *Imagined Communities* (New York: Verso, 1991; 1st pub. *c*.1983), and see also Ana María Alonso, 'The Effects of Truth: Representations of the Past and the Imagining of Community', *Journal of Historical Sociology*, 1/1 (1988), 33–57.

4. Juan José Linz, 'Totalitarianism and Authoritarianism', in Fred Greenstein and Nelson Polsby (eds.), *Handbook of Political Science* (Reading, Mass.: Addison-Wesley, 1975), iii. 175–411; Ruth Berins Collier and David Collier, *Shaping the Political Arena* (Princeton: Princeton University Press, 1990); Guillermo O'Donnell, *Bureaucratic-Authoritarianism:*

Argentina, 1966–1973 (Berkeley and Los Angeles: University of California Press, 1988).

5. On the interplay of intellectuals and the political realm see François Bourricaud, 'The Adventures of Ariel', *Daedalus* (summer 1972), 109–36; W. S. Stokes, 'The Pensadores of Latin America', in G. B. de Huszar (ed.), *The Intellectuals: A Controversial Portrait* (Glencoe, Ill.: Free Press, 1960), 422–9; and Raquel Angel, *Rebeldes y domesticados: los intelectuales frente al poder* (Buenos Aires: El cielo por asalto, 1992).

6. Graciela Fernández Meijide, 'La historia vista por las víctimas', *Paz y justicia* (1989), Año IV, No. 17, 22.

7. Tulio Halperin Donghi, 'Argentina's Unmastered Past', *Latin American Research Review*, 23 (1988), 3–4.

8. Juan E. Corradi, *The Fitful Republic: Economy, Society and Politics in Argentina* (Boulder, Colo.: Westview Press, 1985), 91.

9. Gabriel Salazar, 'Historiografía y dictadura en Chile, 1973–1990', *Cuadernos hispanoamericanos*, 482–3 (1990), 81–94.

10. José Joaquín Brunner, 'La intelligentsia: escenarios institucionales y universos ideológicos', *Proposiciones*, 18 (1990), 181–2.

11. See Néstor Campiglia, *El Uruguay movilizado* (Montevideo: Editorial Girón, 1971).

12. Carlos Martínez Montero, 'Crepúsculo en Arcadia', in *Uruguay hoy* (Buenos Aires; Siglo XXI, 1971), 444.

13. Angel Rama, 'La generación crítica (1939–1969)', in *Uruguay hoy*, 347–8. The entire article (pp. 325–402) is a most comprehensive analysis of that intellectual generation.

14. Mario Benedetti, 'Rebelión de los amanuenses', in id., *El país de la cola de paja* (Montevideo: Arca, 8th edn. 1970), 56 (1st pub. 1960).

15. Fernando Andatch, *Signos reales del Uruguay imaginario* (Montevideo: Trilce, 1992).

16. Jean Franco, *The Modern Culture of Latin America: Society and the Artist* (Harmondsworth: Penguin, 1970; 1st pub. c.1967), 311.

17. Eduardo Galeano, *La venas abiertas de América Latina* (Montevideo: Ediciones del Chanchito, 1987; 1st pub. c.1970), 435–6.

18. Ana Pizarro, *De ostras y caníbales: ensayos sobre la cultura latino-americana* (Santiago: Editorial Universidad de Santiago, 1994), 173.

19. Gonzalo Vial Correa, 'Otros rasgos históricos de la derecha', *La segunda* (Santiago), 27 Feb. 1966.

20. Paradigmatic is Skármeta's *Soñé que la nieve ardía* (Barcelona: Planeta, 1975) and the closing scenes of *Ardiente paciencia* (Madrid: Plaza y Janés, 1986), in which security forces detained Mario Jiménez, the young mailman of Isla Negra who delivered Pablo Neruda's mail. The latter book was originally the script for a Chilean film (1983) and later served as script for the internationally acclaimed Italian film *Il postino*.

21. Claudio Grossman, 'States of Emergency: Latin America and the United States', in Louis Henkin and Albert J. Rosenthal (eds.), *Constitutionalism and Rights* (New York: Columbia University Press, 1990), 185–6.

22. *La república perdida* (1984). The narrator is renowned poet María Elena Walsh.

23. Interview with Adriana Puiggrós, Professor of Education at the University of Buenos Aires and MP of the FREPASO in Buenos Aires, 7 July 1997. According to Puiggrós, this theory was used to free the redemocratized society from any serious search for historical understanding and from deep soul-searching.
24. Tulio Halperin Donghi, 'Argentina's Unmastered Past', *Latin American Research Review*, 23 (1988), 15.
25. Jeffrey C. Alexander and Philip Smith, 'The Discourse of American Civil Society: A New Proposal for Cultural Studies', *Theory and Society*, 22/2 (1993), 156.
26. Jorge Edwards, himself a member of a patrician family and a leftist intellectual, went into exile. *Los convidados de piedra* (Barcelona: Seix Barral, 1978). See also Teresa Cajiao Salas, 'Algunas consideraciones sobre la narrativa chilena en el exilio', *Cuadernos hispanoamericanos*, 372 (1981), 600–15.
27. Marco de la Parra, *La secreta obscenidad de cada día* (Santiago: Planeta, 1988); Juan Radrigan, *La contienda humana* (Santiago: Ediciones Literatura Alternativa, 1989).
28. Diamela Eltit, *The Fourth World*, trans. and with foreword by Dick Gerdes (Lincoln: University of Nebraska Press, 1995; 1st pub. 1988).
29. David Viñas, *Cuerpo a cuerpo* (Mexico: Siglo XXI, 1979); Enrique Medina, *Las muecas del miedo* (Buenos Aires: Editorial Galerna, 1981).
30. While Viñas's book was published abroad, Medina's appeared in Buenos Aires. Two previous books by Medina had been forbidden by the censors for their sexual crudity. To the surprise of the author, no action was taken against his new book. In an interview, Medina indicated that 'personally, with two proscribed books, I should have taken the trouble to write a more metaphoric book and say the same but in a different way', 'Enrique Medina y las Muecas del miedo, un reportaje de Roxana Morduchowicz', *Nueva presencia*, 6 Nov. 1981. We are grateful to Florinda Goldberg for this material.
31. Juan José Saer, another leading writer, traces as well in a non-fictional book the 'informal history' of such tradition of violence in the Río de la Plata, attributing it to the heritage of (Western) civilization in the region (*El río sin orillas* (Buenos Aires: Alianza, 1991), 159). He criticizes Borges's and other leading intellectuals' fascination with violence, e.g. in their writings on the local rogues (*compadritos* and *cuchilleros*).
32. Ricardo Piglia, 'Viñas y la violencia oligárquica', from *La Argentina en pedazos* (Buenos Aires: Ediciones de la Flor, 1993). Internet communication (http://lenti.med.umn.edu/~ernesto/viñas/viñas por piglia.html).
33. Luis Alberto Romero, 'La utopía y el drama', *Clarín* (13 Oct. 1996), 4.
34. Ricardo Piglia, *Respiración artificial* (Buenos Aires: Editorial Pomaire, 1980), 63.
35. Julio Huasi, 'Junio, un mes trágico en la Argentina: la patria asesinada', *Madres de Plaza de Mayo*, 7 (June 1985), 8.
36. Piglia, *Respiración artificial*, 109.
37. Carina Perelli and Juan Rial, *De mitos y memorias políticas* (Montevideo: Ediciones de la Banda Oriental, 1986), 21–8; Gerardo Caetano and

Milita Alfaro, *Historias del Uruguay contemporáneo* (Montevideo: FCU, 1995), 185–95.

38. Jorge Ruffinelli, 'Uruguay, dictadura y redemocratización: un informe sobre la literatura, 1973–1989', *Nuevo texto crítico*, 5 (1990), 50–2.

39. Manuel Flores Mora, '1973 y 1904: cómo terminar una guerra', *Jaque* (13 Apr. 1984), 24. On 9 Feb. 1973 President Bordaberry delegated part of his powers to the armed forces, and the latter deployed troops and armoured vehicles in the streets of Montevideo as a demonstration of force. Cagancha was the main Colorado victory in the civil wars of Uruguay between Blancos and Colorados; peace was achieved only on 8 Oct. 1850.

40. Ibid.

41. 'Es necesaria la amnistía?', *Jaque* (25 Nov. 1983), 9.

42. Interview with Eber Gatto, lawyer and politician, Montevideo, 13 July 1995.

43. Tomás de Mattos, *Bernabé! Bernabé!* (Montevideo: Ediciones de la Banda Oriental, 1988).

44. Abril Trigo, *Caudillo, estado, nación: literatura, historia e ideología en el Uruguay* (Gaithersburg, Md.: Hispamérica, 1990), 202.

45. Ibid. 221–2.

46. From a speech of Rear-Admiral Sansurjo on 23 Sept. 1977, published in *El soldado*, 29 (Sept. 1977), 7 from Trigo, *Caudillo, estado, nación*, 217.

47. Trigo, *Caudillo, estado, nación*, 232.

48. Mattos, *Bernabé, Bernabé!*, 155–6.

49. Hugo Achugar, 'Como el Uruguay no hay. Bernabé! Bernabé! y el referéndum', *Cuadernos de marcha*, 41 (Feb. 1989), 61–4.

50. Hugo Achugar, 'El Parnaso', in id., *La biblioteca en ruinas* (Montevideo: Trilce, 1994), 99.

51. Carlos Demasi, 'La dictadura militar: un tema pendiente', in Alvaro Rico (ed.), *Uruguay: las cuentas pendientes* (Montevideo: Trilce, 1995).

52. As early as 1973 there were politicians and public figures who compared the ongoing military salience with previous dictatorial situations. See Omar Prego, *Reportaje a un golpe de estado* (Montevideo: La República Ediciones, 1988), 30.

53. Rico, *Uruguay: cuentas pendientes* Hugo Achugar and Gerardo Caetano (eds.), *Identidad uruguaya: mito, crisis o afirmación* (Montevideo: Trilce, 1992); Carina Perelli and Juan Rial, *De mitos y memorias políticas*.

54. This was the day authoritarian rule was installed with the support of the military by President Bordaberry, who dissolved the Parliament.

55. For instance, former President Bordaberry referred recently to 'democracy and those other fictions born out of human arrogance'. See 'La dictadura como tema cultural: Memorias de hace un rato', *El País* (http://www.web2mil.com/el país/noticias. htm), 15 Sept. 1996.

56. Augusto Pinochet, 'Clase magistral en la Universidad de Chile', Santiago, 6 Apr. 1979, in *Pinochet: patria y democracia*, 229.

57. Arturo Fontaine, 'Ideas nacionalistas chilenas', in Enrique Campos Menéndez (ed.), *Pensamiento nacionalista* (Santiago: Editora Nacional Grabiela Mistral, 1974), 239–40.

58. José Bengoa, *Historia del pueblo mapuche* (Santiago: Ediciones Sur, 1991: 1st pub. *c*.1985), 5.

59. Jaime Guzmán, 'Mártir para la paz social', in *Jaime Guzmán: su legado humano y político* (Santiago: Ercilla, 1991), 87–8.

60. Fundación Jaime Guzmán, *Los derechos humanos en el pensamiento de Jaime Guzmán Errázuriz* (Santiago: FJG, 1994), serie Documentos No. 7.

61. Jaime Guzmán Errázuriz, *Escritos personales* (Santiago: Zig-Zag, 3rd edn. 1993; 1st pub. *c*.1992), 150–1.

62. A flurry of journalistic articles, interviews, round tables, and essays were published in Sept. 1995. Cf. 'Eramos felices y sin desaparecidos', *Punto final*, 3–16 Sept. 1995; 'Golpe al corazón del pueblo', *El siglo*, 9–15 Sept. 1995; and 'A 25 años de la UP', *La Segunda*, 4 Sept. 1995.

63. 'Moulian: experiencia de la UP era inviable', *La Epoca* (3 Sept. 1995), 12–13.

64. 'Godoy: la derecha cometió muchos errores', *La Epoca* (4 Sept. 1995), 10–11.

65. Isabel Allende, *The House of the Spirits* (New York: Alfred A. Knopf, 1985), 367 (Spanish original: *Las casa de los espíritus* (Barcelona: Plaza y Janes, 17th edn. 1985 (1st edn. *c*.1982), 379).

66. Ibid. 367–8.

67. Ricardo García, 'Cantar de nuevo', *Cuadernos hispanoamericanos*, 482–3 (1990), 197–202; Alberto Martins, 'Popular Music as Alternative Communication: Uruguay, 1973–1982', *Popular Music*, 7 (1987), 77–95; Leo Masliah, 'La música popular, censura y represión', in Sosnowski, *Represión, exilio y democracia*, 113–24.

68. Poetry was a major channel for expression. Chilean poetry during the military period has been illustrative, as it dealt with the themes of exclusion, disencounter, wounds, and suffering, and longing for home and the lost past figure prominently. See Sandra Reyes (ed. and trans.), *One More Stripe to the Tiger* (Fayetteville: University of Arkansas Press, 1989). On narrative see Mario Osser, 'Nosotros, los finiseculares', *Cuadernos hispanoamericanos*, 482–3 (1990), 137–48; Cajiao Salas, 'Algunas consideraciones sobre la narrative chilena en el exilio', 600–19; and Selena Millares, 'Ultima narrativa chilena: la escritura del desencanto', ibid. 113–22.

69. Carlos Guzmán, *La frontera* (Chile, 1991); Fernando Solanas, *Sur* (Argentina, 1988); Héctor Olivera, *La noche de los lápices* (Argentina, 1986); Sergio Bitar, *Isla 10* (Santiago: Pehuén, 1987); Luis Vega, *La caída de Allende: anatomía de un golpe de estado* (Jerusalem: La Semana Publicaciones, 1983); Mauricio Rosencof and Eleuterio Fernández Huidobro, *Memorias del calabozo* (Navarra: Txalaparta-Argitaletxea, 1993).

70. Mario Benedetti, *Pedro y el capitán* (Mexico City: Editorial Nueva Imagen, 1979). The books by Benedetti, together with some of the works by Julio Cortázar, Antonio Machado, and others were prohibited in Uruguay under the dictatorship.

71. Nelson Marra, 'El guardaespalda', *Marcha*, 1671 (8 Feb. 1974); id., *El guardaespalda y otros cuentos* (Stockholm: Nordan, 1981).

72. For example in Vargas Llosa's *Conversación en la catedral*, in which the chauffeur has sex with his master, a respected elite politician, or in David Viñas's *Cuerpo a cuerpo* and Isabel Allende's *La casa de los espíritus*, analysed above.

73. Interview with María Inés Olivella, Buenos Aires, 16 July 1995.

74. Fernando Aínsa, *De aquí y de allá: juegos a la distancia* (Montevideo: Ediciones del Mirador, 1986), 79–80.

75. Fernando Aínsa, *Con acento extranjero* (Buenos Aires: Nordan Comunidad, 1984); Patricia Politzer, *Altamirano* (Buenos Aires: Grupo Editorial Zeta, 1989); Carlos Prats González, *Memorias: Testimonio de un soldado* (Santiago: Pehuén, 1987; 1st pub. *c*.1985); Fernando Solanas, *Tangos: el exilio de Gardel* (Argentina, 1985); José Rodríguez Elizondo, *La pasión de Iñaki* (Santiago: Editorial Andrés Bello, 1996).

76. One of the works that describe these realities is Antonio Skármeta's most recent book, *No pasó nada*, which portrays the milieux of Chilean exiles in Germany. Antonio Skármeta, *No pasó nada* (Barcelona: Plaza y Janés, 1996). See 'Exilio, gran asunto literario', *Copesa* (http://www.copesa.cl), 97 (18–25 Sept. 1996).

77. Alicia Steimberg, 'Cecilia's Last Will and Testament', in Marjorie Agosin (ed.), *Landscapes of a New Land: Short Fiction by Latin American Women* (Buffalo: White Pine Press, 1989), 102–11; cited from 111.

78. Among the more influential have been Joseph Page, *Peron: A Biography* (New York: Random House, 1983); Frederick C. Turner and José Enrique Miguens (eds.), *Juan Peron and the Reshaping of Argentina* (Pittsburgh: University of Pittsburgh Press, 1983); and Tulio Halperin Donghi, *Argentina: la democracia de masas* (Buenos Aires: Paidós, 1986).

79. Halperin Donghi, 'Argentina's Unmastered Past', 22.

80. Tomás Eloy Martínez, *La novela de Perón* (Buenos Aires: Legasa, 1985).

81. Fernando E. Solanas, 'Le sud', *L'avant scène cinema*, 377–8 (1989), 118.

82. Ibid. 124.

83. Alberto Ciria, 'Variaciones sobre la historia argentina en el teatro de Roberto Cossa', *Revista Canadiense de estudios hispánicos*, 18/3 (1994), 445–53. One of the more recent essays in this line is the inspiring cultural analysis of Graciela Scheines, *Las metáforas del fracaso* (Buenos Aires: Sudamericana, 1993).

84. Roberto Cossa, 'Los compadritos' (1985), in *Teatro 4* (Buenos Aires: Ediciones de la Flor, 1991), 123–203. There are other, more direct treatments of the military repression in Cossa's work. Thus, *El sur y después* is probably the most personal and direct allusion to the period of repression; in the piece, a batallion of soldiers successively shoots four women who voice different ideological positions, covering the spectrum from anarchism to Peronism. See 'El sur y después', in *Teatro 3* (Buenos Aires: Ediciones de la Flor, 1990), 243–300.

85. Piglia, *Respiración artificial*, passim and esp. 214–22.

86. Matilde Sánchez, 'ERP y los Montoneros', *Clarín* (13 Oct. 1996), 7.

87. Tomás Eloy Martínez, 'A Culture of Barbarism', in Colin M. Lewis and Nissa Torrents (eds.), *Argentina in the Crisis Years (1983–1990): From*

Alfonsín to Menem (London: Institute of Latin American Studies, 1993), 18.

88. 'El gobierno de Chile avanza con seguridad y sin vacilaciones' (Pinochet's presidential message on the first anniversary of the coup), *El Mercurio* (12 Sept. 1974), 2.

89. *Pinochet: patria y democracia*, 251 (from an interview with *La Tercera de la hora*, 8 Mar. 1981).

90. 'Texto del discurso de S. E.', *El Mercurio* (12 Sept. 1989), C7–C8.

91. Joaquín Lavín, *Chile: revolución silenciosa* (Santiago: Zig-Zag, 1987), 24–6; in the first twelve weeks of its promotion, the book sold 67,000 copies.

92. María Angélica Bulnes, 'José Piñera: dar un golpe de timón, crear esquemas nuevos . . .', *Qué Pasa* (27 Dec. 1979), 6–11; *Objetivo nacional del gobierno de Chile* (Santiago: Impresora Filadelfia, 1975), esp. 19–31.

93. This article was reformed, under democracy, to allow the recreation of political pluralism. *Constitución política de la República de Chile* (Santiago: Publiley, 1989), 10–11; Carlos A. González Moya, *54 reformas a la constitución política de Chile* (Santiago: Publiley, 1989), 4.

94. Jaime Esteves, Socialist MP, in Nathaniel C. Nash, '1973 Coup Still Divides Chile after 3 Years of Civilian Rule', *New York Times*, 12 Sept. 1993.

95. Pilar Vergara, *Auge y caída del neoliberalismo en Chile* (Santiago: FLACSO, 1985), 260.

96. Interview with Ricardo Israel, director of the School of Political Science of the University of Chile, Santiago, 19 July 1995.

97. Manuel Antonio Garretón, *Hacia una nueva era política* (Santiago: Fondo de Cultura Económica, 1995), 150–2.

98. Interview with Hugo Frühling, human-rights activist and researcher, former member of the 'Group of the 24' and adviser at the Ministry of Internal Affairs, Santiago, 20 July 1995. Journalist and TV anchorperson Patricia Politzer too is of the opinion that 'social solidarity has been reduced to zero'. Interview, Santiago, 18 July 1995.

99. Among the latter are Prego ('Desde el exilio', 'Solo para exiliados') and Aínsa ('Con acento extranjero').

100. Jorge Ruffinelli, 'Uruguay y redemocratización', *Nuevo Texto Crítico*, 5 (1990), 50–2; id., 'La crítica y los estudios literarios en el Uruguay de la dictadura (1973–1984)', *Hispamérica*, 56–7 (1991), 21–9.

101. Teresa Porzecanski considers that some of these genres represented an attempt to capture the tragic and paradoxical aspects of the new institutional setting, subverting the conventional line of the official epigones and talking less in terms of the 'good' and 'bad' characters, and more about the shortcomings and partiality of the order and routine that authoritarianism strives to. Already in the 1960s there were some initial works in this line, even though their significance and impact was more restricted to the literary domain. See Porzecanski, 'Ficción y fricción de la narrativa de imaginación escrita dentro de fronteras', in Sosnowski, *Represión, exilio y democracia*, 221–30.

102. Martins, 'Popular Music as Alternative Communication: Uruguay 1973–82', 77–89; Leo Masliah, 'La música popular'.
103. Abril Trigo, 'Rockeros y grafiteros: la construcción al sesgo de una anti-memoria', in Adriana J. Bergero and Fernando Reati (eds.), *Memoria colectiva y política de olvido: Argentina y Uruguay, 1970–1990* (Buenos Aires: Beatriz Viterbo, 1997), 305–34.
104. Hugo Achugar, *La balsa de la medusa*, 47.
105. Roos combines motifs of various genres (i.e. tango, candombe, murga, and rock) in an eclectic style which has been highly appreciated in recent years.
106. 'El día en que Artigas se emborrachó', *Revista tres*, 18 Oct. 1996; 'El primer oriental desertor', Mario Vila Oliveros <mariovi@adinet.com.uy>, 29 Oct. 1996; 'El poder de la música' (http://www.chasque.apc.org/becha/cuarteto.htr), 4 Nov. 1996.
107. Achugar, *La balsa de la medusa*, 109.
108. Hugo Achugar, 'Transformaciones culturales en el Uruguay del fin de siglo', *Hispamérica*, 20 (1991), 44.
109. David Viñas, 'Las astucias de las servidumbre', in Raquel Angel, *Rebeldes y domesticados: los intelectuales frente al poder* (Buenos Aires: Ediciones El Cielo por Asalto, 1992), 56. In the same vein, Florinda Goldberg claims that contemporary Southern Cone literature reflects 'a loss of faith in political solutions and a move toward individual adventure, personal adventure, . . . posing conflicts at an individual level, without promising any vision of future, . . . the social contents disappear'. Interview in Jerusalem, 16 June 1995.
110. Jean Graham-Jones, 'De la euforia al desencanto y avacío: la crisis nacional en el teatro argentino de los '80 y los '90', in Bergero and Reati, *Memoria colectiva y política de olvido*, 253–77.
111. Jean Franco, 'Latin American Intellectuals and Collective Identity', in Luis Roniger and Mario Sznajder (eds.), *Constructing Collective Identities and Shaping Public Spheres: Latin American Paths* (Brighton: Sussex Academic Press, 1998), 231; Franco refers to: Beatriz Sarlo, *Escenas de la vida posmoderna* (Buenos Aires: Ariel, 1994).
112. *Malajunta*, 76 (1996).
113. Lita Stantic, *Un muro de silencio* (Argentina, 1993).
114. León Rozitchner, 'El terror de los desencantados', in Angel, *Rebeldes y domesticados*, 42–5.
115. Achugar, 'Transformaciones culturales en el Uruguay de fin de siglo', 37–47; Ruffinelli, 'Uruguay, dictadura y redemocratización', 57–8; Ronaldo Munck, 'After the Transition: Democratic Disenchantment in Latin America', *European Review of Latin American and Caribbean Studies*, 55 (1993), 7–19. According to political scientist Atilio Borón, a process has occurred of universal degradation of political culture, a process of emptying of political substance, of impoverishment of politics. Interview with Atilio Borón, Buenos Aires, 10 July 1995. On this trend see also María de los Angeles Yannuzzi, 'Identidad, política y crisis: las experiencias canadiense y argentina', in Mario Rapoport (ed.), *Globalización, integración e identidad nacional* (Buenos Aires: Grupo Editor Latinoamericano, 1995), 333–51.

116. Interview with Florinda Goldberg. Jerusalem, 16 June 1995, and id., 'Patterns of Jewish Plight in Argentinean Fiction of the Catastrophe', unpublished paper, Apr. 1995. The 'Holocaust line', to which Goldberg alludes, is illustrated by Beatriz Sarlo, 'La historia contra el olvido', *Punto de vista*, 36 (Dec. 1989), 11–13; and Raúl Beceyro, 'Los límites: sobre la lista de Schindler', ibid. 49 (Aug. 1994), 11–15.

117. On the *Historikerstreit* and the writings of the historians cited see *Forever in the Shadow of Hitler?*, trans. James Knowlton and Truett Cates (New Jersey: Humanities Press, 1994). See also Saul Friedlander (ed.), *Probing the Limits of Representation* (Cambridge, Mass.: Harvard University Press, 1992); and Charles S. Maier, *The Unmasterable Past* (Cambridge, Mass.: Harvard University Press, 1988). On the specific politics of memory in Germany see also Jeffrey K. Olick and Daniel Levy, 'Collective Memory and Cultural Constraint: Holocaust Myth and Rationality in German Politics', *American Sociological Review*, 62 (1997), 921–34.

118. Ralf Dahrendorf, 'After the Twentieth Century: What Role for Liberalism?', paper presented to the Conference in Honour of Shlomo Avineri, on the Impact of Ideas on Twentieth Century History, Hebrew University of Jerusalem, 16 Dec. 1996.

CONCLUSIONS

1. Michael Walzer, *Thick and Thin: Moral Arguments at Home and Abroad* (Notre Dame, Ind.: University of Notre Dame Press, 1994), 1 and 6.

2. Diana Kordon, Lucila Edelman, Darío Lagos, Daniel Kersner, et al., *La impunidad: una perspectiva psicosocial y clínica* (Buenos Aires: Sudamericana, 1995), 21–2.

Select Bibliography

This bibliography includes the books, book chapters, academic articles and contributions in cultural journals used in the book. No mention is made here of the interviews, primary sources and documents, web materials and communications, laws, films, newspaper articles and other media sources used, which are indicated in the notes above.

ABREGÚ, MARTÍN, 'Contra las apologías del "homicidio uniforme": La violencia policial en Argentina', *Nueva Sociedad*, 123 (1993), 68–83.

—— 'La tramitación de las causas judiciales sobre el derecho a la verdad', in CELS, *Informe anual sobre la situación de los derechos humanos en la Argentina, 1995* (Buenos Aires: CELS, 1996), 85–122.

—— 'Democratizando la lucha por los derechos humanos: la difícil relación entre el movimiento de derechos humanos y las instituciones republicanas en la Argentina: una experiencia de trabajo', paper presented to LASA '97, Guadalajara, 17–19 Apr. 1997.

Abuelas de Plaza de Mayo et al., *Culpables para la sociedad, impunes por la ley* (Buenos Aires: self-edition, 1988).

ACHUGAR, HUGO, 'Como el Uruguay no hay: Bernabé! Bernabé! y el referendum', *Cuadernos de Marcha*, 41 (Feb. 1989), 61–4.

—— 'Transformaciones culturales en el Uruguay de fin de siglo', *Hispamérica*, 20 (1991), 37–58.

—— *La balsa de la medusa* (Montevideo: Trilce, 1992).

—— 'El Parnaso es la nación o reflexiones a propósito de la violencia de la lectura y el simulacro,' in id., *La biblioteca en ruinas: Reflexiones culturales desde la periferia* (Montevideo: Trilce, 1994).

—— and CAETANO, GERARDO (eds.), *Identidad uruguaya: mito, crisis o afirmación* (Montevideo: Trilce, 1992).

ACUÑA, CARLOS H., and SMULOVITZ, CATALINA, 'Militares en la transición argentina: del gobierno a la subordinación constitucional', in Acuña et al., *Juicio, castigos y memorias*, 19–100.

—— et al., *Juicio, castigos y memorias: derechos humanos y justicia en la política argentina* (Buenos Aires: Ediciones Nueva Visión, 1995).

AGÜERO, FELIPE, 'Autonomía de las fuerzas armadas en el autoritarismo y la democracia en Chile', in Varas, *La autonomía militar*, 167–97.

AÍNSA, FERNANDO, *Con acento extranjero* (Buenos Aires and Stockholm: Nordan Comunidad, 1984).

—— *De aquí y de allá: juegos a la distancia* (Montevideo: Ediciones del Mirador, 1986).

ALEXANDER, JEFFREY, 'Citizen and Enemy as Symbolic Classification: On the Polarizing Discourse of Civil Society', in Michèle Lamont and Marcel Fournier (eds.), *Cultivating Differences: Symbolic Boundaries and the Making of Inequality* (Chicago: University of Chicago Press, 1992), 289–308.

—— and SMITH, PHILIP, 'The Discourse of American Civil Society: A New Proposal for Cultural Studies', *Theory and Society*, 22/2 (1993), 151–207.

ALIAGA ROJAS, FERNANDO, *Educación para la paz: módulos y dinámicas en resolución no violenta de los conflictos* (Santiago: SERPAJ, 1996).

ALLENDE, ISABEL, *La casa de los espíritus* (Barcelona: Plaza y Janés, 1985).

—— *De amor y de sombra* (México: Edivisión, 1986).

ALLENDE, SALVADOR, *Chile's Road to Socialism* (Harmondsworth: Penguin, 1973).

ALONSO, ANA MARÍA, 'The Effects of Truth: Representations of the Past and the Imagining of Community', *Journal of Historical Sociology*, 1/1 (1988), 35–57.

—— 'The Politics of Space, Time and Substance: State Formation, Nationalism, and Ethnicity', *Annual Review of Anthropology*, 23 (1994), 379–405.

Americas Watch and CELS, *Verdad y justicia en la Argentina* (Buenos Aires: AW and CELS, 1991).

Americas Watch Committee, *Challenging Impunity: The Ley of Caducidad and the Referendum Campaign in Uruguay* (New York: Americas Watch, 1989).

Amnesty International, *Report of an Amnesty International Mission to Argentina*, 6–15 Nov. 1976.

—— *Argentina: The Attack on the Third Infantry Regiment Barracks at La Tablada* (New York: Amnesty International, 1990).

ANDATCH, FERNANDO, *Signos reales del Uruguay imaginario* (Montevideo: Trilce, 1992).

ANDERSON, BENEDICT, *Imagined Communities* (London: Verso, 1991).

ANGEL, RAQUEL (ed.), *Rebeldes y domesticados* (Buenos Aires: Ediciones el Cielo por Asalto, 1992).

ANGELL, ALAN, and CARTAIRS, SUSAN, 'The Exile Question in Chilean politics', *Third World Quarterly*, 9/1 (1987), 148–67.

—— and POLLACK, BENNY, 'The Chilean Elections of 1989 and the Politics of the Transition to Democracy', *Bulletin of Latin American Research*, 9/1 (1990), 1–23.

AN-NA'IM, ABDULLAHI AHMED, 'Problems and Prospects of Universal Cultural Legitimacy for Human Rights', in An-Na'im and Francis Mading Deng (eds.), *Human Rights in Africa* (Washington: Brookings Institution, 1990), 331–67.

—— (ed.), *Human Rights in Cross-Cultural Perspectives. A Quest for Consensus* (Philadelphia: University of Pennsylvannia Press, 1992).

APPADURAI, ARJUN, 'The Past as a Scarce Resource', *Man*, 16/1 (1981), 201–19.

ARENDT, HANNAH, *Between Past and Future* (New York: Viking Press, 1961).

ARRIAGADA, GENARO, *Pinochet: The Politics of Power* (Boston: Unwin Hyman, 1988).

ASTORI, DANILO, *La política económica de la dictadura* (Montevideo: Ediciones de la Banda Oriental, 1989).

BALOYRA, ENRIQUE A. (ed.), *Comparing New Democracies: Transition and Consolidation in Mediterranean Europe and the Southern Cone* (Boulder, Colo.: Westview, 1987).

BARAHONA DE BRITO, ALEXANDRA, *Human Rights and Democratization in Latin America. Uruguay and Chile* (Oxford: Oxford University Press, 1996).

BAYER, OSVALDO, 'Pequeño recordatorio para un país sin memoria', in Sosnowski, *Represión y reconstrucción*, 203–27.

BECEYRO, RAÚL, 'Los límites: sobre la lista de Schindler', *Punto de vista*, 49 (Aug. 1994), 11–15.

BECKER, D., LIRA, E., CASTILLO, M. I., GÓMEZ, E., and KOVALSKY, J., 'Therapy with Victims of Political Repression in Chile: The Challenge of Social Reparation', *Journal of Social Issues*, 46/3 (1990), 133–49.

BENEDETTI, MARIO, 'Rebelión de los amanuenses', in id., *El país de la cola de paja* (Montevideo: Arca, 1970), 56–69.

—— *Pedro y el capitán* (Mexico: Editorial Nueva Imagen, 1979).

BENGOA, JOSÉ, *Historia del pueblo Mapuche* (Santiago: Ediciones Sur, 1991).

BERGERO, ADRIANA J., and REATI, FERNANDO (eds.), *Memoria colectiva y política de olvido: Argentina y Uruguay, 1970–1990* (Buenos Aires: Beatriz Viterbo, 1997).

BERINS COLLIER, RUTH, and COLLIER, DAVID, *Shaping the Political Arena* (Princeton: Princeton University Press, 1990).

BITAR, SERGIO, *Isla 10* (Santiago: Pehuén, 1987).

BLAUSTEIN, EDUARDO, 'La encuesta inolvidable', *Página/30* (Dec. 1994), Año IV, No. 53, 5–36.

BONASSO, MIGUEL, *Recuerdo de la muerte* (Buenos Aires: Editorial Planeta, 1994, 1st edn. *c*.1983).

—— *La memoria donde ardía* (Buenos Aires: El Juglar Editores, 1990).

BOURRICAUD, FRANÇOIS, 'The Adventures of Ariel', *Daedalus* (Summer 1972), 109–36.

BOYARIN, JONATHAN, 'Space, Time and the Politics of Memory' (Center for Studies of Social Change, SSRC/Mac Arthur Foundation, 1991, MS).

BRADFORD BURNS, E., 'Cultures in Conflict: The Implications of Modernization in the 19th Century', in V. Vernhard (ed.), *Elites, Masses and Modernization in Latin America* (Austin: University of Texas Press, 1979), 11–77.

BRAVO MICHELL, CLODOMIRO, and PAZ, NISSIM SHARIM, *Restricciones a las libertades públicas* (Santiago: Editorial Jurídica de Chile, 1958).

BRUNNER, JOSÉ JOAQUÍN, 'La intelligentsia: escenarios institucionales y universos ideológicos', *Proposiciones*, 18 (1990), 180–91.

BRYSK, ALISON, *The Politics of Human Rights in Argentina* (Stanford, Calif.: Stanford University Press, 1994).

BURT, JO-MARIE, *El pueblo decide: A Brief History of the Referendum against the 'Impunity Law' in Uruguay* (Montevideo: SERPAJ, 1989).

BUSTAMANTE, FRANCISCO, and GONZÁLEZ, MARÍA LUISA, *Derechos humanos en el aula* (Montevideo: SERPAJ, 1992).

CAETANO, GERARDO, and ALFARO, MILITA, 'La Suiza de América y sus mitos', in id. (ed.), *Historia del Uruguay contemporáneo: materiales para el debate* (Montevideo: Fundación de Cultura Universitaria and Instituto de Ciencia Política, 1995), 185–92.

—— et al., *De la tradición a la crisis: pasado y presente de nuestro sistema de partidos* (Montevideo: CLAEH and Ediciones de la Banda Oriental, 1985).

CAETANO, GERARDO, and RILLA, JOSÉ, *La era militar* (Montevideo: Ediciones de la Banda Oriental, 1989).

—— —— 'Breve historia de la dictadura', in Caetano and Alfaro, *Historia del Uruguay contemporáneo*, 253–306.

CAIRNS, ALAN C., 'Reflections on the Political Purposes of the Charter: The First Decade', in Gerald A. Beaudoin (ed.), *The Charter: Ten Years Later* (Quebec: Les Editions Yvon Blais, 1992), 163–91.

CAJIAO SALAS, TERESA, 'Algunas consideraciones sobre la narrativa chilena en el exilio', *Cuadernos hispanoamericanos*, 372 (1981), 600–15.

CALHOUN, CRAIG, 'Civil Society and the Public Sphere', *Public Culture*, 5 (1993), 267–80.

CAMP, RODERIC A. (ed.), *Democracy in Latin America: Patterns and Cycles* (Wilmington: Scholarly Resources, 1996).

CAMPIGLIA, NÉSTOR, *El Uruguay mobilizado* (Montevideo: Editorial Girón, 1971).

CASTAGNOLA, JOSÉ LUIS, and MIERES, PABLO, *La ideología política de la dictadura* (Montevideo: Ediciones de la Banda Oriental, 1989).

CASTILLO VELASCO, JAIME, *Hubo en Chile violaciones de derechos humanos? Comentario a las memorias del General Pinochet* (Santiago: Editora Nacional de Derechos Humanos, 1995).

CAVALLO, ASCANIO, SALAZAR, MANUEL, and SEPÚLVEDA, OSCAR, *La historia oculta del régimen militar* (Santiago: Ediciones La Epoca, 1988).

CAVIEDES, CÉSAR N., *Elections in Chile* (Boulder, Colo.: Lynne Rienner, 1991).

CAYUELA, JOSÉ, *Laura Soto: una dama de lila y negro* (Santiago: Planeta, 1991).

CELS, *Informe anual sobre la situación de los derechos humanos en la Argentina—1994* (Buenos Aires: CELS, 1995), and subsequent annual reports.

Centro Uruguay Independiente, *Referéndum* (Montevideo: CUI, 1987).

CHERESKY, ISIDORO, 'Argentina, una democracia a la búsqueda de su institución', *European Review of Latin American and Carribean Studies*, 53 (1992), 7–45.

CHIARAMONTE, JOSÉ CARLOS, *Formas de sociedad y economía en Hispanoamérica* (México: Grijalbo, 1983).

Cien primeros decretos-leyes dictados por la Junta de gobierno de la República de Chile (Santiago: Editorial Jurídica de Chile, 1973).

CIRIA, ALBERTO, 'Variaciones sobre la historia argentina en el teatro de Roberto Cossa', *Revista canadiense de estudios hispánicos*, 18/3 (1994), 445–53.

CLAUDE, RICHARD PIERRE, and WESTON, BURNS H. (eds.), *Human Rights in the World Community* (Philadelphia: University of Pennsylvania Press, 1989).

CODEPU-DIT-T, *La gran mentira: el caso de las 'listas de los 119'* (Santiago: CODEPU-DIT-T, 1994).

—— *Más allá de las fronteras: estudio sobre las personas ejecutadas o desaparecidas fuera de Chile (1973–1990)* (Santiago: CODEPU-DIT-T, 1996).

COHEN, STANLEY, 'State Crimes of Previous Regimes: Knowledge, Accountability and the Policing of the Past', *Law and Social Inquiry*, 20/1 (1995), 12–22.

—— *Denial and Acknowledgement: The Impact of Information about Human Rights Violations* (Jerusalem: Center for Human Rights, 1995).

Comisión Interamericana de Derechos Humanos, 'Informe 28–92: Argentina' (1992).

Comisión Nacional sobre la Desaparición de Personas, *Nunca Más* (Buenos Aires: EUDEBA, 20th edn. 1995, 1st edn. *c*.1984).

Consejo de Educación Secundaria, *Programa: Educación Moral y Cívica; Introducción a la Sociología; Introducción al Derecho* (Montevideo: CES, 1986).

—— *Educación Social y Cívica: programa del ciclo básico único* (Montevideo: CES, 1993).

Constitución Política de la República de Chile—1980 (Santiago: Publiley, 1989).

Corporación Nacional de Reparación y Reconciliación, *Informe a su Excelencia el Presidente de la República sobre las actividades desarrolladas al 15 de mayo de 1996* (Santiago: CNRR, 1996).

—— *Ensayos para la reconciliación* (Santiago: CNRR, 1994).

—— *Catálogo de material didáctico para la educación en derechos humanos* (Santiago: Trama Color, 1994).

—— *Para recrear la cultura escolar* (Santiago: Trama Color, 1994).

—— *Prefeccionamiento del docente: tarea permanente para la educación de derechos humanos* (Santiago: Trama Color, 1994).

—— *Nuevos acercamientos a los derechos humanos* (Santiago: CNRR, 1995).

CORRADI, JUAN E., *The Fitful Republic, Economy, Society and Politics in Argentina* (Boulder, Colo.: Westview Press, 1985).

—— 'Towards Societies without Fear', in Corradi et al., *Fear at the Edge*, 267–92.

—— PATRICIA WEISS FAGEN, and GARRETÓN, MANUEL A. (eds.), *Fear at the Edge: State Terror and Resistance in Latin America* (Berkeley and Los Angeles: University of California Press, 1992).

CORREA, RAQUEL, and SUBERCASEAUX, ELIZABETH, *Ego sum Pinochet* (Santiago: Zig-zag, 1989).

COSSA, ROBERTO, 'Los compadritos' (1985), in *Teatro 4* (Buenos Aires: Ediciones de la Flor, 1991), 123–203.

—— 'El sur y después', in *Teatro 3* (Buenos Aires: Ediciones de la Flor, 1990), 243–300.

CRASSWELLER, ROBERT D., *Perón and the Enigmas of Argentina* (New York: W. W. Norton, 1987).

CRAWFORD, KATHRYN LEE, 'Due Obedience and the Rights of Victims: Argentina's Transition to Democracy', *Human Rights Quarterly*, 12 (1990), 17–52.

CRAWLEY, EDUARDO, *A House Divided, 1880–1980* (New York: St Martin's Press, 1984).

DAHL, ROBERT, *Polyarchy* (New Haven: Yale University Press, 1971).

DAHRENFORD, RALF, 'After the Twentieth Century: What Role for Liberalism?', Paper presented to the Conference in Honor of Shlomo Avineri, on the Impact of Ideas on Twentieth-Century History. Hebrew University of Jerusalem, Dec. 16 1996.

DAVIS, JOHN, 'The Social Relations of the Production of History', in E. Tonkin et al. (eds.), *History and Ethnicity* (London: Routledge, 1989), 104–20.

DE LA PARRA, MARCO, *La secreta obscenidad de cada día* (Santiago: Planeta, 1988).

DELGADO, ARIEL, *Agresiones a la prensa, 1991–1994* (Buenos Aires: Madres de Plaza de Mayo, 1995).

DEMASI, CARLOS, 'La dictadura militar: un tema pendiente', in Alvaro Rico (ed.), *Uruguay: Cuentas pendientes* (Montevideo: Trilce, 1995), 29.

DE RIZ, LILIANA, 'Argentine: les élections de 1991 à 1995', *Problèmes d'Amerique Latine*, 20 (1996), 25–40.

DIAMOND, LARRY J., LINZ, JUAN L., and LIPSET, MARTIN S. (eds.), *Democracies in Developing Countries* (Boulder, Colo.: Lynne Rienner, 1989).

El diario del juicio (Buenos Aires: Editorial Perfil, 1985–6).

DI MAGGIO, PAUL J., and POWELL, WALTER W., 'The Iron Cage Revisited: Institutional Isomorphism and Collective Rationality in Organizational Field', *American Sociological Review*, 48 (1983), 147–60.

DI TELLA, TORCUATO S., *Historia Argentina 1830–1992* (Buenos Aires: Editorial Troquel, 1993).

—— *Historia 3: el mundo contemporáneo* (Buenos Aires: Santillana, 1995).

DORFMAN, ARIEL, *La doncella y la muerte* (Buenos Aires: Ediciones de la Flor, 1993).

DRAKE, PAUL W., and SILVA, EDUARDO (eds.), *Elections and Democratization in Latin America 1980–1985* (La Jolla: UCSD Center of Iberian and Latin American Studies, 1986).

DROMI, ROBERTO, and MENEM, EDUARDO, *La constitución reformada* (Buenos Aires: Ediciones Ciudad Argentina, 1994).

DUNDES RENTELN, ALISON, *International Human Rights: Universalism versus Relativism* (London: Sage, 1990).

DUSSEL, INÉS, FINNOCHIO, SILVIA, and GOJMAN, SILVIA, *Haciendo memoria en el país del Nunca Más* (Buenos Aires: Eudeba, 1997).

DUTRÉNIT, SILVIA, 'Del margen al centro del sistema político: los partidos uruguayos durante la dictadura', in id (ed.), *Diversidad partidaria y dictaduras: Argentina, Brazil y Uruguay* (Mexico: Instituto Mora, 1996), 235–317.

EDWARDS, JORGE, *Los convidados de piedra* (Barcelona: Seix Barral, 1978).

EDWARDS, ALBERTO, *La fronda aristocrática en Chile* (Santiago: Editorial Universitaria, 1982).

EISENSTADT, S. N., *Trust, Meaning and Power* (Chicago: University of Chicago Press, 1995).

—— and GIESEN, B., 'The Construction of Collective Identity', *Archives européennes de sociologie*, 36 (1995), 72–102.

ELTIT, DIAMELA, *The Fourth World*, trans. from the Spanish 1988 edition and with a foreword by Dick Gerdes (Lincoln, Neb.: University of Nebraska Press, 1995).

ERRO, DAVID G., *Resolving the Argentine Paradox: Politics and Development, 1966–1992* (Boulder, Colo.: Lynne Rienner, 1993).

ESPÍNDOLA, ROBERTO, 'Democracy and Redistribution: The Problems of Governance in Chile', in Hojman, *Neoliberalism with a Human Face*, 64–70.

—— (ed.), *Problems of Democracy in Latin America* (Stockholm: Institute of Latin America Studies, Stockholm University, 1996).

FALARDEAU-RAMSAY, MICHELLE, 'The Changing Face of Human Rights in Canada', *Constitutional Forum*, 4/3 (1993), 61–6.

FALCOFF, MARK, *Modern Chile, 1970–1989: A Critical History* (New Brunswick, NJ: Transaction, 1989).

FALCÓN, SUSANA, *20 años: memorias de la impunidad y el olvido, Argentina 1976/1996* (Sevilla: Cromoarte, 1997).

FALETTO, ENZO, and CARDOSO, FERNANDO HENRIQUE, *Dependency and Development in Latin America* (Berkeley and Los Angeles: University of California Press, 1979).

FARIÑA, JUAN JORGE, 'Aspectos psicosociales de la amnesia/amnistía en Argentina: los tres tiempos de exculpación', in Horacio Riquelme (ed.), *Otras realidades, vías de acceso* (Caracas: Nueva Sociedad, 1992), 203–9.

FEITLOWITZ, MARGUERITE, 'Códigos del terror: Argentina y los legados de la tortura', in Senkman and Sznajder with Kaufman, *El legado del autoritarismo*, 79–94.

FERNÁNDEZ MEIJIDE, GRACIELA, 'La historia escrita por las víctimas', *Paz y justicia*, Año IV, No. 17, 21–2.

FERREIRA RUBIO, DELIA, and GORETTI, MATTEO, 'Cuando el Presidente gobierna solo: Menem y los decretos de necesidad y vigencia hasta la reforma constitucional (julio 1989–agosto 1994)', *Desarrollo económico*, 36/141 (1996), 443–74.

FLEET, MICHAEL, *The Rise and Fall of the Chilean Christian Democracy* (Princeton: Princeton University Press, 1988).

FONTAINE, ARTURO, 'Ideas nacionalistas chilenas', in Enrique Campos Menéndez (ed.), *Pensamiento nacionalista* (Santiago: Editora Nacional Gabriela Mistral, 1974), 233–47.

Forever in the Shadow of Hitler?, trans. James Knowlton, and Truett Cates (New Jersey: Humanities Press, 1994).

FRANCK, THOMAS M., *The Power of Legitimacy among Nations* (Oxford: Oxford University Press, 1990).

FRANCO, JEAN, *The Modern Culture of Latin America: Society and the Artist* (Harmondsworth: Penguin, 1970).

—— 'Latin American Intellectuals and Collective Identity', in Roniger and Sznajder, *Constructing Collective Identities and Shaping Public Spheres*, 231–41.

FRASER, NANCY, 'Rethinking the Public Sphere: A Contribution to the Critic of Actually Existing Democracy', in Craig Calhoun (ed.), *Habermas and the Public Sphere* (Cambridge: MIT Press, 1992), 109–42.

FRIEDLANDER, SAUL (ed.), *Probing the Limits of Representation* (Cambridge: Harvard University Press, 1992).

FRIEDMAN, JONATHAN, 'Myth, History, and Political Identity', *Cultural Anthropology*, 7/2 (1992), 194–210.

FRÜHLING, HUGO (ed.), *Derechos humanos y democracia* (Santiago: Instituto Interamericano de Derechos Humanos, 1991).

—— *Determinants of Gross Human Rights Violations: The Case of Chile* (Santiago: author's MS, 1995).

Fundación Jaime Guzmán, *Los derechos humanos en el pensamiento de Jaime Guzmán Errázuriz* (Santiago: FJG, 1994), serie Documentos No. 7.

GALEANO, EDUARDO, 'La dictadura y después: las heridas secretas', in Sosnowski, *Represión, exilio y democracia*, 107–11.

—— *Las venas abiertas de América Latina* (Montevideo: Ediciones del Chanchito, 1987).

GARCÍA, PRUDENCIO, *El drama de la autonomía militar* (Madrid: Alianza, 1995).

GARCÍA, RICARDO, 'Cantar de nuevo', *Cuadernos Hispanoamericanos*, 482–3 (1990), 197–202.

GARRETÓN, MANUEL ANTHONIO, 'Problems of Democracy in Latin America: On the Processes of Transition and Consolidation', *International Journal*, 43 (1988), 357–77.

—— *The Chilean Political Process* (Boston: Unwin Hyman, 1989).

—— 'Fear in Military Regimes', in Corradi et al., *Fear at the Edge*, 13–25.

—— 'Human Rights in Processes of Democratization', *Journal of Latin American Studies*, 26 (1994), 221–34.

—— *Hacia una nueva era política* (Santiago: Fondo de Cultura Económica, 1995).

—— LAGOS, MARTA, and MÉNDEZ, ROBERTO, *Los chilenos y la democracia: la opinión pública, 1991–1994* (Santiago: Editorial Participa, 1992–5), 4 vols.

GARZÓN VALDÉS, ERNESTO, 'La democracia argentina actual: problemas eticopolíticos de la transición', in Valdés Garzón, Manfred Mols, and Arnold Spita (eds.), *La nueva democracia argentina (1983–1986)* (Buenos Aires: Editorial Sudamericana, 1988), 237–58.

GERMANI, GINO, *Política y sociedad en una época de transición: de la sociedad tradicional a la sociedad de masas* (Buenos Aires: Paidós, 1966).

—— DI TELLA, TORCUATO, and IANNI, OCTAVIO, *Populismo y contradicciones de clase en Latinoamérica* (México: ERA, 1977).

GIANNONI, MARIO (ed.), *Aula Nueva* (Buenos Aires: Kapelusz, 1995).

GIDDENS, ANTHONY, *The Nation-State and Violence* (Berkeley and Los Angeles: University of California Press, 1987).

GIL, DANIEL, 'Prólogo: memorias del horror', in Viñar and Viñar, *Fracturas de la memoria*, 5–11.

GILLESPIE, CHARLES G., *Negotiating Democracy: Politicians and Generals in Uruguay* (Cambridge: Cambridge University Press, 1991).

GIRARD, RENÉ, *Violence and the Sacred* (Baltimore: Johns Hopkins University Press, 1977).

GIUSSANI, PABLO, *Por qué, doctor Alfonsín? Conversaciones con Pablo Giussani* (Buenos Aires: Sudamericana-Planeta, 1987).

GLENDON, MARY A., *Rights Talk* (New York: Free Press, 1991).

GOLDBERG, FLORINDA, 'Patterns of Jewish Plight in Argentinean Fiction of the Catastrophe', Unpublished paper, Hebrew University of Jerusalem, Apr. 1995.

GOLDENBERG, JORGE, *Knepp* (Buenos Aires: by the author, 1983).

GÓMEZ, JOSE MARÍA, 'La cuestión de los derechos humanos en una democracia no consolidada', *Punto de vista* (Dec. 1989), 4–5.

GONZÁLEZ, CARLOS A. (ed.), *54 reformas a la constitución política de Chile* (Santiago: Editora Jurídica Publiley, 1989).

—— *Ley de partidos políticos y votaciones populares* (Santiago: Ediciones Publiley, 1995).

GONZÁLEZ, LUIS E., *Political Structures and Democracy in Uruguay* (Notre Dame, Ind.: University of Notre Dame Press, 1991). Spanish version: *Estructuras políticas y democracia en Uruguay* (Montevideo: Fundación de Cultura Universitaria, 1993).

GONZÁLEZ, MÓNICA, and CONTRERAS, HÉCTOR, *Los secretos del comando conjunto* (Santiago: Ornitorrinco, 1991).

GONZÁLEZ BERMEJO, ERNESTO, *Las manos en el fuego* (Montevideo: Ediciones de la Banda Oriental, 1985).

GRAHAM-JONES, JEAN, 'De la memoria al desencanto y al vacío: la crisis nacional en el teatro argentino de los '80 y los '90', in Bergero and Reati, *Memoria colectiva*, 253–77.

GRAZIANO, FRANK, *Divine Violence, Spectacle, Psychosexuality and Radical Christianity in the Argentine 'Dirty War'* (Boulder, Colo.: Westview, 1992).

GREEN, LINDA, 'Fear as a way of life', *Cultural Anthropology*, 19/2 (1994), 227–57.

GREGORICH, LUIS, 'Literatura: una descripción del campo. Narrativa, periodización, ideología', in Sosnowski, *Represión y reconstrucción*, 109–24.

GROSSMAN, CLAUDIO, 'States of Emergency: Latin America and the United States', in Louis Henkin and Albert Rosenthal (eds.), *Constitutionalism and Rights* (New York: Columbia University Press, 1990), 176–96.

GRUGEL, JEAN, 'External Support for Democratization in Latin America: European Political Parties and the Southern Cone', *Estudios Interdisciplinarios de América Latina y el Caribe*, 4/3 (1993), 53–68.

GUELAR, DIEGO, *Crónicas de la transición*, ii: *El pueblo nunca se equivoca (Los dirigentes a veces sí)* (Buenos Aires: Editorial Sudamericana, 1988).

GUERRA, FRANCOIS-XAVIER, and QUIJADA, MÓNICA (eds.), *Imaginar la nación* (Hamburg: LIT Verlag, 1994).

GUEST, IAN, *Behind the Disappearances: Argentina's Dirty War against Human Rights and the United Nations* (Philadelphia: University of Pennsylvania Press, 1990).

GUZMÁN, JAIME, 'Mártir para la paz social', in *Jaime Guzmán: su legado humano y político* (Santiago: Ercilla, 1991).

—— *Escritos personales* (Santiago: Zig-zag, 1993).

GUZMÁN BOUVARD, MARGUERITE, *Revolutionizing Motherhood: The Mothers of the Plaza de Mayo* (Wilmington: Scholarly Resources, 1993).

GUZMÁN ERRÁZURIZ, ROSARIO, *Mi hermano Jaime* (Santiago: Editorial VER, 1991).

HABERMAS, JÜRGEN, *The Structural Transformation of the Public Sphere* (Cambridge: MIT Press, 1989).

HALBWACHS, MAURICE, *The Collective Memory* (New York: Harper and Row, 1980; 1st edn. *c*.1951)

HALPERIN DONGHI, TULIO, *Argentina: la democracia de masas* (Buenos Aires: Paidós, 1986).

—— 'Argentina's Unmastered Past', *Latin American Research Review*, 23 (1988), 3–24.

Historia de las Abuelas de Plaza de Mayo (Buenos Aires: Página/12, 1996).

Historia de las Madres de Plaza de Mayo (Buenos Aires: Página/12, 1996).

HOJMAN, DAVID E., 'Chile after Pinochet: Aylwin's Christian Democrat Economic Policies for the 1990's', *Bulletin of Latin American Research*, 9/1 (1990), 25–47.

—— (ed.), *Neo-Liberalism with a Human Face: The Politics and Economics of the Chilean Model* (Liverpool: Institute of Latin American Studies, 1995).

HUNTINGTON, SAMUEL, CROZIER, MICHEL, and WATANIKI, JOJI, *The Crisis of Democracy: Report on the Governability of Democracies to the Trilateral Commission* (New York: New York University Press, 1975).

HURTADO, MARÍA DE LA LUZ, 'Presencia del teatro chileno durante el gobierno militar', *Cuadernos hispanoamericanos*, 482–3 (1990), 149–60.

HYMES, ROBERT P., and SCHIROKAUER, CONRAD (eds.), *Ordering the World. Approaches to State and Society in Sung China* (Berkeley and Los Angeles: University of California Press, 1993).

Informe de la Comisión Nacional de Verdad y Reconciliación (Santiago: Secretaría de Comunicación y Cultura, Ministerio Secretaría General de Gobierno, 1991), 3 volumes.

Instituto Interamericano de Derechos Humanos, *El referéndum uruguayo del 16 de abril de 1989, Disposiciones legales* (San José de Costa Rica, IIDH, 1989).

IONESCU, GUITTA, and GELLNER, ERNEST, *Populism: Its Meanings and National Characteristics* (London: Weidenfeld & Nicolson, 1969).

ISRAEL ZIPPER, RICARDO, *Politics and Ideology in Allende's Chile* (Tampa: Center for Latin American Studies, Arizona State University, 1989).

IVELIC, MILAN, 'Itinerario de las artes visuales', *Cuadernos hispanoamericanos*, 482–3 (1990), 205–24.

JELIN, ELIZABETH, 'The Politics of Memory: The Human Rights Movement and the Construction of Democracy in Argentina', *Latin American Perspectives*, 21/2 (1994), 35–58.

—— 'La política de la memoria: el movimiento de derechos humanos y la construcción democrática de la Argentina', in Acuña et al., *Juicio, castigos y memorias*, 101–46.

KAUFMAN, EDY, *Uruguay in Transition: From Civil to Military Rule* (New Brunswick, NJ: Transaction Books, 1979).

—— 'El rol de los partidos políticos en la redemocratización del Uruguay', in Sosnowski, *Represión, exilio y democracia*, 25–62.

—— *Crisis in Allende's Chile: New Perspectives* (New York: Praeger, 1988).

—— 'Análisis de los patrones represivos en el cono sur: los regímenes militares argentinos 1976–1983', in Senkman and Sznajder with Kaufman, *El legado del autoritarismo*, 55–78.

KIRCHHEIMER, OTTO, *Political Justice: The Use of Legal Procedure for Political Ends* (Princeton: Princeton University Press, 1961).

KORDON, DIANA, EDELMAN, LUCILA, et al., *La impunidad: una perspectiva psicosocial y clínica* (Buenos Aires: Sudamericana, 1995).

KOZAMEH, ALICIA, 'El encuentro: Pájaros' (Los Angeles, MS. Nov. 1994).

—— 'Dos días en la relación de mi cuñada Inés con este mundo perentorio', *Confluencia* (Fall 1995), 230–40.

—— *Pasos bajo el agua* (Buenos Aires: Contrapunto, 1987). English version: *Steps under Water* (Berkeley and Los Angeles: University of California Press, 1996).

LAVÍN, JOAQUÍN, *Chile: revolución silenciosa* (Santiago: Zig-zag, 1987).

LEDESMA, GUILLERMO A. C., 'La responsabilidad de los comandantes por las violaciones de los derechos humanos', in Senkman and Sznajder with Kaufman, *El legado del autoritarismo*, 121–9.

LEHMANN, DAVID, *Democracy and Development in Latin America* (Cambridge: Polity Press, 1990).

LESSA, ALFONSO, *Estado de guerra: de la gestación del golpe del 73 a la caída de Bordaberry* (Montevideo: Fin de Siglo, 1996).

LEWIS, BERNARD, *History Remembered, Recovered, Invented* (New York: Simon & Schuster, 1975).

LINZ, JUAN JOSÉ, 'Totalitarian and Authoritarian Regimes', in Fred Greenstein and Nelson Polsby (eds.), *Handbook of Political Science* (Reading, Mass.: Addison-Wesley, 1975), iii. 175–411.

LOVEMAN, BRIAN, *Struggle in the Countryside: Politics and Rural Labor in Chile 1919–1973* (Bloomington: Indiana University Press, 1976).

—— *Chile: The Legacy of Hispanic Capitalism* (New York: Oxford University Press, 1988).

—— 'Protected Democracies and Military Guardianship: Political Transitions in Latin America, 1978–1983', *Journal of Interamerican Studies*, 36 (1994), 105–90.

LOWDEN, PAMELA, *Moral Opposition to Authoritarian Rule in Chile 1973–1990* (New York: St Martin's Press, 1996).

LOWENTHAL, ABRAHAM, and FITCH, SAMUEL (eds.), *Armies and Politics in Latin America* (New York: Holmes & Meier, 1986).

LYNN KARL, Terry, 'Dilemmas of Democratization in Latin America', *Comparative Politics*, 23/1 (1990), 1–21.

MACKLEM, PATRICK et al., *Canadian Constitutional Law* (Toronto: Montgomery, 1994).

Madres y Familiares de Detenidos Desaparecidos, *El referéndum desde familiares* (Montevideo: MFDDU, 1990).

—— *María Victoria Moyano: la alegría de una niña uruguaya recuperada* (Montevideo: MFDDU).

MADRID, ALBERTO, 'La escena de la memoria', *Cuadernos hispanoamericanos*, 482–3 (1990), 9–16.

MAGENDZO, ABRAHAM, *Curriculum, Educación para la democracia en la modernidad* (Santiago: PIIE, 1996).

—— and DUEÑAS, CLAUDIA, *La construcción de una nueva práctica educativa* (México: Comisión Nacional de Derechos Humanos, 1994).

MAIER, CHARLES S., *The Unmasterable Past* (Cambridge: Harvard University Press, 1988).

MALAMUD-GOTI, JAIME, 'Punishing Human Rights Abuses in Fledging Democracies: The Case of Argentina', in Roth-Arriaza, *Impunity and Human Rights*, 160–70.

MALLOY, JAMES M., and SELIGSON, MITCHELL (eds.), *Authoritarians and Democrats: Regime Transition in Latin America* (Pittsburgh: University of Pittsburgh Press, 1987).

MALTÉS, JULIO, and CRUZ, CONCHA, *Historia de Chile* (Santiago: Bibliografía Internacional, 1992).

MANDEL, M., *The Charter of Rights and the Legalization of Politics in Canada* (Toronto: Thompson Educational Publishing Co., 1992).

Manual Aula Taller 7° grado (Buenos Aires: Angel Estrada y Cia, 1989).

Manual esencial Santillana (Buenos Aires: Ediciones Santillana, 1993).

Manual Kapelusz Bonaerense (Buenos Aires: Kapelusz, 1992).

Manual métodos sexto grado, educación General Básica (Buenos Aires: Editorial Métodos, 1995).

MARRA, NELSON, *El guardaespalda y otros cuentos* (Stockholm: Nordan, 1981).

MARTÍNEZ, TOMÁS ELOY, *La novela de Perón* (Buenos Aires: Planeta, 1991).

—— 'A Culture of Barbarism', in Colin M. Lewis and Nissa Torrents (eds.), *Argentina in the Crisis Years (1983–1990): From Alfonsín to Menem* (London: Institute of Latin American Studies, 1993), 11–23.

MARTÍNEZ MONTERO, CARLOS, 'Crepúsculo en Arcadia', *Uruguay hoy* (Buenos Aires: Siglo XXI, 1971), 403–55.

MARTINS, ALBERTO, 'Popular Music as Alternative Communication: Uruguay, 1973–1982', *Popular Music*, 7 (1987), 77–95.

MARRA, NELSON, *El guardaespalda y otros cuentos* (Stockholm: Nordan, 1981).

MARRAS, SERGIO, *Palabra de soldado* (Santiago: Ornitorrinco, 1989).

MASLIAH, LEO, 'La música popular, censura y represión', in Sosnowski, *Represión, exilio y democracia*, 113–24.

MATTOS, TOMÁS, *Bernabé! Bernabé!* (Montevideo: Ediciones de la Banda Oriental, 1988).

MEDINA, ENRIQUE, *Las muecas del miedo* (Buenos Aires: Editorial Galerna, 1981).

MÉREGA, HERMINIA (ed.), *Manual Bonaerense 7* (Buenos Aires: Santillana, 1987).

—— *7° Manual esencial* (Buenos Aires, Santillana, 1990).

MIDAGLIA, C., *Las formas de acción colectivas en Uruguay* (Montevideo: CIESU, 1992).

MIGNONE, EMILIO F., *Witness to the Truth: The Complicity of the Church and Dictatorship in Argentina 1976–1983* (Maryknoll, NY: Orbis, 1988).

—— 'The Catholic Church and the Argentine Democratic Transition', in Edward C. Epstein (ed.), *The New Argentine Democracy* (Westport, Conn.: Praeger, 1992), 157–70.

MILLAR, WALTERIO, *Historia de Chile* (Santiago: Zig-Zag, 1987).

MILLARES, SELENA, 'Ultima narrativa chilena: la escritura del desencanto', *Cuadernos hispanoamericanos*, 482–3 (1990), 113–22.

MILNER, NEAL, 'The Denigration of Rights and the Persistence of Rights Talk', *Law and Social Inquiry*, 14/4 (1989), 631–75.

Ministerio de Cultura y Educación de la Nación, Consejo Federal de Cultura y Educación, *Contenidos Básicos Comunes para la Educación General Básica* (Buenos Aires: MCE and CFCE, 1994).

MITSCHERLICHT, ALEXANDER, and MITSCHERLICHT, MARGARETE, *The Inability to Mourn* (New York: Groove Press, 1975).

MORDUCHOWICZ, ROXANA, 'Enrique Medina y las muecas del miedo, un reportaje de Roxana Morduchowicz', *Nueva presencia* (6 Nov. 1981).

MUNCK, RONALDO, 'Democratization and Demilitarization in Argentina, 1982–1985', *Bulletin of Latin American Research*, 4/2 (1985), 85–93.

MUNCK, RONALDO, 'After the Transition: Democratic Disenchantment in Latin America', *European Review of Latin American and Caribbean Studies*, 55 (1993), 7–19.

NAHUM, BENJAMÍN, *Manual de Historia del Uruguay 1903–1990* (Montevideo: Ediciones de la Banda Oriental, 1991).

NINO, CARLOS S., 'The Communitarian Challenge to Liberal Rights', in id., *Rights* (Aldershot: Dartmouth, 1992), 309–24.

—— 'The Duty to Punish Past Abuses of Human Rights Put into Context: The Case of Argentina' and 'The Human Rights Policy of the Argentine Constitutional Government: A Reply', in *Yale Journal of International Law*, 100 (1991), 2537–643 and 217–30.

NOGUEIRA, HUMBERTO (ed.), *Manual de educación cívica: educación para la democracia* (Santiago: Editorial Andrés Bello, 1991).

NORA, PIERRE, 'Between Memory and History: Les lieux de mémoire', *Représentations*, 26 (1989), 7–25.

NORDEN, DEBORAH, 'Democratic Consolidation and Military Professionalism: Argentina in the 1980s', *Journal of Interamerican Studies and World Affairs*, 32/3 (1990), 151–76.

NUNN, FREDERICK, 'The South American Military and (Re)Democratization: Professional Thought and Self Perception', *Journal of Interamerican Studies and World Affairs*, 37/2 (1995), 1–56.

Objetivo Nacional del Gobierno de Chile (Santiago: Impresora Filadelfia, 1975).

O'DONNELL, GUILLERMO, *Bureaucratic-Authoritarianism: Argentina, 1966–1973* (Berkeley and Los Angeles: University of California Press, 1988).

—— *Delegative Democracy* (Notre Dame: University of Notre Dame Press, 1991).

—— 'Delegative Democracy', *Journal of Democracy*, 5/1 (1994), 59–69.

—— SCHMITTER, PHILIPPE, and WHITEHEAD, LAURENCE, *Transitions from Authoritarian Rule* (Baltimore: Johns Hopkins University Press, 1986).

OLICK, JEFFREY K., and LEVY, DANIEL, 'Collective Memory and Cultural Constraint: Holocaust, Myth and Rationality in German Politics', *American Sociological Review*, 62 (1997), 921–36.

O'MALLEY, ANTHONY H., 'Chile's Constitution, Chile's Congress', *Canadian Review of Latin American Studies*, 15 (1990), 85–112.

ORENTLICHTER, DIANE F., 'Settling Accounts: The Duty to Prosecute Human Rights Violations of a Prior Regime' and 'A Reply to Profesor Nino', *Yale Journal of International Law*, 100 (1991), 2537–643.

OSIEL MARK, 'The Making of Human Rights Policy in Argentina: The Impact of Ideas and Interests on a Legal Conflict', *Journal of Latin American Studies*, 18/1 (1986), 135–80.

—— 'Ever again: Legal Remembrance of Administrative Massacre', *University of Pennsylvania Law Review*, 144/2 (1995), 683–91.

—— *Mass Atrocity, Collective Memory and the Law* (New Brunswick, NJ: Transaction Books, 1997).

OSSER, MARIO, 'Nosotros los finiseculares', *Cuadernos hispanoamericanos*, 482–3 (1990), 137–48.

PADILLA BALLESTEROS, ELÍAS, *La memoria y el olvido: detenidos desaparecidos en Chile* (Santiago: Ediciones Orígenes, 1995).

PAGE, JOSEPH, *Perón: A Biography* (New York: Random House, 1983).

PALERMO, VICENTE, 'Argentine: Reformes de structures et régime politique, 1989–1994', *Problèmes d'Amérique Latine*, 20 (1996), 61–80.

PAOLETTI, ALIPIO, *Como los nazis, como en Vietnam: los campos de concentración en la Argentina* (Buenos Aires, Edición Cañón Oxidado, 1987).

PERALTA RAMOS, MÓNICA, and WAISMAN, CARLOS (eds.), *From Military Rule to Liberal Rule in Argentina* (Boulder, Colo.: Westview, 1987).

PERELLI, CARINA, 'Settling Accounts with Blood Memory: The Case of Argentina', *Social Research*, 59/2 (1992), 415–51.

—— and RIAL, JUAN, *De mitos y memorias políticas* (Montevideo: Ediciones de la Banda Oriental, 1986).

PÉREZ AGUIRRE, LUIS, 'Memoria de los detenidos desaparecidos', *Carta SERPAJ* (Nov.–Dec. 1994), 8–9.

PETRAS, JAMES, and VIEUX, STEVE, 'The Transition to Authoritarian Electoral Regimes in Latin America', *Latin American Perspectives*, 21 (1994), 5–20.

PIANCA, MARINA, 'La política de la dislocación (o retorno a la memoria del futuro)', in Bergero and Reati, *Memoria colectiva y política de olvido*, 115–38.

PIGLIA, RICARDO, *Respiración artificial* (Buenos Aires: Editorial Pomaire, 1980).

—— 'Los pensadores ventrílocuos', in Angel, *Rebeldes y domesticados*,

—— 'Viñas y la violencia oligárquica' from *La Argentina en pedazos* (Buenos Aires: Ediciones de la Flor, 1993).

PINOCHET, AUGUSTO, *El día decisivo: 11 de Septiembre de 1973* (Santiago: Empresa periodística La Nación, 1979).

—— *Pinochet: patria y democracia* (Santiago: Editorial Andrés Bello, 1985).

PION-BERLIN, DAVID, *The Ideology of State Terror: Economic Doctrine and Political Repression in Argentina and Peru* (Boulder, Colo.: Lynne Rienner, 1989).

—— 'Between Confrontation and Accommodation: Military and Government Policy in Democratic Argentina', *Journal of Latin American Studies*, 23/2 (1991), 552–60.

—— 'Military Autonomy and Emerging Democracies in South America', *Comparative Politics*, 25/1 (1992), 82–102.

—— 'To Prosecute or to Pardon? Human Rights Decisions in the Latin American Southern Cone', *Human Rights Quarterly*, 15 (1993), 101–30.

PIZARRO, ANA, *De ostras y caníbales: ensayos sobre la cultura latinoamericana* (Santiago: Editorial Universidad de Santiago, 1994).

POGGE, H., *Realizing Rawls* (Ithaca, NY: Cornell University Press, 1989).

POLITZER, PATRICIA, *La ira de Pedro y los otros* (Santiago: Planeta, 1988).

—— *Altamirano* (Buenos Aires: Grupo editorial Zeta, 1989).

—— (ed.), *Fear in Chile: Lives under Pinochet* (New York: Pantheon Books, 1989).

POPKIN, MARGARET, and ROTH-ARRIAZA, NAOMI, 'Truth as Justice: Investigatory Commissions in Latin America', *Law and Social Inquiry*, 20/1 (1995), 79–116.

Popular Memory Group, 'Popular memory: theory, politics, method', in R. Johnson et al. (eds.), *Making Histories* (London: Hutchinson, 1991), 205–52.

PORTILLO, ALVARO, and GALLICCHIO, ENRIQUE, *Montevideo: Geografía electoral 2* (Montevideo: Centro Uruguay Independiente, 1989).

PORZECANSKI, TERESA, 'Ficción y fricción de la narrativa de imaginación escrita dentro de fronteras', in Sosnowski, *Represión, exilio y democracia*, 221–30.

POST, ROBERT, *Constitutional Domains* (Cambridge, Mass.: Harvard University Press, 1995).

PRATTS GONZÁLEZ, CARLOS, *Memorias: testimonio de un soldado* (Santiago: Pehuén, 1987, 3rd edn.).

PREGO, OMAR, *Reportaje a un golpe de estado* (Montevideo: La República Ediciones, 1988).

PUIGGRÓS, ADRIANA, 'World Bank Education Policy: Market, Liberalism Meets Ideological Conservatism', *International Journal of Health Services*, 27/2 (1997), 217–26.

QUIJADA CERDA, ANÍBAL, *Cerco de púas* (La Habana: Casa de las Américas, 1977).

RADRIGAN, JUAN, *La contienda humana* (Santiago: Ediciones Literatura Alternativa, 1989).

RAMA, ANGEL, 'La generación crítica (1939–1969)', in *Uruguay hoy* (Buenos Aires: Siglo XXI, 1971), 325–402.

Rama Argentina de la Asociación Americana de Juristas, *Argentina: juicio a los militares. Documentos secretos, decretos-leyes, jurisprudencia* (Buenos Aires: AAJ, 1988).

RAPOPORT, MARIO (ed.), *Globalización, integración e identidad nacional* (Buenos Aires: Grupo Editor Latinamericano, 1995).

RATNER, STEVEN R., and ABRAMS, JASON S., *Accountability for Human Rights Atrocities in International Law: Beyond the Nuremberg Legacy* (Oxford: Clarendon Press, 1997).

RAWLS, JOHN, 'Justice as Fairness: Political, not Metaphysical', *Philosophy and Public Affairs*, 14 (1985), 225–30.

—— 'The Law of Peoples', in Stephen Shute and Susan Hurley (eds.), *On Human Rights: The Oxford Amnesty Lectures, 1993* (Oxford: Oxford University Press, 1993), 41–82.

RENAN, ERNEST, *Che cos'è una nazione?* (Roma: Donzelli Editore, 1993).

Reparaciones a los familiares de las víctimas a que se refiere el informe de la Comisión de Verdad y Reconciliación (Santiago: Secretaría de Comunicatión y Cultura, 1992).

Report of the Chilean Commission on Truth and Reconciliation (English) (South Bend: University of Notre Dame Press, 1993).

República Argentina, *El gobierno democrático y los derechos humanos* (Buenos Aires: Imprenta del Congreso de la Nación, 1985).

'Respuesta de las Fuerzas Armadas y de Orden al Informe de la Comisión Nacional de Verdad y Reconciliación', *Estudios Políticos*, 41 (1991), 449–504.

REYES, SANDRA (ed. and trans.), *One More Stripe to the Tiger* (Fayetteville: University of Arkansas Press, 1989).

RIAL, JUAN, 'Los militares en tanto "partido político sustituto" frente a la redemocratización en Uruguay', in Varas, *La autonomía militar en América*, 197–229.

—— 'Makers and Guardians of Fear: Control Terror in Uruguay', in Corradi et al., *Fear at the Edge*, 90–103.

—— 'El referéndum del 16 de abril de 1989 en Uruguay', in IIDH, *El referéndum uruguayo*, 15–58.

RICO, ALVARO (ed.), *Uruguay: cuentas pendientes* (Montevideo: Trilce, 1995).

ROCK, DAVID, *Argentina, 1516–1982* (Berkeley and Los Angeles: University of California Press, 1985).

RODRÍGUEZ ELIZONDO, JOSÉ, *La ley es más fuerte* (Buenos Aires: Grupo Editorial Zeta, 1995).

—— *La pasión de Iñaki* (Santiago: Editorial Andrés Bello, 1996).

ROJAS, LUIS EMILIO, *Nueva historia de Chile* (Santiago: Gong Ediciones, 1991).

RONIGER, LUIS, 'Sociedad civil y derechos humanos: una aproximación teórica en base a la experiencia argentina', in Senkman and Sznajder with Kaufman, *El legado del autoritarismo*, 37–54.

—— 'Globalization as Cultural Vision', *Canadian Review of Sociology and Anthropology*, 32/3 (1995), 259–86.

—— and SZNAJDER, MARIO (eds.), *Constructing Collective Identities and Shaping Public Spheres: Latin American Paths* (Brighton: Sussex Academic Press, 1998).

RORTY, RICHARD, *Objectivity, Relativism and Truth* (Cambridge: Cambridge University Press, 1991).

—— 'Human Rights, Rationality and Sentimentality', in *On Human Rights: The Oxford Amnesty Lectures* (Oxford: Oxford University Press, 1993), 111–34.

ROSENCOF, MAURICIO, and FERNÁNDEZ HUIDOBRO, ELEUTERIO, *Memorias del calabozo* (Navarra: Txalaparta: Argitaletxea, 1993).

ROTH-ARRIAZA, NAOMI (ed.), *Impunity and Human Rights in International Law and Practice* (New York: Oxford University Press, 1995).

ROUQUIÉ, ALAIN, 'Hegemonía militar, estado y dominación', in *Argentina hoy* (México: Siglo XXI, 1982).

ROWE, WILLIAM, and WHITFIELD, TERESA, 'Thresholds of Identity: Literature and Exile in Latin America', *Third World Quarterly*, 9/1 (1987), 230–1.

ROZITCHNER, LEÓN, 'El terror de los desencantados', in Angel, *Rebeldes y domesticados*, 42–5.

RUFFINELLI, JORGE, 'Uruguay, dictadura y redemocratización: un informe sobre la literatura, 1973–1989', *Nuevo Texto Crítico*, 5 (1990), 50–2.

—— 'La crítica y los estudios literarios en el Uruguay de la dictadura (1973–1984)', *Hispamérica*, 56–7 (1991), 21–9.

SÁBATO, HILDA, 'Olvidar la memoria', *Punto de vista*, 36 (Dec. 1989), 8.

—— 'Citizenship, Participation and the Formation of the Public Sphere in Buenos Aires, 1850s–1880s', *Past and Present*, 136 (1992), 139–63.

—— 'Historia reciente y memoria colectiva', *Punto de vista* (Aug. 1994), 30–5.

SAER, JUAN JOSÉ, *El río sin orillas* (Buenos Aires: Alianza, 1991).

SALAZAR, GABRIEL, 'Historiografía y dictadura en Chile, 1973–1990', *Cuadernos hispanoamericanos*, 482–3 (1990), 81–94.

SALAZAR, MANUEL, *Contreras: historia de un intocable* (Santiago: Grijalbo, 1995).

SÁNCHEZ, MARÍA PURA, 'Postfoundationalism, Human Rights and Diversity of Cultures', Paper presented at the Conference on Collective Identities and Symbolic Representation, Paris, July 1996.

SANDEL, MICHAEL, 'The Procedural Republic and the Unencumbered Self', *Political Theory*, 12/1 (1984), 81–96.

Santelices y Dinamarca, *Por los chiquitos que vienen . . .* (Montevideo: MFDDU, n.d.).

SARLO, BEATRIZ, 'La Historia contra el olvido', *Punto de vista*, 36 (Dec. 1989), 11–13.

—— *Escenas de la vida posmoderna: intelectuales, arte y videocultura en la Argentina* (Buenos Aires: Ariel, 1994).

SCHEINES, GRACIELA, *Las metáforas del fracaso* (Buenos Aires: Sudamericana, 1993).

SCHEPER-HUGHES, NANCY, *Death without Weeping* (Berkeley and Los Angeles: University of California Press, 1992).

SCHUDSON, MICHAEL, 'The Present in the Past versus the Past in the Present', *Communication*, 11 (1989), 105–13.

SCHWARTZ, BARRY, 'Vengeance and Forgiveness: The Uses of Beneficence in Social Control', *School Review*, 86/4 (1978), 655–68.

—— 'The Social Context of Commemoration: A Study in Collective Memory', *Social Forces*, 61 (1982), 374–402.

SENKMAN, LEONARDO, 'The Right and Civilian Regimes, 1955–1976', in Sandra McGee and Ronald Dolkart (eds.), *The Argentine Right* (Wilington: Scholarly Resources, 1993).

—— and SZNAJDER, MARIO, with the cooperation of KAUFMAN, EDY (eds.), *El legado del autoritarismo: derechos humanos y antisemitismo en la Argentina contemporánea* (Buenos Aires: Grupo Editor Latinoamericano, 1995).

Servicio de Paz y Justicia, *Educación y derechos humanos, cuadernos para docentes: reflexiones y experiencias* (Montevideo: SERPAJ, 1988).

—— *Derechos humanos en Uruguay* (Montevideo: SERPAJ, 1990–4).

Servicio de Rehabilitación Social, *Intercambio* (Montevideo: Productora Gráfica, 1986).

SHILS, EDWARD, *Center and Periphery* (Chicago: University of Chicago Press, 1975).

SHOTTER, JOHN, 'The Social Construction of Remembering and Forgetting', in David Middleton and Derek Edwards (eds.), *Collective Remembering* (Sage: London, 1990), 120–38.

SIEBZEHNER, BATIA B., *La universidad americana y la ilustración: autoridad y conocimiento en Nueva España y el Río de la Plata* (Madrid: MAPFRE, 1994).

SIGAL, SILVIA, 'Argentine, 1992–1995: une société en mutation', *Problèmes d'Amerique Latine*, 20 (1996), 3–24.

SIMPSON, JOHN, and BENNETT, JANA, *The Disappeared: Voices from a Secret War* (London: Robson Books, 1985).

SIVES, AMANDA, 'Elites Behaviour and Corruption in the Consolidation of Democracy in Brazil', *Parliamentary Affairs*, 46/4 (1993), 549–62.

SKÁRMETA, ANTONIO, *Soñé que la nieve ardía* (Barcelona: Planeta, 1975).

—— *Ardiente paciencia* (Madrid: Plaza y Janés, 1986).

—— *No pasó nada* (Barcelona: Plaza y Janés, 1996).

SKIDMORE, THOMAS, *The Politics of Military Rule in Brazil 1964–1985* (Oxford: Oxford University Press, 1988).

SLACK, KEITH M., 'Operation Condor and Human Rights: A Report from Paraguay's Archive of Terror', *Human Rights Quarterly*, 18 (1996), 492–506.

SOLANAS, FERNANDO E., 'Le sud', *L'Avant Scène cinema* (1989), 377–8.

SOSNOWSKI, SAÚL (ed.), *Represión y reconstrucción de una cultura: el caso argentino* (Buenos Aires: Universidad de Buenos Aires, 1984).

—— (ed.), *Represión, exilio y democracia: la cultura uruguaya* (Montevideo: Maryland University Press and Ediciones de la Banda Oriental, 1987).

STEIMBERG, ALICIA, 'Cecilia's Last Will and Testament', in Marjorie Agosin (ed.), *Landscapes of a New Land: Short Fiction by Latin American Women* (Buffalo, Colo.: White Pine Press, 1989), 102–11.

STEPAN, ALFRED, *Estado, corporatismo e autoritarismo* (Rio de Janeiro: Paz e Terra, 1980).

STERNHELL, ZEEV, SZNAJDER, MARIO, and ASHERI, MAIA, *The Birth of Fascist Ideology* (Princeton: Princeton University Press, 1994).

STEWART-GAMBINO, HANNAH, 'Redefining the Changes and Politics in Chile', in Edward L. Cleary and Hannah Stewart-Gambino (eds.), *Conflict and Competition: The Latin American Church in a Changing Environment* (Boulder, Colo.: Lynne Rienner, 1992), 21–44.

STOKES, W. S. 'The Pensadores of Latin America', in G. B. de Huszar (ed.), *The Intellectuals: A Controversial Portrait* (Glencoe, Ill.: Free Press, 1960), 422–9.

SUÁREZ-OROZCO, MARCELO, 'Speaking of the Unspeakable: Toward a Psychosocial Understanding of Responses to Terror', *Ethos*, 18/3 (1990), 353–83.

—— 'A Grammar of Terror: Psychocultural Responses to State Terrorism in Dirty War and Post-Dirty War Argentina', in Carolyn Nordstrom and Jo Ann Martin (eds.), *The Paths to Domination, Resistance and Terror* (Berkeley and Los Angeles: University of California Press, 1992), 219–59.

SZNAJDER, MARIO, 'Ethnodevelopment and Democratic Consolidation in Chile: The Mapuche Question', *Migration*, 28 (1995), 15–35.

—— 'Entre autoritarismo y democracia: el legado de violaciones de derechos humanos', in Senkman and Sznajder with Kaufman, *El legado del autoritarismo*,

—— 'Transition in South America: Models of Limited Democracy', *Democratization*, 3/3 (1996), 360–70.

—— 'Limited Democracy: A Comparative Approach', in Espíndola, *Problems of Democracy*, 52–74.

TAPIA, JORGE ANTONIO, *National Security: The Dual State and the Role of Deception* (Rotterdam: By the author, 1989).

TIMERMAN, JACOBO, *Preso sin nombre, celda sin número* (New York: Random House, 1981). English version: *Prisoner without a Name, Cell without a Number* (New York: Alfred Knopf, 1981).

Toda persona tiene derecho a . . . Concurso de poesía y cuento, 1986–1987: obras premiadas (Comisión regional de derechos humanos de Linares, 1987).

TOURAINE, ALAIN, *Vida y muerte del Chile popular* (México: Siglo XXI, 1974).

TRIGO, ABRIL, *Caudillo, estado, nación: literatura, historia e ideología en el Uruguay* (Gaithersburg, Md.: Hispamérica, 1990).

—— 'Rockeros y grafiteros: la construcción al sesgo de una anti-memoria', in Bergero and Reati, *Memoria colectiva y política de olvido*, 305–34.

TRÓCCOLI, JORGE NÉSTOR, *La ira de Leviatán* (Montevideo: Caelum, 1996).

TURIANSKY, WLADIMIR, *Apuntes contra la desmemoria: recuerdos de la resistencia* (Montevideo: Arca, 1988).

TURNER, FREDERICK C., and MIGUENS, JOSÉ ENRIQUE (eds.), *Juan Perón and the Reshaping of Argentina* (Pittsburgh: University of Pittsburgh Press, 1983).

Uruguay: nunca más. Informe sobre la violación a los derechos humanos (1972–1985) (Montevideo: Servicio Paz y Justicia, 1989).

VALDÉS, HERNÁN, *Tejas verdes: diario de un campo de concentración en Chile* (Barcelona: Ariel, 1974).

VALENZUELA, ARTURO, *The Breakdown of Democratic Regimes: Chile* (Baltimore: John Hopkins University, 1978).

VALENZUELA, J. SAMUEL, and VALENZUELA, ARTURO (eds.), *Military Rule in Chile* (Baltimore: Johns Hopkins University Press, 1986).

VALERGA-ARÁOZ, JORGE A., 'Los juicios a los militares argentinos: significación jurídico-penal', in Senkman and Sznajder with Kaufman, *El legado del autoritarismo*, 143–53.

VANGER, MILTON, *El país modelo: José Battle y Ordóñez, 1907–1915* (Montevideo: Arca-EBO, 1980).

VARAS, AUGUSTO, 'Democratización y reforma militar en Argentina', in id., *La autonomía militar*, 57–83.

—— *La autonomía militar en América Latina* (Caracas: Nueva Sociedad, 1988).

VEGA, LUIS, *La caída de Allende: anatomía de un golpe de estado* (Jerusalem: La Semana Publicaciones, 1983).

VERDUGO, PATRICIA, *André de la Victoria* (Santiago: Editorial Aconcagua, 1985).

—— *Rodrigo y Carmen Gloria* (Santiago: Editorial Aconcagua, 1986).

—— *Los zarpazos del Puma* (Santiago: CESOC, 1989).

—— and HERTZ, CARMEN, *Operación siglo XX* (Santiago: Ornitorrinco, 1990).

VERGARA, PILAR, *Auge y caída del neoliberalismo en Chile* (Santiago: FLACSO, 1985).

VEZZETI, HUGO, 'El juicio: un ritual de la memoria', *Punto de vista* (Oct. 1985), 4–12.

—— 'La memoria y los muertos', *Punto de vista* (Aug. 1994), 4.

—— 'Variaciones sobre la memoria social', *Punto de vista* (Dec. 1996), 2.

VIÑAR, MARCELO, and VIÑAR, MAREN, *Fracturas de la memoria* (Montevideo: Trilce, 1993).

VIÑAS, DAVID, *Cuerpo a Cuerpo* (México: Siglo XXI, 1979).

—— 'Las astucias de la servidumbre', in Angel, *Rebeldes y domesticados*,

WAISMAN, CARLOS, *Reversal of Development in Argentina* (Princeton: Princeton University Press, 1987).

WAKEMAN, FREDERICK, 'The Civil Society and Public Sphere Debate: Western Reflections on China's Political Culture', *Modern China*, 19/2 (1993), 108–38.

WALZER, MICHAEL, *Thick and Thin Moral Arguments at Home and Abroad* (Notre Dame, Ind.: University of Notre Dame Press, 1994).

WARLEY, JORGE, 'Revistas culturales de dos décadas (1970–1990)', *Cuadernos hispanoamericanos*, 517–19 (1993), 195–207.

WARREN, KAY B., 'Transforming Memories and Histories: The Meanings of Ethnic Resurgence for Mayan Indians', in Alfred Stepan (ed.), *Americas: New Interpretative Essays* (Oxford: Oxford University Press, 1992), 189–219.

WATTS, MICHAEL, 'Islamic Modernities? Citizenship, Civil Society and Islamism in a Nigerian City', *Public Culture*, 8 (1996), 251–89.

WHELAN, JAMES R., *Out of the Ashes, Life, Death and Transfiguration of Democracy in Chile, 1833–1988* (Washington, DC: Regney Gateway, 1989).

WHITEHEAD, LAURENCE, 'The Alternatives to "Liberal Democracy": A Latin American Perspective', *Political Studies*, 40 (1992), 146–59.

WILKER, ALEJANDRO, *Prisión en Chile* (México: Fondo de Cultura Económica, 1975).

WILSON, RICHARD A., 'Human Rights, Culture and Context: An Introduction', in id. (ed.), *Human Rights, Culture and Context: Anthropological Perspectives* (London: Pluto, 1997), 1–27.

WOLIN, SHELDON, 'Postmodern Politics and the Absence of Myth', *Social Research*, 52/2 (1985), 217–39.

YANNUZZI, MARÍA DE LOS ANGELES, 'Identidad, política y crisis: las experiencias canadiense y argentina', in Rapoport, *Globalización, integración e identidad nacional*, 333–52.

YERUSHALMI, YOSEF HAYIM, *Zakhor* (Seattle: University of Washington Press, 1982).

ZAGORSKI, PAUL W., 'Civil–Military Relations and Argentine Democracy: The Armed Forces under the Menem Government', *Armed Forces and Society*, 20/3 (1994), 423–37.

ZALAQUETT, JOSÉ, 'Balancing Ethical Imperatives and Political Constraints: The Dilemma of New Democracies Confronting Past Human Rights Violations', *Hastings Law Journal*, 43 (1992), 1425–38.

ZUBILLAGA BARRERA, CARLOS A., *Artigas y los derechos humanos* (Montevideo: Comité Central Israelita del Uruguay, 1966).

—— and PÉREZ, ROMEO, *La democracia atacada* (Montevideo: Ediciones de la Banda Oriental, 1988).

Index